ANNUAL EDITIONS

Education 12/13

Thirty-Ninth Edition

W9-CBK-683

EDITOR

Dr. Rebecca B. Evers

Winthrop University

Dr. Rebecca Evers, a professor in Counseling, Leadership, and Educational Studies at the Richard W. Riley College of Education, attended Illinois College to earn a BA in English education in 1966, an MA in the Rehabilitation Teaching of the Adult Blind from Western Michigan University in 1969, and an EdD in Special Education from Northern Illinois University in 1994. She is actively involved in researching methods to determine and assess the quality of teacher candidate's dispositions. Her primary focus is dispositions for providing equitable access to learning for students with disabilities and other exceptional needs.

Mc Graw Hill

Connect
Learn
Succeed™

The McGraw-Hill Companies

Connect
Learn
Succeed™

ANNUAL EDITIONS: EDUCATION, THIRTY-NINTH EDITION

1 2 3 4 5 6 7 8 9 0 QDB/QDB 1 0 9 8 7 6 5 4 3 2 1

ISBN: 978–0–07–805106–7
MHID: 0–07–805106–1
ISSN: 2162–1799 (print)
ISSN: 2162–1799 (online)

Managing Editor: *Larry Loeppke*
Developmental Editor: *Dave Welsh*
Permissions Coordinator: *DeAnna Dausener*
Marketing Specialist: *Alice Link*
Project Manager: *Melissa Leick*
Design Coordinator: *Margarite Reynolds*
Cover Designer: *Kristine Jubeck*
Buyer: *Susan K. Culbertson*
Media Project Manager: *Sridevi Palani*

Compositor: Laserwords Private Limited
Cover Image Credits: Image Source/SuperStock (inset); Ingram Publishing/SuperStock (background)

www.mhhe.com

Editors/Academic Advisory Board

Members of the Academic Advisory Board are instrumental in the final selection of articles for each edition of ANNUAL EDITIONS. Their review of articles for content, level, and appropriateness provides critical direction to the editors and staff. We think that you will find their careful consideration well reflected in this volume.

ANNUAL EDITIONS: Education 12/13
39th Edition

EDITOR

Dr. Rebecca B. Evers
Winthrop University

ACADEMIC ADVISORY BOARD MEMBERS

Editors/Academic Advisory Board continued

Preface

In publishing ANNUAL EDITIONS we recognize the enormous role played by the magazines, newspapers, and journals of the public press in providing current, first-rate educational information in a broad spectrum of interest areas. Many of these articles are appropriate for students, researchers, and professionals seeking accurate, current material to help bridge the gap between principles and theories and the real world. These articles, however, become more useful for study when those of lasting value are carefully collected, organized, indexed, and reproduced in a low-cost format, which provides easy and permanent access when the material is needed. That is the role played by ANNUAL EDITIONS.

The public conversation on the purposes and future direction of education is lively as ever. Alternative visions and voices regarding the broad social aims of schools and the preparation of teachers continue to be presented. *Annual Editions: Education 12/13* attempts to reflect current mainstream as well as alternative visions as to what education ought to be. This year's edition contains articles on important issues facing educators such as educational reforms; effective teaching practices for reading and mathematics; teaching all students in communities of caring learners, with an emphasis on students who live in poverty; and effectively using technology to teach all students.

We face a myriad of quandaries to our schools today, not unfamiliar to our history as a nation, which are not easily resolved. Issues regarding the purposes of education, as well as the appropriate methods of educating, have been debated throughout the generations of literate human culture. Today, we are asking ourselves and others to provide our children a *quality education* for the twenty-first century. But first we must answer the questions: What is a quality education? How do we provide such an education for all children? There will always be debates over the purposes and the ends of "education," as it depends on what the term means at a given place or time and as each generation constructs its definition of "education" based on its understanding of "justice," "fairness," and "equity" in human relations. Each generation must establish its understanding of social justice and personal responsibility for our children and youth.

All of this is occurring as the United States continues to experience important demographic shifts in its cultural makeup. Furthermore, our ability to absorb children from many cultures into our schools has become a challenge in troubled economic times. Teachers in large cities have worked with immigrant populations since this nation began, but now schools in mid-size cities and rural towns are experiencing increasing numbers of children who speak a language other than English. Several articles in this edition address teaching methods for English

Language Learners throughout the units on diversity, caring communities, and managing student behavior. Further, we address the larger issues of teaching reading and mathematics and the use of technology. Technological breakthroughs in the information sciences have an impact on how people learn. The rate of change in how we learn and obtain information increases at a rapid pace that will certainly continue. The articles in this section address how technology can change the fundamental delivery of content and expand options for personalizing learning, as well as research on the effects of technology use on our children.

In assembling this volume, we make every effort to stay in touch with movements in educational studies and with the social forces at work in schools. Members of the advisory board contribute valuable insights, and the production and editorial staffs at the publisher, McGraw-Hill Contemporary Learning Series, coordinate our efforts.

The readings in *Annual Editions: Education 12/13* explore the social and academic goals of education, the current conditions of the nation's educational system, the teaching profession, and the future of American education. In addition, these selections address the issues of change and the moral and ethical foundations of schooling. As always, we would like you to help us improve this volume. Please rate the material in this edition on the postage-paid *article rating form* provided at the back of this book and send it to us. We care about what you think. Give us the public feedback that we need.

Rebecca B. Evers
Editor

The Annual Editions Series

VOLUMES AVAILABLE

Adolescent Psychology

Aging

American Foreign Policy

American Government

Anthropology

Archaeology

Assessment and Evaluation

Business Ethics

Child Growth and Development

Comparative Politics

Criminal Justice

Developing World

Drugs, Society, and Behavior

Dying, Death, and Bereavement

Early Childhood Education

Economics

Educating Children with Exceptionalities

Education

Educational Psychology

Entrepreneurship

Environment

The Family

Gender

Geography

Global Issues

Health

Homeland Security

Human Development

Human Resources

Human Sexualities

International Business

Management

Marketing

Mass Media

Microbiology

Multicultural Education

Nursing

Nutrition

Physical Anthropology

Psychology

Race and Ethnic Relations

Social Problems

Sociology

State and Local Government

Sustainability

Technologies, Social Media, and Society

United States History, Volume 1

United States History, Volume 2

Urban Society

Violence and Terrorism

Western Civilization, Volume 1

Western Civilization, Volume 2

World History, Volume 1

World History, Volume 2

World Politics

Contents

UNIT 1
School Reforms: The Debate Continues

The concepts in bold italics are developed in the article. For further expansion, please refer to the Topic Guide.

UNIT 2
Teaching All Students in All Schools

UNIT 3
Cornerstones to Learning: Reading and Math

The concepts in bold italics are developed in the article. For further expansion, please refer to the Topic Guide.

UNIT 4
Creating Caring Communities of Learners

The concepts in bold italics are developed in the article. For further expansion, please refer to the Topic Guide.

UNIT 5
Addressing Diversity in Your School

The concepts in bold italics are developed in the article. For further expansion, please refer to the Topic Guide.

UNIT 6
Technology: Are We Effectively Using Its Potential in Our Schools?

The concepts in bold italics are developed in the article. For further expansion, please refer to the Topic Guide.

The concepts in bold italics are developed in the article. For further expansion, please refer to the Topic Guide.

Correlation Guide

The *Annual Editions* series provides students with convenient, inexpensive access to current, carefully selected articles from the public press. **Annual Editions: Education 12/13** is an easy-to-use reader that presents articles on important topics such as *learning, diversity, behavior management,* and many more. For more information on *Annual Editions* and other *McGraw-Hill Contemporary Learning Series* titles, visit www.mhhe.com/cls.

This convenient guide matches the units in **Annual Editions: Education 12/13** with the corresponding chapters in three of our best-selling McGraw-Hill Education textbooks by Sadker/Zittleman and Spring.

Annual Editions: Education 12/13	Teachers, Schools, and Society: A Brief Introduction to Education, 3/e, by Sadker/Zittleman	American Education, 15/e, by Spring
Unit 1: Reformatting Our Schools	**Chapter 5:** The Multicultural History of American Education **Chapter 6:** Philosophy of Education **Chapter 9:** Reforming America's Schools	**Chapter 1:** The History and Goals of Public Schooling **Chapter 4:** The Economic Goals of Schooling: Human Capital, Global Economy, and Preschool **Chapter 8:** Local Control, Choice, Charter Schools, and Home Schooling
Unit 2: Preparing Teachers to Teach All Students in All Schools	**Chapter 1:** The Teaching Profession and You **Chapter 2:** Different Ways of Learning **Chapter 3:** Teaching Your Diverse Students **Chapter 6:** Philosophy of Education **Chapter 8:** School Law and Ethics **Chapter 11:** Becoming an Effective Teacher	**Chapter 8:** Local Control, Choice, Charter Schools, and Home Schooling **Chapter 10:** The Profession of Teaching
Unit 3: Cornerstones to Learning: Reading and Math	**Chapter 10:** Curriculum, Standards, and Testing	
Unit 4: Caring Communities for Creating Learners	**Chapter 4:** Student Life in School and at Home	**Chapter 2:** The Social Goals of Schooling **Chapter 8:** Local Control, Choice, Charter Schools, and Home Schooling **Chapter 10:** The Profession of Teaching
Unit 5: Addressing Diversity in Your School	**Chapter 3:** Teaching Your Diverse Students **Chapter 5:** The Multicultural History of American Education	**Chapter 3:** Education and Equality of Opportunity **Chapter 5:** Equality of Educational Opportunity: Race, Gender, and Special Needs **Chapter 6:** Student Diversity **Chapter 7:** Multicultural and Multilingual Education
Unit 6: Rethinking Behavior Management: Getting the Behavior You Want and Need to Effectively Teach	**Chapter 4:** Student Life in School and at Home **Chapter 11:** Becoming an Effective Teacher	
Unit 7: Technology: Are We Effectively Using Its Potential in Our Schools?		

Topic Guide

This topic guide suggests how the selections in this book relate to the subjects covered in your course. You may want to use the topics listed on these pages to search the Web more easily.

On the following pages a number of websites have been gathered specifically for this book. They are arranged to reflect the units of this Annual Editions reader. You can link to these sites by going to www.mhhe.com/cls.

All the articles that relate to each topic are listed below the bold-faced term.

Achievement gaps
27. Meeting Students Where They Are: The Latino Education Crisis
37. Tech Tool Targets Elementary Readers
38. Digital Readers: The Next Chapter in E-Book Reading and Response
39. Digital Tools Expand Options for Personalized Learning
40. Differentiate Teaching and Learning with Web 2.0 Tools

Authentic learning
8. A Diploma Worth Having
39. Digital Tools Expand Options for Personalized Learning

Behavior management
25. She's Strict for a Good Reason: Highly Effective Teachers in Low-Performing Urban Schools

Bullying
20. The Power of Positive Relationships
26. What Educators Need to Know about Bullying Behaviors

Caring communities of learners
20. The Power of Positive Relationships
21. Teachers Connecting with Families—In the Best Interest of Children
22. Motivation: It's All About Me
23. Start Where Your Students Are
24. Leaving Nothing to Chance
25. She's Strict for a Good Reason: Highly Effective Teachers in Low-Performing Urban Schools

Critical thinking skills
32. Using Guided Notes to Enhance Instruction for All Students
33. Strategies for Every Teacher's Toolbox

Diversity
27. Meeting Students Where They Are: The Latino Education Crisis
28. What Does Research Say about Effective Practices for English Learners?
31. Literacy and Literature for 21st Century Global Citizenship

Early childhood education
29. Strategies and Content Areas for Teaching English Language Learners

Education leadership
1. 'Quality Education Is Our Moon Shot'
2. Duncan's Strategy Is Flawed
3. Grading Obama's Education Policy
4. Dictating to the Schools
5. Response to Intervention (RTI): What Teachers of Reading Need to Know
6. Responding to RTI
7. The Why Behind RTI
8. A Diploma Worth Having
24. Leaving Nothing to Chance
25. She's Strict for a Good Reason: Highly Effective Teachers in Low-Performing Urban Schools

Education
33. Strategies for Every Teacher's Toolbox
34. Methods for Addressing Conflict in Cotaught Classrooms
35. "For Openers: How Technology Is Changing School"
38. Digital Readers: The Next Chapter in E-Book Reading and Response

Education policies
1. 'Quality Education Is Our Moon Shot'
2. Duncan's Strategy Is Flawed
3. Grading Obama's Education Policy
4. Dictating to the Schools

Elementary education
25. She's Strict for a Good Reason: Highly Effective Teachers in Low-Performing Urban Schools
29. Strategies and Content Areas for Teaching English Language Learners

Engaging students
23. Start Where Your Students Are
24. Leaving Nothing to Chance
27. Meeting Students Where They Are: The Latino Education Crisis

English language learners
27. Meeting Students Where They Are: The Latino Education Crisis
28. What Does Research Say about Effective Practices for English Learners?
29. Strategies and Content Areas for Teaching English Language Learners
30. Teaching Photosynthesis with ELL Students

Families
21. Teachers Connecting with Families—In the Best Interest of Children

Future of education
1. 'Quality Education Is Our Moon Shot'
2. Duncan's Strategy Is Flawed
3. Grading Obama's Education Policy
4. Dictating to the Schools
8. A Diploma Worth Having

Gaming
37. Tech Tool Targets Elementary Readers
41. Effects of Video-Game Ownership on Young Boys' Academic and Behavioral Functioning: A Randomized, Controlled Study

Gender issues
19. Do Girls Learn Math Fear from Teachers?
41. Effects of Video-Game Ownership on Young Boys' Academic and Behavioral Functioning: A Randomized, Controlled Study

Inclusion
10. Teacher's Perspectives on Teaching Students Who Are Placed At-Risk
18. Strategies for Teaching Algebra to Students with Learning Disabilities: Making Research to Practice Connections

Technology

Internet References

The following Internet sites have been selected to support the articles found in this reader. These sites were available at the time of publication. However, because websites often change their structure and content, the information listed may no longer be available. We invite you to visit www.mhhe.com/cls for easy access to these sites.

Annual Editions: Education 12/13

General Sources

Education Week on the Web
www.edweek.org

At this Education Week home page you will be able to open its archives, read special reports on education, keep up on current events in education, look for job opportunities, and access articles relevant to educators today.

Educational Resources Information Center
www.eric.ed.gov

This invaluable site provides links to all ERIC sites: clearinghouses, support components, and publishers of ERIC materials. You can search the ERIC database, find out what is new, and ask questions about ERIC.

National Education Association
www.nea.org

Something about virtually every education-related topic can be accessed via this site of the 2.3-million-strong National Education Association.

Great Schools
www.greatschools.org

This privately funded organization was established to provide parents information about specific school districts and schools. In addition, there are useful tips to support parents who wish to be involved.

National Parent Information Network/ERIC
www.npin.org

This is a clearinghouse of information on elementary and early childhood education as well as urban education. Browse through its links for information for parents and for people who work with parents.

U.S. Department of Education
www.ed.gov

Explore this government site for examination of institutional aspects of multicultural education. National goals, projects, grants, and other educational programs are listed here as well as many links to teacher services and resources.

UNIT 1: School Reforms: The Debate Continues

U.S. Department of Education: Overview of the Educational Recovery Act
www.ed.gov/policy/gen/leg/recovery/programs.html

This page offers links to the various recovery acts passed during 2009. Here, you can learn what the acts are and how they are being implemented to improve public schools.

No Child Left Behind
www2.ed.gov/policy/elsec/guid/stateletters/index.html

This source links to the policy letters regarding NCLB. Reading these will increase your knowledge of a variety of topics of interest to teachers who must implement No Child Left Behind.

American School Board Journal
www.asbj.com

The National School Boards Association publishes a monthly magazine where educational issues of national interest are discussed. It offers the journal online (free of cost) and solicits reader comments at www.asbj.com/readerpanel. Further, at the Resources tab, are links to special reports and a topic archive that is a rich source of information on current topics.

The Response to Intervention Action Network
www.rtinetwork.org

The goal of the RTI Action Network, sponsored by the National Center for Learning Disabilities, is to inform educators and families about the large-scale implementation of RTI so that each child has equitable access to instruction and that struggling students are identified early, in order to receive the necessary supports to meet their individual needs. Materials and links offered at this website cover all grade levels and content areas. They bring leaders to the website to answer questions and offer webinars.

Teacher Magazine
www.edweek.org/tsb/articles/2010/04/12/02allington.h03.html

This link to *Teacher Magazine* will allow you to read or make comments in response to Dr. Richard Allington's article about Response to Intervention. In addition, in this online copy of the article you will find a link to allow you to sign up for the Education Week Teacher Book Club.

Wrightslaw
www.wrightslaw.com/info/rti.index.htm

Wrightslaw is the website of a lawyer who specializes in special education law and has argued special education cases before the U.S. Supreme Court. The link above leads you to his page on Response to Intervention where you will find additional links to national experts who helped frame the law and who offer their perspective on RTI.

The Bill & Melinda Gates Foundation
www.gatesfoundation.org/topics/Pages/high-schools.aspx

The Gates Foundation provides grants and donations to schools. Visit this website to learn how the foundation is working to improve educational opportunities across the country.

What Works Clearinghouse
www.ies.ed.gov/ncee/wwc

The Clearinghouse is a source for programs with scientific evidence that they work. You are able to create a summary of the research findings on a topic, such as beginning reading, and then read summaries of the research on all of the reviewed programs.

The Center for Comprehensive School Reform and Improvement
www.centerforcsri.org

Information about research-based strategies and assistance for schools wishing to make positive changes is available on this U.S. Department of Education sponsored website. You can search the database by topic, listen to podcasts, and view videos to learn how schools are working to reform the educational experience for students.

Internet References

Unit 2: Teaching All Students in All Schools

National Center for Children in Poverty
www.nccp.org

Explore this website to find the demographics of your state's population and to learn more about children living in poverty.

U.S. Census Bureau: Poverty
www.census.gov/hhes/www/poverty/poverty.html

The Census Bureau collects and maintains a comprehensive database about poverty in America. This rich source has many reports and tables of data to help you understand the effects of poverty.

Southern Poverty Law Center Teaching Diverse Students Initiative
www.tolerance.org/tdsi/cb_achievement_gaps

On this page of the SPLC, you will find articles and videos regarding how race and underachievement are stereotypically linked, when poverty is really the issue.

Donors Choose
www.donorschoose.org

On this website teachers can post projects and solicit funds to complete those programs, projects, or lesson plans. Donors can choose which programs, projects, and lessons they wish to fund.

Doing What Works
http://dww.ed.gov/index.cfm

As stated on the homepage, this website provides articles that translate research-based practices into practical tools to improve classroom instruction. Many of these teaching practices are needed to help children who live in poverty learn and thrive.

Center on Rural Education
www2.ed.gov/nclb/freedom/local/rural/index.html

This agency within the federal government will provide additional information about funding and programs designed specifically for rural schools.

The Rural School and Community Trust
www.ruraledu.org

On the homepage, find the *Customized Content for* title on the left, click on *Teacher* at the bottom of the list to find information about being a teacher in rural America.

Edutopia
www.edutopia.org

Regardless of SES and locations of a school, teaching methods such as Project-based Learning can be used to teach all children the problem-solving and critical-thinking skills needed for adulthood. This website has many video examples and articles about how teachers are integrating the real world into their teaching.

Unit 3: Cornerstones to Learning: Reading and Math

The National Council of Teachers of English (NCTE)
www.readwritethink.org/professional-development/strategy-guides/supporting-comprehension-strategies-english-30106.html

NCTE provides teaching strategies for supporting language learning for students who are not native-English speakers. In addition, it provides information about other resources and professional readings.

International Association of Reading
www.reading.org/General/Default.aspx

This international association for reading offers resources on many reading topics such as adolescent literacy, reading comprehension, the history of reading, Response to Intervention, and technology. In addition, it provides information on conferences, workshops, and books about teaching reading.

Jim Trelease's Read-aloud Home Page
www.trelease-on-reading.com

Did you know you can use rain gutters for book shelves? Or do you know where to find an online interview with a favorite author? Or do you know how to read a book you don't want to read? Answers can be found on the website noted above.

Literature Circles Resource Center
www.litcircles.org

The comprehensive website will help you start a literature circle in your classroom. Begin with the link to *How to use this site.*

Read, Write, Think
www.readwritethink.org

This resource-rich website is sponsored by the International Reading Association and National Council of Teachers of English. You can find lesson plans, student materials, and Web resources for teaching language and reading.

Visible Thinking
www.pzweb.harvard.edu/vt/index.html

Visible Thinking is one of several programs that are part of Project Zero at Harvard University. The goal is to help students develop thinking dispositions that support thoughtful learning—in the arts, and across school subjects. Also visit the Artful Thinking website at www.pzweb.harvard.edu/tc/index.cfm.

National Council of Teachers of Mathematics
www.nctm.org

The National Council of Teachers of Mathematics (NCTM) has a resource-rich website for any teacher who wants professional development, suggestions for teaching, or is interested in attending conferences and workshops. Membership in this professional organization offers opportunities to network with teachers who share an interest in mathematics.

National Library of Virtual Manipulatives
www.nlvm.usu.edu/en/nav/vlibrary.html

This site, sponsored by Utah State University, offers a wide variety of online manipulatives that teachers and students can use to enhance learning of mathematical principals.

Unit 4: Creating Caring Communities of Learners

American School Board Journal
www.asbj.com/TopicsArchive/Bullying/default.aspx

Editors of this journal compiled a set of resources for teachers and school administers to use for professional development. Regardless of your reason for interest in bullying, this page contains valuable information.

Teacher Vision
www.teachervision.fen.com/education-and-parents/resource/3730.html

This website has links to many topics of interest to all teachers. The link will take you to a page of tips, strategies, and free *printables* to use as you collaborate and consult with parents of your students. Under the tab *Classroom Management* you will find more information about conduction-effective and collaborative conferences with parents.

Coalition of Essential Schools
www.essentialschools.org

The Coalition is about creating and sustaining personalized, equitable, and intellectually challenging schools. While you will have access to many resources on this website, if you register you can participate in blogs and discussions online.

Internet References

The National Coalition for Parent Involvement in Education (NCPIE)
www.ncpie.org

On this website you will find information and ideas about research, programs, and policies to increase family involvement in education. You will find access to resources, tools, and legislative updates to assist you in promoting parent and family involvement in their child's education.

Office of Safe and Drug-Free Schools
www2.ed.gov/about/offices/list/osdfs/index.html

This office of the U.S. Department of Education is devoted to programs for drug and violence prevention. In addition, you can find data for your state and information about professional development.

GLSEN: Gay, Lesbian and Straight Education Network
www.glsen.org/cgi-bin/iowa/all/home/index.html

On this website you will find information about GLSEN and its programs to develop school climates where difference is valued for the positive contribution it makes in creating a more vibrant and diverse community.

Unit 5: Addressing Diversity in Your School

The Literacy Web
www.literacy.uconn.edu/index.htm

The University of Connecticut sponsors this website devoted to literacy. You will find many useful resources for teaching reading to all students. If you are interested in teaching English Language Learners, go to the *Literacy Topics* page and scroll down to find the link to ESL/EFL.

New Horizons for Learning
www.newhorizons.org

This site has many resources for teachers who work with diverse students. The topics addressed by the group are news from the neurosciences, teaching strategies, student voices, lifelong learning, and special needs. Resources include articles to read online, lists of additional recommended reading, and related links.

National Association for Multicultural Education (NAME)
www.nameorg.org

NAME is a professional organization for persons interested in multicultural education. However, there are many resources available for nonmember teachers in the Resource Center.

Multicultural Education Internet Resource Guide
www2.nau.edu/~jar/Multi.html

This website offers links to over 50 additional websites of educational resources. These include information about multicultural education, culturally diverse holidays, libraries, artwork, and lesson plans.

Everything ESL
www.everythingesl.net

You WILL find everything at this website! This veteran teacher offers lesson plans ready to use, teaching tips, discussion topics where you can ask questions and read teaching tips from other teachers, and links to additional resources.

The Center for Comprehensive School Reform and Improvement
Center's Home page: www.centerforcsri.org

Center's link for resources on English Language Learners and Diverse Students: www.centerforcsri.org/index .php?option=com_content&task=view&id=678&Itemid=126

These two links will provide additional information on best-practices for teaching and supporting students who are diverse, including those who are ELL, Gifted/Talented, or who have a disability.

The Power of Two
www.powerof2.org

Collaboration is a powerful tool for teachers to use in their classrooms. Teachers who coteach share the fun of teaching as well as the load of planning, grading, and managing behavior. This website will provide videos of teachers who are masters of collaboration as well as materials and ideas for ways to do collaboration. You will need to log in but it is free.

Unit 6: Technology: Are We Effectively Using Its Potential in Our Schools?

Educational Technology
www.edtech.sandi.net

Are you concerned that you do not know enough to help your students learn with technology. Visit the San Diego School District website link found above. Under the category of *Resources* you will find helpful tutorials, lesson plans, and other resources to get you started teaching with technology.

Center for Applied Special Technology
http://cast.org

CAST is the primary source for information about Universal Design for Learning. There are interactive activities, a hyperlinked, digital text, and sample lesson plans at www.cast .org/teachingeverystudent/. This is a must-see website.

Curriculum Connections
www.edtech.sandi.net/old305/handouts/digitalclassroom /curriculumconnections.html

This is a comprehensive resource for lesson plans, teaching materials, and online resources for your students. Content is offered by grade level and content area. You will find resources to U.S. national parks, libraries, zoos, and many other websites that will enhance your teaching and student learning.

Open Thinking Wiki
http://couros.wikispaces.com/TechAndMediaLiteracyVids

This wiki is meant as a resource for courses I teach related to ICT in education and media studies. The creator, Alec Couros, is the ICT Coordinator of the Faculty of Education, University of Regina. The link *About* will take you to a page of resources all teachers will find helpful.

No limits 2 learning: Celebrating human potential through assistive technology
www.nolimitstolearning.blogspot.com

Lon Thornburg is an educator and assistive technology specialist and trainer. His blog is updated regularly with the latest information on technology tools that all students can use. However, he does offer clear descriptions and reviews that all of us can understand.

Quest Garden
www.questgarden.com

Looking for a way to include Project-based Learning into your lesson plans? This is the website for you. Regardless of the content area, topic, or size of your class, you will find a Web Quest you can use at this site. All Web Quests found here have been peer previewed.

Go2web20
www.go2web20.net

Some schools and teachers do not have the funds to purchase software every year. At Go2Web20 you will find 68 pages of Web 2.0 tools and applications. Some of these are just for fun, but many can be used for educational purposes. Enjoy searching here.

UNIT 1

School Reforms:
The Debate Continues

Unit Selections

1. **'Quality Education Is Our Moon Shot',** Joan Richardson
2. **Duncan's Strategy Is Flawed,** ASBJ Reader's Panel
3. **Grading Obama's Education Policy,** Michael W. Apple
4. **Dictating to the Schools,** Diane Ravitch
5. **Response to Intervention (RTI): What Teachers of Reading Need to Know,** Eric M. Mesmer and Heidi Anne E. Mesmer
6. **Responding to RTI,** Anthony Rebora
7. **The Why Behind RTI,** Austin Buffum, Mike Mattos, and Chris Weber
8. **A Diploma Worth Having,** Grant Wiggins

Learning Outcomes

After reading this unit, you will be able to:

- Explain the issues that make revisions of the No Child Left Behind (NCLB) Act necessary.
- Discuss the merits of the five strategies that Secretary Duncan thinks will support school improvement under a new NCLB Act.
- Synthesize the public responses to the policies and strategies suggested for the revision of NCLB.
- Construct your own response to the policies and strategies in NCLB.
- Paraphrase each of the levels of Response to Intervention (RTI) process.
- Explain how to complete each of the five steps to implementation of RTI.
- Prepare a plan for using the RTI process in your classroom.
- Present an argument for or against the implementation of RTI in general education classrooms.
- Assess the criticism of RTI's value as a method for finding and remediating students who are struggling to learn.
- Debate the purposes of secondary education.

Student Website

www.mhhe.com/cls

Internet References

U.S. Department of Education: Overview of the Educational Recovery Act
www.ed.gov/policy/gen/leg/recovery/programs.html

No Child Left Behind
www2.ed.gov/policy/elsec/guid/stateletters/index.html

American School Board Journal
www.asbj.com

The Response to Intervention Action Network
www.rtinetwork.org

Teacher Magazine
www.edweek.org/tsb/articles/2010/04/12/02allington.h03.html

Wrightslaw
www.wrightslaw.com/info/rti.index.htm

The Bill & Melinda Gates Foundation
www.gatesfoundation.org/topics/Pages/high-schools.aspx

What Works Clearinghouse
www.ies.ed.gov/ncee/wwc

The Center for Comprehensive School Reform and Improvement
www.centerforcsri.org

As school districts have implemented "No Child Left Behind" (NCLB) legislation, they have restructured the schools to emphasize core content proficiency. In other words, the emphasis has been on preparing students to meet college entrance requirements. We are left to decide the equity issues involved. We are also left to answer the most fundamental question of all: What constitutes a "well-educated high school graduate"? What educational background should the person have? We are a democratic society, committed to the free education of all our citizens, but are we accomplishing that goal? The Clinton administration established Goals 2000 under the *Educate America Act*. Two of these goals are important to the discussion of what constitutes a well-educated graduate.

Goal 2 states that "The high school graduation rate will increase to at least 90%" (U.S. Department of Education n.d.). The data indicate that we have not reached this goal, and are far from achieving it. While there is some disagreement on the exact percentages, most researchers agree that we have not reached the goal of 90 percent.

Goal 5 states that "Every adult American will be literate and will possess the knowledge and skills necessary to compete in a global economy and exercise the rights and responsibilities of citizenship" (U.S. Department of Education n.d.). Educators have acknowledged that high school graduates get more satisfactory jobs, are happier in their job choices, and earn higher salaries than nongraduates. Heckman and LaFontaine (2008) note the decline in high school graduation since 1970 (for cohorts born after 1950) has flattened growth in the skill level of the U.S. workforce. We must, at the very least, confront the drop-out problem to increase the skill levels of the future workforce. We must also consider how high schools that respond only to higher education demands may be ignoring the needs of the nation at-large for a skilled workforce that can compete in a global market. Bridgeland, Dilulio, and Morrison (2006) found in a survey of dropouts that 47 percent reported a major reason why they left school was the classes were not interesting. We must consider that by simply preparing students to attend traditional four-year institutions we may be ignoring their interests and desires, thus alienating them.

Educational law and policy issues of NCLB and Response to Intervention are hot-button topics in most schools of education.

Each of the articles in this unit relates to the tension involved in conceiving how educational development should proceed in response to all the dramatic social and economic changes in society.

In the first article, Secretary of Education, Arne Duncan, responds to questions and lays out the rationale for the educational reform proposed by the Obama administration. These reforms are informed in part by his experiences as the CEO of the Chicago Public School system, and his belief that a quality education for all children is the civil rights issue of his generation. In the interview, he lays out several actions he believes will achieve these goals. However, he is not without detractors. In the article, "Duncan's Strategy Is Flawed," we can read the comments and concerns of educators across the country. As readers discuss these articles, perhaps a basic question to ask

© Blend Images/Getty Images

might be how will these reforms change the data presented in the paragraphs above under Goals 2 and 5 of *Goals 2000*?

On the other hand, the articles regarding Response to Intervention in this unit present direct actions that may be taken to address the primary and devastating educational problem of struggling students who do not read well and who constitute 80 percent of the students identified for special education. Response to Intervention (RTI) was introduced in the Public Law 108-446 (IDEA-2004) as a method to identify students with learning disability. Mesmer and Mesmer provide a straightforward explanation of the legislation with clear definitions and details supported with examples. All educational professionals will benefit from reading this article. In "Responding to RTI" Allington expresses strong opinions about its use to achieve full literacy in our country by stating that RTI is possibly "our last, best hope." He has much more to say about how we assess and teach reading in public schools, and in the end, he states we must " . . . ask the questions about what we are doing or not doing, rather than asking what is wrong with the child." In the third RTI article, Buffum suggests we consider the why behind RTI in order to ask the right questions. Asking the right questions is critical as local school districts implement and use the results of collected data. Finally, Wiggins asserts there is only one valid measure of the high school curriculum. How well does it prepare students for their adult lives? Going back to the beginning of the twentieth century, he asks us to consider the foundational purposes for education and face the future by reconsidering the past.

As we consider reformatting the educational system of the United States, we must engage in an intensively reflective and analytical effort. Further, we must give considerable contemplation and forethought to the consequences, because our actions will shape not only the students' futures, but also the future of our country as a member of the global community. Prospective teachers are being encouraged to question their own individual educational experiences as they read the articles presented in this section. All of us must acknowledge that our values affect both our ideas about curriculum and what we believe is the purpose of educating others. The economic and demographic changes in the last decade and those that will occur in the future necessitate a fundamental reconceptualization of how schools ought to respond to social and economic environments in which they are located. How can schools, for instance, reflect the needs of and respond to the diverse group of students they serve while meeting the needs of our democratic society?

References

Bridgeland, J. M., Dilulio, J. J., & Morrison, K. B. 2006. "The Silent Epidemic: Perspectives of High School Dropouts." Bill & Melinda Gates Foundation. Retrieved on 28 May 2008 from www.gatesfoundation.org/Pages/home.aspx.

U.S. Department of Education. Summary of Goals 2000: Educate America Act. Author. Retrieved on 28 May 2008 from www.ed.gov/legislation/GOALS2000/TheAct/sec102.html.

'Quality Education Is Our Moon Shot'

An interview with Secretary of Education Arne Duncan.

JOAN RICHARDSON

KAPPAN: Whenever we embark on any project, we're always encouraged to "begin with the end in mind," so that's where I want to start this interview. The last Administration will be forever tagged with No Child Left Behind as its legacy. When Arne Duncan and Barack Obama leave Washington in four years or eight years, what do you hope folks will be saying about what you contributed to education?

DUNCAN: Well, the President has drawn a line in the sand. He has said that by 2020, we want to again have the largest percentage of college graduates in the world. We used to have that a couple of decades ago. We've lost our way. We've flat lined. Other countries have passed us by. That's our Moon shot.

But we have to get dramatically better to get there. That's the goal. We're going to push as hard as we can to hit that goal. The President and I both believe that we have to educate our way to a better economy. It's the only way we're going to get there.

Achieving a quality education for all children is the civil rights issue of our generation. We have to give children a chance to fulfill their potential and be successful. And the way to do that is by giving them quality educational opportunities.

Achieving a quality education for all children is the civil rights issue of our generation.

That means that we have to reduce the dropout rate significantly. We have to increase the graduation rate. We have to make sure that the students who graduate are prepared to go on to be successful in some form of higher education, whether it's a two-year college, a four-year university, vocational, or technical training.

We want to get dramatically better in every piece of the education continuum: early childhood, K-12, higher ed. as well. It's an ambitious agenda, but we think it's all critically important.

KAPPAN: Is there one phrase that you could use to describe what you just said?

DUNCAN: We want to become the most educated country in the world. That's the goal.

The Future of NCLB

KAPPAN: I want to talk about the reauthorization of ESEA (Elementary and Secondary Education Act). As you make plans to move ahead with that, I want to know how you think you can change No Child Left Behind from what many perceive to be a test-and-punish law to a law that is really focused on improving student learning?

DUNCAN: Let me start by telling you what I like about No Child Left Behind. I always try to give the previous Administration credit for its focus on the achievement gap and its use of disaggregating student data.

As a country, we used to sweep that conversation under the rug and not talk about the tremendous disparities in outcomes between white children and African-American and Latino children. Forever-more, we will keep that front and center.

I think that's an important conversation. It's sometimes uncomfortable. It's sometimes tough. But, as a country, we have a tremendous achievement gap that we have to continue to close. Having transparency around that and challenging ourselves to both raise the bar and close the gap is hugely important.

Having said that, there are things that need to change pretty fundamentally. The opportunity that we have is to be very pragmatic. If it worked, then let's keep it. If it didn't work, then let's blue sky it and think in very different ways.

First, as you know, No Child Left Behind was dramatically underfunded. We've put over $100 billion into education. While it's never enough, it's a huge investment.

Second, from a management standpoint, you have to figure out what you manage loose and what you manage tight. I think they got this one fundamentally backwards. NCLB was very, very loose on the goals. So there are 50 different goal posts, 50 different measurements at the state level.

And the vast majority of those got dummied down due to political pressure. In some states, including my state of Illinois,

The Four Reforms

Secretary Arne Duncan and President Barack Obama have pledged federal money to four central areas of reform that they believe will drive school improvement:

- Adopt internationally benchmarked standards and assessments that prepare students for success in college and the workplace;
- Recruit, develop, retain, and reward effective teachers and principals;
- Build data systems that measure student success and inform teachers and principals how they can improve their practices; and
- Turn around the lowest-performing schools.

Learn more about programs being supported by the American Recovery and Reinvestment Act and the Race to the Top funds.

www.ed.gov/policy/gen/leg/recovery/programs.html

have access to art or drama or music is in school. So how are we going to think differently about that? How are we going to make sure that we're giving all children a well-rounded education from the earliest ages on?

Then, finally, to your original starting point: No Child Left Behind did a lot of labeling of schools as failures. I'm much more interested in gain and growth than in absolute test scores. There were a lot of schools that were labeled as failures that were actually improving every year. That was wrong. That's tremendously demoralizing to staff and confusing to parents. That needs to be corrected.

No Child Left Behind is what I would call a blunt instrument. Schools that were improving got labeled as failures. Schools that were struggling didn't get the help that they needed. Schools at the bottom that need to be fundamentally and absolutely transformed got incremental help, which doesn't get us where we need to go.

If we have a much more finely tuned instrument that would understand those really important distinctions between schools, it would help us dramatically improve student outcomes. It would help us turn around schools that need dramatic, fundamental change and do it with a real sense of urgency.

Urban Districts

KAPPAN: You came into this job with dramatically different on-the-ground experience than most of your predecessors in this job. You had some demonstrated success in a very challenged urban district. What do you say to other urban superintendents about where they begin the hard work of improving student learning in those districts? How do you create systems of success? Where do you start?

DUNCAN: It's very complex, but it starts with real leadership at the top. You have to have strong, courageous leadership. You can't do anything without that. You have to rally the entire community behind these efforts. I've argued that if it's just the school system by itself trying to get better, you're not going to get there. You need the business community, the philanthropic community, the religious community; you need the not-for-profits, you need the parks and recreation, health and human services. This has to be a citywide effort. You cannot have a world-class city without a world-class school system.

we're actually lying to children. When you tell the parent that their child is meeting the 'state standard,' the logical assumption is that they're on track to be successful.

I would argue that, in many places, the standard has been dummied down so much that those children who are just meeting the standard are barely able to graduate from high school and absolutely inadequately prepared to go on to a competitive four-year university, much less graduate.

So, they were very loose on the goal but very prescriptive on how you get there. Very tight on that. I think that's backwards. I want to fundamentally flip that on its head.

We want common, career-ready, college-ready standards that would be internationally benchmarked. We would let people be creative and innovative about how they get to those standards, but we'd hold them accountable for results. Have people at the local level figure out the best way to get there.

I often joke that before I came to Washington, I didn't believe that all of the good ideas came out of Washington. Now that I'm in Washington, I *know* that all of the good ideas don't come out of Washington. The best ideas are always going to come at the local level.

So fundamentally, we want to be loose and tight. To become tight on the goals but to allow people to become much more entrepreneurial, much more creative, innovative to get there.

I also worry a lot about the narrowing of the curriculum under No Child Left Behind. Too many schools are focusing on just what's tested so there's a loss of P.E., music, art, the nontested subjects, even science in some places.

It's so important that all children at the early ages have exposure to those things. That's how children develop their skills and discover their passions. I worry particularly about disadvantaged children who don't have those opportunities in their homes or their communities. The only place they're going to

You cannot have a world-class city without a world-class school system.

You've seen a series of mayors—Mayor (Richard) Daley in Chicago, Mayor (Michael) Bloomberg in New York, Mayor (Adrian) Fenty here in Washington—provide real leadership at the top to rally an entire city, not just the school district by itself.

Leadership at the top, all hands on deck, everyone pushing hard in the right direction, and a commitment for the long haul. None of this is about an overnight success. You have to be willing to stick with it. But I can't imagine a more important activity for a city and one that a city can rally behind than dramatically improving the quality of public education.

It combines a real sense of self-interest. If you want to attract and retain jobs, you have to have an educated workforce. And the sense of altruism that our children deserve more than what we're giving them.

At the end of the day, it brings together a set of interests.

Mayoral Control

KAPPAN: I assume that all of the ideas that are in your plan, all of the ideas in the Obama plan for education, that all of those are driven by your belief that they will improve student learning.

DUNCAN: Yes, absolutely. That's what it's all about, driving student achievement. It's about closing the gap and raising the bar.

KAPPAN: Let's tick through some of those ideas and help me make the link between those ideas and improving student learning. You touched on mayoral control, so let's start there. What's the connection between mayoral control and improving student learning?

DUNCAN: It's not always the right answer. It's a piece of an answer. It's not a magic bullet. In some places, it might be the wrong answer. But I would argue that in large urban cities with a history of fairly dysfunctional school systems, the work is so hard and the challenges so intractable that you have to have strong leadership at the top to give you a chance to get there.

It doesn't guarantee success, but it puts you in the ball game. The problem is so large, the needs are so great that everyone in the city needs to rally around the effort.

The best person I can think of to rally all those different sectors together to achieve that is the mayor.

Charter Schools

KAPPAN: Same question related to charter schools. By the way, in the Gallup Poll, charter schools got a lot of support, even though people still seem to be confused by exactly what they are.

DUNCAN: I've always said I'm not a fan of charters, I'm a fan of good charters.

Three things have to happen for charter schools to be successful. First, you have to have a very high bar for entry. This is not "let a thousand flowers bloom." I would argue that there are far too many low-performing charters. We had a lot of charters in Chicago, but I closed three charter schools because they weren't performing.

This is not "let a thousand flowers bloom."

Arne Duncan

POSITION: U.S. Secretary of Education. Oversees a staff of 4,200 employees and a budget of $62.6 billion in regular FY 2009 discretionary appropriations and $96.8 billion in discretionary funding provided under the American Recovery and Reinvestment Act of 2009. Operates programs that touch every area and level of education—elementary and secondary programs annually serve nearly 14,000 school districts and about 56 million students attending some 98,000 public schools and 34,000 private schools. Department programs also provide grant, loan, and work-study assistance to more than 13 million postsecondary students.

AGE: 45

EDUCATION: Graduated magna cum laude from Harvard University with a bachelor's degree in sociology, 1987. Senior thesis: "The Values, Aspirations and Opportunities of the Urban Underclass" (unpublished) which he wrote after taking a year off and working at his mother's education center in Chicago. Attended University of Chicago Laboratory School, a private school that President Obama's children later attended.

PROFESSIONAL HISTORY: Played professional basketball with the Eastside Spectres in Australia, 1987 to 1991. Returned to Chicago in 1992 to run the Ariel Education Initiative, which helped fund a college education as part of the I Have a Dream program. Joined the Chicago Public Schools in 1998 as deputy chief of staff to then-CEO Paul Vallas. Replaced Vallas in 2001 and served as CEO for seven years. Became Secretary of Education in January 2009.

FAMILY: Wife, Karen, and two children (Claire, 7, Ryan, 4). Claire attends a public school in Northern Virginia. Mother, Sue Duncan, runs the Sue Duncan Children's Center (sueduncanchildrenscenter.org), an independent early-learning center on Chicago's South Side; father, the late Starkey Duncan Jr., was a psychology professor at the University of Chicago and a leading researcher in the study of nonverbal and verbal interactions.

PERSONAL: 6'5" tall. Plays basketball with the President. Grew up without a television at home.

The chance to educate our kids is like a sacred obligation. You really need to have a very clear vetting process so you're only allowing the best of the best to do that.

Once you've done that, two other things have to happen. You have to give these schools real autonomy. These are by definition educational entrepreneurs who have a different vision of education. You have to free them from the bureaucracy and give them the chance to innovate and create.

Third, you have to tie that autonomy to real accountability. We had five-year performance contracts. If they're not performing, you need to close them down.

When those three things happen, you can have remarkable, remarkable results for children. It's a piece of the answer. It's by no means the whole answer.

Merit Pay

KAPPAN: Another question that we asked in the Gallup Poll was about merit pay. We found that there was very high public support for merit pay. Are you surprised by that? Why do you think there was so much support? To the bigger question, why do you think that could be a lever for improving student learning?

DUNCAN: In education, we've been so scared to talk about excellence. I don't understand that. Great teachers and great principals make a tremendous difference in students' lives. Talent matters tremendously in education. Great teachers and great principals are the unsung heroes in our society. They perform miracles every day. They change student lives on a daily basis.

Somehow as a country, we've been scared to talk about that. In every other sector, in your world, in the media, business, sports, entertainment, music, excellence gets recognized. It gets rewarded. You learn from it. It gets replicated. In education, we're scared to do that. We have to do a much better job of identifying, rewarding, recognizing, spotlighting, and learning from excellence.

We have to do a much better job of identifying, rewarding, recognizing, spotlighting, and learning from excellence.

Nobody goes into education to make a million dollars. People go into education for the most altruistic of reasons. They want to make a difference. It's a phenomenally committed group of folks. But there's no reason we can't provide some recognition for those who go beyond the call of duty every day and make a huge difference in students' lives. I don't think we can do enough of that. There's a lot that we can do, not just at the individual teacher level, but at the school level.

When I see a high-performing school, it's every adult in the building working together. It's not just the teachers and the principal, it's the custodians, the security guards, the social workers, the lunchroom attendants; they're all working hard and working together. We need to know who's doing a great job and shine a spotlight on them.

KAPPAN: Your proposal is to tie those pay increases into teacher evaluations and to testing data.

DUNCAN: Well, that's a piece of it. Teachers are concerned that that will be the only measure. I couldn't agree more. It should never be the only measure.

I'm fighting the reverse fight. I'm fighting the fight against those folks who say there should never be a tie between student achievement and teacher performance.

I'm fighting the fight against those folks who say there should never be a tie between student achievement and teacher performance.

There are actually states that prohibit linking student data with teacher data. (Editor's note: California prohibits using its teacher-identification database for making decisions about teacher pay, promotion, evaluation, and other employment issues. New York prohibits using student achievement data in making tenure decisions.) That, to me, is stunning. That totally devalues the profession. It basically says that teaching doesn't matter, that anybody can do this. We know there's tremendous variation there. In those situations, everyone loses. Teachers who are successful don't get rewarded. Teachers who are struggling don't get the support that they need. Teachers who shouldn't be teaching don't get moved out. So every adult loses. And when the adults lose, guess what? The children lose, too. That doesn't make sense to me.

So we're creating significant incentives to encourage folks to think about this in a different way.

Grading the Public Schools

DUNCAN: Here's another Gallup result that I think is fascinating. This is the most remarkable finding. Everyone thinks their own school is good and that everybody else's school is bad. That's a constant theme.

KAPPAN: Why do you think that exists?

DUNCAN: Too many people don't understand how bad their own schools are. They always think it's somebody else's kid who's not being educated. They don't understand that it's their own kid who's being short-changed. That's part of our challenge. How do you awaken the public to believe that your own kid isn't getting what they need and you don't know it. If they would wake up, they could be part of the change. We need to wake them up.

Duncan and Sports

KAPPAN: OK, last question. This is the basketball question, but I'm not going to ask you whom you're playing, where you're playing, and who's winning. But talking about basketball is a required part of every interview with you, right?

DUNCAN: Absolutely.

KAPPAN: I'm assuming again that basketball, sports, played a big part in your life as you were growing up, or you wouldn't have gone on to do what you did, playing basketball at Harvard, playing professional basketball in Australia after graduation.

In this test-crazy environment where, as you noted, so many things are being lost at schools, what's the role of competitive athletics in schools today? What role do you think that ought to play in a kid's education?

DUNCAN: Sports can be a tremendous vehicle for teaching students really important life lessons. When you talk about student athletes, as long as that student piece is kept front and center, I think great things can happen. Too often, it gets flipped and becomes athlete first and student second. That has a very damaging impact on students. I worry about the skewed or warped sense of priorities and values there.

But when it's kept in perspective, the life lessons that you can learn on the court or the playing field—hard work, selflessness, teamwork, working for the greater good, not about yourself—those life lessons can be hugely important. I absolutely believe that I would not be doing what I'm doing today if I had not had a chance to learn those lessons. For me, that was on the basketball court.

With the proper coaching in the right context with a laser-like focus on academics first and sports being the carrot, the reward for good academic work, I think sports can have a huge and positive role.

What I worry about are adults living their own dreams through students and chasing a dream of going pro. When students don't focus academically, that ends up dooming a kid to academic failure.

It can be a tool for good or it can be really destructive to children, depending on the quality and character of the adults who are engaged with those children.

KAPPAN: And I won't ask you who wins when you play horse.

DUNCAN: (Laughs) I plead the fifth.

Critical Thinking

1. List and explain the issues that Secretary of Education Duncan thinks make revision of the No Child Left Behind (NCLB) Act necessary. Your explanation should include a discussion of why these are important to you as a teacher.

2. Share the Duncan interview with a P–12 teacher. Engage the teacher in a conversation about the five strategies that are suggested to improve schools. Write a summary of your conversation to share with peers in class.

3. If you disagree with Secretary Duncan's four reform goals, what would be your top three goals for public education in the United States?

4. Secretary Duncan stated that "by 2020, we want to again have the largest percentage of college graduates in the world." Should this be the primary goal of our public schools? Provide a rationale for your answer.

JOAN RICHARDSON is editor-in-chief of *Phi Delta Kappan* magazine.

Duncan's Strategy Is Flawed

He's definitely racing somewhere, just maybe not to "The Top." That's what many of you seemed to be saying when asked if Arne Duncan is "on the right track" concerning his ambitious plan to reform the public schools. Just 16 percent said that the education secretary's plan is sound, compared with 26 percent who found it seriously flawed. The biggest group—48 percent—weighed in with "maybe," and 10 percent chose "none of the above."

Is this NCLB all over again? That thought scares Missouri board member Peggy Taylor.

"It appears we are selling out for big bucks, while compromising if not eroding local control," said Taylor, who is also president of the Missouri School Boards' Association. "Big bucks are owed to public education for all the broken promises over the years. The 'rush' to the race certainly guarantees another federal mess at a time we are challenged to survive with our budgets and save teaching positions. Secretary Duncan's enthusiasm for education is refreshing, but firing principals and 50 percent of the teachers is not the answer. Is this the preliminary test run for the new look of the replacement for NCLB? That is scary to me!"

More comments:

I believe he is on the right track, but I am not convinced he will be successful. To be successful, he will need many educational leaders to be willing to accept change that they have been unwilling to accept in the past. We need talented teachers to enter the classroom and better ways to evaluate their success. We need state governments to be prepared to uphold teacher quality and de-tenure teachers when it is warranted. We need to be willing to try to bring innovation back into schools by trying new things supported by research to determine when it works and when it does not work. This is all dependent on the willingness of current and future educators to be prepared to accept change. I hope Secretary Duncan can pull it off, and I am rooting for his side. —*Paul Herman, New Jersey*

Until they quit the procedure of "the whippings will continue until morale improves," they will continue to have issues. They need to treat educators as professionals and not the enemy. Most of the panels are made up of non-educators. Most educators now are working very hard to make sure that their students achieve; however, their opinions are not valued. Who will the experts get to put their plans and visions into action? Of course, the educators in the field. —*Ron Saunders, Superintendent, Georgia*

Duncan's desire to put mayors in control of public schools is a recipe for disaster. We need to talk about how money can matter when it is focused on specific academic interventions, tied to measureable outcomes, and embedded in a system with quality professional development and support. Just pouring more money into education won't solve our country's education problems. I'm waiting to hear a plan based on a foundation of local control, not Washington D.C., control. —*Fred Deutsch, Board Member, South Dakota*

There are so many endeavors that focus on "systemic change" in school reform. The one area that *always* engenders better results is when the students are blessed with a superb teacher. When the power of the teachers' unions is blunted, and poorly performing teachers can be removed more easily, then real reform will happen. The sad part is that these poor performers are probably only 5 percent of the profession. That is what we are protecting at such a great cost to kids. —*Paul Vranish, Superintendent, Texas*

The current system is functioning exactly as it was intended—play to the bell curve and prepare citizens for a life in an industrial world. Throwing money at a system that does not serve the needs of the current and future marketplace is insane. Substantive changes must occur in the way the education system is conceived. . . . Putting a high priority on teacher excellence is a good start and the subject of research by Battelle for Kids [a nonprofit focused on school improvement]. However, extending the school day and adding charter schools will do little to address the fundamental problem—outdated methods, buildings, and expectations. —*Anna Bucy, Board Member, Ohio*

Certainly the call for higher standards is warranted, and perhaps even [Duncan's] call for international standards. NAEP is just the latest "test" to come down the line. Until assessments are scored by third parties who truly are in the international arena, assessment will remain a political football. It is my hope that his insistence of tying performance to pay will make a difference. —*Michael R. Martin, Superintendent, Tennessee*

Critical Thinking

1. Summarize the public responses to Duncan's suggested revision of NCLB.
2. Based on what you have read in this unit, your conversation with active teachers, and your own experiences as a public school student, construct your own response to Duncan's plans to revise NCLB.

Grading Obama's Education Policy

Michael W. Apple

For those of us who slogged through the years of No Child Left Behind and its damaging effects on education, Barack Obama's election promised what we hoped was a major shift in educational policies. The threat of privatization would no longer hang over schools. Curricula would no longer be simply made up of low-level facts to be mastered for seemingly mindless tests. Teachers would no longer have to spend weeks doing nothing but test preparation with their students. Poor children of color would no longer be so overrepresented in special education classes, shunted there as an excuse for not dealing with the realities of racism in the larger society.

Schools would finally get the resources they needed to try to compensate for the loss of jobs, ever increasing impoverishment, lack of health care, massive rates of incarceration, and loss of hope in the communities that they served. A richer and more vital vision of education would replace the eviscerated vision of education that now reigned supreme.

Ah yes, all would change. And even if all did not change, we would see vastly different approaches to education than those that had dominated the Bush years.

Some things have changed. But much still remains the same. Obama's signature education initiative, the Race to the Top, includes some partly progressive elements and intuitions. For instance, schools will be given more credit for raising student achievement, even if a school's average scores do not meet the goals of adequate yearly progress. The culture of shaming schools has been lessened. There is no longer a hidden agenda of privatizing all of our major public institutions. These changes should not be dismissed.

Obama's signature education initiative, the Race to the Top, includes some partly progressive elements and intuitions.

But even with this more flexible approach, Race to the Top continues some of the same tendencies that made No Child Left Behind so deeply problematic. We still have corporate-style accountability procedures, the employment of divisive market mechanisms, the closing of schools, an uncritical approach to what counts as important curricular knowledge, the weakening of teachers' unions, and strong mayoral control of school systems.

The policies advocated by Obama and Secretary of Education Arne Duncan aren't as aggressive as before. They don't see schools as simply factories producing workers and profits. But overall, these policies still bear some of the hallmarks of the neoliberal agenda that has been pushed on schools for years. Competition eats cooperation. Nationalist rhetoric dominates as well.

Throughout the last decade, we repeatedly were told that public is necessarily bad and private is necessarily good. Powerful groups argued that the more that schools mirror the goals and procedures of the corporate sector, the more that we hold teachers' and schools' feet to the fire of competition, the better they will be. These arguments are almost religious, since they seem to be nearly impervious to empirical evidence.

Even such a stalwart supporter of these policies as Diane Ravitch has finally concluded that none of these measures will lead to more democratic, substantive, and high quality education. But the criticisms of these kinds of "reforms" have not made it any easier for states to resist them. States and school districts face a serious economic crisis, so federal stimulus dollars tempt them to engage in these problematic reforms, a key part of Race to the Top.

In Obama's plan, competition will still be sponsored. But rather than an emphasis on vouchers and privatization—the ultimate goal of many on the right during the Bush years—the focus is on charter schools. Choice will largely be limited to the public sector. This is clearly an improvement over the ways in which public institutions and public workers were vilified during the Bush years.

However, the research on charter schools shows that their results are mixed at best. While some good charter schools flourish, charter schools as a whole have often fared worse than regular public schools. And they seem to be even more racially segregated than regular public schools.

But unlike a number of other progressive commentators who have been quite critical of nearly all of the major aspects of Obama's educational policies, I believe that our criticisms need to be a bit more subtle and open.

For me, there is a complex politics surrounding larger issues of race at work here. The reality that a very large proportion of black and brown children face in schools is not pretty, to say the least. We should never romanticize what is happening to all too many children of color in our public schools. Many parents of black children will understandably do anything they can to save their children's future.

We should never romanticize what is happening to all too many children of color in our public schools.

Because of this distressing reality, Obama's commitment to choice can be read as partly a critique of dominance. When so much of the media and other aspects of popular culture and mainstream discourse treat African Americans as criminals, as out of control, and basically as not fully rational, choice plans do offer something different. By appropriating a new public identity, an identity that resoundingly says one is a rational economic actor who can make rational choices, people of color are saying that the usual stereotypes about them are both reprehensible and wrong.

Yet, understanding some of the reasons behind Obama's policies doesn't necessarily mean that we should agree with all of his concrete educational proposals, including his embrace of competitive models.

Take performance pay for individual teachers. Teachers' pay is to be linked to test results. Are there teachers who are ineffective and who need help? Undoubtedly. Is this the best way to judge the immensely complicated job of teaching? No. And given the well-known technical problems of judging teachers' work in more complicated ways, I have very few doubts that student scores on standardized achievement tests will be the norm.

The situation is made worse by the large amount of criticism that the rightwing media have made of teachers, something that is deeply disrespectful of how hard it is to teach in schools now. This combination is a formula for even more of an emphasis on simply teaching for the tests.

I do not doubt either President Obama's or Secretary Duncan's concern for improving achievement, especially for the least advantaged members of our society. But good intentions do not guarantee worthwhile outcomes. Indeed, this is one of those times when the opposite will probably be the result: even more uncreative curricula and teaching, ever more testing and more emphasis on it, and increasingly alienated students and teachers.

Are there alternatives to these kinds of policies? Here the answer is yes. James Beane and I offer in our recent book, *Democratic Schools,* powerful examples of public schools that work. We tell the stories of an array of real public schools in places as diverse as Boston, Chicago, Madison, Milwaukee, and New York. These are schools where expectations and standards are high, where students achieve, where poor and minority students are not pushed out, where teachers have created substantive and serious curricula, and where both students and the local communities are deeply involved in the life of the school.

Take Fratney Elementary School in Milwaukee. Eschewing the never-ending pressure to teach only those things that can be easily tested, the school took a different path. The teachers and administrators engaged in close consultations with the multiethnic community served by the school. Together, they discussed the goals and curriculum of the school. They connected the curriculum to the culture of the students and the problems of the community. In a situation where half of the students spoke Spanish and the other half English, they established a two-way bilingual program in which all subjects for all students were taught in Spanish for a period of time and then in English for the next period of time. The aim was to make all students bilingual and to interrupt the all too common results that have Spanish-speaking children falling further and further behind the longer they stay in school.

We also have much to learn from other nations. Many people point to what has been done in Finland to reduce the achievement gap. We do have something of importance to learn from these policies, including much more support and professional education for teachers, less emphasis on tracking and standardized testing, more creative curricula, and an emphasis on higher levels of thinking.

But I also think that we have much to learn from the nations of the global South. One of the best examples can be found in Porto Alegre, Brazil. There, you actually have a Citizen School and "participatory budgeting." The curricula are closely linked to the lives and cultures of children and communities, and all people affected by school policies and programs are able to become deeply involved in making decisions about them.

These examples put into practice three insights of the great Brazilian educator Paulo Freire. First, that an education worthy of its name must begin in critical dialogue. Second, that a school should serve as a site both for community mobilization and transformation. And third, that schools should create citizens who can fully participate in building a society that responds to the best in us. These insights are hard to find in the top down policies being advocated in Race to the Top.

I take the position of being an optimist with no illusions. These are difficult times, but a large number of educators and activists in the United States and elsewhere are deeply committed to both defending and building policies and practices that expand the sphere of democratic and critical dialogue and keep emancipatory educational possibilities alive. This remains our homework.

Critical Thinking

1. Consider what grade you might give to President Obama's educational policy. Justify your grade with reasons based on your K-12 learning experiences, higher education programs, and the readings in this unit.

2. At the end of the article, Apple provides an example of school that reflects Paulo Freire's insights on education. Write a brief reflection explaining why very few schools in this country have adopted these ideals.

3. You have been outspoken about your opinion on "performance pay" for teachers in your local schools. Now you are being asked to share that opinion with local business leaders at their monthly luncheon. You will have 15 minutes to share your thoughts. What are your top three reasons for either your positive or negative opinion of pay for performance?

MICHAEL W. APPLE is John Bascom Professor of Curriculum and Instruction and Educational Policy Studies at the University of Wisconsin-Madison. Among his recent books are "Educating the 'Right' Way: Markets, Standards, God, and Inequality" (second edition) and "Democratic Schools: Lessons in Powerful Education" (second edition).

Dictating to the Schools

A nationally-known educator looks at the effects of the Bush and Obama administrations on our schools.

DIANE RAVITCH

Momentous changes are occurring in American education, and they are occurring at a rapid pace, with far too little deliberation about the value and the likely consequences of these changes.

The most dramatic of these changes, and possibly the most significant, is the federal Department of Education's quiet but firm assumption of control of the nation's public schools. This is not an overnight development. Secretary of Education Arne Duncan is building on the precedent established by President George W. Bush's No Child Left Behind program, which established a strong federal presence in every public school district. NCLB not only required the states to create a testing and accountability regime for every public school in the nation, but prescribed the sanctions that would be applied to schools that did not make adequate yearly progress. Acting in a spirit of either ambition or ignorance (or both), NCLB dictated that every student in every school would be proficient by 2014, a goal that has never been attained by any state or nation. As that date draws nearer, more and more schools will be stigmatized as failing because of their inability to reach a goal that was unrealistic from the start. And, as they fail, they will suffer harsh penalties: They will be compelled to close, to fire the principal, to fire all or part of the staff, to be taken over by the state or a private management organization, or to "restructure" in some other fashion.

NCLB has been a costly disaster. None of its prescribed remedies has been successful as a template for turning around a low-performing school. No school was ever improved by closing it. Few schools see results if they are handed over to the state or private management, and thus far, restructuring has demonstrated little or no success. Low-performing schools can improve, and there are many examples of such improvement, but there is no model that Washington can prescribe or dictate to make it happen. When low-performing schools improve, it is almost always the work of an inspiring principal and a dedicated staff, whose efforts are enhanced by professional development, a strengthened curriculum, greater access to resources, better supervision, reduced class size, extra instructional time, and other commonsense changes.

NCLB's legacy is this: State accountability systems that produce inflated results; widespread cheating to meet the annual targets; a curriculum with less time for history, science, and the arts; teaching to the test; and meager academic gains on the National Assessment of Educational Progress. This too is the legacy of NCLB: a widespread public perception that the public schools have "failed," because they are unable to meet the law's demand for 100 percent proficiency. This perception of failure erodes public confidence in public education and sets the stage for privatization.

Instead of admitting that NCLB has been an expensive and demoralizing failure, President Obama and Secretary Duncan have accepted its fundamental premise that students must be tested annually and that schools and teachers must be subject to harsh punishment if they are unable to raise test scores. Their Race to the Top program will make student test scores even more consequential than they were under NCLB.

Race to the Top received funding of $4.3 billion from the economic stimulus plan enacted by Congress in 2009. Secretary Duncan used this money to launch a competition among the states at a time when every state was facing fiscal meltdown. To become eligible, the states had to enact changes that most were unlikely to do without the lure of the federal cash. Hoping to win a share of the billions, some states lifted their caps on charter schools; some passed laws to evaluate teachers in relation to their students' test scores; others agreed to "turn around" low-performing schools by adopting the punitive measures favored by the Obama administration; many embraced newly created national standards in mathematics and English language arts.

Secretary Duncan recognized early on that NCLB is a toxic brand and will drop the name in the administration's proposal for reauthorization of the Elementary and Secondary Education Act. But much will remain familiar. Like the Bush administration, the Obama administration will continue to emphasize test-based accountability, merit pay and choice. All of these are traditional elements of the Republican approach to school reform. Now, they have become the bipartisan consensus.

The mainstream media have applauded the Obama administration's bold plans to remake American education, but have been strangely uncurious about the evidence supporting it. In fact, there is little to no evidence for any part of this agenda. It is a risky venture, not only because it involves the expenditure of billions of dollars (leveraging billions more that will be spent by the states), but because it sets the nation's schools on a course that is unlikely to lead to meaningful improvement in the quality of education. This strategy may ultimately lead to even greater public dissatisfaction with public education and accelerate the movement towards privatization.

The Obama education reform program is indeed muscular. It is brash and confident in claiming to know precisely what is needed to reform American schools and raise student achievement. It represents a remarkable expansion of the federal role into what has traditionally been the province of state and local decision-making. If there was incontrovertible proof that the nation's schools would improve dramatically by taking the required steps, then there might be good reason for the federal government to take such assertive action. But incontrovertible proof does not exist for the federal government's agenda. Neither President Obama nor Secretary Duncan can point to any district that has applied their reforms and seen dramatic improvement.

Consider charter schools, which are now receiving royal treatment by the media. In 2010, three commercial films featured charters as the miracle cure for education, a beacon of hope especially for disadvantaged and minority students. There are currently about 5,000 charter schools in the nation. Some are excellent, some are terrible, and most are somewhere in the middle. On the whole, charter schools do not produce higher test scores than regular public schools. The CREDO national study, conducted by Stanford economist Margaret Raymond, compared nearly half the nation's charter schools to similar public schools and concluded that only 17 percent of the charters got higher math scores than the public schools. The remaining 83 percent of charters were either no different or worse than neighboring public schools.

When viewed through the scores on the National Assessment of Educational Progress (NAEP), the federal testing program that is considered the gold standard, charter schools achieve no miracles. Having been compared to regular public schools by NAEP in 2003, 2005, 2007 and 2009, charters have never outperformed regular public schools, not in reading or mathematics. Whether one looks at the performance of black students, Hispanic students, low-income students or urban students, there is no significant difference between the two sectors.

Nonetheless, the Obama administration is betting on charters as one of its key levers to reform American education.

Another reform that is supposed to lead to dramatic improvement is evaluating teachers by their students' test scores. In hopes of winning federal dollars, several states have passed laws to base as much as 50 percent of teachers' evaluation on test scores. The results of tying teacher evaluation, compensation and tenure to student test scores are predictable: There will be more teaching to the test; more time devoted to test preparation rather than instruction; and a consequent narrowing of the curriculum. The current generation of multiple-choice standardized tests are designed to measure a band of skills, not teacher quality.

Researchers have found that teacher effects, when measured this way, vary from year to year because scores are influenced by many factors other than teacher quality. Students are not randomly assigned to teachers. A teacher will get great results one year because she had a "good" class, but poor results the next year because the class had a few disruptive students. Test scores will also be affected by extraneous events, such as whether students got a good night's sleep, had a quarrel with a friend, or were distracted.

While the public, the press, and the administration seem keen on the idea of judging teachers by student test scores, it is important to remember that the tests are subject to random variation and measurement error. Furthermore, the more that policymakers attach high stakes—rewards and punishments—to test scores, the more they should expect to see cheating, gaming the system, inflated scores, and other efforts to hit the target. In recent years, even state education departments have gamed the system by lowering the passing mark on state tests, thus lifting their results without improving education.

Once this regime is well established, we can expect to see more attention to basic skills and less time for history, science, the arts, geography, civics, foreign language, even physical education. And as test preparation intensifies, we can expect to see students who master test-taking skills without necessarily becoming better at reading and mathematics. After eight years of NCLB, remediation rates in college have not declined. Some districts and states are producing higher test scores but no better education because students are learning to pass the state tests but not learning to comprehend complex material—that requires background knowledge—nor have they mastered the mathematics required for entry-level courses in college.

Another hallmark of federal policy in this administration is punitive action against low-performing schools. When the President and the Secretary saluted education officials in Rhode Island for threatening to close the only high school in the state's poorest urban center, they sent a message that was heard across the nation: Schools that have low scores should be shut down or turned into charters or privatized; their staffs should be fired. The problem with these approaches is that there is no evidence that any of them will consistently produce better education for the students in those schools. Closing a school is no guarantee that whatever replaces it will be better. Most of the schools that are identified as low-performing are sure to be schools that enroll large numbers of poor students, students who speak limited English, students who are homeless or transient. By its words and actions, the administration seems to assume that the school gets low scores because it has a bad principal or bad teachers. But the staff may be heroic in the face of daily challenges; they may be operating with fewer resources than schools in affluent neighborhoods. Absent individual evaluations, it seems unfair to conclude that the staff is failing.

No nation with a high-performing school system is following the policies advocated first by the Bush administration and now by the Obama administration. High-performing nations make sure that students have access to a rich and balanced curriculum, not just a steady diet of test preparation and testing. High-performing nations place their bets on a strong and well-prepared education profession. They prize highly-educated teachers and treat them with respect. They insist on having principals who are experienced educators. And at the same time, our own policymakers seem to be promoting the de-professionalization of education, as more districts hire non-educators as superintendents and create programs to train new-comers and inexperienced teachers to become principals. This approach is not a good bet for the future.

If we are serious about improving our schools, we must select well-educated teachers, give them the support and mentors they need to succeed, and make sure that they are evaluated by principals who are themselves master teachers. We must insist that all students receive a curriculum that inspires a love of learning, one that includes the arts, history, science, civics and other important and engaging studies. We must use tests for information and diagnosis, we must use them as part of an improvement strategy, not as a means to hand out money or pink slips. We must stop blaming educators for the social ills that get in the way of learning.

The work of school improvement involves small victories and occasional defeats. We must forego the search for silver bullets and dramatic transformations. Such strategies produce spectacular gains and equally spectacular losses in the financial markets. But these are risks we cannot take with our children, our schools and our communities. Above all, we must treasure public education as one of the prime elements of our democracy. We must not privatize it or give it away or outsource it. Nor should we set unrealistic goals that demoralize and punish those who do the daily work of schooling.

In this important work, the federal government certainly has a role to play. But it does not have all the answers. And we must take care not to invest our hopes in unproven, untried strategies.

Critical Thinking

1. When the Bush administration developed No Child Left Behind, Ravitch supported the legislation. Why has Ravitch changed her mind?

2. What are the principal reasons she is critical of No Child Left Behind?

3. Now that you have read Secretary Duncan's vision for school improvement and the various criticisms from the public as well as educational leaders, what are your own concerns about and suggestions for school reform? Provide a suggestion for each concern.

DIANE RAVITCH, a widely renowned education historian, is research professor of education at New York University. She has written numerous books and has served as Assistant Secretary of Education in the U.S. Department of Education and as a member of the National Assessment Governing Board. In addition, she currently blogs for Education Week, Politico.com and the Huffington Post. For more information, visit www.DianeRavitch.com.

From *Virginia Education Association*, December 2008/January 2009, pp. 1–5. Copyright © 2009 by Virginia Education Association. Reprinted by permission.

Response to Intervention (RTI): What Teachers of Reading Need to Know

Clear definitions, details of relevant legislation, and examples of RTI in action help explain this approach to identifying and supporting learners who may be struggling.

ERIC M. MESMER AND HEIDI ANNE E. MESMER

I n the most recent "What's hot, what's not for 2008?" *Reading Today* survey, 75% of prominent literacy researchers believed that Response to Intervention (RTI) was "very hot" and the same percentage believed that it should be "hot" (Cassidy & Cassidy, 2008). RTI is a new approach to identifying students with specific learning disabilities and represents a major change in special education law, the Individuals With Disabilities Act (IDEA). This change shifts the emphasis of the identification process toward providing support and intervention to struggling students early and is similarly reflected in the Reading First provisions of No Child Left Behind, which calls for proven methods of instruction to reduce the incidence of reading difficulties. RTI will alter the work of reading teachers because more than 80% of students identified for special education struggle with literacy (Lyon, 1995), and the law names "reading teachers" as qualified participants in the RTI process because of the International Reading Association's (IRA, 2007) lobbying efforts. However, RTI has only recently attracted the attention of the reading community (Bell, 2007), despite having roots in approaches such as prereferral intervention (Flugum & Reschly, 1994; Fuchs, Fuchs, & Bahr, 1990), curriculum-based measurement (Shinn, 1989), and Reading Recovery (Clay, 1987; Lyons & Beaver, 1995).

RTI in Theory
Background and Rationale
RTI was developed because of the many problems with the discrepancy model for identifying students with learning disabilities (e.g., Francis et al., 2005; O'Malley, Francis, Foorman, Fletcher, & Swank, 2002; Stanovich, 2005; Vellutino, Scanlon, & Lyon, 2000; Walmsley & Allington, 2007). In 1977, a learning disability was defined as "a severe discrepancy between achievement and intellectual ability" (U.S. Department of Education, 1977, p. G1082). In practice, this involves schools administering IQ

tests and achievement tests and then examining scores for discrepancies between intellect and achievement to identify a learning disability (see Table 1). The discrepancy model has drawn four major criticisms. First, it requires that a learning problem becomes considerably acute in terms of an IQ/achievement discrepancy before a learner can receive additional support, a problem called "waiting to fail" (Vaughn & Fuchs, 2003, p. 139). Second, establishing a discrepancy is not necessary to improve outcomes for struggling readers, as students both with and without a discrepancy are qualitatively the same in their literacy instructional needs (Fuchs, Mock, Morgan, & Young, 2003; Vellutino et al., 2000). Third, the IQ/achievement discrepancy has shifted focus away from understanding the impact of other possible factors, such as opportunities to learn (Walmsley & Allington, 2007). These factors need to be considered prior to determining that a learning disability exists. Fourth, under the discrepancy model, many districts and states have seen skyrocketing percentages of students identified as learning disabled, particularly minorities (IRA, 2007; Walmsley & Allington, 2007).

The Law
In 2004, IDEA, Public Law 108-446, introduced RTI language (U.S. Department of Education, 2006). In Table 2, the section entitled "Specific learning disabilities" (§ 300.307) asserts that states cannot be required to use the discrepancy model for identifying learning disabilities but may "permit the use of a process based on the child's response to scientific, research-based intervention." This is RTI, a process measuring whether a learner's academic performance improves when provided with well-defined, scientifically based interventions. In an RTI model, the "tests" of whether students possess learning disabilities are not standardized measures but students' measured responses to interventions. Within RTI, student potential (IQ) is replaced by a goal that allows for the evaluation of a performance relative to a defined academic standard (e.g., performance of other students

Table 1 Definitions of RTI Terms

Term	Definition
Discrepancy model	The standard for identifying students with learning disabilities based on the 1977 federal regulations. This process required that a significant difference be documented between a student's ability (IQ) and achievement in order for a learning disability to be identified. RTI models respond to the many problems identified with the discrepancy model.
Intervention	Targeted instruction provided in addition to the regular classroom program that addresses a student's documented instructional needs.
	Instruction that intends to prevent students who are struggling from falling farther behind their peers and intends to improve their future educational trajectory.
Level data	Information that reflects how students are performing in comparison to peers at a specific point in time.
	Slope data information that reflects how a student is learning across time in comparison to his or her previous learning. These data capture rate of learning and can also be called growth rates. Slopes that are steeper show more growth over a smaller period of time than slopes that are flatter. Slope data are obtained by repeatedly measuring student performance in a particular area. They are displayed using a line graph.
Student progress monitoring	An assessment technique required by RTI regulations. Teachers administer quick assessments (1–5 minutes) frequently (weekly) to gauge the improvement of a student. The assessments provide information about the student's rate of learning and the effectiveness of a particular intervention (National Center on Student Progress Monitoring, 2007).
Literacy screening	The process of assessing the most basic and predictive literacy skills for all students in a school. The goal of screenings is to select learners whose reading achievement is significantly below standards. Literacy screenings are intended to identify students who require additional help so that further slippage and literacy failure can be prevented.

in the class or grade level). Students responding quickly and significantly to interventions are less likely to possess a disability than students responding more slowly or not at all. However, data showing a student's response to an intervention serves as only one source of information for determining whether a learning disability is present. Learning disabilities cannot be diagnosed when appropriate instruction, socioeconomic status, culture, sensory issues, emotional issues, or English as a second language may be of concern.

In the section entitled "Determining the existence of a specific learning disability" (§ 300.309), the law states that a learning disability may be present when a student's performance is not adequate to meet grade-level standards when provided with appropriate instruction and research-based interventions. The term *appropriate* refers to instruction in the classroom that matches a student's skill level. The descriptors *scientific* or *research-based* indicate that interventions should be based on practices that have produced verifiable results through research studies.

RTI Processes

The processes undergirding RTI have been used for evaluating the success of schoolwide supports, individualized interventions, and special education (O'Connor, Fulmer, Harty, & Bell, 2005; Powell-Smith & Ball, 2002; Taylor-Greene et al., 1997). However, in this article we focus on RTI as an initial referral and identification process for students suspected of having learning disabilities.

Step 1

Universal literacy practices are established. Prevention begins with universal literacy screenings to identify students who could be at risk (see Table 3). Any state receiving Reading First monies has identified a literacy screening in grades K–3. All students are screened on basic literacy skills approximately three times per year. Typically, student performance is compared with minimal benchmark scores and students not meeting benchmarks receive help.

Step 2

Scientifically valid interventions are implemented. When students do not meet benchmarks, they need additional instruction. Within most RTI models, interventions are first delivered to a small group and are intended to assist students in developing skills that will allow them to improve their reading skills.

Step 3

Progress of students receiving intervention instruction is monitored. RTI requires that progress-monitoring data are continuously collected as students receive interventions. Progress-monitoring assessments should address the skills that are being targeted for intervention and should indicate if the intervention is changing the student's reading. Also, the assessments should be administered repeatedly (weekly or biweekly) without introducing test-wise bias, which occurs when the results of an assessment reflect the testtaker's acquired knowledge about a test rather than true performance. In addition, the

Table 2 Additional Procedures for Identifying Children
with Specific Learning Disabilities

IDEA terminology	IDEA definition
§ 300.307 Specific learning disabilities.	A State must adopt, consistent with 34 CFR 300.309, criteria for determining whether a child has a specific learning disability as defined in 34 CFR 300.8(c)(10). In addition, the criteria adopted by the State:
	• Must not require the use of a severe discrepancy between intellectual ability and achievement for determining whether a child has a specific learning disability, as defined in 34 CFR 300.8(c)(10);
	• Must permit the use of a process based on the child's response to scientific, research-based intervention; and
	• May permit the use of other alternative research-based procedures for determining whether a child has a specific learning disability, as defined in 34 CFR 300.8(c)(10).
	A public agency must use the State criteria adopted pursuant to 34 CFR 300.307(a) in determining whether a child has a specific learning disability.
	[34 CFR 300.307] [20 U.S.C. 1221e-3; 1401(30); 1414(b)(6)]
§ 300.309 Determining the existence of a specific learning disability.	The group described in 34 CFR 300.306 may determine that a child has a specific learning disability, as defined in 34 CFR 300.8(c)(10), if:
	• The child does not achieve adequately for the child's age or to meet State-approved grade-level standards in one or more of the following areas, when provided with learning experiences and instruction appropriate for the child's age or State-approved grade-level standards:
	• Oral expression.
	• Listening comprehension.
	• Written expression.
	• Basic reading skills.
	• Reading fluency skills.
	• Reading comprehension.
	• Mathematics calculation.
	• Mathematics problem solving.
	• The child does not make sufficient progress to meet age or State-approved grade-level standards in one or more of the areas identified in 34 CFR 300.309(a)(1) when using a process based on the child's response to scientific, research-based intervention; or the child exhibits a pattern of strengths and weaknesses in performance, achievement, or both, relative to age, State-approved grade-level standards, or intellectual development, that is determined by the group to be relevant to the identification of a specific learning disability, using appropriate assessments, consistent with 34 CFR 300.304 and 300.305; and the group determines that its findings under 34 CFR 300.309(a)(1) and (2) are not primarily the result of:
	• A visual, hearing, or motor disability;
	• Mental retardation;
	• Emotional disturbance;
	• Cultural factors;
	• Environmental or economic disadvantage; or
	• Limited English proficiency.
	To ensure that underachievement in a child suspected of having a specific learning disability is not due to lack of appropriate instruction in reading or math, the group must consider, as part of the evaluation described in 34 CFR 300.304 through 300.306:
	• Data that demonstrate that prior to, or as a part of, the referral process, the child was provided appropriate instruction in regular education settings, delivered by qualified personnel; and
	• Data-based documentation of repeated assessments of achievement at reasonable intervals, reflecting formal assessment of student progress during instruction, which was provided to the child's parents.

Note. From U.S. Department of Education. (2006). *Assistance to states for the education of children with disabilities and preschool grants for children with disabilites* (Federal register 34 CFR Parts 300 and 301). Washington, DC: Author.

Table 3 Examples of Literacy Screening Assessments

Screener	Authors
Dynamic Indicators of Basic Early Literacy Skills (DIBELS)	Good & Kaminski, 2002
Phonological Awareness Literacy Screening (PALS)	Invernizzi, Juel, Swank, & Meier, 2005
Texas Primary Reading Inventory (TPRI)	Texas Education Agency & University of Texas System, 2006
Illinois Snapshots of Early Literacy (ISEL)	Illinois State Board of Education, 2008

assessments should be sufficiently sensitive to small changes in the student's reading performance (i.e., those that might occur within a few days) because if students are showing growth on the more sensitive, microlevel progress-monitoring measures, they will also be showing growth in the more comprehensive measures (Deno, Mirkin, & Chiang, 1982; Fuchs & Deno, 1981; Riedel, 2007). Finally, progress-monitoring measures must be reliable, valid, and brief (National Center on Student Progress Monitoring, 2007). For a list of tools for progress monitoring, see the National Center on Student Progress Monitoring website at www.studentprogress.org/chart/chart.asp.

Step 4

Individualize interventions for students who continue to struggle. Students who continue to struggle despite receiving initial intervention instruction will require more intense, targeted interventions. These interventions may require additional assessments to clarify the nature of the difficulty. The data generated from these additional assessments should be used collaboratively by teachers, reading specialists, school psychologists, and parents to develop more intensive intervention strategies. Upon implementation, the student's progress continues to be monitored.

Step 5

A decision-making process to determine eligibility for special education services occurs when necessary. In the last step, a team of school-based professionals and the student's parents review all data to determine whether the student is eligible for special education services. Special services may be indicated when the student has not responded to interventions that have been well implemented for a sufficient period of time. If the team suspects that the student's lack of response may be explained by some other factor (i.e., not explained by a learning disability), then it should request additional assessment of the student's social, behavioral, emotional, intellectual, and adaptive functioning.

RTI in Real Life: Making a Difference for Mark

To illustrate RTI processes, we use a vignette (with pseudonyms) based on our experiences in schools. This vignette shows how a team including Donisha, a reading teacher, Julie, a special educator, Carol, a second-grade teacher, and Sandra, a school psychologist, worked collaboratively (and sometimes painstakingly) within an RTI model to assist a student named Mark.

Step 1: Universal Literacy Practices Are Established

In September, Mark was administered the Phonological Awareness and Literacy Screening (PALS; Invernizzi, Juel, Swank, & Meier, 2005), an assessment that begins with two screening measures, the first-grade word list, given in the fall of grade 2, and a spelling assessment. From these measures, an entry benchmark score is formed. If the benchmark score does not meet the grade-level minimum, then additional diagnostics are administered (preprimer and primer lists, letter naming, letter sounds, concept of word, blending, and sound-to-letter). Students also read passages through which accuracy, reading rate, phrasing (a 3-point subjective scale), and comprehension scores are collected.

In the fall, Mark received a benchmark score of 22 (7/20 on the first-grade word list) and 15/20 on the spelling assessment. An expected benchmark score of 35, based on 15 words on the first-grade list, and 20 spelling feature points is expected for the beginning of second grade. Mark read instructionally at the primer level (1.1) with moderate phrasing and expression and answered five-sixths of the questions correctly. He read the 120 words in the primer story in 4 minutes and 20 seconds, a rate of about 28 words correct per minute (WCPM) and 20 words below the 50th percentile for second graders in the fall (Parker, Hasbrouck, & Tindal, 1992). When diagnostic assessments were administered, data showed that Mark had mastered alphabetic skills, such as phonemic awareness and letters. Carol described her initial analysis: "Mark seemed to have the basic building blocks for reading but needed more practice at his level." Initially, Mark received small-group classroom instruction, including reading daily in on-level materials and working with Carol on comprehension and decoding. In September, October, and November, Carol took running records on the books that Mark and the other students had been reading. Although the accuracy and book levels of other students were steadily increasing, Mark's accuracy was averaging 90% in less difficult books. Carol explained, "I felt like Mark needed more help, and we needed to act because I was concerned that he would continue to fall behind."

Step 2: Scientifically Valid Interventions Are Implemented

RTI requires that instructional interventions be scientifically valid, public, implemented with integrity, and systematically evaluated. Julie, who had recently attended the district's RTI workshop, explained that "The who, what, when, where, and how of interventions must be clear." The content of the intervention should be designated, the teacher responsible for implementing it identified, and the assessments determined. Often different team members plan, implement, or assess the intervention based on availability and expertise. For this reason, educators must collaborate and share information.

The team discussed Mark's needs and designed an intervention. Based upon its review of the data, the team determined that accurate, fluent reading in connected text seemed to be the problem. Mark could easily understand books above his reading level, but his progress was being impeded by word recognition. The group decided that an intervention increasing the amount of reading practice for Mark would build up his reading level. The designed intervention comprised the following components: modeling of fluent reading, repeated readings, error correction, comprehension questions, and self-monitoring. They decided that Donisha would implement the intervention with three other students in the classroom in 20-minute sessions, three times per week. In addition, Carol continued to work with Mark in the classroom during small-group instruction. Specifically, she had Mark read from the same materials used by Donisha to further increase practice opportunities, and she set a daily goal for Mark on comprehension questions. Mark checked his answers each day and provided the results to his teacher at the end of the reading block.

Step 3: Progress of Students Receiving Intervention Instruction Is Monitored

As the intervention was implemented, Sandra tracked Mark's accuracy and fluency in reading passages at the primer and second-grade levels, because the goal was to understand Mark's progress toward grade-level norms. She used a PDA device loaded with passages at different levels. As Mark read these passages weekly, Sandra kept track of his accuracy (percentage of words correct) and reading rate (WCPM). Figure 1 shows Mark's accuracy and Figure 2 shows his reading rate before and after implementing the intervention for six weeks. Mark demonstrated some gains in accuracy and fluency, but his progress was not increasing at a rate that would allow him to meet established second-grade goals.

As we have described RTI to this point, it sounds smooth and trouble free. But it was anything but that for the professionals involved. Donisha's first reaction to RTI was strong:

> At first, I felt like this group was shrinking reading down to something very simplistic. I had to advocate for comprehension questions to be included in the intervention. Even though Mark's comprehension was fine, we did not want him to believe that comprehension didn't matter. We also clarified that interventions are *additive* and by nature narrower because their power lies in solving specific problems. The comprehensive reading program is broad and multifaceted, and it keeps going on while a child is receiving an intervention. So Carol wasn't going to stop guided reading or doing the rest of her program.

We liken the intervention and the reading program to a balanced diet. The intervention is like an extra serving of milk, but it doesn't replace meat, fruits, or vegetables.

Donisha was also concerned that the intervention would be scripted. Scripts are directions to teachers that are read verbatim during instruction. Interventions are specific and systematic, but nothing in the law requires them to be scripted.

Carol also had concerns. "I was not used to people asking me specific questions about exactly what I was doing, and how often, and what my results were. At first, it felt invasive and suspicious." Given the frequency with which blame is placed on classroom teachers, Carol's reaction was understandable. However, the team members pointed out that the instruction was working well for almost all of the other students and acknowledged the time limitations and demands placed on Carol as a classroom teacher. Although she had felt it in the past, Carol did not feel as though fingers were being pointed at her. Sandra had faced equal frustration before:

> I come in because a teacher has a concern and when I start asking questions, I get tight responses and defensiveness. It's like asking questions is stepping on toes. I can't help others further understand the problem or contribute to a useful intervention if we can't talk nitty-gritty. Once I had a teacher tell me, "You're not a teacher. You won't be able to help." While I am not a teacher, I can contribute to the development of interventions, and I have particular skill in measuring effects.

In addition to reviewing Mark's progress during the six weeks of intervention instruction, Mark's midyear PALS scores were evaluated by the team. He was independent at the primer (1.1) level and barely instructional at the first-grade level with 14 errors and a reading rate of 42 WCPM. Despite his increase in instructional level and fluency, the team remained concerned about the lack of reduction in the number of errors that Mark was making. The team decided that these errors would ultimately become detrimental to Mark's fluency and comprehension, particularly as text increased in difficulty. The team determined that individualized intervention was warranted.

Step 4: Individualize Interventions for Students Who Continue to Struggle

Because they had no measure of decoding, the team decided to assess Mark using the Word Attack Test from the Woodcock Reading Mastery Test. Results from this assessment revealed that Mark was having difficulty decoding words with more than one syllable or those that contained difficult vowel patterns. This resulted in reduced accuracy and fluency. The team enhanced the intervention by adding practice with problem words. Mark practiced incorrectly read words, received instruction in how to analyze word parts, extended analytic skills to similar words, and practiced through word sorts. Following word sorts, Mark read each word within a sentence. Donisha implemented this individualized intervention for 10 minutes each day following the reading practice intervention (discussed earlier in the article).

Mark's reading accuracy and fluency continued to be monitored weekly by Sandra. The team determined that the intervention would be implemented for a minimum of 6 weeks, as this time frame would correspond with the end of the school year. However, the team recognized that interventions in early

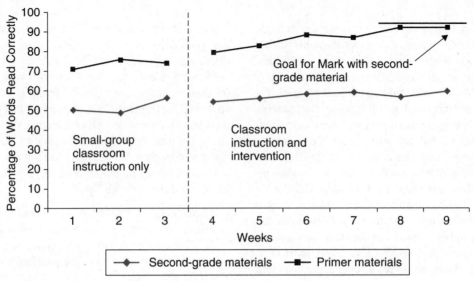

Figure 1 Mark's accuracy during intervention instruction.

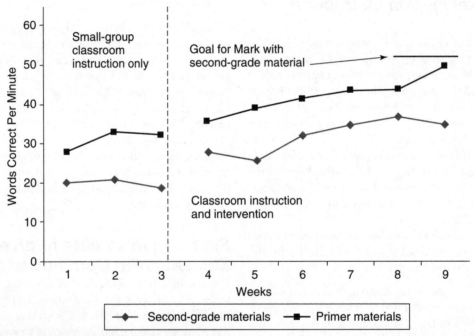

Figure 2 Mark's fluency during intervention instruction.

literacy often need to run longer, between 10 and 20 weeks, depending on factors such as the needs of the student and the intensity of the intervention (University of Texas Center for Reading and Language Arts, 2003; Wanzek & Vaughn, 2008). Moreover, Mark's progress was measured each week so that the intervention could be modified if he failed to make adequate gains. His response to the individualized reading intervention is provided in Figures 3 and 4. Figure 3 shows that Mark quickly responded to the word attack intervention. Data were collected once per week on the percentage of words read correctly from second-grade passages. Mark's response to the intervention contrasted dramatically with his performance reading unknown

words prior to the intervention. By the sixth week, Mark correctly read 100% of words presented when prior to intervention he was only reading 55% to 60% accurately. Figure 4 shows that Mark improved in reading fluency as well. Prior to word attack intervention, the effects of the fluency intervention had leveled off. With the addition of the word attack intervention, Mark's fluency steadily improved until he met the second-grade goal. By the end of May, Mark met the PALS summed score benchmark. His end-of-the-year PALS (58 summer score) showed him meeting the benchmark, reading instructionally at second-grade level with comprehension, and reading at a rate of about 60 WCPM.

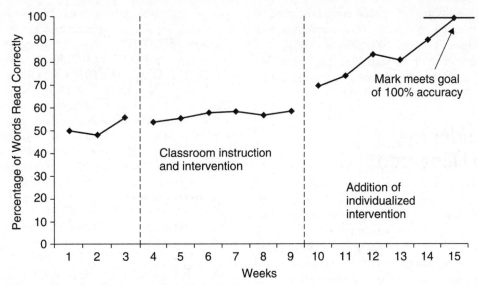

Figure 3 Mark's accuracy during individualized intervention.

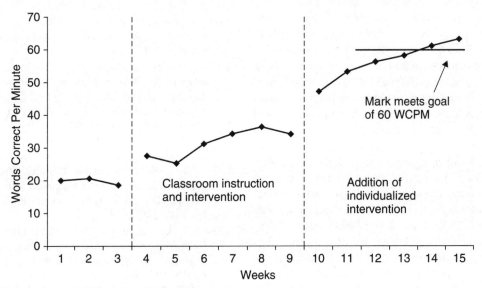

Figure 4 Mark's fluency during individualized intervention.

Step 5: Decision-Making Process to Determine Eligibility for Special Education Services

Despite falling below the second-grade benchmark in September, Mark demonstrated growth on accuracy, fluency, and decoding as a result of the efforts of school personnel. The team reviewed Mark's intervention data and determined that special education services were not necessary. However, Julie voiced concerns about Mark and the continued need for support:

I could see that Mark had made great progress, but I knew that summer could potentially influence his starting point in the rail and that his progress was the result of substantive instruction *in addition* to the regular classroom. So I insisted that a meeting be scheduled for him in the fall to be proactive about his needs.

Mark's progress was significant relative to where his skills were at the beginning of the year. If the interventions had not met Mark's needs, the team would have been charged with determining whether the lack of response was indicative of a learning disability.

Why RTI?

As illustrated, RTI is a process that incorporates both assessment and intervention so that immediate benefits come to the student. Assessment data are used to inform interventions and determine the effectiveness of them. As a result of the intervention-focused nature of RTI, eligibility services shift toward a supportive rather than sorting function. A testing model that identifies and sorts students into programs or services is predicated upon the effectiveness of those services.

Unfortunately, the effectiveness of special education, particularly placement of students in separate classrooms, has been variable at best (Bentum & Aaron, 2003; Kavale, 1990), even as an increasing percentage of students have been identified as learning disabled over the past 30 years (Gresham, 2002). Within the RTI model, instruction can at last be addressed.

Queries, Concerns, and Future Research

We have worked with state departments of education, school districts, schools, and teachers long enough to have questions about RTI. The first issue is that definitions of scientific research privilege experimental and quasi-experimental research (Eisenhart & Towne, 2003; Pressley, 2003). Experiments occur when subjects are randomly assigned to different conditions and the results measured, and they are the best way to know if a practice is causing a certain learning outcome. However, they depend on delivering an instructional treatment in a standardized way, often with study personnel. When teachers do participate in experiments, they often receive intensive support that may not be available when the strategy is widely implemented. The artifices of experiments can limit the degree to which the instructional treatment can be implemented in the real world (Pressley, 2003).

Second, if scientifically based interventions are to be implemented, then research findings must get to schools. We are concerned that the label *scientifically based* will be misused and will proliferate as publishers and companies slap it on everything they market to schools. The final issue is that diverse ways to screen in literacy are still emerging (Gersten & Dimino, 2006). Researchers note that phonologically based competencies, such as phoneme awareness, letter/sound knowledge, and decoding, contribute to part of what makes a student a successful reader (Gersten & Dimino, 2006; Paris, 2005; Scarborough, 2005). Readers must also have a deep knowledge of word meanings and be able to comprehend text. We know oral reading fluency is a good predictor of grade 1 comprehension (Riedel, 2007) but powerful, direct screenings in the areas of vocabulary and comprehension have yet to be developed for elementary learners. Nonetheless, intervening in these areas is important despite the fact that few screening tools exist.

Despite the challenges with RTI, we have seen this approach increase the quantity and quality of instruction for struggling readers. RTI is an initial attempt to provide an alternative to the dominant and damaging discrepancy model in which so much time is spent admiring the student's reading problem. By this we mean people discuss the problem, collect data on it, and write about it, months before they *do* anything about it. IDEA 2004 provides school districts with a choice to opt out of the discrepancy model.

References

Bell, M. (2007). *Reading teachers play key role in successful response to intervention approaches.* Retrieved May 31, 2007, from www.reading.org/downloads/resources/IDEA_RTI _teachers_role.pdf.

Bentum, K.E., & Aaron, P.G. (2003). Does reading instruction in learning disability resource rooms really work?: A longitudinal study. *Reading Psychology, 24*(3–4), 361–382. doi:10.1080/02702710390227387.

Cassidy, J., & Cassidy, D. (2008). What's hot, what's not for 2008? *Reading Today, 25*(4), 1, 10–11.

Clay, M.M. (1987). Learning to be learning disabled. *New Zealand Journal of Educational Studies, 22*(2), 155–173.

Deno, S.L., Mirkin, P.K., & Chiang, B. (1982). Identifying valid measures of reading. *Exceptional Children, 49*(1), 36–45.

Eisenhart, M., & Towne, L. (2003). Contestation and change in national policy on "scientifically based" education research. *Educational Researcher, 32*(7), 31–38. doi:10.3102/0013189X032007031.

Flugum, K., & Reschly, D. (1994). Prereferral interventions: Quality indices and outcomes. *Journal of School Psychology, 32*(1), 1–14. doi:10.1016/0022-4405(94)90025-6.

Francis, D.J., Fletcher, J.M., Stuebing, K.K., Lyon, G.R., Shaywitz, B.A., & Shaywitz, S.E. (2005). Psychometric approaches to the identification of LD: IQ and achievement scores are not sufficient. *Journal of Learning Disabilities, 38*(2), 98–108. doi:10.1177/00222194050380020101.

Fuchs, D., Fuchs, L., & Bahr, M. (1990). Mainstream assistance teams: A scientific basis for the art of consultation. *Exceptional Children, 57*(2) 128–139.

Fuchs, D., Mock, D., Morgan, P.L., & Young, C.L. (2003). Responsiveness-to-intervention: Definitions, evidence, and implications for the learning disabilities construct. *Learning Disabilities: Research & Practice, 18*(3), 157–171. doi:10.1111/1540-5826.00072.

Fuchs, L.S., & Deno, S.L. (1981). *The relationship between curriculum-based mastery measures and standardized achievement tests in reading* (Research Report No. 57). Minneapolis: University of Minnesota Institute for Research on Learning Disabilities. (ERIC Document Reproduction Service No. ED212662).

Gersten, R., & Dimino, J.A. (2006). RTI (Response to Intervention): Rethinking special education for students with reading difficulties (again). *Reading Research Quarterly, 41*(1), 99–108. doi:10.1598/RRQ.41.1.5.

Good, R., & Kaminski, R. (2002). *DIBELS oral reading fluency passages for first through third grades* (Technical Report 10). Eugene: University of Oregon.

Gresham, F. (2002). Responsiveness to intervention: An alternative approach to the identification of learning disabilities. In R. Bradley, L. Danielson, & D. Hallahan (Eds.), *Identification of learning disabilities: Research to practice* (pp. 467–519). Mahwah, NJ: Erlbaum.

Illinois State Board of Education. (2008). *Illinois Snapshots of Early Literacy.* Retrieved June 5, 2007, from www.isbe.state.il.us /curriculum/reading/html/isel.htm.

International Reading Association. (2007). *Implications for reading teachers in Response to Intervention (RTI).* Retrieved May 31, 2007, from www.reading.org/downloads/resources/rti0707 _implications.pdf.

Invernizzi, M., Juel, C., Swank, L., & Meier, J. (2005). *Phonological awareness literacy screening.* Virginia: The Rector and The Board of Visitors of the University of Virginia.

Kavale, K. (1990). Effectiveness of special education. In T.B. Gutkin & C.R. Reynolds (Eds.), *Handbook of school psychology* (2nd ed., pp. 868–898). New York: Wiley.

Lyon, G.R. (1995). Research initiatives in learning disabilities: Contributions from scientists supported by the National Institute of Child Health and Human Development. *Journal of Child Neurology, 10*(Suppl. 1), S120–S126.

Lyons, C., & Beaver, J. (1995). Reducing retention and learning disability placement through reading recovery: An educationally sound cost-effective choice. In R. Allington & S. Walmsley (Eds.), *No quick fix: Rethinking literacy programs in America's elementary schools* (pp. 116–136). New York: Teachers College Press.

National Center on Student Progress Monitoring. (2007). Common questions for progress monitoring. Retrieved May 20, 2007, from www.studentprogress.org/progresmon.asp#2.

O'Connor, R.E., Fulmer, D., Harty, K.R., & Bell, K.M. (2005). Layers of reading intervention in kindergarten through third grade: Changes in teaching and student outcomes. *Journal of Learning Disabilities, 38*(5), 440–455. doi:10.1177/00222194050380050701.

O'Malley, K., Francis, D.J., Foorman, B.R., Fletcher, J.M., & Swank, P.R. (2002). Growth in precursor and reading-related skills: Do low-achieving and IQ-discrepant readers develop differently? *Learning Disabilities Research & Practice, 17*(1), 19–34. doi:10.1111/1540-5826.00029.

Paris, S.G. (2005). Reinterpreting the development of reading skills. *Reading Research Quarterly, 40*(2), 184–202. doi:10.1598/RRQ.40.2.3.

Parker, R., Hasbrouck, J., & Tindal, G, (1992). Greater validity for oral reading fluency: Can miscues help? *The Journal of Special Education, 25*(4), 492–503.

Powell-Smith, K., & Ball, P. (2002). Best practices in reintegration and special education exit decisions. In A. Thomas & J. Grimes (Eds.), *Best practices in school psychology-IV* (pp. 541–557). Bethesda, MD: National Association of School Psychologists.

Pressley, M. (2003). A few things reading educators should know about instructional experiments. *The Reading Teacher, 57*(1), 64–71.

Riedel, B. (2007). The relation between DIBELS, reading comprehension, and vocabulary in urban first grade students. *Reading Research Quarterly, 42*(4), 546–567. doi:10.1598/RRQ.42.4.5.

Scarborough, H. (2005). Developmental relationships between language and reading: Reconciling a beautiful hypothesis with some ugly facts. In H.W. Catts & A.G. Kamhi (Eds.), *The connections between language and reading disabilities* (pp. 3–24). Mahwah, NJ: Erlbaum.

Shinn, M, (1989). *Curriculum-based measurement: Assessing special children.* New York: Guilford.

Stanovich, K. (2005). The future of a mistake: Will discrepancy measurement continue to make the learning disabilities field a pseudoscience? *Learning Disability Quarterly, 28*(2), 103–106. doi:10.2307/1593604.

Taylor-Greene, S., Brown, D., Nelson, L., Longton, J., Cohen, J., Swartz, J., et al. (1997). School-wide behavioral support: Starting the year off right. *Journal of Behavioral Education, 7*(1), 99–112. doi:10.1023/A:1022849722465.

Texas Education Agency & University of Texas System. (2006). *Texas Primary Reading Inventory.* Retrieved from www.tpri.org/products/.

University of Texas Center for Reading and Language Arts. (2003). *Three-tier reading model: Reducing reading difficulties for kindergarten through third grade students.* Austin, TX: Author.

U.S. Department of Education. (1977). *1977 code of federal regulations.* Washington, DC: Author.

U.S. Department of Education. (2006). *Assistance to states for the education of children with disabilities and preschools grants for children with disabilities, final rule.* Retrieved May 17, 2007, from eric.ed.gov/ERICDocs/data/ericdocs2sql/content_storage_01/0000019b/8011b/e9/95.pdf.

Vaughn, S., & Fuchs, L.S. (2003). Redefining learning disabilities as inadequate response to instruction: The promise and potential problems. *Learning Disabilities Research & Practice, 18*(3), 137–146. doi:10.1111/1540-5826.00070.

Vellutino, F.R., Scanlon, D.M., & Lyon, G.R. (2000). Differentiating between difficult-to-remediate and readily remediated poor readers: More evidence against the IQ-discrepancy definition of reading disability. *Journal of Learning Disabilities, 33*(3), 223–238. doi:10.1177/002221940003300302.

Walmsley, S., & Allington, R. (2007). *No quick fix, the RTI edition: Rethinking literacy programs in America's elementary schools.* Newark, DE: International Reading Association.

Wanzek, J., & Vaughn, S. (2008). Response to varying amounts of time in reading intervention for students with low response to intervention. *Journal of Learning Disabilities, 41*(2), 126–142. doi:10.1177/0022219407313426.

Critical Thinking

1. Write a summary for each level of Response to Intervention.

2. Review the five steps used to implement RTI. Prepare a detailed outline of the actions you would take to implement each step. Actions should be appropriate for the content or grade you will be teaching.

3. Outline a plan that uses RTI to meet the NCLB goals set by Secretary Duncan.

4. What do you believe are the critical issues of RTI for educators who will be implementing these procedures?

Eric M. Mesmer teaches at Radford University, Radford, Virginia, USA; e-mail emesmer@radford.edu. **Heide Anne E. Mesmer** teaches at Virginia Polytechnic Institute and State University, Blacksburg, USA; e-mail hamesmer@vt.edu.

From *The Reading Teacher,* December 2008/January 2009, pp. 280–290. Copyright © 2009 by International Reading Association. Reprinted by permission.

Responding to RTI

Early-reading expert Richard Allington believes response to intervention is possibly "our last, best hope" for achieving full literacy in the United States. So why does he sound so unhopeful?

Richard Allington, a professor of education at the University of Tennessee and the author of a number of prominent books on reading policy and instruction, is one of the country's most recognized experts on early literacy. A former president of the International Reading Association and the National Reading Council and co-editor of **No Quick Fix: Rethinking Literacy Programs in America's Elementary Schools** *(Teachers College Press, 1995), Allington has long advocated for intensifying instructional support for struggling readers, and he is often credited with helping lay the groundwork for the response to intervention concept. But while he believes RTI is "our last, best hope" for achieving full literacy in the United States, he is critical of the way it has been conceptualized and implemented in many schools. Allington's most recent book, tellingly, is titled* **What Really Matters in Response to Intervention** *(Allyn & Bacon, 2008).*

ANTHONY REBORA

I**n *No Quick Fix: The RTI Edition,* you describe response to intervention as an "old wine with a new label." What do you mean by that?**

Well, I'm 62. And literally, since I entered the education field at 21 and became a reading specialist the following year, the promise has been held that we're going to teach all kids to read. The good news is that, in the past five or 10 years, we've had large-scale demonstrations that show that in fact we could do that if we wanted to. We have studies involving multiple school districts and hundreds or thousands of kids demonstrating that, with quality instruction and intervention, 98 percent of all kids can be reading at grade level by the end of 1st or 2nd grade.

So it's not a question that we don't know what to do. It's a question of having the will to develop full literacy in this country, and to organize schools and allocate money in ways that would allow us to do that. Instead, we've tended to come up with flim-flam excuses for why it's not possible.

So you see RTI as a way of building on the research that's been done on successful literacy instruction?

I'd like to think it could be. I've called it perhaps our "last, best hope."

Why do you think it holds promise?

If for no other reason that, for the first time in many years, the federal government wrote a law that is not very

prescriptive. It simply says: Take up to 15 percent of your current special education allocation and use that money instead to *prevent* the development of learning disabilities or reading disabilities. And do it in a way that, while there's no mention of specific intervention tiers, incorporates increasingly expert and increasingly intensive instruction. It's just telling schools to stop using money in ways that haven't worked over the past half-century and start investing at least some of that money in interventions that are designed to actually solve kids' reading problems.

So it's not so much the specific framework of RTI that you see as promising as the emphasis it puts on intensive reading instruction?

Yes. For me the most important part of the proverbial three tiers is the first one: regular classroom instruction. In my view, RTI works best if it's started in kindergarten and 1st grade—we know how to solve those problems. Unfortunately, we have good evidence that a lot of kindergarten and 1st grade teachers in this country are just not very skilled in teaching reading. They may offer solid social and emotional support, but when it comes to delivering high-quality academic instruction, they just don't do it. And a lot of them also assume that if a kid is struggling and is way behind in reading, he must have some neurological problem, and therefore it's not their job to teach him.

So you can do a lot by strengthening instruction. The evidence is there in the research literature. We can reduce the number of kids who have trouble in the 1st grade by half just by improving the quality of kindergarten. And by 2nd grade, we can reduce the number of kids who are behind by another half just by improving the quality of 1st grade instruction.

How do you do that? I mean, if you were an administrator who was implementing RTI, what would you do in terms of professional development? How do you help teachers so they can deliver that high level of instruction?

I think it takes someone who knows what they're doing to start with, and virtually every school system already has those people on their staff. Again, we know from the research literature that, while a lot of kindergarten and 1st grade teachers might not be that strong in academic instruction, at least 25 percent of kindergarten and 1st grade teachers are in fact very skilled. So that 25 percent is out there whose expertise can be built on. The problem is they're just typically ignored.

But, yes, the most successful training models are those that involve teachers who are actually working with each other, where the teachers who don't know what to do in delivering reading instruction are given a few days each to observe a teacher who does know what to do. The skilled teacher, that is, becomes a mentor teacher who helps others acquire those types of skills.

And the effects of a little high-quality training can be significant. One of the studies on reading professional development that the [U.S. Department of Education's] What Works Clearinghouse has rated as having strong evidence—actually I think it's the only one—was done by my wife [University of Tennessee Professor **Anne McGill-Franzen**] in Philadelphia with kindergarten teachers. This program primarily involved using mentor teachers and some staff from an organization called the **Children's Literacy Initiative.** And it really only required about three days of work before the school year started and about three hours a month of professional development and, for some teachers, a little in-class support. But the difference in performance was dramatic: Students in the classes of the teachers who got the training ended the year in about the 45th percentile in reading, while those with teachers who didn't get the training ended the year at the 13th percentile.

And I'll tell you, I actually went down to help my wife with some of the debriefing interviews at the end of the year. We had veteran teachers—people my age—breaking down in the interview and starting to cry, saying, "Why didn't anyone ever teach us this before? Why have I been teaching for 30 years and never knew how to teach kids to read?"

What mistakes do schools commonly make in implementing RTI?

Letting the interventions be done by paraprofessionals or parent volunteers or special education teachers who have limited reading-instruction expertise. If you want a kid to remain illiterate and ultimately end up in special ed., send him out to work with someone who lacks expertise in teaching reading. If you want him to develop literacy, put him with someone with expertise in teaching kids at that age to read.

The idea behind RTI was for a district to actually take some of its special education budget to fund reading specialists, but in most cases, they haven't done that. In too many cases, they simply have paraprofessionals work with those kids. So the amount of expert reading instruction the kids are getting under RTI is typically very slight.

My question to superintendents is always, "Would you let me randomly select one of your paraprofessionals to be your assistant superintendent for finance, or to be the head football coach, or teach AP chemistry?" No, of course not, because those jobs require that you know something. But when you take people who are not reading experts and put them with the hardest kids to teach, and then blame the kids when they don't make progress, you penalize the children for the rest of their lives because of your decision.

You've been critical of the use of so-called packaged reading programs in schools. Why?

Well, the problem is that the concept of a packaged reading program doesn't have any scientific validity to start with, because we know that if you take 100 kids or even 10 kids, there are no prescribed programs that will work with all of them. What kids need are teachers who know how to teach and have multiple ways of addressing their individual needs. And the evidence that there's a packaged program that will make a teacher more expert is slim to none.

So the alternative would be to focus on building on teachers' expertise and knowledge?

Right. And one good example of how to do that is the much-criticized **Reading Recovery** program, which isn't a scripted program in the sense that most commercial programs are. Instead, it's a year long—or even life long—professional development plan. Of the 150 reading-intervention programs that the What Works Clearinghouse looked at, it was the only one determined to have strong evidence that it worked. And I've been telling principals for 20 years that the good thing about a program like Reading Recovery is that, if your district ever decides not to continue funding it, your teachers still have that expertise, and you can't take that away from them. You can take away the one-to-one tutoring that's part of the program, but even more important than that is the expertise of the teachers. Another example of a large-scale program that schools ought to be looking at is the **Interactive Strategies Approach,** developed by researchers F.R. Vellutino and Donna Scanlon. That is also a kind of extended PD plan.

When schools implement RTI, they often use digital screening and monitoring tools for assessment . . .

It's idiotic.

Those tools aren't effective?

No. We don't have any evidence that any computerized screening and monitoring tools are related to reading growth. It just doesn't exist. In fact, I think we have enough evidence in the opposite direction with the problems of Reading First.

So what do you advise schools to use to determine where a student is in his reading ability?

Well, I tell them, if the student is in kindergarten or 1st grade, to listen to the child read. And you have to have some sense of the difficulty level of the books, and you need to be expert enough to know what strategies students at different stages should be demonstrating in their reading.

OK, say I'm a principal, and I say to you, "Listen, I'm not sure my teachers have the expertise at this point to make those kinds of judgments without the help of available tools."

I'd say you're a principal who doesn't have a clue, and you probably need to go off and develop some expertise yourself. Or maybe find another job.

Look, the problem isn't that teachers don't know which students are in trouble and need help. I mean, you could try an experiment: Call 100 1st grade teachers around the country and ask them, "Do you have any kids who are in trouble in learning to read?" They're not going to say, "Gosh, I don't know. I haven't DIBEL'd them yet." Teachers know who needs help. If they don't know, they shouldn't be teaching.

But you just said that many teachers aren't skilled in teaching reading?

But that doesn't mean they don't know who's in trouble. They just don't know what to do with a kid who's in trouble. The point is we need to free teachers up from spending their time using an assessment program on kids every few weeks, or having reading or LD specialists going around doing it. Educators need to be working with kids and teaching them rather than continuing to document that they can't do something.

Do you have any guidelines for the amount of intervention time that should be provided for a struggling reader?

Well, let's talk about kindergarten and 1st grade. In kindergarten, amazingly, it takes as little as 15 to 20 minutes a day, working in a one-on-one or very small group setting with a child. That's it. In 1st grade, most of the studies have recommended either a half-hour or 45 minutes a day, five days a week, usually for a period of roughly 20 weeks, as an initial shot at it. At that point, some kids still may not be up to grade level. But if you give them another 20 weeks, you can be down to 2 percent of kids who aren't reading at grade level. And that 2 percent, according to the large-scale studies, are typically those students who are highly mobile and come in and out of the program, or are part of that very small portion of the school population who have very severe or profound cognitive disabilities. But you have to look around and ask, how many schools do we currently have that have any kind of intensive expert intervention in place in kindergarten, much less 30 or 45 minutes a day of one-to-one or one-to-three expert intervention for up to a year in the 1st grade? The answer is, there are virtually no schools like that in this country.

None?

None. And they'll say they don't have enough money to provide that kind of intervention. And I'm saying, wait a second, we're spending between $5,000 and $10,000 a year on every child who's identified as having a learning disability, and you don't have enough money to try to prevent that?

Can RTI work with older students or adolescents?

Well, we don't have a lot of research on how well it works with older children, but I certainly think it can. The problem is that you really have to ramp up instruction because, as they get older, the kids get further and further behind in the current setting. Let me give you an example: Let's say you have a 4th grader who's reading at the 2nd grade level. So you've got evidence that whatever you've been doing up to this point has produced about a half grade's growth per year. So even if you can provide something that will double his rate of growth, up to a year's growth per year, by the time he gets to 9th grade, he'll only be reading at a 7th grade level. Now, if we can triple his rate of growth—to a year and a half grade level per year—he'd be caught up by 9th grade. If we could quadruple it, he'd be caught up by 6th grade and in even better shape.

How do you do that?

I think you could do that, with a substantial amount of high-quality instruction—and that means, in effect, that his reading instruction has to take place all day long. In other words, if he's reading at a 2nd grade level in 4th grade, this child would need texts in social studies, science, and math that are written at the 2nd grade level but cover the 4th grade curriculum, so he has a book in his hands all day long that he can actually read. If we did that in addition to high-quality classroom reading instruction and then provided 45 minutes every day after school of one-on-one expert instruction, and maybe did something in the summer that wasn't as useless as what we usually see going on in summer school, we might be able to catch him up.

How realistic is that scenario?

I think it's pretty realistic, and it's not very expensive compared to what we're doing now to keep the child essentially illiterate. If you look at the research on the quality and quantity of reading instruction given to students in special education or Title I classes (some of which both my wife and I conducted), I mean, it's not a rosy scenario. Too often, no one gets worse or less instruction in reading than the kids who need it most. Did you know there are only 19 states that require special education teachers to take even one course in teaching reading? In other words, special education teachers often know less about teaching reading than the regular classroom teachers who turn to them for help.

When do you think a determination for special education should be made under an RTI framework?

I think if you've spent most of kindergarten and 1st grade giving a child expert, intensive instruction and he or she is still lagging way behind, it might be time. But I'd be awfully hesitant to classify any child given the lack of expectations for academic growth in special education. If we had evidence that special education programs were actually declassifying a third of their kids each year—in other words that two or three years of treatment in special education could get them caught up—I'd be more optimistic.

So, in most cases, you'd just continue the interventions and expert reading instruction?

Yes.

Even if a student failed to make it to grade level for several years running?

Yep. Now, you could define special education such that the whole point was that kids who go into it were getting more and better instruction every day, such that special education was likely to catch them up and perhaps lead to declassification. But I don't see any will in schools to do that. And I worry about RTI, in some states and schools, being run by special ed. personnel. Again, though it was created in a special education law and has potential bearing on how special education determinations are made, it's not intrinsically a spec. ed. program. It's about strengthening regular classroom instruction and general education interventions for students so they can stay out of special ed. But I'm afraid some schools just see it as a way to find more LD kids faster.

What advice would you have for a teacher who is in a school that is implementing RTI and wants to make it work?

Well, the best advice is to make sure you know what you're doing with struggling readers in your classroom, all day long. And then work to ensure that, when a student leaves your classroom for intervention, he or she is going out to work with someone who knows as much or even more than you do about what to do with that child.

Any particular resource or book you would recommend to start with?

I think one of the most powerful resources is a skinny little book called **Choice Words** by Peter Johnston. I think it's all of 68 pages long, and the subtitle is *How Our Language Affects Children's Learning.* It's simply a careful and close look at how effective teachers talk to their children and how less effective teachers talk to their children. How do you foster a child's sense of agency and identity? Think about it: By the end of 1st grade, most struggling readers already know they're terrible at reading and they think they're the problem. And at that point they start working very hard on any number of schemes to try to hide the fact that they can't read or aren't very good at it. And not surprisingly, they don't do much reading independently. This is a cycle that teachers need to and can break.

In the end it's us, educators, who really matter in the case of struggling readers. We have to understand that and ask the questions about what we are doing or not doing, rather than asking what is wrong with the child.

Critical Thinking

1. Based on what you have read in the other articles regarding RTI, prepare an argument for or against implementation of RTI in your future classroom.

2. Do you believe that Allington's criticism of RTI implementation in public schools is valid? Prepare two to three reasons for your assessment with a rationale for each reason.

The Why Behind RTI

Response to Intervention flourishes when educators implement the right practices for the right reasons.

AUSTIN BUFFUM, MIKE MATTOS, AND CHRIS WEBER

We educators are directly responsible for crucial, life-saving work. Today, a student who graduates from school with a mastery of essential skills and knowledge has a good chance of successfully competing in the global market place, with numerous opportunities to lead a rewarding adult life. In stark contrast, students who fail in school are at greater risk of poverty, welfare dependency, incarceration, and early death. With such high stakes, educators today are like tightrope walkers without a safety net, responsible for meeting the needs of every student, with little room for error. Fortunately, compelling evidence shows that Response to Intervention (RTI) is our best hope for giving every student the additional time and support needed to learn at high levels (Burns, Appleton, & Stehouwer, 2005).

RTI's underlying premise is that schools should not wait until students fall far enough behind to qualify for special education to provide them with the help they need. Instead, schools should provide targeted and systematic interventions to *all* students as soon as they demonstrate the need. From one-room schoolhouses on the frozen tundra of Alaska to large urban secondary schools, hundreds of schools across the United States are validating the potential of these proven practices.

In light of this fact, why are so many schools and districts struggling to reap the benefits of RTI? Some schools mistakenly view RTI as merely a new way to qualify students for special education, focusing their efforts on trying a few token regular education interventions before referring struggling students for traditional special education testing and placement. Others are implementing RTI from a compliance perspective, doing just enough to meet mandates and stay legal. For still others, their RTI efforts are driven by a desire to raise test scores, which too often leads to practices that are counter productive to the guiding principles of RTI. Far too many schools find the cultural beliefs and essential practices of RTI such a radical departure from how schools have functioned for the past century that they are uncomfortable and unwilling to commit to the level of change necessary to succeed. Finally, some schools refuse to take responsibility for student learning, instead opting to blame kids, parents, lack of funding, or society in general for students' failures.

Although the specific obstacles vary, the underlying cause of the problem is the same: Too many schools have failed to develop the correct thinking about Response to Intervention. This has led them to implement some of the right practices for the wrong reasons.

The Wrong Questions

The questions an organization tries to answer guide and shape that organization's thinking. Unfortunately, far too many schools and districts are asking the wrong questions, like these.

How Do We Raise Our Test Scores?

Although high-stakes testing is an undeniable reality in public education, this is a fatally flawed initial question that can lead to incorrect thinking. For example, many districts that focus first on raising test scores have concluded that they need strictly enforced pacing guides for each course to ensure that teachers are teaching all required state standards before the high-stakes state tests. Usually, these guides determine exactly how many days each teacher has to teach a specific standard. Such thinking makes total sense if the goal is to *teach* all the material before the state assessments, but it makes no sense if the goal is to have all students *learn* essential standards. This in itself is problematic because, as Marzano (2001) notes, "The sheer number of standards is the biggest impediment to implementing standards" (p. 15). Assigning arbitrary, pre-determined amounts of time to specific learning outcomes guarantees that students who need additional time to learn will be left in the wake as the teacher races to cover the material.

This faulty thinking also leads to misguided intervention decisions, such as focusing school resources primarily on the "bubble kids" who are slightly below proficient. Administrators who adopt this policy conclude that if these students can improve, the school's test scores will likely make a substantial short-term jump. Consequently, the students far below basic often receive less help. This is deemed acceptable, as the primary goal of the school is to make adequate yearly progress, and the lowest learners are so far behind that providing them intensive resources will likely not bring about immediate gains in the school's state assessment rankings.

How Do We "Implement" RTI?

Frequently, we have worked with schools that view RTI as a mandated program that they must "implement." Consequently, they create an abundance of implementation checklists and time lines. Like obedient soldiers, site educators take their RTI marching orders and begin to complete the items on their RTI to-do list, such as administering a universal screening assessment, regrouping students in tiered groups, or creating a tutorial period.

Such an approach is fraught with pitfalls. First, it tends to reduce RTI to single actions to accomplish, instead of ongoing *processes* to improve teaching and learning. In addition, this approach fails to understand that what we ask educators to "do" in RTI are not ends in themselves, but means to an end. In other words, a school's goal should not be to administer a universal screening assessment in reading but to ensure that all students are able to read proficiently. To achieve this goal, it would be essential to start by measuring each student's current reading level, thus providing vital information to identify at-risk students and differentiate initial instruction.

How Do We Stay Legal?

Because RTI was part of the reauthorization of the Individuals with Disabilities Education Improvement Act (IDEIA) in 2004, many schools view its implementation from the perspective of legal compliance. This concern is understandable, as special education is by far the most litigated element of public education, and the potential costs of being out of compliance or losing a fair hearing can cripple a district.

Unfortunately, a large number of schools and districts are making RTI unreasonably burdensome. We find many districts creating unnecessarily complicated, laborious documentation processes for every level of student intervention, in fear that the data may be needed someday if a specific student requires special education services.

Teachers tell us that they often decide against recommending students for interventions "because it's not worth the paperwork." Other teachers complain that they "hate" RTI because they spend more time filling out forms than working with at-risk students. We have also worked with districts that refuse to begin implementing RTI until there is a greater depth of legal interpretation and case precedent; all the while, their traditional special education services are achieving woefully insufficient results in student learning.

If there is one thing that traditional special education has taught us, it's that staying compliant does not necessarily lead to improved student learning—in fact, the opposite is more often the case. Since the creation of special education in 1975, we have spent billions of dollars and millions of hours on special education—making sure we meet time lines, fill out the correct forms, check the correct boxes, and secure the proper signatures. A vast majority of schools are compliant, but are students learning?

Consider These Facts:

- In the United States, the special education redesignation rate (the rate at which students have exited special education and returned to general education) is only 4 percent (U.S. Department of Education, 1996).
- According to the U.S. Department of Education, the graduation rate of students with special needs is 57 percent (National Center on Secondary Education and Transition [NCSET], 2006).
- It is estimated that up to 50 percent of the U.S. prison population were identified as students with special needs in school (NCSET, 2006).

There is little evidence to suggest that greater levels of legal compliance lead to greater levels of learning. If schools or districts would like to stay legal, they should start by focusing on student learning; parents rarely file for a fair hearing because their child is learning too much.

What's Wrong with This Kid?

At most schools, when a student struggles in the regular education program, the school's first systematic response is to refer the student for special education testing. Traditionally, schools have believed that "failure to succeed in a general education program meant the student must, therefore, have a disability" (Prasse, 2009). Rarely does special education testing assess the effectiveness and quality of the *teaching* that the student has received.

RTI is built on a polar opposite approach: When a student struggles, we assume that we are not teaching him or her correctly; as a result, we turn our attention to finding better ways to meet the student's specific learning needs. Unless schools are able to move beyond this flawed question, it is unlikely that they will ever see RTI as anything more than a new way to identify students for special education.

The Right Questions

Schools cannot succeed by doing the right things for the wrong reasons. So what are the right questions that should lead our work?

What Is the Fundamental Purpose of Our School?

Our schools were not built so educators would have a place to work each day, nor do they exist so that our government officials have locations to administer high-stakes standardized tests each spring. If we peel away the various layers of local, state, and federal mandates, the core mission of every school should be to provide every student with the skills and knowledge needed to be a self-sufficient, successful adult.

Ask parents what they want school to provide their child, and it is doubtful the answer would be, "I just want my child to score proficient on state assessments," or "I want my child to master standard 2.2.3 this year." Learning specific academic standards and passing state tests are meaningless if the student does not become an intelligent, responsible adult who possesses the knowledge and quality of character to live a happy, rewarding adult life.

What Knowledge and Skills will Our Children Need to Be Successful Adults?

Gone are the days when the only skills a child needed to become a successful adult were a desire to work and some "elbow grease." Today's economy is driven by technology, innovation, and service. Because technology and human knowledge are changing at faster and faster rates, the top 10 in-demand jobs today probably didn't exist five or six years ago (Gunderson, Jones, & Scanland, 2004). Our high school graduates will most likely change careers at least four times by the age of 40—not jobs or employers, but *careers*. Alvin Toffler has been said to have suggested that, because of this acceleration of human knowledge, the definition of *illiterate* in the 21st century will not be "Can a person read and write?" but rather "Can a person learn, unlearn, and relearn?"

How do we prepare students for jobs that don't exist? How do we teach our students knowledge that we've not yet discovered? Teaching them comprehension and computation skills will not be enough—they need to be able to analyze, synthesize, evaluate, compare and contrast, and manipulate and apply information. We will erode our children's and world's future by limiting our vision to teaching only the skills and knowledge presented in our state assessments.

What Must We Do to Make Learning a Reality for Every Student?

If we took the research on effective teaching and learning and condensed it into a simple formula for learning, it would look like this:

$$\text{Targeted Instruction} + \text{Time} = \text{Learning}$$

Because learning styles and instructional needs vary from student to student, we must provide each student with *targeted instruction*—that is, teaching practices designed to meet his or her individual learning needs. We also know that students don't all learn at the same speed. Some will need more time to learn. That is the purpose of RTI—to systematically provide every student with the additional time and support needed to learn at high levels.

Transforming the Tiers

If a school has asked the right questions, then how would this new way of thinking affect a school's RTI efforts? Quite honestly, it would transform every tier.

Tier 1

In Tier 1, the school would start by ensuring that every student has access to rigorous, grade-level curriculum and highly effective initial teaching. The process of determining essential student learning outcomes would shift from trying to cover all required standards to a more narrow focus on standards that all students must master to be able to succeed in the future.

A collective response will be required to ensure that all students learn, so teacher teams would work collaboratively to define each essential standard; deconstruct the standard into discrete learning targets (determine what each student must be able to know and do to demonstrate proficiency); identify the prior skills needed to master the standard; consider how to assess students on each target; and create a scope and sequence for the learning targets that would govern their pacing. Schools may continue to use such resources as textbooks as primary Tier 1 resources, but only by selecting those sections that align to what the team of teachers has determined to be essential for all students to master.

The school would understand that differentiation for individual student needs cannot be optional at Tier 1. Whether in an elementary math lesson or a secondary social studies lesson, teachers must scaffold content, process, and product on the basis of student needs, setting aside time to meet with small groups of students to address gaps in learning.

The direct, explicit instruction model contains the structures through which differentiation can take place. This thinking contradicts the approach taken by many schools that have purchased a research-based core instructional program and dictated that this program constitutes the *only* instructional material that teachers can use. This quest for fidelity sometimes becomes so rigid that each teacher is required to teach the same lesson, on the same day, following the same script.

Although we agree that schools should implement scientifically research-based resources, we also know that not all students learn the same way. In addition, because not all students learn at the same speed, we would plan flexible time into our master schedule to allow for reteaching essential standards for students who require it as well as providing enrichment learning for students who have already demonstrated mastery. To achieve these collective Tier 1 outcomes, we firmly believe that the only way for an organization to successfully implement RTI practices is within the professional learning community (PLC) model (Buffum, Mattos, & Weber, 2009).

Tier 2

At Tier 2, the school would use ongoing formative assessment to identify students in need of additional support, as well as to target each student's specific learning needs. In addition, teachers would create common assessments to compare results and determine which instructional practices were most and least effective in Tier 1. Giving students more of what *didn't* work in Tier 1 is rarely the right intervention!

Most Tier 2 interventions would be delivered through small-group instruction using strategies that directly target a skill deficit. Research has shown that small-group instruction can be highly effective in helping students master essential learnings (D'Agostino & Murphy, 2004; Vaughn, Gersten, & Chard, 2000).

Intervention is most effective when the interventions are timely, structured, and mandatory; focused on the *cause* of a student's struggles rather than on a symptom (for example, a letter grade); administered by a trained professional; and part of a system that guarantees that these practices apply no matter which teacher a student is assigned to (Buffum, Mattos, & Weber, 2009). Finally, because the best intervention is prevention, the effective RTI school would use universal screening data to identify students lacking the prerequisite skills for an essential standard and then provide targeted Tier 2 or Tier 3 support before delivering core instruction on that standard.

Tier 3

At Tier 3, we would start by guaranteeing that all students in need of intensive support would receive this help in *addition* to core instruction—not in place of it. If our goal is to ensure that all students learn at high levels, then replacing core instruction with remedial assistance not only fails to achieve this outcome, but also tracks at-risk students into below-grade-level curriculum.

Because Tier 3 students often have multiple needs, intensive help must be individualized, based on a problem-solving approach. It is unlikely that a single program will meet the needs of a student in Tier 3, as many of these students are like knots, with multiple difficulties that tangle together to form a lump of failure. Because of this, a school focused on meeting the needs of every student would develop a problem-solving team, composed of a diverse group of education experts who can address the students' social, emotional, and learning needs. The purpose of this team would not be to determine what is wrong with the student but to identify the specific needs the student still experiences after Tier 2 intervention, quantify them, and determine how to meet them.

Schools need to deliver Tier 3 interventions with greater intensity than Tier 2 interventions. They can do this by increasing both the duration and frequency of the intervention and lowering the student–teacher ratio (Mellard, 2004). At Tier 3, it is also important to quantify the student's specific learning needs. It would not be enough to say that a student's problem is "reading." Instead, a school team might find that a 2nd grade student is reading grade-level passages at a rate of 20 words read correctly (WRC) per minute compared with the expectation of 45 WRC for 2nd grade students at that point in the school year.

If a school diligently applies these practices, a vast majority of students will never need to be referred for special education testing. When all students have guaranteed access to rigorous curriculum and effective initial teaching, targeted and timely supplemental support, and personalized intensive support from highly trained educators, few will experience failure (Sornson, Frost, & Burns, 2005). In the rare case that this level of support does not meet a specific students' needs, the student may indeed have a learning disability. In this case, special education identification would be fair and appropriate.

Although the purpose of RTI is not special education identification, a school will identify far fewer students for these services if they ask the right questions and take preventative steps. Schools that fail to do so will continue to blame students for failing, which will perpetuate the over-identification of minority, English language learning, and economically disadvantaged students into special education.

Doing the Right Work for the Right Reasons

The secret to capturing the right way of thinking about RTI comes down to answering this question: Why are we implementing Response to Intervention?

The answer lies in why we joined this profession in the first place—to help children. Our work must be driven by the knowledge that our collaborative efforts will help determine the success or failure of our students. RTI should not be a program to raise student test scores, but rather a process to realize students' hopes and dreams. It should not be a way to meet state mandates, but a means to serve humanity. Once we understand the urgency of our work and embrace this noble cause as our fundamental purpose, how could we possibly allow any student to fail?

References

Buffum, A., Mattos, M., & Weber, C. (2009). *Pyramid response to intervention: RTI, professional learning communities, and how to respond when students don't learn*. Bloomington, IN: Solution Tree.

Burns, M. K., Appleton, J. J., & Stehouwer, J. D. (2005). Meta-analytic review of response-to-intervention research: Examining field-based and research-implemented models. *Journal of Psycho-educational Assessment, 23*, 381–394.

D'Agostino, J. V., & Murphy, J. A. (2004). A meta-analysis of reading recovery in United States schools. *Educational Evaluation and Policy Analysis, 26*(1), 23–38.

Gunderson, S., Jones, R., & Scanland, K. (2004). *The jobs revolution: Changing how America works.* n.p.: Copywriters Inc.

Marzano, R. J. (2001). How and why standards can improve student achievement: A conversation with Robert J. Marzano. *Educational Leadership, 59*(1), 14–18.

Mellard, D. (2004). *Understanding responsiveness to intervention in learning disabilities determination.* Retrieved from the National Research Center on Learning Disabilities at www.nrcld.org/about/publications/papers/mellard.pdf.

National Center on Secondary Education and Transition (NCSET). (2006, March). Promoting effective parent involvement in secondary education and transition. *Parent Brief.* Retrieved from www.ncset.org/publications/viewdesc.asp?id=2844.

Prasse, D. P. (2009). *Why adopt an RTI model?* Retrieved from the RTI Action Network at www.rtinetwork.org/Learn/Why/ar/WhyRTI.

Sornson, R., Frost, F., & Burns, M. (2005). Instructional support teams in Michigan: Data from Northville Public Schools. *Communique, 33*(5), 28–29.

U.S. Department of Education. (1996). Eighteenth Annual Report to Congress on the Implementation of the Individuals with Disabilities Education Act. Retrieved from www2.ed.gov/pubs/OSEP96AnlRpt/chap1c.html.

Vaughn, S., Gersten, R., & Chard, D. J. (2000). The underlying message in LD intervention research: Findings from research syntheses. *Exceptional Children, 67,* 99–114.

Critical Thinking

1. These authors are also critical of how schools implement RTI; however, they believe that school personnel misunderstand the true purpose for RTI. What are those misunderstandings? Do you agree?

2. The authors suggest that placing students into special education may not be the right intervention for many failing students. What are their reasons? Do you agree?

3. Return to the first RTI article for reading teachers; compare the implementation of RTI tiers with the suggestions for transforming the tiers in this article. Are there differences in the implementation process? What are they?

4. Now what do you think? Write a brief reflection summarizing what you believe are the most important points for you to understand, why these points are important, and how you might implement them for a student struggling in your content area.

Austin Buffum is former senior deputy superintendent of the Capistrano Unified School District, California, and is currently a PLC associate with Solution Tree; austinbuffum@cox.net. **Mike Mattos** is a former elementary and middle school principal; mikemattos@me.com; and **Chris Weber** is director of K–6 instructional services in Garden Grove Unified School District in Orange County, California; chrisaweber@me.com.

Editor's note—This version corrects a proofing error in the print version of the October *EL.* On page 15, the printed article incorrectly stated that "Intervention is most effective when the interventions are timely, structured, and not mandatory." The word *not* is incorrect. The statement should read, "Intervention is most effective when the interventions are timely, structured, and mandatory."

A Diploma Worth Having

There's only one valid measure of the high school curriculum: How well does it prepare students for their adult lives?

GRANT WIGGINS

I have a proposal to make: It's time we abolished the high school diploma as we know it. In a modern, unpredictable, and pluralistic world, it makes no sense to demand that every 18-year-old pass the same collection of traditional courses to graduate.

Instead, we should do away with most course requirements, make *all* courses rigorous, and simply report what students have accomplished from year to year. Students should prepare for adult life by studying subjects that suit their talents, passions, and aspirations as well as needs. They should leave when they are judged to be ready for whatever next challenge they take on—whether it be college, trade school, the military, or playing in a band. Let's therefore abolish the diploma, if by *diploma* we mean that all students must graduate as though they were heading for the same 20th-century future.

> **Students should prepare for adult life by studying subjects that suit their talents, passions, and aspirations.**

This plan would enable us to finally deal with the key weakness of high school, summarized in that term virtually all students and adults use to describe it: *bor-ing.* High school is boring in part because diploma requirements crowd out personalized and engaged learning. It is also boring because our graduation requirements have been produced the way our worst laws are; they are crude compromises, based on inadequate debate. Because of arbitrary policies that define preparation in terms of content instead of useful abilities, schools focus on "coverage," not meaningful learning.

A Historical Perspective

Our belief in lockstep adherence to rigid curriculum requirements appears especially myopic and misguided if we look through the lens of the fundamental question, How well does the high school curriculum prepare all students for their adult lives? The Commission on the Reorganization of Secondary Education thought that asking this question was not only sensible but sorely needed—in 1918! Its report, *Cardinal Principles of Secondary Education,* yielded a sound set of criteria by which to rationally judge the high school curriculum. The commission underscored that these criteria must flow from the mission of schooling:

> Education in a democracy, both within and without the school, should develop in each individual the knowledge, interests, ideals, habits, and powers whereby he will find his place and use that place to shape both himself and society toward ever nobler ends. (p. 9)

The Cardinal Principles were a deliberate counterbalance to the policies that had arisen from the work of the Committee of Ten in 1892. That group had famously argued that a college-prep education, including multiple years of Latin and Greek, was appropriate for all students—even though fewer than 10 percent of high school students went to college. Chaired by the president of Harvard, the Committee of Ten was organized into subject-area groups and staffed by professors and teachers of those subjects. (Our current system, with its attention to a narrow collection of "traditional" academic subjects, still embodies the worst consequences of the work of this group.)

The Cardinal Principles, in contrast, were intentionally external to the traditional subjects and were based on an understanding of the broad mission of schooling as enabling individuals to better themselves and society. They proposed the following "main objectives of education": (1) health; (2) command of fundamental processes (reading, writing, arithmetical computations, and the elements of oral and written expression); (3) worthy home membership; (4) vocation; (5) citizenship; (6) worthy use of leisure; and (7) ethical character.

It's a bit startling to see health first in the list, ahead of "readin', writin', and 'rithmetic," isn't it? But that shock is also a helpful reminder of how much schools have lost their way. What could be more important in moving into adulthood than learning how to lead a healthy life, in the broadest sense?

This idea actually has much older roots. Herbert Spencer arguably wrote the first modern critique of out-of-touch college-prep education in his famous essay, "What Knowledge Is of Most Worth?" Spencer (1861) asserts that school exists to help us answer the essential question of how to live. Under this vision of education, health as an area of study rises to the top. Spencer writes that

> as vigorous health and its accompanying high spirits are larger elements of happiness than any other things whatever, then teaching how to maintain them is a teaching that yields in moment to no other whatever. (p. 13)

Spencer anticipates the protests with rapier wit:

> Strange that the assertion should need making! Stranger still that it should need defending! Yet are there not a few by whom such a proposition will be received with something approaching to derision. Men who would blush if caught saying Iphigénia instead of Iphigenía . . . show not the slightest shame in confessing that they do not know where the Eustachian tubes are, what are the actions of the spinal cord, what is the normal rate of pulsation, or how the lungs are inflated. . . . So overwhelming is the influence of established routine! So terribly in our education does the ornamental over-ride the useful! (p. 14)

But Spencer saves his greatest scorn for the failure to make child-rearing a core subject:

> If by some strange chance not a vestige of us descended to the remote future save a pile of our school-books or some college examination papers, we may imagine how puzzled an antiquary of the period would be on finding in them no sign that the learners were ever likely to be parents. "This must have been the curriculum for their celibates," we may fancy him concluding. (p. 20)

Spencer wisely notes that every subject will, of course, make a plea for its importance. Therefore, a curriculum can only be fairly justified using criteria about the purpose of schooling that are *outside* all "content."

In other words, we need to decide to include or exclude, emphasize or deemphasize any subject based on criteria related to school mission—a mission centered on improving the behavior and lives of students. Otherwise, our curricular decisions are arbitrary and school is aimless. Indeed, when we fail to seriously question the inclusion of algebra or the exclusion of ethics from graduation requirements, we can only fall back on custom: "We've always done it this way." But if that were the only real argument, we would still be requiring Greek of all graduates, as the Committee of Ten recommended.

Standards committees reflect typical people with typical backgrounds in education, charged to tinker with, but not radically overhaul, typical schooling.

The Unwitting Harm of the Standards Movement

Our current situation is no better than when the Committee of Ten did its work. Think about it: We are on the verge of requiring every student in the United States to learn two years of algebra that they will likely never use, but no one is required to learn wellness or parenting.

The current standards movement, for all its good intentions, is perilously narrowing our definition of education, to the great harm of not only students but also entire fields of study: the arts, the technical arts and trades, and the social sciences. Gone are excellent vocational programs—as powerfully described by Matthew Crawford in *Shop Class as Soul Craft* (Penguin, 2010), arguably the best book on education in the last five years. Threatened are visual arts, theater, music, and dance programs despite their obvious value. Indeed, there are more musicians in this country than mathematicians, but you would never know it from the work of standards committees.

The current standards movement, for all its good intentions, is perilously narrowing our definition of education.

Not Which Standards, but Whose Standards

At a meeting many years ago, I heard Ted Sizer respond to a proponent of national standards, "It's not *which* standards, it's *whose* standards!" In other words, don't make this sound so objective. It's a political determination, made by whoever has a seat at the table.

And who sits at the table? Representatives of all the traditional academic subjects. When have standards committees included working artists, journalists, web designers, or doctors who could critique the usefulness or uselessness of traditional content standards? When have professors of bioethics, anthropology, or law been invited to critique content standards? Rather, the people who care most about their little corner of the traditional content world dictate that it is required.

True story: When I did a workshop as part of a standards-writing project in a large eastern state, I mentioned the problem of arcane elements in the history standards, in particular a mention of an obscure Chinese dynasty. A gentleman cried out, "But that was my dissertation topic, and it is important for students to know!" Worse: The speaker was the social studies coordinator for the state and had made sure to put this topic in the previous version of the standards.

Having worked with three different states on their standards writing and revision process, I can say with confidence that the way we organize standards-based work at the state and national levels dooms it from the start. The committees reflect typical people with typical backgrounds in education, charged to tinker with, but not radically overhaul, typical schooling; no criteria for choices are ever put forward to weed the document of pet topics. In short, these committees merely rearrange the furniture of the traditional core content areas; they replicate the past that they feel comfortable with rather than face the future that is on its annoying but inexorable way.

A Case in Point: Mathematics

For proof of the lack of forward thinking, look at the Common Core math standards. The recommended high school mathematics is unchanged from when I was a kid in prep school 45 years ago: four years of conventional topics in algebra, geometry, trigonometry, and calculus. The only improvement is greater emphasis on modeling and statistics. But the laying out of the standards in isolated lists of content (as opposed to summarizing the kinds of performance standards student work must meet) undercuts the likelihood of vital reform to make mathematics more engaging and useful to the majority of students.

Consider this dreary summary of a high school strand from the Common Core:

Trigonometric Functions

- Extend the domain of trigonometric functions using the unit circle.
- Model periodic phenomena with trigonometric functions.
- Prove and apply trigonometric identities.

This is a standard? With what justification? It almost goes without saying (but in the current myopia, it needs to be said): *Few people need to know this.*

Today, algebra is the new Greek that "all educated persons" supposedly need. This is clear from the work of the American Diploma Project (2004), launched a few years ago by Achieve, a group created by governors and corporate leaders. Achieve deserves credit for taking the idea of "backward design" of high school requirements from college and workplace readiness seriously, buttressed by research and analysis. But we should be cautious about accepting its narrow view of the high school curriculum, especially its claim that advanced algebra should be a universal requirement (Achieve, 2008). The data Achieve cites to justify this claim include the following:

- Completing advanced math courses in high school has a greater influence on whether students will graduate from college than any other factor— including family background. Students who take math beyond Algebra II double their chances of earning a bachelor's degree.
- Through 2016, professional occupations are expected to add more new jobs—at least 5 million—than any other sector; within that category, computer and mathematical occupations will grow the fastest.
- Simply taking advanced math has a direct impact on future earnings, apart from any other factors. Students who take advanced math have higher incomes 10 years after graduating—regardless of family background, grades, and college degrees.

But hold on: All that this really says is that people who take advanced math courses are more likely to do well in college and be prepared for jobs that involve advanced math. But that doesn't mean that broad success in life depends on those courses. I have no doubt, for example, that most students who study Greek or astrophysics also end up in satisfying careers. Algebra is not the cause of adult success any more than Greek is. It is most likely the reverse: Those who take advanced courses are smart, motivated students who will succeed in any career they choose. As a recent study pointed out, only about 5 percent of the population actually need algebra in their work (Handel, 2007).

Much the same criticism was made by the Partnership for 21st Century Skills (2010), whose critique of the draft Common Core math standards asserted that the standards should include more emphasis on practical mathematical application (for example, analyzing financial data); include statistics and probability in the elementary grades and emphasize these areas more in the secondary grades; and focus less on factual content mastery in favor of better integrating higher-order thinking skills throughout the curriculum.

Lerman and Packer (2010) remind us that employers tend to call for something far more general and useful than advanced algebra skills:

Every study of employer needs made over the past 20 years . . . has come up with the same answers. Successful workers communicate effectively, orally and in writing, and have social and behavioral skills that make them responsible and good at teamwork. They are creative and techno-savvy, have a good command of fractions and basic statistics, and can apply relatively simple math to real-world problems such as those concerning financial or health literacy. Employers never mention polynomial factoring. (p. 31)

For a more enlightened approach to mathematics instruction, there is a fine body of work developed over the past 15 years under the heading of Quantitative Literacy (or Quantitative Reasoning). The *Quantitative Literacy Manifesto* (National Council on Education and the Disciplines, 2001) shares the concern of organizations like Achieve that most U.S. students leave high school without the math skills they need to succeed in either college or employment. But this report proposes a different solution—one better suited to the goal of universal education in a modern society:

Common responses to this well-known problem are either to demand more years of high school mathematics or more rigorous standards for graduation. Yet even individuals who have studied trigonometry and calculus often remain largely ignorant of common abuses of data and all too often find themselves unable to comprehend (much less to articulate) the nuances of quantitative inferences. As it turns out, it is not calculus but numeracy that is the key to understanding our data-drenched society. (p. 2)

The *Quantitative Literacy Manifesto* calls for developing in students a predisposition to look at the world through mathematical eyes, to see the benefits (and risks) of thinking quantitatively about commonplace issues, and to approach complex problems with confidence in the value of careful reasoning. (p. 22)

Alas, the Quantitative Literacy movement simply has less political clout than Achieve does. Again we see: It's not *which* standards, but *whose* standards.

Revisiting High School Requirements

Mindful of the mission of schooling to prepare students to prosper in and contribute to a pluralistic and ever-changing democracy, I humbly offer my own update of Spencer's proposal and the work of the Cardinal Principles group. I think that if we consider future usefulness in a changing world as the key criterion, the following subjects represent more plausible candidates for key high school courses in the 21st century than those on the Achieve list:

- Philosophy, including critical thinking and ethics.
- Psychology, with special emphasis on mental health, child development, and family relations.
- Economics and business, with an emphasis on market forces, entrepreneurship, saving, borrowing and investing, and business start-ups.
- Woodworking or its equivalent; you should have to make something to graduate.
- Mathematics, focusing primarily on probability and statistics and math modeling.
- Language arts, with a major focus on oral proficiency (as well as the reading and writing of nonfiction).
- Multimedia, including game and web design.
- Science: human biology, anatomy, physiology (health-related content), and earth science (ecology).
- Civics, with an emphasis on civic action and how a bill *really* becomes law; lobbying.
- Modern U.S. and world history, taught backward chronologically from the most pressing current issues.

Instead of designing backward from the traditions of college admission or the technical demands of currently "hot" jobs, this list designs backward from the vital human capacities needed for a successful adulthood regardless of school or job. How odd, for example, that our current requirements do not include oral proficiency when all graduates will need this ability in their personal, civic, social, and professional lives. How unfortunate for us personally, professionally, and socially that all high school and college students are not required to study ethics.

The financial meltdown of recent years underscores a related point: Understanding our economic system is far more important than learning textbook chemistry. In science, how sad that physics is viewed as more important than psychology and human development, as parents struggle to raise children wisely and families work hard to understand one another. (The principle of inertia from physics may explain it!)

Do not misunderstand my complaints as somehow too utilitarian or opposed to the liberal arts and higher math. I was educated in the classic tradition at St. John's College. I learned physics and calculus through Newton's *Principia* and geometry through Euclid and Lobachevski—in a college program with *no* electives—all based on the Great Books. I had arguably the best undergraduate education in the United States, if the aim is intellectual power. But would I mandate that all colleges look like St. John's? Absolutely not, any more than I would mandate that all schools adopt my proposed course list as graduation requirements. On the contrary, my advocacy for injecting philosophy, economics, and human development into the terribly narrow conventional curriculum is a call to bring a richer array of options to students.

Everyone agrees that high school needs to be more rigorous. No one wants to perpetuate inequity of opportunity. But can't there be greater student choice that opens up rather than closes off opportunities? Can't vocational courses and courses in the arts be as demanding as upper-level courses in math or chemistry?

Setting standards in the way we do—mandating requirements for all by looking at our own generation's academic experience rather than forward to the developmental needs of all students—impedes progress rather than advancing it. Then, we add insult to injury: a one-size-fits-all diploma. In sum, it seems to me that we still do not have a clue about how to make education *modern*: forward-looking, client-centered, and flexible; adapted to an era where the future, not the past, determines the curriculum.

What Do Our Students Need from School?

I am not arguing for throwing out the Common Core Standards. At least they will impose reason on the current absurd patchwork of state standards and finally make it possible for authors, software designers, test makers, and textbook publishers to provide the most resources at the least expense. But let's not treat these standards as anything more than a timid rearrangement of previous state standards, promulgated by people familiar only with traditional courses and requirements.

Instead, let us face the future by pausing to consider anew the wisdom of Herbert Spencer and the authors of the Cardinal Principles. Let us begin a serious national conversation (all of us, not just the policy wonks, selected employers, and college admissions officers) about the questions, What is the point of high school? What do our society and our students need from school, regardless of hidebound tradition or current policy fads?

Then we might finally have a diploma worth giving and receiving in the modern age.

References

Achieve. (2008). *Math works: All students need advanced math.* Washington, DC: Author. Retrieved from www.achieve.org/files/Achieve-MathWorks-FactSheet-All%20StudentsNeedAdvancedMath.pdf.

American Diploma Project. (2004). *Ready or not: Creating a high school diploma that counts.* Washington, DC: Achieve.

Commission on the Reorganization of Secondary Education. (1918). *Cardinal principles of secondary education: A report of the Commission on the Reorganization of Secondary Education, appointed by the National Education Association.* Washington, DC: U.S. Department of the Interior.

Handel, M. J. (2007, May 23). *A new survey of workplace skills, technology, and management practices (STAMP): Background and descriptive statistics.* Boston: Department of Sociology, Northeastern University.

Lerman, R. I., & Packer, A. (2010, April 21). Will we ever learn? What's wrong with the common-standards project. *Education Week, 29*(29), 30–31.

National Council on Education and the Disciplines. (2001). *Mathematics and democracy: The case for quantitative literacy.* Princeton, NJ: Author. Retrieved from Mathematical Association of America at www.maa.org/ql/mathanddemocracy.html.

Partnership for 21st Century Skills. (2010). *P21 comments on Common Core state standards initiative—mathematics.* Retrieved from www.p21.org/documents/P21_CCSSI _Comments_MATH_%20040210.pdf.

Spencer, H. (1861). What knowledge is of most worth? In H. Spencer, *Essays on education and kindred subjects* (pp. 1–44). London: Author.

Critical Thinking

1. Wiggins takes a new look at the general education curriculum in public high schools and finds it wanting. Why does he think educators have a myopic and misguided focus on a rigid curriculum for all students?

2. Take some time to reflect on what you learned in high school to determine which courses prepared you for your adult life. Briefly describe why you selected these courses and what classes contributed to your success as an adult.

3. Which students would benefit from the changes Wiggins suggests? Explain your reasons.

4. Could these changes have a positive effect on our country's future? Why?

5. Do Wiggins's ideas fit with what you think about NCLB and RTI? Explain your answer with specific reasons.

GRANT WIGGINS is the coauthor with Jay McTighe of *Understanding by Design* (ASCD, 2005) and *Schooling by Design: Mission, Action, and Achievement* (ASCD, 2007). He is president of Authentic Education in Hopewell, New Jersey; grant@authenticeducation.org.

UNIT 2

Teaching All Students in All Schools

Unit Selections

9. **Who Are America's Poor Children?: The Official Story,** Vanessa R. Wright, Michelle Chau, and Yumike Aratani
10. **Teacher's Perspectives on Teaching Students Who Are Placed At-Risk,** Raji Swaminathan and Thalia Mulvihill
11. **Dismantling Rural Stereotypes,** James Bryant
12. **Examining the Culture of Poverty: Promising Practices,** Kristen Cuthrell, Joy Stapleton, and Carolyn Ledford
13. **Exploring Educational Material Needs and Resources for Children Living in Poverty,** Indra Kumar Mahabir

Learning Outcomes

After reading this unit, you will be able to:

- Summarize the data regarding students who live in poverty.
- Discuss the needs and resources of persons living in poverty.
- Define the term "at-risk."
- Explain how teacher beliefs about at-risk students affect their practice.
- Summarize the actions teachers and their schools can take to counteract their perceptions of students who are at-risk.
- Compare and contrast the unique issues of rural, suburban, and urban schools.
- Debate the idea that rural schools should not be forced to adhere to reforms that have no relevance in their districts.
- Describe the socioeconomic context of schools.
- Explain how teachers' beliefs about poverty may determine their teaching practices.
- Select appropriate strategies for working with students who live in poverty.
- Determine what educational materials are generally needed by students who live in poverty.

Student Website

www.mhhe.com/cls

Internet References

National Center for Children in Poverty
www.nccp.org

U.S. Census Bureau: Poverty
www.census.gov/hhes/www/poverty/poverty.html

Southern Poverty Law Center Teaching Diverse Students Initiative
www.tolerance.org/tdsi/cb_achievement_gaps

Donors Choose
www.donorschoose.org

Doing What Works
http://dww.ed.gov/index.cfm

Center on Rural Education
www2.ed.gov/nclb/freedom/local/rural/index.html

The Rural School and Community Trust
www.ruraledu.org

Edutopia
www.edutopia.org

The problem of high levels of poverty in urban and rural areas of our country is of great concern to American educators. One in four American children does not have all of his/her basic needs met and lives under conditions of poverty. Almost one in three lives in a single-parent home, which in itself is no disadvantage, but under conditions of poverty, it may become one. Children living in poverty are in crisis if their basic health and social needs are not adequately met, and their educational development can be affected by crises in their personal lives. We must teach and support these students and their families, even when it appears that they are not fully invested in their education. As a teacher, you may not have much control over the factors that shape the lives of our students, but hopefully you will begin with these readings to see how you can help students in other ways.

What is poverty? Jensen (2009) defines poverty as "a chronic and debilitating condition that results from multiple adverse synergistic risk factors and affects the mind, body and soul" (p. 6). Some of the risk factors frequently mentioned in the literature on poverty include 1) violence in the community, 2) stress and distress felt by the adults in the child's life, 3) disorganized family situation, including physical and substance abuse, 4) negative interactions between parents and children, and 5) parents lack understanding of developmental needs. Rawlinson (2007) grew up in poverty and later wrote about her experiences in *A Minds Shaped by Poverty: Ten things educators should know.* These words give us a peek into the mind of the children we teach.

> When I entered school, I took all the pain, anger, frustration, resentment, shame, low self-esteem, debilitating worldview, and dehumanizing effects of poverty with me. I had a poverty mind-set (p. 1).

After looking at the list of risk factors and Rawlinson's admitted poverty mind-set, what are teachers to do? Can teachers ignore these concerns to treat and teach all students as NCLB requires? Smiley and Helfenbein (2011) found that how teachers see themselves, their students, and the larger community plays a powerful role in planning and instructing students from poverty. That study leaves us with new questions. So what can we do about our beliefs? If a majority of teachers in the United States are non-minority, middle-class, and female how do they relate to students who are so unlike themselves? The articles in this unit were selected so that the readers could begin that conversation about relating to the children born into or living in poverty. Further, the articles offer some new ideas about how to change the mind-set of both teachers and the children of poverty. And lastly, the articles will offer examples of schools and teachers who are making a difference for children, not just by raising test scores, but also by changing lives.

This unit begins with the article *Who Are America's Poor Children?: The Official Story* because it is important to understand what we mean by the phrase "living in poverty." This article will frame the issues and provide a context for the remaining articles in this section. The next four articles explore the issues of bias and prejudice surrounding those who live in poverty. The common question of teachers' perspectives about students who live in poverty is explored in three of the studies and the fourth investigates how students who live in poverty view themselves.

© Comstock/PictureQuest

Each of the articles offers strategies and interventions for teachers to use in their work. Swaminathan and Mulvihill investigate how preconceived beliefs about poverty and those who are poor relate to teacher behavior and student learning. These researchers argue that for teachers to have an appropriate perspective of students placed at-risk, they need to have repertoire of strength-based models. Bryant looks at the differences found in rural schools. He suggests that most of us have quaint ideas of the "little red schoolhouse" when in reality rural schools are in some of the hardest hit economic areas. One issue is coping with school-reform regulations that are not realistic because rural schools have limited funds they are forced to spend on complying with government regulations. In the fourth article, Cuthrell, Stapleton, and Ledford listened to the discussions of preservice teachers who thought that their beliefs about poverty would not affect their teaching. Those conversations were the impetus for this research study that focused on developing a curriculum for their teacher-education program. Children who live in poverty generally attend schools in areas of high unemployment, high-minority population, and low-levels of funding. If the school does not have enough funds to provide programs and materials to break the cycle of generational poverty, how can teachers make a difference? Mahabir's two-part study explored the educational material needs of children living in poverty and the programs that are in place to provide materials. The researcher's conclusions have implications for both schools and agencies serving in high-poverty areas.

References

Jensen, E. 2009. *Teaching with Poverty in Mind: What Being Poor Does to Kid's Brains and What Schools Can Do About It.* Alexandria, VA: Association for Supervision and Curriculum Development.

Rawlinson, R.M. 2007. *A Mind Shaped by Poverty: Ten Things Educators Should Know.* New York: iUniverse, Inc.

Smiley, A.D., and R.J. Helfenbein. 2011. "Becoming Teachers: The Payne Effect." *Multicultural Perspectives, 13*(1): 5–15.

Who Are America's Poor Children?

The Official Story

VANESSA R. WIGHT, MICHELLE CHAU, AND YUMIKO ARATANI

O ver 15 million American children live in families with incomes below the federal poverty level, which is $22,050 a year for a family of four.[1] The number of children living in poverty increased by 33 percent between 2000 and 2009. There are 3.8 million more children living in poverty today than in 2000.

Not only are these numbers troubling, the official poverty measure tells only part of the story. Research consistently shows that, on average, families need an income of about twice the federal poverty level to make ends meet.[2] Children living in families with incomes below this level—for 2010, $44,100 for a family of four—are referred to as low income. Forty-two percent of the nation's children—more than 31 million in 2009—live in low-income families.[3]

Nonetheless, eligibility for many public benefits is based on the official poverty measure. This fact sheet describes some of the characteristics of American children who are considered poor by the official standard.[4]

How many children in America are officially poor?

The percentage of children living in poverty and extreme poverty (less than 50 percent of the federal poverty level) has increased since 2000.

- Twenty-one percent of children live in families that are considered officially poor (15.3 million children).
- Nine percent of children live in extreme poor families (6.8 million).

Rates of official child poverty vary tremendously across the states.

- Across the states, child poverty rates range from 10 percent in New Hampshire to 30 percent in Mississippi.

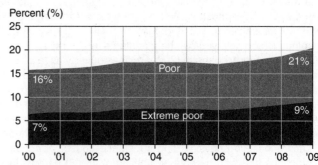

Children living in poor and extreme poor families, 2000–2009

What are some of the characteristics of children who are officially poor in America?

Black, American Indian, and Hispanic children are disproportionately poor.

- Twelve percent of white children live in poor families. Across the 10 most populated states,[5] rates of child poverty among white children do not vary dramatically; the range is nine percent in California and Texas to 16 percent in Ohio.
- Thirty-six percent of black children live in poor families. In the 10 most populated states, rates of child poverty among black children range from 30 percent in California and New York to 46 percent in Ohio and Michigan.
- Fifteen percent of Asian children, 34 percent of American Indian children, and 24 percent of children of some other race live in poor families (comparable state comparisons are not possible due to small sample sizes).[6]
- Thirty-three percent of Hispanic children live in poor families. In the 10 most populated states, rates of child poverty among Hispanic children range from 25 percent in Florida and Illinois to 41 percent in North Carolina and Georgia.

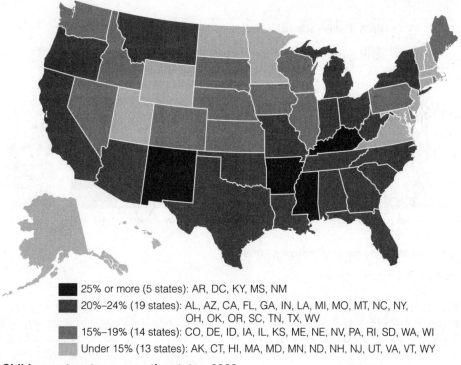

25% or more (5 states): AR, DC, KY, MS, NM

20%–24% (19 states): AL, AZ, CA, FL, GA, IN, LA, MI, MO, MT, NC, NY, OH, OK, OR, SC, TN, TX, WV

15%–19% (14 states): CO, DE, ID, IA, IL, KS, ME, NE, NV, PA, RI, SD, WA, WI

Under 15% (13 states): AK, CT, HI, MA, MD, MN, ND, NH, NJ, UT, VA, VT, WY

Child poverty rates across the states, 2009

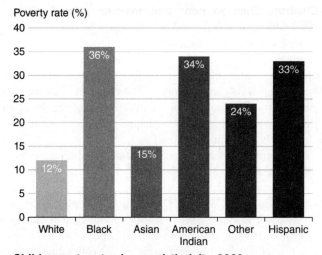

Child poverty rates by race/ethnicity, 2009

Having immigrant parents can increase a child's chances of being poor.

- Twenty-seven percent of children in immigrant families are poor; 19 percent of children with native-born parents are poor.

- In the six states with the largest populations of immigrants —California, Florida, Illinois, New Jersey, New York, and Texas—the poverty rate among children in immigrant families ranges from 16 percent to 34 percent.

Official poverty rates are highest for young children.

- Twenty-four percent of children younger than age 6 live in poor families; 19 percent of children age 6 or older live in poor families.

- In about two-thirds of the states (35 states), 20 percent or more of children younger than age 6 are poor, whereas only about a half (24 states) have a poverty rate for all children (younger than age 18) that is as high.

What are some of the hardships faced by children in America?

Food insecurity, lack of affordable housing, and other hardships affect millions of American children, not just those who are officially poor.

- Twenty-one percent of households with children experience food insecurity. The share of households with children experiencing food insecurity was split with about half (10 percent) reporting food insecurity among adults, only, and the other half (about 11 percent) reporting low and very low food security among children.[7]

- Nearly 50 percent of tenants living in renter-occupied units spend more than 30 percent of their income on rent.[8]

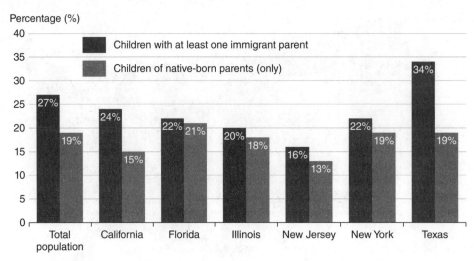

Poor children by parents' nativity, 2009

- Although crowded housing is relatively uncommon, five percent of poor households and nearly two percent of all households are moderately crowded with 1.01–1.50 persons per room. Severe crowding with 1.51 or more persons per room characterizes about 1.1 percent of poor households and 0.3 percent of all households.[9]
- Compared to white families with children, black and Latino families with children are more than twice as likely to experience economic hardships, such as food insecurity.[10]

Many poor children lack health insurance.

- Sixteen percent of poor children lack health insurance, whereas 11 percent of all children (poor and non-poor) lack health insurance.[11]
- In the 10 most populated states, the percentage of poor children who lack health insurance ranges from 12 percent in New York to 38 percent in Texas.[12]

Measuring Poverty: Needs and Resources[13]

The official U.S. poverty rate is used as one of the nation's primary indicators of economic well-being. The measure of poverty, which was developed in the 1960s, is calculated by comparing a family's or person's resources to a set of thresholds that vary by family size and composition and are determined to represent the minimum amount of income it takes to support a family at a basic level.[14] Families or people with resources that fall below the threshold are considered poor.

The current poverty measure is widely acknowledged to be inadequate.[15] The method of calculating the poverty thresholds is outdated. Originally based on data from the 1950s, the poverty threshold was set at three times the cost of food and adjusted for family size. Since then, the measure has been updated only for inflation. Yet food now comprises only about

one-seventh of an average family's expenses, while the costs of housing, child care, health care, and transportation have grown disproportionately. The result? Current poverty thresholds are too low, arguably arbitrary, and they do not adjust for differences in the cost of living within and across states.

Further, the definition of resources under the current poverty measure is based solely on cash income. So while the measure takes into account a variety of income sources, including earnings, interest, dividends, and benefits, such as Social Security and cash assistance, it does not include the value of the major benefit programs that assist low-income families, such as the federal Earned Income Tax Credit, food stamps, Medicaid, and housing and child care assistance. Therefore, the way we measure poverty does not tell us whether many of the programs designed to reduce economic hardship are effective because the value of these benefits is ignored.

Considerable research has been done on alternative methods for measuring income poverty.[16] In 2010, the Office of Management and Budget formed the Interagency Technical Working Group (ITWG) on Developing a Supplemental Poverty Measure to create a set of starting points that would allow the Census Bureau and the Bureau of Labor Statistics to produce a supplemental poverty measure for estimating poverty at the national level. The group targeted two main issues: 1) establishing a threshold and 2) estimating family resources.[17] First, the ITWG suggested that the poverty threshold represent a dollar amount that families need to purchase a basic bundle of commodities that include food, shelter, clothing and utilities (FSCU), along with a small amount for additional expenses. The threshold should be based on the expenditure data of families with two children and then adjusted to reflect different family types and geographic differences in housing. Finally, the threshold should be set to the 33rd percentile of the spending distribution for the basic bundle. Second, the ITWG suggested that family resources represent the sum of cash income from all sources along with near-cash benefits that families can use to purchase the basic FSCU bundle. In addition, expenses not included in the threshold, such as taxes, work and child care

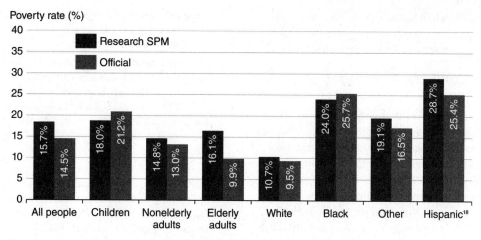

Poverty rate (%)

■ Research SPM

■ Official

	Research SPM	Official
All people	15.7%	14.5%
Children	18.0%	21.2%
Nonelderly adults	14.8%	13.0%
Elderly adults	16.1%	9.9%
White	10.7%	9.5%
Black	24.0%	25.7%
Other	19.1%	16.5%
Hispanic[18]	28.7%	25.4%

Percent of people in poverty by different poverty measures, 2009

Source: Short, K. S. 2010 "Who is Poor? A New Look with the Supplemental Poverty Measure." Paper presented at the 2011 Allied Social Science Associations, Society of Government Economists, Denver, CO.

expenses, and medical out of pocket expenses should be subtracted from the sum of cash income and near-cash benefits.

Recently, the Census Bureau released estimates of poverty based on the research SPM, a preliminary measure of poverty incorporating the ITWG recommendations.[18] In general, the findings in this report indicate that poverty is higher with the new measure when compared with the official measure. Approximately 14.5 percent[19] of the population is poor using the official measure compared with 15.7 percent using the research SPM (see figure). Children have lower poverty rates while adults, particularly the elderly, have higher rates using the new measure. Differences by race/ethnicity suggest higher poverty among most groups using the research SPM.

These differences are partly a function of the new measure's higher thresholds that consequently capture more people. However, some of the differences are explained by the new definition of resources, which subtracts medical out-of-pocket expenses from income—a large expenditure among the elderly population—as well as other work-related and child care expenditures.

What should be done about child poverty?

Research suggests that being poor during childhood is associated with being poor as an adult.[21] Yet, child poverty is not intractable. Policies and practices that increase family income and help families maintain their financial footing during hard economic times not only result in short-term economic security, but also have lasting effects by reducing the long-term consequences of poverty on children's lives. NCCP recommends a number of major policy strategies to improve the well-being of children and families living in poverty:

Make work pay

Since research is clear that poverty is the greatest threat to children's well being, strategies that help parents succeed in the labor force help children.[22] Increasing the minimum wage is important for working families with children because it helps them cover the high cost of basic necessities, such as child care and housing.[23] Further, policies aimed at expanding the Earned Income Tax Credit and other tax credits such as the Additional Child Tax Credit and the Making Work Pay Tax Credit are particularly instrumental in putting well-needed dollars back into the hands of low-earning workers. Finally, many low-wage workers need better access to benefits such as health insurance and paid sick days. Reducing the costs of basic needs for low-income families Medicaid/SCHIP not only increase access to health care, but also helps families defray often crippling health care costs by providing free or low-cost health insurance. The Patient Protection and Affordable Care Act signed into law by President Obama promises to provide more affordable coverage and to prevent families from bankruptcy or debt because of health care costs. Further, housing is known to be a major expense for families. However, current housing subsidy programs are available for a small percentage of eligible families due to inadequate funding.[24] Housing subsidies have been shown to be positively related to children's educational outcomes.[25] Thus, it is important to increase funding for housing subsidies for families with children.

Support parents and their young children in early care and learning

To thrive, children need nurturing families and high quality early care and learning experiences. Securing child care is particularly important for working parents with young children. Research has found that child care subsidies are positively associated with the long-term employment and financial well-being of parents.[26] Along with providing child care subsidies, policies and practices that ensure high-quality child care are also important. For example, programs that target families with infants and toddlers, such as Early Head Start, have been shown to improve children's social and cognitive development, as well as improve parenting skills.[27] Investments in preschool for 3- and

4-year-olds are just as critical. In short, high-quality early childhood experiences can go a long way toward closing the achievement gap between poor children and their more well-off peers.[28]

Support asset accumulation among low-income families

Many American families with children are asset poor, which means they lack sufficient savings to live above the poverty line for three months or more in the event of parental unemployment or illness when no earnings are available.[29] This type of economic vulnerability is typically masked by conventional poverty measures based on income. Unlike wages, income generated from assets provides a cushion for families. Further, parental saving promotes both positive cognitive development and subsequent college attendance among children.[30] There are two ways to support asset accumulation among low-income families. First, eliminating asset tests from major means-tested programs reduces the risk of running up large amounts of debt and increases the amount of financial resources parents have to invest in children. Second, there are programs that actively promote and encourage the development of saving habits among asset-poor families through matching funds incentives, such as the Individual Development Accounts (IDA) program and the Saving for Education, Entrepreneurship, and Down-payment (SEED) National Initiative programs.

Endnotes

1. Unless otherwise noted, national data were calculated from the U.S. Current Population Survey, Annual Social and Economic Supplement, March 2010, which represents information from calendar year 2009. State data were calculated by NCCP analysts from the 2009 American Community Survey, which represents information from 2009. Estimates include children living in households with at least one parent and most children living apart from both parents (for example, children being raised by grandparents). Children living independently, living with a spouse, or in group quarters are excluded from these data. Children ages 14 and under living with only unrelated adults were not included because data on their income status were not available. Among children who do not live with at least one parent, parental characteristics are those of the householder and/or the householder's spouse. In the most recent CPS and ACS, parents could report children's race as one or more of the following: "white," "black," "American Indian or Alaskan Native," or "Asian and/or Hawaiian/Pacific Islander." In a separate question, parents could report whether their children were of Hispanic origin. For the data reported, children whose parent reported their race as white, black, American Indian or Alaskan Native, or Asian and/or Hawaiian/ Pacific Islander and their ethnicity as non-Hispanic are assigned their respective race. Children who were reported to be of more than one race were assigned as Other. Children whose parent identified them as Hispanic were categorized as Hispanic, regardless of their reported race.

2. Lin, J.; Bernstein, J. 2008. What We Need to Get By: A Basic Standard of Living Costs $48,779, and Nearly a Third of Families Fall Short. Washington, DC: Economic Policy Institute.

Pearce, D.; Brooks, J. 1999. *The Self-Sufficiency Standard for the Washington, DC Metropolitan Area*. Washington, DC: Wider Opportunities for Women.

3. For more information about children living in low-income families (defined as families with incomes below 200 percent of the official poverty level), see: Chau, M.; Thampi, K.; Wight, V.R. 2010. *Basic Facts About Low-income Children, Children Under Age 18, 2009*. New York, NY: National Center for Children in Poverty, Columbia University, Mailman School of Public Health.

4. To learn more about child poverty and family economic hardship, see Cauthen, Nancy K.; Fass, Sarah. 2008. *Ten Important Questions About Child Poverty and Family Economic Hardship*. New York, NY: National Center for Children in Poverty, Columbia University, Mailman School of Public Health.

5. The 10 most populated states in 2009 were California, Texas, New York, Florida, Illinois, Pennsylvania, Ohio, Michigan, Georgia, and North Carolina.

6. Data for Asian, American Indian, and children of some other race are unavailable due to small sample sizes.

7. Wight, V. R.; Thampi, K.; Briggs, J. 2010. *Who Are America's Poor Children?: Examining Food Insecurity Among Children in the United States*. National Center for Children in Poverty, Columbia University, Mailman School of Public Health.

8. American Community Survey. 2009. Table B25070: Gross Rent as a Percentage of Household Income in the Past 12 Months. American FactFinder. Washington, DC: U.S. Census Bureau. American Community Survey.

9. U.S. Census Bureau. 2008. American Housing Survey for the United States in 2009. Washington, DC: U.S. Government Printing Office.

10. Wight, V.R.; Thampi, K. 2010. *Basic Facts About Food Insecurity Among Children in the United States, 2008*. National Center for Children in Poverty, Columbia University, Mailman School of Public Health.

11. Chau, M.; Thampi, K.; Wight, V.R. 2010. *Basic Facts About Low-income Children, Children Under Age 18, 2009*. New York, NY: National Center for Children in Poverty, Columbia University, Mailman School of Public Health.

12. Authors' calculations from the 2009 American Community Survey.

13. For more information about the official poverty measure, see: Fass, Sarah. 2009. *Measuring Income and Poverty in the United States*. New York, NY: National Center for Children in Poverty, Columbia University, Mailman School of Public Health; Cauthen, Nancy K. 2007. Testimony before the House Subcommittee on Income Security and Family Support, Committee on Ways and Means. August 1, 2007; NYC Center for Economic Opportunity. 2008. The CEO Poverty Measure: A Working Paper by the New York City Center for Economic Opportunity. New York: New York City Center for Economic Opportunity.

14. Iceland, John. 2005. Measuring Poverty: Theoretical and Empirical Considerations. *Measurement* 3: 199–235.

15. See Iceland, John. 2003. *Poverty in America*. Berkeley: University of California Press.; Citro, Constance F., and Robert T. Michael (eds.), Measuring Poverty: A New Approach, Washington, DC: National Academy Press, 1995.; Ruggles, P.

1990. *Drawing the Line: Alternative Poverty Measures and their Implications for Public Policy.* Washington, DC: Urban Institute.

16. Citro, Constance F., and Robert T. Michael (eds.), Measuring Poverty: A New Approach. Washington, DC: National Academy Press, 1995.

17. ITWG. 2010. "Observations from the Interagency Technical Working Group on Developing a Supplemental Poverty Measure" available at: www.census.gov/hhes/www /poverty/SPM_TWGObservations.pdf.

18. Short, K. S. 2010. "Who is Poor? A New Look with the Supplemental Poverty Measure." Paper presented at the 2011 Allied Social Science Associations, Society of Government Economists. Denver, CO.

19. This estimate is slightly higher than the published poverty rate that appears in the Census publication, Income, Poverty, and Health Insurance Coverage in the United States: 2009 (P60-238) because it includes unrelated individuals under age 15 in the poverty universe.

20. People of Hispanic origin may be of any race. In this figure, persons of Hispanic origin, whatever their race, are shown by their origin but not by their race and persons not of Hispanic origin are shown by race.

21. Wagmiller, Robert L. Jr.; Adelman, Robert M. 2009. *Childhood and Intergenerational Poverty: The Long-term Consequences of Growing up Poor.* New York, NY: National Center for Children in Poverty, Columbia University, Mailman School of Public Health.

22. Duncan, Greg J.; Brooks-Gunn, Jeanne. 1997. *Consequences of Growing up Poor.* New York: Russell Sage Foundation.

23. Purmort, Jessica. 2010. *Making Work Supports Work: A Picture of Low-wage Workers in America.* New York, NY: National Center for Children in Poverty, Columbia University, Mailman School of Public Health.

24. Ibid.

25. Currie, J.; Yelowitz, A., 2000. Are Public Housing Projects Good for Kids? *Journal of Public Economics* 75: 99–124

26. Martinez-Beck, Ivelisse; George, Robert M. 2009. Employment Outcomes for Low-income Families Receiving Child Care Subsidies in Illinois, Maryland, and Texas. Final Report to U.S. Department of Health and Human Services Administration for Children and Families. Office of Planning, Research, and Evaluation. Chicago, Chapin Hall at the University of Chicago. Forry, Nicole D. 2008. The Impact of Child Care Subsidies on Low-income Single Parents: An Examination of Child Care Expenditures and Family Finances. *Journal of Family and Economic Issues* 30(1): 43–54.

27. Stebbins, Helene; Knitzer, Jane. 2007. *State Early Childhood Policies.* New York, NY: National Center for Children in Poverty, Columbia University, Mailman School of Public Health.

28. Knitzer, Jane. 2007. Testimony on the Economic and Societal Costs of Poverty. Testimony before the U.S. House of Representatives, Committee on Ways and Means. Jan. 24, 2007.

29. Aratani, Yumiko; Chau, Michelle. 2010. *Asset Poverty and Debt among Families with Children in the United States.* New York, NY: National Center for Children in Poverty, Columbia University, Mailman School of Public Health.

30. Conley, Dalton. 2001. Capital for College: Parental Assets and Postsecondary Schooling. Sociology of Education 74: 59–72. Yeung, W. Jean; Conley, Dalton. 2008. Black–white Achievement Gap and Family Wealth. *Child Development* 79(2): 303–324.

Critical Thinking

1. Does what you learned when reading this information support what you are hearing and seeing on the nightly news?

2. Why do we, as teachers, need to be concerned about the rising level of poverty in our country?

3. Based on this article, what are some actions you can take to support families in your school district and state?

4. How will what you have learned impact how you teach? Give specific actions with details.

5. Do you know the levels of poverty in your school district or the school district where you go to college? To know more about poverty in your area, you can go to the websites provided in this unit's section at the front of this edition, such as the National Center for Children in Poverty www.nccp.org or the U.S. Census Bureau www.census.gov /hhes/www/poverty/poverty.html

VANESSA R. WIGHT, PhD, is senior research associate at the National Center for Children in Poverty. Her research focuses on the contribution of early childhood experiences and involved parenting to children's well-being. **MICHELLE CHAU** is a research analyst on the Family Economic Security team at the National Center for Children in Poverty. **YUMIKO ARATANI, PhD,** is senior research associate and acting director of Family Economic Security at the National Center for Children in Poverty. Her research has focused on the role of housing in stratification processes, parental assets and children's well-being.

Acknowledgments—This research was supported by funding from Annie E. Casey Foundation. Special thanks to Morris Ardoin, Lee Kreader, Amy Palmisano, Curtis Skinner, and Telly Valdellon.

Teacher's Perspectives on Teaching Students Who Are Placed At-Risk

How do teachers make meaning of the term "students-at-risk"? What are their beliefs about learners who are at-risk? How do their beliefs impact the ways in which they teach? How do teachers move students from an at-risk status to a status of promise?

RAJI SWAMINATHAN AND THALIA MULVIHILL

These questions guided our initial inquiry into the phenomenon of the meaning and use of the term "at-risk" when it is applied to students. In this article we examine the perspectives of twelve teachers from two schools. Both schools had programs specifically designed to meet the needs of students placed "at-risk." Our analyses revealed that teachers were either facilitated or obstructed in large part by systemic issues such as program philosophy. Teachers acted on their personal beliefs that either coincided with or enhanced the mission and vision of the program. In cases where the teachers' beliefs collided with the program philosophy, teachers tended to reinterpret the mission or vision of the program to suit their own beliefs.

For example, teachers who were part of the "discipline," i.e. behavior modification program focused on rewards and punishments, defined success in terms of behavior and not academics! Teachers who focused on discipline-defined-as-subject matter, motivated students and attempted to engage them through academic innovations. The latter group, operating from a strength-based perspective, tended to have a holistic view of students, put academics first and offered several alternative explanations for students' behaviors that did not blame the student.

We argue that while teachers did the best they could, both groups of teachers worked within the "at-risk" framework and were therefore in some ways trapped by it. They found explanations for the at-risk status within students, the situational context or the school. They consistently attempted to combat the status by balancing the risks encountered by students with building resilience in them.

Such a mental model, while it is somewhat strength-based, continues to centralize the notion of risk. In this article, we argue that for teachers to have a different perspective of students placed at-risk, they need to have in their repertoire several strength-based models. While resilience is one way to think about moving students out of the at-risk status, we advocate the use of Luis Moll's (2005) funds-of-knowledge approaches to teach students at-risk.

Background

The term "at-risk" has been used as a catch-all term to predict youth failure in terms of behavior, situations such as family circumstances or structural issues such as poverty. In the state of Wisconsin, where the study was conducted, at-risk students include "dropouts, habitual truants, parents or adjudicated delinquents who are either in grades 5 through 12 and two or more years behind their age group in basic skill levels or in grades 9 through 12 and are one or more years behind their age group in number of high school credits attained" (Wisconsin Statutes, 118.153).

In a world where there are increasing demands for an educated workforce; large numbers of youth are not graduating. According to the Manhattan-Institute, the national graduation rate for the class of 1998 was 71%. For White students, the rate was 78%, while it was 56% for African-American students and 54% for Latino students (www.Manhattan-Institute.org, 2002). The U.S. Department of Labor indicates that students not earning a diploma earn approximately 30% less income than those who have a diploma, are less likely to vote, plus the unemployment rate is significantly higher for dropouts (www.bls.gov, 2010).

Several dropout prevention programs exist, however one of the significant school reforms that promised a quality and innovative education for students was the Charter school reform movement that began in Minnesota in 1991.

Charter schools in the state of Wisconsin were seen as an opportunity to provide innovative instructional practices to cater to the needs of students placed at-risk. The assumptions were that in light of lesser bureaucratic measures, schools were expected to have the freedom to focus on and improve the performance of those who are likely to be at highest risk of failure or of not graduating high school. This study was conducted in two charter schools which self-identified as innovative schools with successful programs.

Literature Review

At-Risk

The use of the term "at-risk" is notorious for being controversial because the surrounding discourse often includes implications for who (such as parents, teachers, administrators, school, community, government) or what (such as the way schools are organized, the inequitable funding formulas used for school budgets, inadequate teacher preparation, the design of the larger economic system) is responsible for the condition and who holds the power to change it.

Educational Responses to the at-risk Student by Teachers

The literature on educating the at-risk student is replete with suggestions to increase performance (Epstein, 1995; Rossi, 1994; McClendon, 1998) and improve instruction (Knapp, 1995; Ladson-Billings, 1994). While teacher support emerges as a key factor in facilitating school engagement for middle- and high-school students at-risk of school failure (Brewster and Bowen, 2004), that support is often dependent on how teachers perceive students or their beliefs about students. For example, Weisz and Weiss (1991) suggested that to interpret behavior ratings of children, one must examine both the child's behavior as well as the appraiser's interpretation of the behavior.

Schools are often primary sites where behavior is identified and interventions implemented (Edens, 1998). While most often behavior problems are conceptualized within educational settings as "acting out," teachers who have a caring relationship with their students are also aware of the invisible over controlled behaviors that may point to underlying stress among students (Chang & Sue, 2003). In the case of students placed at-risk, the teacher–student relationship is especially important since teachers often represent one of the few if not the only adult role model in their lives with whom they have everyday contact.

Teacher quality is seen to be a key reason for student success in the effective schools literature (Wayne & Youngs, 2003; Rockoff, 2004). Caring relationships with teachers along with high standards are essential components of effective schools. Research shows us that teacher beliefs influence their practice (Elliott, 1985; Tatto, 1998). By thinking about work differently, teachers can change their practice (Collins, Harkins & Nind, 2002). However, while the broad strokes are clear, it is less clear how teacher beliefs about students relate to practice and why some teachers are more successful with at-risk students than others. Very little is known about teachers' perceptions about their students who carry the label of at-risk and how those perceptions impact their teaching practices.

Purpose of the Study and Research Questions

The purpose of our study was to examine the perspectives of teachers who were educating students placed at-risk to help us understand how their beliefs about students who carry the label of at-risk impacted their teaching practices.

The following research questions guided the study:

- What are teacher beliefs about students who are termed "at-risk"?
- How do their beliefs relate to their practice?

Study Design—Interpretive Paradigm and Portraiture

Sample

The purposive sample (Patton, 1990) for this study comprised twelve teachers from two charter schools which self-identified as innovative schools with successful programs specifically designed to meet the needs of students placed "at-risk."

Data Collection and Analysis

The data sources for this research included interviews, observations, and institutional documents. The main focus of the data gathering, however, centered on teachers' perspectives, which were captured through interviews.

The interviews focused on teachers' beliefs about students and how they thought it impacted their practice. Interviews also went into topics such as student attendance, retention and addressing truancy and creating classroom engagement and how teachers defined success. Twelve individual interviews of two hours with each teacher in the sample, and two full-day observations at the sites completed the data gathering. In presenting the findings, the names of the participants have been changed to protect their confidentiality.

The two schools are referred to in this article as County Charter School (CCS) and Urban Charter School (UCS). Both schools were high schools and fell into the definition of an optimal small school (Meier, 1995) with a population of 180–225 students. They had similar demographics with all the students being identified as "at-risk" under the state statute. Additionally, over 75% students in both schools qualified for free or reduced lunch; and both schools had a majority student of color population (Charter School Yearbook, 2007). County Charter School (CCS) referred to its curriculum as a "boot camp" while Urban Charter (UCS) defined its program as "science based" (Charter School Yearbook, 2007).

We combined the interpretive interview method (Carr and Kemmis, 1986) with Sarah Lawrence Lightfoot's (1997) concept of portraiture in order to document teachers' perceptions of students at-risk. The interview protocols were designed to capture a full range of teachers' perceptions about the challenges and the possibilities they encountered while educating students placed at-risk.

For Lightfoot, portraiture as a methodology serves as a "counterpoint to the dominant chorus of social scientists whose focus has largely centered on the identification and documentation of social problems" (1997, xvi). Lightfoot's portraiture research looks for strengths and how challenges are being met and effectively handled. It includes the rhythm of schools and classrooms, the ways in which students are treated, and the expectations set forth by the teachers and administrators. This method was deemed most appropriate for the context under examination because it more readily embraces the complexity of social contexts holistically rather than other methods designed to break apart pieces of the experiences for a more microanalysis.

Results of the Study

Making meaning of the term "at-risk"

Teachers in this study gave a variety of responses with regard to how they made meaning of the term "at-risk." For the most part, the responses may be categorized into *two broad themes*—teachers who blamed the individual student and teachers who blamed the context.

The teachers who blamed the individual saw students as "at-risk" of failing in school and in society. They worried that the students they saw everyday in their classroom were "troublemakers" who would find themselves on the wrong side of the law. As one of the teachers put it, "at-risk can mean falling behind or failing or in trouble with the law—adjudicated."

Teachers who blamed the context described the term "at-risk" to mean circumstances over which the student had little control—for example, family or economic situations. As one teacher put it,

"I see the students as being placed at-risk or at-risk of factors over which they have no control. It is not their fault that they were born in circumstances that are challenging beyond what most people have experienced or seen in their lives. I see the school as a safe haven and as an exit route for them."

Therefore there were two ways in which teachers described the meaning of "at-risk." One group saw the term as a descriptor of student behavior; the second group of teachers saw the term as meaning structural issues over which the student had little control. They saw the students as "placed at-risk" of adverse circumstances. There was a mix of these sentiments at both schools, although in large part, teachers tended to be loyal to the program philosophy. Therefore at County Charter High School, teachers were likely to refer to individuals' being at fault, while at the Urban Charter High School the teachers were more likely to refer to the situation or context as placing the student at-risk.

Relating Teachers' Beliefs about Learners "at-risk" to Practice

Teachers' views of the term "at-risk" related to their practice in different ways. All teachers were keen on making a difference in their classrooms and in the lives of their students regardless of whether or not they saw their at-risk students as being adjudicated or whether they positioned them as suffering due to situational contexts. They were dedicated to their work and saw themselves as the one point of contact that students had in the day that was enlivening, safe and affirming. However, the ways in which teachers attempted to create solutions for the problems they saw depended on how they framed the problem.

Teachers who framed *the problem as the individual* also tended to put behavior modification or attitude correction ahead of academic learning. They were quick to deal out punishments and give the students referrals. They saw their primary role as correcting behavior. In this, their practice resembled wardens and they created a culture of surveillance to watch for any misstep from the students.

Teachers who saw *the issue as the context* tended to blame the students' parents or the home life or the neighborhood in which the student lived for the academic performance of the students.

These teachers tended to think of the students' with sympathy and attempted to help them to become resilient. To them, it was imperative that students escape the neighborhood and poverty through education and the school and by securing a job when they left school. Such teachers often cited stories of famous figures such as Thomas Edison or Eleanor Roosevelt as examples of people who overcame difficult circumstances in their lives. They pointed to the resilience of such historical figures and encouraged the students to build their own inner resilience.

While teachers' practice reflected their views of students and the ways in which they made meaning of the term "at-risk," their practice was also in large part either facilitated or obstructed by the academic and school program. In the next section, we discuss how teachers negotiated their beliefs and practices with the program philosophy.

Program Philosophy: Promise or Challenge?

Both schools were charter schools and self-identified as meeting the needs of at-risk students in innovative ways. The schools had very different program philosophies and curricula emphases. In our research, we found that teachers negotiated their relationship with the school policies to align with their personal beliefs. Before we move into a discussion of the beliefs, we briefly describe the two school philosophies and curricular emphases here.

County Charter School

Focus—Disciplining the Body

The County Charter School (CCS) was started by Keith Jackson. He had previously been involved with setting up and designing a reform program for incarcerated youth in conjunction with the Department of Corrections. While that program enjoyed an overall high success rate, a high recidivism rate was also evident among the Midwest City urban youth.

In Jackson's view, the problem stemmed from a lack of follow up and continuity in the immediate vicinity of youth after they returned to their communities.

. . . when the kids returned to most communities throughout the state, three out of every four were having pretty good success. In Midwest City, only one out of four. . . . They were returning to parents who were either non-existent or couldn't handle it and the kids just went south.

Disturbed by the high recidivism rate among the urban city youth, Jackson started the CCS with a firm belief in the benefits of behavior modification for youth through a strong disciplinary structure.

Several teachers at the County Charter School saw the school as a holding space for students until they were ready to go back to the original school. In their view, the students were "at-risk" in terms of behavior and once their behavior was modified, they could begin to learn. Success for many teachers meant transferring the student out of the school. Mike, another faculty member, explained the idea:

. . . I think the ultimate goal is to break them like wild horses and move them on to the next school where their academics can be made stronger.

Implementation—Attitude First, Attendance Second & Academics Third

For most teachers at the County Charter School, it was not possible to teach students in the class unless students were "ready to learn." Readiness in the words of several teachers meant having the "right attitude." Jackson put it bluntly,

"The way we look at education is attitude, attitude, attitude. . . . You cannot concentrate on the behavior change and at the same time present them with an entire curriculum of academics."

For most teachers at the County Charter School, their beliefs were consistent with the school philosophy and they bought into the idea that it was necessary and possible to separate attitude from content area learning. There were however, some teachers such as Maria and Jane at the school who resisted this idea and thought that they were little more than babysitters and needed to do more. Maria, who did not buy fully into this idea said,

"attitude will come once we get the student interested in what is going on here at school and within the classroom. If I make my English lesson interesting, his attitude is going to change. He is going to sit up straight and want to know what is going on."

Maria and Jane did not agree with several of their colleagues regarding physical education being a vehicle for redirecting negative behavior. Moreover, they interpreted the behaviors of students differently from their peers. Jane, for example said,

They are rude as a way to get your attention. Also, sometimes, in their situation, when going home, they encounter dangers. They have to show some attitude there to survive. Some of that attitude is going to come to school as well. It isn't easy to switch on and off. Giving them 30 pushups as a way to get their attitude straight isn't going to help. They will soon give you 40 pushups and attitude with it.

Therefore, within the County Charter School, while most teachers' beliefs about learners were consistent with the program of the school, there were some teachers like Maria and Jane who resisted the program philosophy in different ways and created a classroom experience for students that was different from the rest.

If the emphasis at the County Charter School was on disciplining the body, at the Urban Charter School it was on disciplining the mind through science. There were more teachers like Maria and Jane at the Urban Charter School where the emphasis was on building resilience of the mind.

Urban Charter School
Focus—Disciplining the Mind

The Urban Charter School founders noticed the low numbers of Midwest City youth going into careers in medicine and science and looked at early science training as the answer.

Implementation—Improving Educational Experiences through Science

In contrast to the County Charter School goal to improve behavior, the Urban Charter School had the goal of providing a good science foundation for all students. As the principal put it:

My vision is that we create a school where kids in Midwest City can have enough science experiences and knowledge that if they choose to go on to careers in sciences, they can do that. Beyond that, I hope that we turn out students who are going to be productive citizens and can make a contribution to society.

The staff members who were interviewed acknowledged the tremendous challenges of teaching in an environment plagued with disciplinary problems. To counter such issues, teachers tried to make their courses interesting and to create curiosity in students. The school instituted a new system for Wednesdays called Wednesday University. While students had the option of taking a half-day off or staying to participate in activities, teachers were engaged in staff development activities every week for a half-day. The Wednesday University allowed teachers to train to make curricular decisions, develop new and exciting curriculum and to participate in planning and decision making. Teachers' reported the experience of the Wednesday University as generally positive although the evidence was anecdotal and no formal evaluation of the Wednesday University has been conducted so far.

Urban Charter School (UCS) is organized around the concept of scientific discovery through exploration. The focus on science is evident from the elementary school. The science curriculum coordinator discussed the ways in which she taught science literacy to one group of students:

I take one of those words each week and turn it into a little mini-lesson. For example, one that I did last was we had some words like bacteria, microorganism, and words like that, yeast, fungi. So I did a lesson where I took a lump of dough in and I also took some yeast crystals and started out and said, look at those. What do they look like? Little rock! So then I took them and put them all in a container and I said these are alive. I poured hot water on them and put a little sugar on them. They like warmth, they like food, and they like it nice and dark. Then I set them aside and then I brought little containers full of yogurt along and they ate the yogurt and we talked about eating bacteria and that there is good bacteria and there is bad bacteria. Then I showed them the yeast that had grown. It is a lot of fun. It is a 15-minute lesson and we do it everyday.

The Urban Charter School teachers saw their roles in the school as filling in the void that existed in the students' academic experiences. Their goal was to help students reclaim the academic opportunities that they had lost. Although they too described some students as being academically behind because of behavior or absences, they agreed that the students, by coming to the school, now had a second chance to acquire their academic competencies. As one of the teachers explained,

I would say that a large number of students that are very interested in getting a good education, but maybe weren't

challenged as much as they wanted to be in their regular local school. We also get a good number of students who have not been successful in the regular school because of excessive absences, or whatever; they fell behind or have fallen through the cracks. So their families look at our school as a second chance I think

An administrator reiterated this impression of the students and the primary tasks of the teachers.

Our students are a wonderful group of kids. But I think, sometimes, they haven't learned the skills that they need to be successful in school. I think school is a hard place for a lot of kids, the way it is structured and the expectations on them. I think they all want to do their best. Some days are harder than others for them.

At the Urban Charter School, teachers' beliefs about learners led them to try to make the classroom interesting and exciting. Despite the belief that the student was not to blame, their conviction that the schools were to blame for their lack of academic preparation led them to offer compensatory or remedial education. Often, they taught basic skills which they thought students had not yet received in their schooling until now.

At the Urban Charter School, teacher beliefs about learners drove the teaching. Here too, the beliefs of teachers were mostly consistent with the program philosophy. However, some teachers fell into the "attitude first" bracket and adjusted their practice to this belief. For example, Henrietta, a science teacher, refused to allow students to use the lab if their dress and behavior showed "attitude." In her words, "That chewing of gum and the untucked shirt is not going to work. I believe that it is for their own good that I set these rules."

Overall, with the exception of one or two teachers, for the most part teachers at Urban Charter School believed in getting "kids excited about learning." Teacher beliefs about learners' also drove what teachers considered "success" in teaching and learning.

Examples of "Success" in the Schools

County Charter School—Success Is Getting Students on the Right Road

Behavior modification was the goal of the County Charter School and success was seeing the student leave with a sense of confidence in their ability to control their behavior and to choose to refuse to participate in activities or behaviors that would lead them into trouble. According to a teacher,

Success can be measured in a couple of ways. If a kid is doing what he needs to do inside this hallway, that is one manner of success. I really don't think our success can be graded inside these halls. I don't think they can be graded at the end of the school year. I think our success will not be really determined until three to four years down the road where the young man or the young woman starts making good sound decisions for themselves and looks back to see the change in them.

Another teacher at the school explained their perception of success quite eloquently when she said:

That they have a positive attitude, that they are willing to take criticism without becoming aggressive or acting out; that they use their ears more than their mouth, become active listeners, that they are respectful of themselves and respect others. I have an opinion that if a child is smiling, has a positive outlook, and uses more eye contact, that is a determining factor that we are making progress with them.

This philosophy seems to suggest that if students can develop positive behavior, develop a caring attitude, be humane in the treatment of each other, develop respect for self and others, then there will be a greater likelihood that learning can take place in the traditional classroom environment. However, some of those interviewed emphasized that in order for learning to take place, there must be evidence of genuine care and support for students, particularly those who have been classified as being at-risk. In other words, students must have access to social capital resources in the learning environment, particularly where such resources are lacking in the home.

Urban Charter School—Success Is Resiliency for Learning

Unlike the County Charter School, the Urban Charter School was intent on academic improvement of all students first.

However, there too, the teachers and administrator felt strongly that for such success to occur, they needed to teach students *resilience*. If students could learn how to overcome their problems and switch into a learning mode, the teachers felt that they had succeeded. The principal of the school voiced this collective sentiment in the following way:

I would define success for our school when we feel that our kids are all coming to the school understanding that this is a place to learn despite some of the challenges that they might face at home, but they know they are here to learn. On the other hand, they also know that there are adults who care about them, who will help them with some of the challenges that they bring to school, which might keep them from learning. I think we have to say student achievement when we see scores increasing. I hate to measure things by test score, but I also know that that is the reality of life today. So for us to be successful, we have to see our kids learning to read and write and do math at a level that is acceptable for kids their age, not just at the bare minimum.

Success, therefore, for the Urban Charter School was measured by a sense of resilience to withstand the social and economic problems that exist in the lives of urban kids and a demonstration of academic progress as evidenced by test scores.

Implications

The results of this study have wide-ranging implications for teachers of at-risk students. If we are serious about teachers acting on the belief that all students can learn, it is important for teachers to examine their own perceptions and the way those perceptions impact their teaching practices (Mulvihill and Swaminathan, 2006). If teachers need to begin where the children are in their classrooms, we also need to remember to approach students in holistic ways so that we do not fragment their minds and bodies.

In our research, we found that one group of teachers felt they were responsible for the minds while the other group thought they had to regulate the bodies before approaching the mind. In both cases, it was a fragmentary approach that did not take into account the "wealth" of experiences that students brought with them into the classroom.

For teachers to move from a "risk" approach to a "wealth" or asset-based approach, teachers may need to reflect on the strengths that students bring into the classroom in new ways and consider ways to access those strengths in their teaching and learning. For example, some strengths and "funds of knowledge" (Moll, 2005) that students may bring with them would include budgeting, cooking, childcare, repairing skills, ethics and storytelling. How might teachers refocus their perceptions of at-risk students in order to reshape educational possibilities? To view students as having strengths rather than weakness moves teachers from offering a compensatory education to one that emphasizes critical thinking. Luis Moll describes the "funds of knowledge" approach as based on the premise that "people are competent, they have knowledge and their life experiences have given them that knowledge" (2005, x).

Teachers at both schools were ultimately operating within a "risk" framework. At the County Charter School, most teachers believed that the risk could be overcome through building control of the self. At the Urban Charter, teachers believed that learners could overcome "risk" in their lives through building mental resilience to study and work.

While the second is certainly a more productive approach than the first, neither approach ultimately moved away from the "risk" framework. In some sense, teachers' beliefs were tied to the "risk" framework, and how they, themselves, were socialized to accept this framework, and limited the range of options they might otherwise have considered for their students. When a school, and/or program, adopts an at-risk framework and infuses it's curricula with an attending philosophy, and arranges it's organizational structure to respond to a concept of at-risk students, surrounds their teachers and students with a discourse that makes at-risk students a problem, and constructs the definition of success as dependent upon ameliorating the concept of at-risk, then the stage is set in ways that both amplify certain possibilities and makes other possibilities invisible!

Recognizing how teachers' perceptions are formed and how those perceptions impact the range of teaching practices deemed possible is an important set of understandings that may lead to new and more productive questions. For example, what might help teachers reorganize their own perceptions in ways that allow them to reappropriate the term "at-risk" and convert it's meaning to a state of being that is ready for transformation?

Conclusion

This study highlighted the multivocal nature of the term at-risk as it played out in two charter school environments designed to respond to at-risk students, and the hidden opportunity teachers may have when they understand a term to be in-flux rather than static.

When teachers believe that they can positively impact not only the experiences of individual students, but also contribute to the reconceptualization of a whole category of children, then the direct impact of teacher beliefs on teacher practices will be more fully understood. The need to further explore the perceptions of teachers and understand how teachers translate their beliefs into their teaching practices continues to be high.

References

Brewster, A.B. & Bowen, G.L. (2004). Teacher support and the school engagement of Latino middle and high school students at risk of school failure. *Child and Adolescent Social Work Journal 21*(1) 47–67.

Broman, S., Bien, E. & Shaughnessy, P. (1985) *Low achieving children: The first seven years.* New Jersey: Lawrence Erlbaum.

Brophy, J. (1998). *Motivating students to learn.* Boston, MA: McGraw-Hill.

Carr, W. & Kemmis, S. (1986). *Becoming critical: Education knowledge and action research.* London: Falmer Press.

Casey, L. (2000). The charter conundrum. *Rethinking schools 4*(3), Spring 2000.

Chang, D.F. & Sue, S. (2003). The effects of race and problem type of teachers' assessments of student behavior. *Journal of Counseling and Clinical Psychology, 71*(2), 235–242.

Collins, J., Harkins, J., & Nind, M. (2002). *Manifesto for Learning.* London: Continuum Press.

Comer, J. (2000). *Child by child: The comer process for change in education.* New York: Teachers College Press.

Edens, J.F. (1998). School-based consultation services for children with externalizing behavior problems. In L. VandeCreek & S. Knapp (Eds). *Innovation in clinical practice: A source book.* Sarasota, FL: Professional Resource Press.

Epstein, J.L. (1995). School/family/community partnerships: Caring for the children we share. *Phi Delta Kappan, 76*(9), 701–712.

Elliott, J. (1985). *A Class Divided.* Frontline Documentary on Jane Elliott. www.pbs.org/wgbh/pages/frontline/shows/divided. Retrieved on March 31, 2010.

Fullan, M.G. (1995). *Successful school improvement.* Buckingham: Open University Press.

Fuller, B. (2000) *Inside charter schools: The paradox of radical decentralization.* MA: Harvard University Press.

Glasser, W. (1998). *Choice theory: A new psychology of personal freedom.* New York: HarperCollins.

Gray, J. & Wilcox, B. (1994). *The challenge of turning around ineffective schools.* Buckingham: Open University Press.

Kennedy, R. & Morton. J.H. (1999). *A school for healing: Alternative strategies for teaching at-risk students.* New York: Peter Lang.

Knapp, M.S. (1995). *Teaching for meaning in high poverty classrooms.* New York: Teachers College Press.

Ladson-Billings, G. (1994). *The Dreamkeepers: Successful teachers of African-American children.* San Francisco: Jossey-Bass.

Lightfoot, S.L. (1997). *The art and Science of portraiture.* San Francisco: Jossey-Bass.

Masten, A.S. & Coatsworth, J.D. (1998). The development of competence in favorable and unfavorable environments. Lessons from research on successful children. *American Psychologist, 53,* 205–220.

Nathan, J. (1996). *Charter schools: Creating hope and opportunity for American education.* San Francisco: Jossey-Bass.

Manhattan Institute for Policy Research (2002). High school graduation rates in the United States.

McClendon, C. (1998). *Promoting achievement in school through sport (PASS): An evaluation Study.* Unpublished Dissertation, University of Maryland, College Park.

Meier, D. (1995) *Central Park East: Lessons for America from a small school in Harlem.* Boston: Beacon Press.

Merriam, S.B. (1998). *Qualitative research and case study applications in education.* San Francisco, CA: Jossey-Bass Publishers.

Moll, Luiz. (2005). Reflections and Possibilities. In Gonzalez, N.; Moll, L.C.; Amandti, C. (Eds). *Funds of Knowledge: Theorizing practices in households, communities and classrooms.* New Jersey: Lawrence Erlbaum Publishers.

Mortimore, P., Mortimore, J., & Sammons, P. (1991). *The Use of indicators, Effectiveness of schooling and of educational resource management.* OECD July 1991, London: Institute of Education, University of London.

Mulvihill, T. and Swaminathan, R. (2006) "I Fight Poverty. I Work!": Examining Discourses of Poverty and their Impact on Pre-Service Teachers, *International Journal of Teaching and Learning in Higher Education, 18*(2), pp. 97–111.

Patton, M.Q. (1990). *Qualitative Evaluation and Research Methods (2nd ed.).* Newbury Park, CA: Sage Publications, Inc.

Rockoff, J.E. (2004). The impact of individual teachers on student achievement: Evidence from panel data. *American Economic Review, 94*(2), 247–252.

Rossi, R.J. (1994). *Schools and students at Risk: Context and framework for positive change.* New York: Teachers College Press.

Sammons, P., Hillman, J. & Mortimore, P. (1994). *Key characteristics of effective schools: A review of school effectiveness research.* London: Office of Standards in Education.

Sanders, M. (2001). *Schooling students placed at risk.* New Jersey: Lawrence Erlbaum Associates.

Spivack, G., Marcuso, J., Swift, M. (1986). Early classroom behavior and later misconduct. *Developmental Psychology, 22,* 124–131.

Tatto, M.T. (1998). The influence of teacher education on teachers' beliefs about purposes of education, roles and practice. *Journal of Teacher Education, 49*(1), 66–77.

US Department of Labor: Bureau of Labor Statistics. Employment pays. Retrieved on 5.12.2010 from www.bls.gov/emp/ep_chart_001.htm.

Viadero, D. (2001). Scholars turn to evaluating charter schools from the Inside. *Education Week, 21*(2).

Wayne, A.J., and Youngs, P. (2003). Teacher characteristics and student achievement gains: A Review. *Review of Educational Research, 73*(1), 89–122.

Werner, E.E. (1993). Risk, resilience, and recovery: Perspectives from the Kauai longitudinal study. *Developmental Psychopathology, 5,* 503–515.

Weisz, J.R., & Weiss, B. (1991). Studying the 'referability' of child clinical problems. *Journal of Consulting and Clinical Psychology, 59,* 266–273.

Wisconsin State Department of Public Instruction. (1998). *Wisconsin charter schools, bulletin No. 99069.* Madison: DPI Publication.

Wisconsin State Department of Public Instruction. (2009). Charter School Yearbook. Madison: DPI Publication.

Wisconsin General School Operations, Chapter 118, 153. *Children at risk of not graduating from high school.*

Yin, R.K. (1994). *Case study research: Design and methods. (2nd Ed.)* Thousand Oaks, CA: Sage.

Critical Thinking

1. What are the research questions? Why did the authors choose these questions?

2. How did the teachers in the study define students who are at-risk?

3. Construct a chart that compares and contrasts the philosophy and programs of the two charter schools.

4. What were the conclusions of the researchers when the study was completed?

5. What are the implications for your teaching? Make your answer personal; talk about your perceptions and conclusions about teaching students who are at-risk and what this study means for your teaching.

Raji Swaminathan is associate professor in the Dept. of Educational Policy & Community Studies at the University of Wisconsin–Milwaukee. She coordinates the Alternative Education Program and teaches the required courses for the Alternative Education Certification on Students at Risk. You can contact her at: swaminar@uwm.edu.

Thalia Mulvihill is professor in the Dept. of Social Foundations and Higher Education at Ball State University. Her research agenda includes critical theory and pedagogies that focus on democracy and social justice issues, including conflict resolution/group development strategies. You can contact her at: tmulvihi@bsu.edu.

From *Journal of Educational Alternatives,* volume 4, no. 2, 2011, pp. 1–23. Copyright © 2011 Raji Swaminathan & Thalia Mulvihill. Reprinted by permission of the authors.

Dismantling Rural Stereotypes

One-size-fits-all solutions don't meet the needs of ignored and misunderstood rural schools.

JAMES A. BRYANT JR.

A springtime drive down North Carolina Highway 194 in Watauga County is a feast for the senses. Once the rains recede, the trees and fields explode in green. The scent of honeysuckle hangs heavy in the air, a sure sign that summer is around the corner. Cattle graze beside old barns while horses swish their tails. White-framed churches dot the hillsides, looming over the granite markers of their faithful departed. It is, in a word, idyllic.

Seated back from the road on a hill with a breathtaking view of a fertile valley and nearby mountains is Green Valley Elementary School. The school looks like a postcard, but its students do not live picture-postcard lives. According to the North Carolina Department of Public Instruction's Child Nutrition Services (2009), 48 percent of children attending Green Valley live at or below the poverty line. Other elementary schools in Watauga County share similar statistics: Valle Crucis, 35.53 percent; Parkway, 36.76 percent; Cove Creek, 50.36 percent; Mabel, 60 percent; and Bethel, 61.94 percent. As one historian writes, "The region's natural beauty [makes] its poverty all the more ironic" (Drake, 2001, p. 174). And, one might add, inconvenient.

The Extent of the Problem

The quaint image of the little red schoolhouse that many Americans cling to is, sadly, utter fantasy. Situated in some of the hardest hit economic areas in the United States, rural schools are struggling. But federal mandates such as No Child Left Behind (NCLB) have forced rural schools to choose whether to spend money where it may be most needed—for example, to improve deteriorating facilities or attract more qualified teachers—or spend it complying with government regulations to meet less urgent needs.

Federal mandates have forced rural schools to choose whether to spend money where it may be most needed or spend it complying with government regulations.

The National Center for Education Statistics reports that 35 percent of rural students live below the poverty level and 38 percent qualify for free or reduced-price lunch programs (Provasnik et al., 2007). The report goes on to state that 45 percent of public school students in remote rural areas attend a moderate-to-high-poverty school, a percentage that was only topped in large and midsize cites, where 66 and 49 percent of students, respectively, attend moderate-to-high-poverty schools.

These numbers may not tell the whole story, however. Because 26.3 percent of rural residents live "just above the poverty line," rural families are "particularly vulnerable to changes in national and regional economies and setbacks in their personal lives" (Huang, 1999, p. 3). Low per capita income, low housing standards, high unemployment, and high illiteracy rates have been characteristic of rural Appalachia, for example, since the government began tracking these data (Drake, 2001).

For minority students in rural areas, these numbers become more frightening. Eighty-seven percent of rural black U.S. schoolchildren and 79 percent of rural American Indian schoolchildren live in poverty (Provasnik et al., 2007). Both of these numbers are higher than their counterparts in urban areas. Poverty in rural America tends to be "widely uneven across demographic categories" and is therefore often difficult to quantify (Huang, 1999, p. 3).

The students in these districts are paying the price. In a report from the Center on Education Policy detailing rural schools' perspectives on NCLB, 68 percent of rural schools reported achievement gaps in both English language arts and math between students with disabilities and nondisabled students, and 50 percent reported gaps between low-income and non-low-income students (Zhang, 2008).

Mollenkopf (2009) has written about the low salaries and geographic isolation teachers face in rural areas, both of which make it a challenge for rural districts to attract and retain highly qualified teachers—another NCLB requirement. Teachers may be unwilling to move to areas with limited social and cultural opportunities, and the low salaries that many rural districts must offer are not much of an enticement. Sometimes even when teachers are willing to work in a rural area, the working conditions may make them reluctant to stay for the long term. Teachers of special education, music, and art, for example, often serve multiple schools and must make long drives from one school to the other. They may also face professional isolation because they are the only teachers in the district with their specialization.

Invisible Schools

Americans have often wrapped rural life in a snug cocoon of fantasy. Thus, one of the primary obstacles for rural education, perhaps *the* primary obstacle, is a willful ignorance— particularly on the part of the federal government—of the conditions in rural areas and schools. The challenges of rural schools seem to always be overshadowed by a focus on urban districts. The federal government provides rural districts with fewer resources—9 percent of rural district budgets are covered by federal funds, compared with 11 percent of budgets in urban districts—while requiring them to meet mandates that do not take their situation into account (Provasnik et al., 2007; Roellke, 2003).

In March 2010, Sam Dillon of *The New York Times* wrote about a growing concern among local, state, and federal lawmakers that education policy was out of touch with the needs of rural educators and children. Wyoming Senator Michael B. Enzi, the ranking Republican on the Senate education committee, worried to Dillon that recent education policies—from No Child Left Behind to Race to the Top—"seem to be urban-centered" (Dillon, 2010). In September 2009, Katie Redding of the *Colorado Independent* asked a simple question: "Does the Race to the Top—Education Secretary Arne Duncan's $4.3 billion education reform contest among the states—handicap rural states?"

The possibility of an "urban bias" should not come as a surprise to those who have kept track of the U.S. Department of Education over recent decades (McNeil, 2009). The three most recent heads of the department have all hailed from urban districts. Current secretary of education Arne Duncan is the former superintendent of Chicago's massive school system, and the two immediately previous education secretaries, Roderick Paige and Margaret Spellings, both claimed the ultra-urban Houston, Texas, school system as the primary source of their experience.

The lack of representation of rural education has led to some difficulties for rural educators as solutions geared toward urban issues are foisted on schools of all demographics. The disastrous effort to standardize everything in education—the laughable notion that one size fits all—leaves rural schools forced to implement policies that are poorly suited for their communities. There is no better example of this policy disconnect than the issue of "choice" and charter schools.

Unhelpful Reforms

Diane Ravitch (2010) has traced the development of the choice movement from its earliest days as a way around desegregation to its growth into magnet schools and its current fascination with charter schools. "Every president lauded charter schools," she writes, "from George H. W. Bush to Bill Clinton to George W. Bush to Barack Obama" (pp. 132–133). This bipartisan consensus has culminated in President Obama's Race to the Top initiative, which enjoins states to remove caps on charter schools to have a better chance of receiving a piece of the $4.3 billion fund. Secretary Duncan has "repeatedly said that states with limits on charter schools will be at a 'competitive disadvantage' when it comes to getting the money" (Niolet, 2009).

In the past, North Carolina had placed a cap of 100 on the number of charters that it would grant, but massive budget shortfalls and the possibility of draconian cuts to education and social services money made Race to the Top dollars look incredibly appealing. The North Carolina legislature leapt into action to remove the charter cap. Although Governor Beverly Purdue attempted to put a positive spin on the move, Senate Minority Leader Phil Berger of Rockingham was more direct: "The purpose of this is mainly, quite frankly, to draw down federal dollars" (Robertson, 2010).

Perhaps removing the cap on charter schools in exchange for an infusion of federal funding seems reasonable, but that may not be the point. The real issue lies in the fact that Duncan's reforms have not considered the needs of rural schools (McNeil, 2009) Timothy Collins (1999) notes that many rural areas lack the capital and facilities needed to establish a charter school. And if founding and operating a brand-new school were not difficult enough, attracting high-quality faculty and administrators would also present a challenge.

Low scores on proficiency tests in math and reading make rural schools highly vulnerable to sanctions, even though closing schools and replacing them with charters will do nothing about the inadequate funding at the root of many rural schools' problems. Even with NCLB success, rural schools face the constant threat of being shuttered in cost-saving measures. In Burke County, North Carolina, two rural elementary schools— Hillcrest and Mountain View—have been consolidated in an effort to stem a tide of red ink in the county (Welker, 2010, April 29). This move came one year after Burke County teachers agreed to a salary cut (Welker, 2010, May 11) and despite both schools' having met their NCLB adequate yearly progress targets (North Carolina Department of Public Instruction, n.d.). Consolidation has become such a pandemic in rural school districts that the Rural Schools and Community Trust's website offers a "Consolidation Fight Back Toolkit" (www.ruraledu.org/articles.php?id=2425).

Consolidation often makes sense from a purely fiduciary viewpoint, but it's frequently detrimental to students. As Purcell and Shackelford (2005) have noted, consolidation "may threaten the educational and social environment of rural communities in ways that would not impact the urban environment" (p. 2). The authors looked at the effects of consolidation of West Virginian rural schools and found that many of the outcomes were distinctly negative. These included sleep deprivation and a loss of study time due to longer commutes and bus rides, as well as social disruptions "brought about by students living and going to school in two separate environments" (p. 5). Money may be saved, but it comes at a high cost.

Competition with a charter school would not have kept the two Burke County schools from being merged—it might even have accelerated the process. Such challenges may be what South Dakota State Senator Sandy Jerstad had in mind when she told *Education Week,* "Charter schools just don't work for us" (McNeil, 2009). In South Dakota, more than half of the school districts serve fewer than 300 students, and in Montana half the districts serve fewer than 100 students (McNeil, 2009). With such demographics, the notion of choice and competition seems fanciful at best. Opening a charter school in these areas would cause a battle over students and funds at a time when the public schools are struggling to survive.

Such a battle has already occurred in Texas, where in 2002 nearly 40 percent of the funds from a $72 million school repair and renovation program was granted to charter schools "even though they educate only 1 percent of students in the state" (Stutz, 2002). Like Race to the Top, the allocation of this money was based on a points system in which schools and school districts applied for state grants, and "charter schools received priority points in the process," according to Robert Muller of the Texas Education Agency (Stutz, 2002).

How to Make Changes

There are steps that could be taken, of course, to meet these challenges and alleviate these difficulties. First, and most obviously, the federal government must rid itself of the disastrous tendency to see U.S. schools as monolithic and static entities. Rural school districts are neither urban districts nor suburban districts. Each has a distinct character, and each has distinct challenges and issues.

Second, the U.S. Department of Education should devote time, funds, and manpower to rural schools and their issues. Answering to the secretary of education should be an undersecretary of rural education (as well as urban and suburban). This model would be similar to that of U.S. State Department, which employs a number of undersecretaries for different regions of the globe. This individual should be an expert on rural policy and education who could provide rural schools with a desperately needed voice in federal policies.

Third, and finally, all school systems should demand that the federal government revisit NCLB and the Race to the Top initiative with the understanding that education policy must speak to the diversity of U.S. schools. No one denies that every child should receive a first-rate education under the tutelage of a highly qualified educator. However, as long as the property tax remains the basis for school funding, poor rural districts will need a significant infusion of federal funding. It's cash, not rhetoric, that these districts need. States and districts are now beginning to speak out: Vermont has sent a letter to the federal government—signed by the education commissioners of 12 other states—"stating that the Obama administration's education policies are leaving too many rural school children behind" (Weiss-Tisman, 2010).

When traveling through rural West Virginia while running for president in 1960, John F. Kennedy was both shocked and appalled by what he saw. After meeting a family existing on relief rations and nothing else, he remarked to an aide, "Imagine . . . just imagine kids who never drink milk" (White, 1961, p. 126). These children are not, however, imaginary. The climate of poverty that so appalled Kennedy still exists in too much of rural America, and too few Americans—particularly policymakers—have taken adequate notice. The romantic version of an idyllic rural United States must be replaced with an accurate appraisal of the challenges that face rural children, teachers, and administrators and a concerted effort to meet those challenges. Rural educators must not be forced to swallow reforms that have no relevance for their districts. Let's start by acknowledging the reality—not the fantasy—of rural schools and making a commitment to providing rural reforms for rural students. The children of rural America deserve no less.

Rural educators must not be forced to swallow reforms that have no relevance for their districts.

References

Collins, T. (1999). *Charter schools: An approach for rural education?* (ERIC No. ED425896). Charleston, WV: ERIC Clearinghouse on Rural Education and Small Schools.

Dillon, S. (2010, March 18). Lawmakers say needs of rural schools are overlooked. *The New York Times.* Retrieved from www.nytimes.com/2010/03/18/education/18educ.html.

Drake, R. B. (2001). *A history of Appalachia.* Lexington: The University of Kentucky Press.

Huang, G. G. (1999). *Sociodemographic changes: Promise and problems for rural education* (ERIC No. ED425048). Charleston, WV: ERIC Clearinghouse on Rural Education and Small Schools.

McNeil, M. (2009, September 2). Rural areas perceive policy tilt. *Education Week.* Retrieved from www.edweek.org/ew/articles/2009/09/02/02stim-rural.h29.html.

Mollenkopf, D. L. (2009). Creating highly qualified teachers: Maximizing university resources to provide professional development in rural areas. *The Rural Educator, 30*(3), 34–39.

Niolet, B. (2009, September 1). NC set in "race" for federal grants [blog post]. Retrieved from Under the Dome at http://projects.newsobserver.com/under_the_dome/nc_set_in_race_for_federal_grants.

North Carolina Child Nutrition Services. (2009). *Free and reduced application data by site.* Retrieved from www.ncpublicschools.org/childnutrition/financial.

North Carolina Department of Public Instruction. (n.d.). *2008–2009 NC School Report Cards.* Retrieved from www.ncschoolreportcard.org/src.

Provasnik, S., Kewal Ramani, A., Coleman, M. M., Gilbertson, L, Herring, W., Xie, Q. (2007). *Status of education in rural America.* Retrieved from the National Center for Education Statistics at http://nces.ed.gov/pubs2007/2007040.pdf.

Purcell, D., & Shackelford, R. (2005, January). *An evaluation of the impact of rural school consolidation: What challenges may a new round of rural school consolidations have on the safety, educational performance, and social environment of rural communities?* Presentation to the National Rural Education Association.

Ravitch, D. (2010). *The death and life of the great American school system: How testing and choice are undermining education.* New York: Basic Books.

Redding, K. (2009, September 3). Federal race to the top education program suffers criticism, but not in Colorado. The *Colorado Independent.* Retrieved from http://coloradoindependent.com /37071/federal-race-to-the-top-education-program-suffers -criticism-but-not-in-colorado.

Robertson, G. D. (2010, May 27). NC legislature gives final OK to schools reform. *reflector.com* [Associated Press story]. Retrieved from www.reflector.com/state-news /nc-legislature-gives-final-ok-schools-reform-36564.

Roellke, C. (2003). *Resource allocation in rural and small schools* (ERIC No. ED482323). Charleston, WV: ERIC Clearinghouse on Rural Education and Small Schools.

Stutz, T. (2002, June 17). Big share of grants going to charters; State agency selected schools to get federal money for repairs. *The Dallas Morning News.* Retrieved from www.lexisnexis.com.

Weiss-Tisman, H. (2010, April 29). State sends letter on education grants. *Brattleboro Reformer.* Retrieved from www.lexisnexis.com.

Welker, S. (2010, May 11). School board approves budget. *The News Herald.* Retrieved from www2.morganton.com/news/2010 /may/11/school-board-approves-budget-ar-207640.

Welker, S. (2010, April 29). Board votes to consolidate schools. *The News Herald.* Retrieved from www2.morganton.com /news/2010/apr/29/board-votes-consolidate-schools-ar-69649.

White, T. H. (1961). *The making of the president 1960.* New York: Signet.

Zhang, Y. (2008). *Some perspectives from rural school districts on the No Child Left Behind Act.* Retrieved from Center on Education Policy at www.cep-dc.org/document/docWindow.cfm?document id=240&documentFormatId=3884.

Critical Thinking

1. What are the stereotypes about schooling in rural areas? What was your first thought as you read this article?

2. How extensive is the poverty in rural areas?

3. What are the distinct issues of rural schooling that make it different from urban or suburban schooling?

4. How do rural school issues impact teachers in those districts?

5. How can we make changes in these rural areas that will support schools, teachers, and students?

JAMES A. BRYANT JR. is an assistant professor in the Department of Curriculum and Instruction at Appalachian State University in Boone, North Carolina; bryantja@appstate.edu.

From *Educational Leadership,* November 2010, pp. 54–58. Copyright © 2010 by ASCD. Reprinted by permission. The Association for Supervision and Curriculum Development is a worldwide community of educators advocating sound policies and sharing best practices to achieve the success of each learner. To learn more, visit ASCD at www.ascd.org.

Examining the Culture of Poverty: Promising Practices

Kristen Cuthrell, Joy Stapleton, and Carolyn Ledford

Kirby, a 6-year-old first-grade student, would come in from the bus with a concern about the way someone talked to or about him. His face was usually serious, with few smiles. However, in late spring, our class was going on a field trip to the local airport. The children were excited about their trip to tour the airport and actually sit on an airplane. Knowing that the school cafeteria would prepare box lunches, I explained that we would need to bring our lunches with us to eat at the airport. Misinterpreting the directions, Kirby, excited on the day of the field trip, came to school carrying an old sock and a half-eaten donut. He had always entered the classroom with concerns, but today he was excited and prepared with his lunch to go on the field trip.

How does a teacher-education program ensure that its graduates are prepared to meet the diverse needs of all learners such as Kirby? How do universities take into consideration each preservice teacher's individual identity and the effect of that identity on his or her teaching? To begin the dialogue, a group of professors reviewed the demographic information of their region and the placement of the majority of program graduates. In terms of race, the schools surrounding the university were high in minorities and low in wealth, with a poverty rate that exceeded the national rate. The preservice teachers that the university enrolled did not reflect these demographics, although 66% of them took a job teaching in the surrounding areas upon graduation.

To examine this concept further, perception surveys of current students were administered to gauge their awareness of issues of diversity and identity with a specific focus on poverty. Results from those surveys indicate that students felt issues of poverty would not affect their teaching. With this shocking revelation, poverty became the immediate focus of our examination.

The Landscape of Poverty

As the number of children living in poverty continues to rise, poverty is garnering more attention as a factor in determining identity. According to the Children's Defense Fund (CDF) statistics from 2006, 1.3 million children have fallen into poverty since 2000. After reaching a historic low in 2000, the number of children living in poverty in the United States is approaching 13 million, and a child's likelihood of being poor has increased by almost 9%. In more concrete terms, one of six children is poor, and one in three Black children is living in poverty. Although the United States leads other industrialized nations with 12.3% of children living in poverty (CDF, 2006; Reid, 2006), the number of children around the world living in extreme poverty has increased 22% since 2000, reaching almost 5.6 million children. *Extreme poverty* is defined as living with an annual income of less than $7,870 for a family of three. Because of the importance of poverty's influence and the growing need to better prepare preservice teachers in meeting the needs of diverse students, we discuss the following areas: (a) the possible effects of poverty on student learning, (b) strategies that are effective in working with students and families from the culture of poverty, and (c) recommendations for infusing instruction of these strategies into teacher-education programs.

Views of Poverty

Individuals have used various terms to describe characteristics and circumstances of poverty. *Situational poverty* is caused by specific circumstances, such as illness or loss of employment, and generally lasts for a shorter period of time. Alternatively, *generational poverty* is an ongoing cycle of poverty in which two or more generations of families experience limited resources. Generational poverty is described as having its own culture, with hidden rules and belief systems. Furthermore, *absolute poverty* equates to a focus on sustenance and the bare essentials for living with no extra resources for social and cultural expenditures.

In the literature, researchers have examined poverty from two perspectives: absence of resources and risk versus resilience. Payne (2005) defined *poverty* as the "extent to which an individual does without resources" (p. 7). Leading experts in the field of poverty have suggested that the problem is much more than financial hardship. Payne identified eight resources whose presence or absence determines the effect of poverty: financial, emotional, mental, spiritual, physical, support systems, relationships and role models, and knowledge of hidden rules. If an individual has limited financial resources but strong emotional, spiritual, and physical support, the burden of poverty may be lessened. Although teachers may not be able to change financial resources, they can affect some of the other areas.

Rather than focusing on risk factors and taking the view of a damage model, a resilience model focuses on protective factors—individual, familial, community, or all three—and allows for positive adaptation despite significant life adversity (Rockwell, 2006). This model examines characteristics of individuals who have "made it" despite coming from an impoverished background. Factors that seem to support resilience are the following: having an internal locus of control, an ability to form warm relationships, a caregiver who values education, and opportunities to participate in recreational and service-oriented activities (Rockwell).

Poverty's Effect on Children

Researchers have linked poverty to several key issues of child welfare including low birth weight, infant mortality, growth stunting, lead poisoning, learning disabilities, and developmental delays (Brooks-Gunn & Duncan, 1997). Children from families in poverty experience more emotional and behavior problems than do children from middle- and upper-class families (Brooks-Gunn & Duncan). Eamon (2001) identified lower self-esteem, lower popularity, and conflictual peer relationships as socioemotional effects of poverty.

Poverty's Effect on Children in Schools

Although all children go to school, the background of some puts them behind their peers academically from the start. Impoverished students are far more likely to enter school as linguistically disadvantaged because they have not had experiences that promote literacy and reading readiness (Strickland, 2001). The achievement gap increases as students progress through school. Alexander, Entwhistle, and Olson (2001) found that children from low-income families are at a disadvantage during the summer when children from middle- and upper-income families are exposed to museums and camps—activities that promote children's social and intellectual development (Koppelman & Goodhart, 2005). According to educators, early childhood education is the most effective intervention for closing this achievement gap (e.g., Karoly et al., 1998; Ramey & Ramey, 1998; Thomas & Bainbridge, 2001), but it should be noted that the United States is the only industrialized nation without universal preschool and child care programs (Koppelman & Goodhart).

With the No Child Left Behind Act of 2001, schools, administrators, and teachers are accountable for the academic success of their students. Although administrators are interested in the best practices associated with student achievement, Pascopella (2006) suggested that teachers make the difference for students living in poverty and highlighted the need to better educate teachers about poverty and student achievement (Burch et al., 2001). Grissmer, Flannagan, Kawata, and Williamson (2000)

noted that the achievement gap could be addressed by targeting resources to disadvantaged families and schools, lowering class size in early grades, strengthening early childhood and early intervention programming, and improving teacher education and professional development. Schools, teachers, and families working together can create strong academic gains for all students. (For a complete list of the strategies, see the Appendix.)

Strategies for Working with Students and Families Living in Poverty
School Environment

The school environment is an essential component to the success of the school and its students. Reeves (2003) conducted a study of what he called *90/90/90 schools* with 90% minority, 90% free or reduced lunch, and 90% of their learning outcomes met. Six strategies emerged from his research on these successful schools; these strategies are repeated in other literature on school improvement.

The first and perhaps most important strategy is to hire and retain teachers who believe in their students (Center for Public Education [CPE], 2005; Danielson, 2002; Reeves, 2003). Reeves found that these teachers go beyond just believing that all students can learn by taking responsibility for their students' learning and by expecting results from students regardless of their background. Expressing sentiments that begin with "My students can't" or "My students aren't ready for" is not acceptable, and administrators in these successful schools were not afraid of making personnel changes if teachers did not believe in or have high expectations for their students.

The second strategy is to focus on academic achievement (CPE, 2005; Marzano, 2003; Reeves, 2003; Schomoker, 2001). In the schools in which these researchers conducted their studies, the curriculum was specifically defined by narrowing the focus to small achievable goals, particularly in mathematics and reading (Marzano). Although little time was spent teaching other subjects, test scores in these areas increased, revealing the importance of reading ability in assessment outcomes (Reeves).

The third strategy is to give assessment a prominent role in the daily activities of students and teachers (CPE, 2005; Marzano, 2003; Reeves, 2003; Schomoker, 2001). Faculty members assess students daily, weekly, and yearly (Marzano), and when reviewing test scores, the focus is on where they ended the year, not where they began. Yearly test scores are deemphasized, and daily or weekly test scores are highlighted as a form of continuous feedback to the students. Teachers use daily and weekly assessments to create academic interactions that closely resemble active coaching by the teachers (Reeves).

In addition, faculty members who are within the successful high-poverty schools work together on their assessments. Students must submit answers to questions from all content areas, requiring them to process the information and to "write to think." By providing answers that document their understanding, teachers are able to get a better diagnostic picture of the student's grasp on the content. Through this process, students also work on creating good nonfiction writing, and a rubric is used to evaluate the students' writing (Reeves, 2003).

Another strategy that successful schools use is creating common assessments for each grade level, establishing consistency in teacher expectations. For this strategy to work, teachers must discuss curriculum outcomes and expectations for each assignment. Following discussions, teachers are better equipped to grade work equitably (Reeves, 2003).

The fourth strategy is to increase collaboration throughout the school (CPE, 2005; Marzano, 2003; Reeves, 2003). In this case, the collaborative assessment is taken one step further by having teachers and principals regularly exchange and grade student work. After faculty members discuss expectations for each common assignment, collaboration is extended throughout the school by holding everyone accountable for student learning, including physical education teachers, librarians, music teachers, and even bus drivers. Teachers collaborate to determine the best ways to cover the content. In addition to the school community, families are also an important part of the collaborative process (CPE; Marzano).

The fifth strategy is to use creative scheduling (Danielson, 2002). Administrators play a key role in freeing up time for activities that promote teacher success, including scheduling time for instruction based on the needs of the students. For example, some elementary school principals who wanted to focus more on certain aspects of the curriculum created 3-hr literacy blocks, whereas some middle and high school principals created double periods of English and mathematics. Similarly, school principals used faculty meetings and replaced professional development sessions—which teachers had found to be a waste of time—to allow for collaborative discussions among teachers. Announcements were sent via e-mail, and the faculty meetings were spent by collaborating with colleagues (Reeves, 2003).

The sixth and final strategy involved administrators who spent money on things that worked. Reeves (2003) found that, overall, effective teachers and teaching strategies obtain results, not programs. Assessment with collaboration and consistent instructional practices were vital to the continued success of these schools. This collaboration in determining what strategies were effective enabled teachers to overcome many of the academic deficits that are often observed in children from low-income families and communities.

Classroom Environment

In addition to schoolwide strategies, creating a positive environment within the classroom is one of the most powerful actions that a teacher can implement to ensure that all children belong, especially children living in poverty. The following research indicates that strategies specifically designed to establish a positive classroom environment can greatly affect the school experience of a child living in poverty.

Often, children living in poverty give up on school because of low self-esteem. Almost as often, teachers give up on children because of a perceived lack of trying and unwillingness to learn. Research has shown that one person can and does make a difference in the life of a child, and children living in poverty

need the teacher to be the person who believes in them and provides a reliable, positive relationship. Researchers have concluded that focusing on assets—not on deficits—significantly contributed to a child's success in school (Cooter, 2006; Dorrell, 1993; Marzano & Marzano, 2003; Payne, 2005; Pellino, 2006; Pugach, 2006).

Researchers have found that creating ongoing relationships with families and communities was equally positive in maintaining positive classroom environments (Cooter, 2006; Epstein, 2001; Machan, Wilson, & Notar, 2005; Mapp, 2002; Pugach, 2006). It is necessary not only to value and assure the child of his or her importance, but also to appreciate what families know and can do. Educators can do this by celebrating differences and showing respect for all families. Educators must be knowledgeable of the cultures in which students live to have clear expectations in the classroom. Chrispeels and Rivero (2001) and Payne (2005) have suggested that teachers need to investigate what hidden rules govern the child's life and be willing to teach the child and the child's family about the school's hidden rules.

According to Pellino (2006) and Pugach (2006), planning lessons and activities that are appropriate and meaningful to the child is important when building a positive classroom environment. Classrooms should be high in challenge and low in terms of threat. Activities and lessons that are neither appropriate nor meaningful can be highly threatening to a child. An example is an activity that many educators use in teaching mapping skills but is often not meaningful for all students: A teacher asks his or her students to draw a map of their bedrooms. In this scenario, the child living in poverty may put his or her head down and not complete the assignment. When asked why he or she is not drawing the map, the child replies that he or she does not have a bedroom or bed. As a teacher, it is important to think beyond personal experiences and help children develop a base of knowledge and experiences for themselves. In terms of appropriateness, teachers should consider the following example: By the time a child gets home in a Vermont town, it is rather dark. The child's home does not have electricity, yet the child is expected to complete homework at home and will be punished the next day for not doing so. Is this assignment appropriate for this child? Would a more appropriate activity be to review the information in the morning at school or as part of differentiated group work during the day?

Setting high expectations is a strategy that sets the stage for a successful year for all children. Children can and do rise to a teacher's expectations, and educators must not assume that because a child is living in poverty that he or she lacks the ability to achieve. The educator's job is not to expect less but to focus on learning and overcoming the challenges associated with poverty (Pellino, 2006; Tableman, 2004).

Marzano and Marzano (2003) and Tableman (2004) suggested that teachers use simple positive reinforcement strategies for establishing a classroom environment. It is important to learn names quickly. Teachers can have children use each others' names positively and often in the classroom. Integrating quick team-building exercises throughout the week to establish positive relationships among the children is also key to reinforcing a positive classroom environment. Something as simple as tossing a smiley face beach ball into a circle of children and telling them they are responsible for keeping the beach ball happy and off the ground unites children and makes them feel like they belong. This activity teaches children not only how to problem solve, but why they must work as a team to do it. The best part is that there is more than one way to solve the problem. Educators can also give hugs or high-fives throughout the day—especially at the end of the day—to let that child know that someone cares. It is imperative in building a positive classroom environment that the teacher continues to model genuine acceptance of all the children.

By believing in a child, cultivating positive relationships, and offering meaningful activities, teachers can build positive classroom environments that affect the child for much longer than a single school year. These positive classroom environments can affect a child for life.

Family Involvement

The earlier in a child's educational process that family involvement begins, the more powerful are the effects. The most effective forms of family involvement are those that engage families in working directly with their children on learning activities at home (Cotton & Wickelund, 2001).

At times, teachers and schools struggle to interact effectively with families of poverty. Research conducted to better understand the interactions between families and schools has revealed three overarching roles that are created in the development and implementation of parent and community involvement programs (Lyons, Robbins, & Smith, 1983). Each of these roles is actualized differently in relationships in classrooms, schools, and school districts. The roles include (a) parents as the primary resource in education of their children, (b) parents and community members as supporters and advocates for the education of their children, and (c) parents and community members as participants in the education of all children.

In addition, the following strategies for working with families are based on the National Standards for Family Involvement. The first strategy is to design effective forms of school-to-home and home-to-school communications about school programs and children's progress. Schools and teachers need to think outside the box when determining communication strategies. For example, a parent conference held at McDonald's is equally as valid as a parent conference held at school.

Another strategy for family involvement is to provide information and ideas to families about how to help students at home with homework and other curriculum-related activities, decisions, and planning. One example of this is a teacher's videotaping him- or herself helping a child read a story. The teacher could explain why each step in reading aloud is important. This video could be made in multiple languages.

A final strategy is the need for schools and teachers to identify and integrate resources and services from community health, cultural, recreational, social support, and other programs or services. Schools and teachers may adopt the Head Start model of serving the whole child. Everyone benefits from this strategy when the family's needs are met.

Recommendations for Infusing Strategies Into Teaching Programs

If strategies like those previously discussed are to be implemented by preservice students, it is critical that administrators of teacher-preparation programs consider ways to model and infuse these strategies within programs. On the basis of our experiences, we recommend the following in the instructional design, program design, and faculty considerations of a teacher-preparation program.

Instructional Design

Increasing and varying practicum experiences in diverse settings may provide students the opportunity to observe and engage in the use of multiple strategies in working with children living in poverty. Requiring practicums as early as the sophomore year in undergraduate programs and in the 1st year of graduate programs assists students in developing a greater understanding of the classroom. Students need to experience the reality of the classroom and how teachers best meet the needs of students. Establishing virtual learning communities that specifically address topics of classroom environment, family involvement, and school leadership may serve as valuable corequisites of the practica. If the supply of practicum placements are a concern, building a video library of local teachers who demonstrate use of the strategies in diverse classrooms is an alternative. These videos could be used in common assignments across courses. The creation of standard rubrics to guide and assess student reactions to videos may lead to greater consistency in providing appropriate instruction in the strategies across courses.

Additional course requirements across all methods courses could include the creation of common assessments in courses that include family involvement, classroom environment, and school leadership strategies. These assignments would be in relation to a particular content methods course and may provide a systematic approach in determining students' understanding of the strategies. An example could involve a senior portfolio that includes one artifact documenting how students participate in and reflect on a family-involvement activity (e.g., "Literacy Night").

Program Design

The development of stand-alone courses in family and school partnerships, classroom environment and management, and diversity is also an important tool for determining multiple strategies of working with students. However, the harsh reality of credit-hour crunches in many teacher-preparation programs may prohibit the development of additional courses. If that is the case, educators could develop modules that focus on the different strategies to use when working with children living in poverty. Completion of these modules may then serve as transition gateways into senior year.

Programs could establish a teacher resource center, both on campus and on the Internet. A teacher center may provide the infrastructure for coordinating student, community, school, and family resources and programs. In addition to providing resources and collaboration opportunities for all stakeholders, these centers may facilitate the training of school personnel, students, and faculty members on the various strategies of working with students from families living in poverty.

Faculty Considerations

Training is essential for faculty members to model the best practices in using multiple strategies to work with children living in poverty. Following structured training, faculty members may explicitly model strategies in courses. These strategies may be highlighted in a daily class blueprint (i.e., the agenda for each class session) that is shared with students on the day of class. In these blueprints, faculty members identify the course objectives and topics to be covered in the class. Faculty members then describe what strategies they are modeling in that class session and why those particular strategies were chosen to be modeled during that class. For example, choosing to begin each class with an icebreaker is a classroom environment strategy that may be described in the blueprint. In the blueprint, the description of the icebreaker may be accompanied by an explanation that the strategy was chosen to build team skills among classmates and to allow the faculty member to learn more about the students. The blueprint may indicate that this is important because it would build student motivation both collaboratively and individually, which in turn would affect student achievement. Providing a blueprint [for] each class session gives students clear examples of how to effectively use the varying strategies in a class setting and offers clear justifications of why strategies are selected. It also ensures that faculty members practice what they preach and model great teaching for students. As a result, students begin to build a greater understanding of how and when to use multiple strategies appropriately in the classroom.

When modeling strategies, it is equally important to model within the same parameters that the students would be working with in their future classrooms. If expensive technology or other resources are needed, faculty members need to equip students with methods for searching for funding or alternative resources.

Furthermore, expanding faculty members' teaching roles to include the supervision of practica allows students to cement their learning from the practica experiences. The feedback that is given and the discussions that arise when faculty members are present during practica experiences can be powerful. Students make connections immediately and faculty members are able to strengthen or reshape those connections as needed. Supervised practica enable the growth of strong school–university partnerships. These partnerships are vital as preservice students learn how to teach all children. Faculty members can also forge individual partnerships with classroom teachers and participate in faculty–teacher exchanges. During these types of exchanges, classroom teachers instruct on campus, while faculty members teach in the classroom. Again, this type of partnership supports the continual professional growth of faculty members and teachers in the classroom and provides invaluable teaching case

studies for faculty members to share how to best use multiple strategies when working with children living in poverty.

In addition, it is crucial that faculty members conduct course-alike meetings so that all instructors of the same course are on the same page in strategy instruction and use of common products. In these meetings, all faculty members who are teaching a certain course—whether full or part time—meet to discuss the primary course content and requirements for the semester or quarter. Although preserving academic freedom in how a faculty member teaches the content is important, students have the right to be taught the same basic content in a course regardless of the section number. Instructional strategies for working with children living in poverty must be included in that discussion of content and in the final decisions of topics and assignments.

Summary

The literature clearly shows that poverty has a great effect on a child's life and subsequently on a teacher's life. For this reason, it is imperative that teacher-preparation programs and public schools continue to explore the effect and strategies that affect the development of children. Strategies must be used by teachers, modeled by professors, and applied by preservice students. How else would preservice teachers be prepared to best meet the needs of the diverse children in their classrooms? Only after recognizing and studying this effect would preservice teachers be prepared for the future Kirbys in their classrooms.

References

Alexander, K., Entwhistle, D., & Olson, L. (2001, Summer). Schools, achievement, and inequality: A seasonal perspective. *Educational Evaluation and Policy Analysis, 23,* 171–191.

Brooks-Gunn, J., & Duncan, G. J. (1997). The effects of poverty on children. *Future of Children, 7*(2), 55–71.

Burch, K., Haberman, M., Mutua, N., Bloom, L., Romeo, J., & Duffield, B. (2001). A tale of two citizens: Asking the Rodriguez question in the twenty-first century. *Educational Studies, 32,* 264–278. Retrieved September 28, 2006, from the Academic Search Premier Database.

Center for Public Education. (2005, August). *Key lessons: High-performing, high-poverty schools.* Retrieved November 28, 2006, from www.centerforpubliceducation.org/site/apps/nl /content2.asp?c=kjJXJ5MPIwE&b=1498887&ct =2040773.

Children's Defense Fund (CDC). (2006). *2004 facts on child poverty in America.* Retrieved February 16, 2006, from www.childrensdefense.org/familyincome/childpoverty /default/aspx.

Chrispeels, J. H., & Rivero, E. (2000, April). *Engaging Latino families for student success: Understanding the process and impact of providing training to parents.* Paper presented at the annual meeting of the American Educational Research Association, New Orleans, LA.

Cooter, K. (2006). When mama can't read: Counteracting inter-generational illiteracy. *Reading Teacher, 59,* 698–702.

Cotton, K., & Wikelund, K. R. (2001). *Parent involvement in education.* Retrieved July 25, 2003, from www.nwrel.org/scpd /sirs/3/cu6.html.

Danielson, C. (2002). *Enhancing student achievement: A framework for school improvement.* Alexandria, VA: Association for Supervision and Curriculum Development.

Dorrell, L. D. (1993). *You can't look forward to tomorrow, while holding on to yesterday: Rural education and the at-risk student.* Paper presented at the 85th annual conference of the National Rural Education Association, Burlington, VT. Retrieved August 31, 2006, from ERIC database.

Eamon, M. (2001). The effects of poverty on children's socioemotional development: An ecological systems analysis. *Social Work, 46,* 256–267.

Epstein, J. (2001). *School, family, and community partnerships: Preparing educators and improving schools.* Boulder, CO: Westview.

Grissmer, D. W., Flanagan, A., Kawata, J. H., & Williamson, S. (2000). *Improving student achievement: What state NAEP test scores tell us.* Santa Monica, CA: RAND.

Karoly, L. A., Greenwood, P., Everingham, S., Hoube, J., Kilburn, M., Rydell, C., et al. (1998). *Investing in our children: What we know and don't know about the costs and benefits of early childhood interventions.* Santa Monica, CA: RAND.

Koppelman, K. L., & Goodhart, R. L. (2005). *Understanding human difference: Multicultural education for a diverse America.* Boston: Pearson.

Lyons, P., Robbins, A., & Smith, A. (1983). *Involving parents: A handbook for participation in schools.* Ypsilanti, MI: High/Scope Press.

Machan, S., Wilson, J., & Notar, C. (2005). *Parental involvement in the classroom. Journal of Instructional Psychology, 32,* 13–16.

Mapp, K. L. (2002, April). *Having their say: Parents describe how and why they are involved in their children's education.* Paper presented at the annual meeting of the American Educational Research Association, New Orleans, LA.

Marzano, R. J. (2003). *What works in schools: Translating research into action.* Alexandria, VA: Association for Supervision and Curriculum Development.

Marzano, R. J., & Marzano, J. S. (2003). The key to classroom management. *Educational Leadership, 61,* 6–13.

No Child Left Behind Act. (2001). Pub. L. No. 107-110 (2001).

Pascopella, A. (2006). Teachers are still the most important tool. *District Administration, 42*(8), 20. Retrieved September 28, 2006, from Academic Search Premier Database.

Payne, R. K. (2005). *A framework for understanding poverty* (4th ed.). Highlands, TX: aha! Process.

Pellino, K. (2006). *The effects of poverty on teaching and learning.* Retrieved September 21, 2006, from www.teachnology.com/tutorials/teaching/poverty/print.htm.

Pugach, M. (2006, March 9). *Preparing teachers to work with diverse students.* Retrieved April 26, 2006, from http://wiley.breezecentral.com/_a444336939/e85406735.

Ramey, C. T., & Ramey, S. L. (1998). Early intervention and early experience. *American Psychologist, 53,* 109–120.

Reeves, D. B. (2003). *High performance in high poverty schools: 90/90/90 and beyond. . . .* Retrieved November 20, 2006, from www.sabine.k12.la.us/online/leadershipacademy/high%20performance%2090%2090%2090%20and%20beyond.pdf.

Reid, J. (2006, August 30). *New census data shows 1.3 million children have fallen into poverty since 2000.* Retrieved October 30, 2006, from www.childrensdefense.org/site/News2?page=NewsArticle&id=7887.

Rockwell, S. (2006). Facilitating the fourth *r:* Resilience. *Kappa Delta Pi Record, 43*(1), 14–19.

Schmoker, M. (2001). *The results handbook: Practical strategies from dramatically improved schools.* Alexandria, VA: Association for Supervision and Curriculum Development.

Strickland, D. S. (2001). Early intervention for African American children considered to be at risk. In S. Neuman & D. Dickenson (Eds.), *Handbook of early literacy research* (pp. 322–333). New York: Guilford Press.

Tableman, B. (2004, February). Characteristics of effective elementary schools in poverty areas. *Best Practice Brief, 29,* 1–4.

Thomas, M. D., & Bainbridge, W. (2001, Winter). All children can learn: Facts and fallacies. *Education Research Service Spectrum, 82*(9), 1–4.

Critical Thinking

1. Do you believe having students who live in poverty will affect your teaching? Provide justification for your answer.

2. Based on what you have read in the other articles in this unit, where are you most likely to find *situational, generational,* and *absolute* poverty? What is the basis for your answer?

3. Consider the strategies for working with students and families offered in the article. Which do you believe you were most prepared to implement by your teacher preparation program? Explain.

Address correspondence to Kristen Cuthrell, East Carolina University, Department of Curriculum and Instruction, College of Education, 119 Speight Building, Greenville, NC 27858, USA; cuthrellma@ecu.edu (e-mail). Copyright © 2010 Heldref Publications.

Author Notes—KRISTEN CUTHRELL is an assistant professor in the Department of Curriculum and Instruction at East Carolina University. Her primary research areas are teacher education, diversity issues, and assessment. **JOY STAPLETON** is an associate professor also in the Department of Curriculum and Instruction at East Carolina University. Her research interests are children and poverty, teacher education, and new teacher induction. **CAROLYN LEDFORD** is also an associate professor in the Department of Curriculum and Instruction at East Carolina University. Her research interests are social studies education, diversity, and global education.

From *Preventing School Failure,* vol. 54, no. 2, 2010, pp. 104–110. Copyright © 2010 by Routledge/Taylor & Francis Group. Reprinted by permission via Rightslink.

APPENDIX
Key Strategies for Working with Students and Families

Type of environment

School	Classroom	Family
• Hire and retain teachers who believe in their students. • Focus on academic achievement. • On a daily basis using common grade assessments, assess achievement through collaboration with faculty. • Increase collaboration throughout the school. • Use creative scheduling. • Spend money on things that work.	• Create a positive environment. • Focus on assets, not deficits. • Create ongoing relationships with families and communities. • Believe in all students. • Plan lessons and activities that are appropriate and meaningful. • Set high expectations. • Use simple, positive reinforcement strategies. • Create a classroom that is high in challenge and low in threat.	• Design effective forms of communication: School to home and home to school. • Provide information and ideas to families on how to help with home work and curriculum-related activities. • Identify and integrate resources and services from the community.

Paper presented at the Annual Meeting of the American Educational Research Association, April 2010, Denver, Colorado

Exploring Educational Material Needs and Resources for Children Living in Poverty

In this qualitative study, I explored the needs for educational materials for children living in poverty in the United States. The purpose of this study was two-fold. It was first to find out what the educational material needs were for children living in poverty, and second, to learn of the challenges, obstacles, and strengths of the programs already in place that were supplying educational materials to these children.

INDRA KUMAR MAHABIR, EdD

Theoretical Framework

In this study, I drew from the Invitational Model, based on Purkey's (1992) rule of five C's (Concern, Confer, Consult, Confront, and Combat). Even though no conflict was involved, the first two steps were applied in this study. It was during an exploratory trip to Mizoram, India, that I saw first-hand the inequity of education in that part of the world compared to the United States. While thinking of an action plan to funnel educational materials to that part of the world, I realized that those same inequities existed in my own back yard, Philadelphia. This self-reflecting and ponderance of the problem is the first rule of Purkey's, the concern, followed by confer. I began talking with educators and found out that this was the situation in many parts of the United States. A formal consultation with professors and the writing of a concept paper served as a prelude to this study. A visit to schools in Philadelphia and interviews with program leaders to confront the issue gave me better insights into the problems and possible solutions. Although the problem still exists, and will for many years to come, attention has been raised to combat this important issue of lack of educational materials and resources for children living in poverty.

Invitational Theory examines quandaries that educators and schools face within their communities. What type of learning environment is more inviting to students—one in which the students do not have the basic materials for learning, or a rich environment in which they have what they need to learn? According to Purkey and Novak (1996), "invitational education

practitioners work toward developing caring behaviors, nurturing environments, person-centered policies, engaging programs, and democratic processes" (p. 5). By providing the materials that children of poverty need in order to learn, educators are providing "nurturing environments" and demonstrating "caring behaviors" (p. 5). Children of poverty deserve for their teachers to be "intentionally inviting" (Purkey & Novak, p. 58) by providing them with the materials that they need. In discussing what is in the best interests of the children, Purkey and Novak (1984) cautioned educators against being intentionally disinviting through their own prejudices. Hilliard (1991) questioned whether or not educators had the will to educate all poor children. Through invitational theory, educators can overcome prejudices that will help them to provide the best education to all children (Reed, 1996).

Invitational teachers treat students with "trust" (Purkey & Novak, 1996, p. 50), "respect" (p. 51), "optimism" (p. 52), and "intentionality" (p. 53), and as a result, students learn to trust teachers who provide what they need in order to learn. Teachers act intentionally as they demonstrate optimism and respect by searching and providing materials that students need. Some schools have gone a step further by inviting parents into schools by giving them access to washers and dryers in the basement (Dryfoos, 2002). Relationships began to build while clothes were being washed and dried, thus furthering the development of commitment and success for their students. Invitational theory focuses on the care and respect in the lives of others.

Children Living in Poverty

Children living in poverty tend to continue in a cycle of poverty. Almost 50 million American adults do not have adequate reading skills to read to a child or fill out a job application (Cooter, 2006). The children's low status in school mirrors their family's status in the community. They "happen" to live in an impoverished ghetto (Conley, 1999; Oliver & Shapiro, 1995). They attend schools and classes with the fewest resources, (Anyon, 1997; Kozol, 1991) and the least academic push (Chazan, 2000). Schools with the fewest resources end up with even less, including loss of funds because of the inability of these impoverished schools to show test scores that the government demands (Kozol, 2008).

Research has shown that poverty is one of the contributing factors to illiteracy (Chall, 1990; Cook, 1996; Kozol, 1991; Newman & Newman, 1995), which results in few reading resources for children in poorer areas. First grade students who fall behind in reading diminish their opportunities to catch up or advance (Chall, 1990). If students do not develop linguistic skills early in their education, they may never develop proficient reading skills. As a result, according to Cavazos (1989), students in these poorer communities fall behind their more affluent counterparts. They have a higher dropout rate and get involved with crimes, while some become teenage parents. Kids Count Data (2008) reported that 7% of teens 16- to 19-years-old were high school dropouts in 2007.

Bursuck et al. (2010) discussed what rural high schools in the southeastern United States face in trying to meet the demands of the No Child Left Behind Act, when so many high school students living in poverty in rural areas do not have adequate reading skills. These rural high schoolers who had difficulties with their reading also found problems in keeping up with their fluent counterparts in class. Although they were willing to do anything to read better, they wanted an after-school hours reading class, where they could learn discreetly and avoid being labeled.

Rural schools that did not offer reading programs explained that they could neither afford them, nor were they able to find qualified reading teachers. Some department chairs said that reading was the responsibility of elementary schools, not high schools. Bursuck et al. (2010) suggested that doing nothing to help struggling readers in high school is too great a cost, as the impact of being low in basic literacy skills affects many aspects of adult life. Lastly, this study found that there seemed to be a lack of collaboration between teachers, parents, and students.

Schools that are funded by low tax revenues (such as urban areas) have relatively few resources, while more affluent areas (such as wealthy suburbs) have access to higher tax revenue and, therefore, more available resources (Hess, 1991). The wealthier the community, the more tax dollars are available to schools. In a report prepared by 17 Chicago-based nonprofit organizations, the level of funding available to support public schools varied significantly across Illinois (Hess). The ability of some school districts to spend five times as much on each student as other districts is primarily related to differences in the value of property located within those districts, since school districts' local revenues come primarily from local property taxes (Hess). A third-grader from the Bronx, New York, wrote the following to Kozol (2005):

> It is not fair that other kids have a garden and new things. But we don't have that. I wish that this school was the most beautiful school in the whole why [sic] world. (para. 21)

Health, education, and literacy are closely interrelated; when children receive a basic education, it leads to healthier families (Greaney, 1996). Children living in poverty come to school hungry, often sick with low energy, with no motivation or confidence, and are thus ill-prepared for learning (Cavazos, 1989). From a psychological perspective, Vygotsky (1978), a cognitive developmentalist, believed that when parents spend time with their young ones, they serve as a greater resource for their children's increased knowledge and ways of thinking. He theorized that children and infants adopt ways of thinking and solving problems by watching others and by being taught formally. Many kindergartners come to school not knowing how to hold a book or never having been read to at home (Wheaton & Kay, 1999). In an effort to study the traits of gifted children, Terman (1926) engaged 1400 children, ages 8 through 15, in an unprecedented study. In this study, only 1.1% of the gifted children said they had no books at home, while 33% reported having over 500 books in the home. He also found that all of the parents of gifted children had finished high school, a little more than one-fourth of them had a college degree, and some had post-graduate degrees.

Methods and Data Sources

This study employed interviews and surveys as data gathering methods to gain interactions with people about their thoughts on what educational materials were needed for children living in poverty. The two research questions addressed in this study were: 1) What educational materials are needed for children living in poverty in the United States? and 2) What can be learned from existing programs that are providing educational materials to children living in poverty?

The participants in this exploratory study consisted of 32 educators from eight states in the United States. Seventeen educators participated in the electronic survey, and 15 education leaders and program directors were interviewed by telephone.

A survey of 10 questions was sent electronically to 244 educators who were in a geographically dispersed doctoral program in educational leadership and change. Questions included the kinds of educational materials that were needed at their schools, and whether or not they had excess materials to donate to schools [in] need. Interview and survey data were collected from participants in California, Florida, Illinois, Massachusetts, New Mexico, North Carolina, Pennsylvania, and Wisconsin. Of the 244 surveys sent, 17 survey responses were returned.

In addition, 15 key informants were chosen because of their personal and professional knowledge about the specific needs for educational materials when working with children living in poverty. These key informants were asked, based on what they knew and had seen, to identify some of the needed educational materials for children living in poverty, and to provide their thoughts on how these materials could be sought. Because of the various geographic locations of the interviewees, most of the interviews were conducted over the telephone. They ranged from 15 minutes to one hour.

Implementing a naturalistic inquiry is not an easy task (Lincoln & Guba, 1985). A naturalistic researcher must make initial contacts, as well as gain, build, and maintain trust with persons being interviewed before accurate data can be collected. Because this naturalistic inquiry was a small study, educators who had knowledge about the needs for educational materials were selected from a convenience sample. According to Creswell (1994), a convenience sample saves time, money, and effort. Lincoln and Guba have suggested that by virtue of their positions, key informants can provide an "inside" view of the processes and culture to the inquirer who is not able to do it herself.

After each interview was completed, member checks were performed by providing excerpts of the interview to the interviewees, along with a copy of the transcribed data. This ensured the accuracy of the transcripts by allowing the parties interviewed to agree or disagree with what was recorded. "It gives the respondent an immediate opportunity to correct errors of fact, and challenge what are perceived to be wrong interpretations" (Lincoln & Guba, 1985, p. 314). The data were analyzed based on my perceptions as a researcher. Dey (1995) said that qualitative data analysts use insight intuition, and impressions when analyzing data, as people learn by doing. Agar (1980) suggested reading the transcripts in their entirety several times before dividing them into segments. This was essential in order to situate each person's point of view before dissecting the interview transcript for the grouping of common themes.

Results

Results are presented for the two research questions.

Research Question #1: What Educational Materials Are Needed for Children Living in Poverty in the United States?

As shown in Figure 1, books were the most needed item in both classrooms and in homes. More specific needs were bilingual books, magazines, newspapers, pens, pencils, paper, current maps and globes, art supplies, educational videotapes, and computers. All of the participants stated that any books or reading materials would be of help to the children. In addition, books, newspapers, sport magazines, technical magazines, computer magazines, and other reading materials were essential to children from homes where families could not afford to buy a daily newspaper. Participants reported that children living in poverty seemed to have no magazines in the home that would

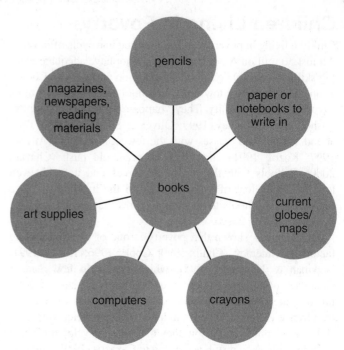

Figure 1 *Educational materials that are needed for children living in poverty.*

spark their interest because no extra money is available when both parents are working in order to pay the bills.

Interviewees stressed the need for educational materials in the homes of children living in poverty. They said that children who are not in a learning environment at home are at a disadvantage because they lack basic information and skills necessary to be on the same level with other children entering school who are their same age. When family priorities dictate that they choose food and clothes over the purchase of books, parents and caregivers must next rely on public schools to provide a good education for their children.

Invitational educators care about students' academic growth and what they can achieve. In the findings of this study, teachers sometimes used their own personal funds to buy books for children in their classrooms. Instead of birthday presents for their children, some parents had donated books in their child's name. These books helped to increase the library count. One participant spoke of the relationship between the giver and receiver of books or other items. She reiterated what Comer (1995) stated that unless the educational materials are accompanied by a significant relationship of mutual respect, not much will be done with them.

Role of the Teachers

From the data, it is evident that the teachers were the ones who take an active role in soliciting the educational materials that were needed in their classrooms. Of the 17 educators (teachers and principals) who participated in the survey, only one teacher reported that she did not know how to disseminate unused books in her school. She wrote the following:

At the end of the year, stuff piles up. They get thrown away if none of the kids take them. There's no place to deploy them—no system within the school district to trade these books among schools.

All of the other teachers reported that they continually sought aid from anyone in their community who was willing to donate school supplies, books, and educational games for their classrooms. Some teachers wrote:

> They could donate materials, school supplies, scissors, colors, colored pens, crayons—you give them a pack of 32, and they are like, "Wow," and 64 are overwhelming!

> The needs are very deep, and people just don't seem to have the time needed to really do what is necessary to assist the children in higher levels of achievement.

> Go through and ask [other schools] how many books they have from first and second grade that are not being used and donate them.

Teachers felt fortunate when they found bargains for school supplies, or when they received money or book donations for their schools. They also appreciated the general benevolence of businesses and people in their community. Teachers reported that they continually sought aid from anyone who was willing to donate school supplies, books, and educational games for their classrooms.

Research Question #2: What Can be Learned from Existing Programs That Are Providing Educational Materials to Children Living in Poverty?

Very few programs or organizations could be found that specifically supplied educational materials to children living in poverty. Representatives from the organizations who supplied educational materials said in their interviews that the children they serve came from (a) low-income families, based on census bureau information, (b) schools in urban areas that are high-poverty and under-resourced communities, (c) schools' at-risk urban children, (d) early intervention programs in local school districts, and (e) specifically, children living below the federal poverty level found through public clinics and hospitals.

Eighty-three percent of the organizations interviewed said that they did not personally conduct ongoing evaluations of the children they served. A lack of funding and resources prevented the organizations from assessing their programs. Program leaders who provided books and educational materials unintentionally disinvited the commitment and success of the students by not evaluating the students, just the performance of their staff.

Here are some excerpts from some of the program leaders who did not conduct evaluations:

> We are so young; we haven't had time to [evaluate].

> The children that are school age are evaluated using their school grades, and the other programs, I know that they do evaluations.

A big piece for us that we have learned is that it's hard for a very small clinic, a small rural clinic, to raise the money to sustain the program after we give them money for the first year.

The organizations that conducted evaluations of the children found that most children improved in their vocabulary and in their school grades as a result of the educational materials they received, while some made the honor roll for the first time.

Scholarly Significance of the Study

While some authors have written from their personal experiences about the poor conditions of the schools in the U.S., no studies have reported what schools in poverty need in their classrooms or what educational materials children living in poverty need, from the point of view of an equal education for all children. Kozol (2000) observed that textbooks were scarce in inner city schools, and that teachers often had to buy books using their own salaries. Educators in this study reported that the very basic necessities, such as pencils, paper, and teaching aids, were bought using their own personal funds. Participants expressed concern about children entering public school without having prior exposure to books and reading materials. This finding supports Cook's (1996) theory that children who live in poor areas may not know how to read because of probable lack of educational materials at home or in schools.

Legal Cases on Equality of Education

Residents of poorer districts have filed lawsuits against their school districts charging that they violated the constitutional rights of children in poorer districts to an "equal education." In New Jersey, parents claimed that their children were not receiving the same educational opportunities as students in school districts with greater tax revenues. This lawsuit was brought against state officials who were responsible for administering the finance provisions of the public education laws and assuring that a thorough and efficient education was provided in all public school districts (Abbott v. Burke, 1984).

In another case in San Antonio, Texas, Mexican Americans claimed that each independent school district was collecting taxes for use exclusively within their school district, thus allowing little or no tax dollars to be spent on poorer schools (Rodriguez v. San Antonio, 1969). In Washington, DC, parents on behalf of their minority children charged the school superintendent and school board members with racial discrimination because they deprived their children of educational opportunities equal to those provided to White students in the public schools in Washington (Hobson v. Hansen, 1966).

Recommendations

The following recommendations evolved from interviews with key informants and program directors during this research study. First, a website could be created for teachers to communicate with one another. Teachers in low-income schools share a universal struggle to gather educational materials for their classrooms. This website could be established for the sole purpose of teachers in the U.S. or possibly around the world sharing ideas and communicating with one another about their classroom needs, and the availability of excess materials for children living in poverty.

Next, teachers should be encouraged to solicit books and other materials from their communities. The data indicated that some teachers have been successful in doing this by posting their classroom needs in heavily frequented shopping areas. Teachers said that people are willing to donate, and sometimes, for a little recognition, books can be donated to a school's library in a child's name in lieu of giving birthday presents. Third, principals and teachers should be encouraged to connect or work with their city to create a Reads organization through a federally funded program called America Reads Challenge. Fourth, principals and teachers could build communication with other schools. At the end of each school year, school districts could host a book fair at a school or township building and invite neighboring schools to participate in the sharing of books and materials.

Until the federal government can provide adequate instructional resources in order to have fully functional schools to produce well-educated children, teachers have no choice but to continue to depend on private citizens, businesses, networking among themselves, and connecting with programs such as America Reads Challenge for the educational materials that they need.

According to Capra (1996),

> The behavior of every living member of the ecosystem depends on the behavior of many others. The success of the whole community depends on the success of its individual members, while the success of each member depends on the success of the community as a whole. (p. 298)

Bursuck et al. (2010) found little collaboration among parents, teachers, and students, in rural schools where students were struggling to read. In order to ensure the educational success of a student, it is important that parents and teachers work collaboratively to meet mutual goals (Musti-Rao & Cartledge, 2004). While solutions exist to major problems, they require a radical change in the way people think and how they perceive their values (Capra, 1996). School lessons can be taught outside the classrooms in innovative and interesting ways, while providing for life's basic needs.

In seeking to understand the connection between humans and the environment, Torrise (2010), a library media specialist, used a community-based approach to teaching today's needed skills on the streets of Chicago, on rooftops, and in community gardens. Lessons included identifying critical resources that were needed, engaging disconnected youth through community-based learning, designing opportunities for inquiry-based learning, and responding to issues around a disconnect between life experiences and what was being taught in schools. A curriculum was designed in which the youth connected with their community in a problem-solving manner, resulting in learning about growing local foods that allowed them to stay healthy. This program created sustainability while bringing about meaningful changes in their lives and community. Students received lifelong lessons such as critical thinking, problem solving, communication, and collaboration.

Conclusion

This study first explored the needs for educational materials for children living in poverty. Findings indicated that books and reading materials, new and used, are needed both in the classroom and in the home. Teachers are continually finding ways to acquire materials they need. According to the respondents, some children did not mind receiving free, used items; however, some did not like the idea that books came to them already used. Quality books, as well as new books, were suggested as better reading materials, yet those were dependent on funding. In the second part of this study, interviews were conducted with directors of programs that provided educational materials to children in need. Based on the data, it is recommended that directors of existing programs conduct research on how the children benefit from their services in order to match what is required with what is provided. The data suggested a huge need for program evaluation. Most of the organizations did not have measures in place to assess the children in relation to the services they provided to the children, due to lack of funding.

A larger study could have provided more compelling results by gaining more perspectives from a larger cross-section of the U.S. or by seeking a better representation of low-income schools in the nation.

This study completed the "look" and "think" sections of Stringer's (1996) action research cycle. These were done by conducting interviews and collecting surveys to gather data on the needs for educational materials for children in poverty. The discovery was made that books and other learning materials are necessary in classrooms and homes of children living in poverty. The next step is to implement the "act" component to complete Stringer's cycle of "look," "think," "act" (p. 19). This will involve finding and providing the needed educational materials and placing them in the hands of the children who need them with a follow-up study and evaluation.

References

Abbott v. Burke, Supreme Court of New Jersey, 97 N.J. 669; 483 A.2d 187; 1984 N.J. LEXIS 3099, July 12, 1984.

Agar, M.H. (1980). *Speaking of ethnography.* Beverly Hills, CA: Sage Publications.

Annie E. Casey Foundation. (2008). *Kids Count Data Book: State profiles of child well-being.* Baltimore, MD: Annie E. Casey Foundation.

Anyon, J. (1997). *Ghetto schooling: A political economy of urban educational reform.* New York, NY: Teachers College Press.

Bursuck, W.D., Robbins, S., & Lazaroff, K. (2010). Meeting the needs of struggling readers in high school. *The Rural Educator, 31*(2), 27–32.

Capra, F. (1996) *Web of life*. New York, NY: Anchor Books.

Cavazos, L. (1989). Building bridges for at-risk children. *Principal, 68*(5), 6–8.

Chall, J. (1990). *The reading crisis: Why poor children fall behind*. Cambridge, MA: Harvard University Press.

Chazan, D. (2000). *Beyond formulas: Mathematics and teaching: Dynamics of the high school algebra class*. New York, NY: Teachers College Press.

Comer, J. (1995). Lecture Given at Education Service Center, Region IV, Houston, TX.

Conley, D. (1999). *Being Black, living in the red: Race, wealth, and social policy in America*. Berkeley, CA: University of California Press.

Cook, J. (1996). On the brink of illiteracy. *Teaching PreK-8, 27*, 24–5.

Cooter, K.S. (2006, April). When Mama can't read: Counteracting intergenerational illiteracy. *The Reading Teacher, 59*(7), 698–702.

Creswell, J.W. (1994). Research design, qualitative and quantitative approaches. Thousand Oaks, CA: Sage Publications.

Dey, I. (1995). Reducing fragmentation in qualitative research. In U. Keele (Ed.), Computer-aided qualitative data analysis. Thousand Oaks, CA: Sage Publications.

Dryfoos, J. (2002). Full service community school: Creative new institutions. *Phi Delta Kappan, 1,* 393–399.

Greaney, V. (1996). *Promoting reading in developing countries*. Washington, DC: World Bank.

Hess, G.A., Jr. (1991). *The inequity in Illinois school finance. An analysis of the current situation, the historical record, and alternative solutions*. Chicago, IL: EdEquity Coalition.

Hilliard, A.G., III. (1991). Do we have the will to educate all poor children? *Educational Leadership, 49*(l), 31–36.

Hobson v. Hansen, Civ. A No. 82-66. United States District Court for the District of Columbia, 269F. Supp. 401; 1967 U.S. Dist. LEXIS 10662, June 19, 1967.

Kids Count Data Book: State profiles of child well-being. (2008). Baltimore, MD: Annie E. Casey Foundation.

Kozol, J. (1991). *Savage inequalities*. New York, NY: Crown Publishers.

Kozol, J. (2000). *Ordinary resurrections*. New York, NY: Crown Publishers.

Kozol, J. (2005). Still separate, still unequal. *Harper's Magazine, 311*(1864). Retrieved from www.learntoquestion.com/resources/database/archives/000711.html.

Kozol, J. (2008). *Letters to a young teacher.* New York, NY: Crown Publishers.

Lincoln, Y.S., & Guba, E.G. (1985). *Naturalistic inquiry*. Newbury Park, CA: Sage Publications.

Musti-Rao, S., & Cartledge, G. (2004). Making home an advantage in the prevention of reading failure: strategies for collaborating with parents in urban schools. *Preventing School Failure, 48*(4), 15–21.

Newman, B.M., & Newman P.R. (1979). *Development through life: A psychosocial approach*. Chicago, IL: Dorsey Press.

Oliver, M.L., & Shapiro, T.M. (1995). *Black wealth/white wealth*. New York, NY: Routledge.

Purkey, W.W., & Novak, J.M. (1996). *Inviting school success: A self-concept approach to teaching, learning, and democratic practice*. Belmont, CA: Wadsworth.

Reed, C. (1996). Overcoming prejudices: an invitational approach. *Urban Review 28*, 81–93.

Stinger, E.T. (1996). *Action research: A handbook for practitioners*. Thousand Oaks. CA: Sage Publications.

Terman, L.M. (1926). *Genetic studies of genius: Mental and physical traits of a thousand gifted children* (vol. 1). Stanford, CA: Stanford University Press.

Torrise, M.L. (2010). Role of the library media specialist in greening the curriculum: a community-based approach to teaching 21st century skills outside of the school library through the practice of urban agriculture. *Library Media Connection, 28*(4), 18–20.

Vygotsky, L.S. (1978). *Mind in society*. Cambridge, MA: Harvard University Press.

Wheaton, C., & Stephen, K. (1999). Every child will read—We guarantee it. *Educational Leadership, 57*(2), 52–56.

Critical Thinking

1. Why did the researcher select this issue for study?

2. What were the research questions?

3. What were the findings?

4. How do these findings impact you and other teachers?

5. List specific actions you can take to find and obtain the materials and resources needed to help schools and students.

From *A paper presented at the Annual Meeting of the American Educational Research Association,* April 2010, pp. 2–14. Copyright © 2010 by Indra Kumar Mahabir. Reprinted by permission of the author.

UNIT 3

Cornerstones to Learning: Reading and Math

Unit Selections

Learning Outcomes

After reading this unit, you will be able to:

- Define *print referencing*.

- Explain the importance of *print referencing* to reading achievement of emergent readers.

- Demonstrate your ability to select appropriate books for teaching print referencing.

- Explain how student perceptions support individual and small-group reading lesson.

- Demonstrate how to support literacy for students in poverty and homeless shelters.

- Explain why and how students learn to fear a subject from their teachers.

- Generate ideas to avoid transferring gender and personal bias about subject matter to students.

- Plan algebra lessons that include research-based interventions.

Student Website

www.mhhe.com/cls

Internet References

The National Council of Teachers of English (NCTE)
www.readwritethink.org/professional-development/strategy-guides/supporting-comprehension-strategies-english-30106.html

International Association of Reading
www.reading.org/General/Default.aspx

Jim Trelease's Read-Aloud Home Page
www.trelease-on-reading.com

Literature Circles Resource Center
www.litcircles.org

Read, Write, Think
www.readwritethink.org

Visible Thinking
www.pzweb.harvard.edu/vt/index.html

National Council of Teachers of Mathematics
www.nctm.org

National Library of Virtual Manipulatives
www.nlvm.usu.edu/en/nav/vlibrary.html

In this unit of the Annual Edition we focus on core skills that are taught in all public schools: reading and math. We have selected this topic because these skills are fundamental skills acquired from printed materials that are a primary source of knowledge. Additionally, being able to read and calculate are fundamental rights of all citizens in a democratic society. Many of us who read for both learning and pleasure cannot imagine a life without reading. Just as reading is an essential skill for learning and living a successful life, so are math skills. Imagine not being able to balance your account checking, keep a budget, or understand and check the deductions on your paycheck. Good math skills are even more important when you try to read the fine print on car and home mortgage loans or credit card bills. These issues are a reality for persons who lack basic math skills. In school, students may have the intellectual ability to attend college, but cannot pass those higher level math classes required in college prep programs. Thus, we are have several articles about math in this section on cornerstones to learning.

© Purestock/Getty Images

The first article in the unit asks us to think about the teaching of reading in a new way: print referencing. The article was chosen because it offers us ways of looking at and thinking about reading books with children. Most of us have fond memories of sitting on a rug in a classroom, listening to our happy teacher read a story to us. She (most early childhood teachers are women) spoke in a lilting voice and pointed to the pictures to call attention to important characters or environmental elements. But did she help us learn print-related skills? According to Zucker, Ward, and Justice, during story time children spend very little time actually looking at the print in the book if teachers do not call specific attention to the print. Referencing Vygotskian theory, the authors emphasize the importance for increasing children's interest in and knowledge of print through meaningful social interactions. After defining this important set of skills, the authors give us a clear scientific basis and suggestions for print referencing, followed by examples of teaching techniques, a list of books containing print-salient features, and the three steps to beginning print referencing.

Seglem and Witte assert that reading is more than text; it is about visual literacy as well. As we move from picture books to chapter books, visuals disappear from our books and the reader is called upon to make his or her own pictures. In fact, the authors note that creating mind movies is an essential element for engaging with, comprehending, and reflecting on the text. As the title of the article suggests, visual literacy should be taught to ensure that all students are able to use this important skill throughout their lives. After defining terms, the authors have a detailed description of how they teach visual literacy in their ninth-grade English classes using tattoos, collages, paintings, and poetry comics. Fingon supports the integration of literacy learning and physical activity. In this article we give suggestions for reading activities using books that emphasize exercise, good nutrition, or are about sports heroes who are good role models. All suggestions can be used independently by general or physical education teachers or in collaboration.

Reading is the single skill every child must have to be successful in school, at work, and in life activities. However, poverty and homelessness can have profound effects on learning to read. These two factors alone can detrain all that is done in classrooms. MacGillivray, Ardell, and Curwen suggest that teachers should extend literacy learning beyond the classroom. They suggest giving high levels of literacy support to children who are living in homeless shelters. First, they define and describe the types of shelter that are available and what services they offer. Second, they describe the literacy practices one author found in shelters she visited. Third, they teach us about literacy from the perspectives of five people who work with children. And last, they provide suggestions to those of us who may teach students in these circumstances.

The article from *Teacher Magazine* may spark an interesting debate. Do female educators transfer their fear about math to your children? Does this lead to poor math skills in young girls that perpetuate math fear in older girls? Does all of this lead to more female teachers who do poorly in college math classes? A quick poll might be an interesting class activity. However, we can no longer allow students to go through grade after grade without understanding the manipulation of numbers, because mathematics counts in today's schools. Graduation requirements for higher math are difficult for students who have learning disabilities and some students without disabilities, such as students who are ELL or who are not motivated to think about college requirements. Strickland and Maccini provide an overview of practical, research-based teaching methods including explicit instruction, graduated instructional sequence, technology, and graphic organizers.

This collection of articles is presented to stimulate your thinking about ways to help your students (or prospective students) become lifelong readers and competent users of math.

Print Referencing during Read-Alouds: A Technique for Increasing Emergent Readers' Print Knowledge

Daily classroom read-alouds provide an important context for supporting children's emergent literacy skills.

Tricia A. Zucker, Allison E. Ward, and Laura M. Justice

Daily classroom read-alouds provide a versatile context for supporting a range of emergent literacy skills. Yet most adults view read-alouds as a time to discuss story meaning or comprehension skills and rarely take advantage of opportunities to talk about print-related skills (Ezell & Justice, 2000). This article describes how early childhood educators can readily increase emergent readers' print knowledge by using an evidence-based technique called *print referencing* to ensure that classroom read-alouds include not only a focus on comprehension and meaning but also a complementary focus on print. Chief motivations for using print referencing with young readers include the following:

- Increasing children's print knowledge
- Developing children's metalinguistic understanding of print
- Fostering children's interest in print during a familiar and highly contextualized social activity

Print referencing is a technique that is integrated with one's existing language arts program and that provides a developmentally appropriate means for achieving curriculum and state standards that specify the importance of systematically addressing children's development of print knowledge.

This article describes how classroom teachers and reading specialists can effectively employ this technique. Because of the strong research base supporting use of print referencing, it was described in *The Reading Teacher* as one of three "particularly compelling approaches to reading aloud" (Lane & Wright, 2007, p. 670). This claim is well supported (see What Works Clearinghouse, Institute of Education Sciences, 2007); nonetheless, research makes a strong contribution to evidence-based practice when findings are put in a useable form and translated for end users (Teale, 2003). In what follows, we provide explicit guidance on translating use of print referencing to the classroom environment by defining print referencing, outlining evidence on the efficacy of print referencing, and providing suggestions for reading teachers and classroom teachers to successfully implement print referencing.

What Is Print Referencing?

Print referencing refers to techniques educators use to increase emergent readers' knowledge about and interest in print by highlighting the forms, functions, and features of print during read-alouds (see Justice & Ezell, 2002, 2004; Justice, Kaderavek, Fan, Sofka, & Hunt, 2009). To implement print referencing, educators call children's attention to print with verbal and nonverbal referencing techniques that include the following:

Questions
- How many words are on this page?
- There are words in the wolf's speech bubble; what do you think they say?

Requests
- Show me where I would start reading on this page.
- Point to a letter that's in your name.

Comments
- The illustrator wrote the word *bus* on this yellow school bus.
- These words are exactly the same.

Nonverbal techniques
- Track print from left to right while reading.
- Point to print.

For many years, researchers have argued that adults play an essential role in actively mediating children's attention to print during book reading (Adams, 1990; Snow & Ninio, 1986). Indeed, eye-gaze studies confirm that children spend very little time looking at print when adults do not use specific behaviors, like questioning about print and pointing to print, that elicit attention to print during read-alouds (Evans & Saint-Aubin, 2005; Justice, Pullen, & Pence, 2008). It is likely no surprise to teachers that pictures grab children's attention more often than the printed words; in fact, unless adults strategically and deliberately highlight print, young children spend less than 6% of read-aloud time looking at print (Evans, Williamson, & Pursoo, 2008). However, estimates suggest that when preschool-age children are read to with a print-referencing style every day for 10 minutes they may fixate on print 20,000 times more often than children who are read to in a way that does not draw their attention to print (Justice et al., 2008). As stipulated by Vygotskian theory, these studies indicate the importance of teachers for increasing children's interest in and knowledge about print through meaningful social interactions (Vygotsky, 1978).

What Aspects of Print Knowledge Are Taught?

The print-referencing technique is used primarily to develop children's emergent literacy skills and knowledge within the domain of print knowledge. Emergent literacy can be defined as the time before conventional reading and writing begins, including the skills, knowledge, attitudes, and experiences within a literate culture that precede conventional literacy (Sulzby & Teale, 1996). Marie Clay is credited as the leader of the movement toward viewing emergent literacy as an important and observable period of reading development (see Clay, 2000). As discussed by Clay and others, children progress through a series of developmental stages as they acquire literacy; from ages 3 to 5 years, typically, children are in the emergent stage of reading (Chall, 1996). The emergent reader is developing important knowledge about the forms and functions of print that, coupled with developing skills in oral language and phonological awareness, will serve as a foundation for later achievements in word recognition and reading comprehension.

Regarding print knowledge, specifically, children learn concepts such as book handling and print conventions or that letters and words convey a message (see Clay, 2000). The following four broad domains of print knowledge may be addressed using print referencing (Justice & Ezell, 2000, 2002, 2004):

1. Print as an object of meaning
2. Book organization and print conventions
3. Alphabet knowledge
4. Concept of word

Although not a lockstep hierarchy, children typically understand early developing concepts, such as print conventions and functions of print, before later developing concepts, such as learning to recognize letters and words (Justice & Ezell, 2004; Lomax & McGee, 1987). Adults use print referencing to target different aspects of print knowledge according to children's level of understanding so that instruction occurs within the child's zone of proximal development (ZPD; Vygotsky, 1978), including increasing the complexity of talk about print as children's understanding of print increases. The four broad domains of print knowledge encompass 15 specific *print targets* (Justice, Sofka, Sutton, & Zucker, 2006). Table 1 provides a definition of each print target followed by specific examples that are ordered in the hypothetical progression of the four broad print knowledge domains.

A central goal of print referencing is to engage emergent readers in conversations about print that foster metalinguistic awareness. Metalinguistic awareness is one's ability to consider language—whether spoken or written—as an object of attention. When adults use print referencing in read-alouds, they promote children's metalinguistic awareness by encouraging children to consider written language (i.e., print) as an object of attention while also modeling specific words one may use to talk about and negotiate the forms and functions of written language. This vocabulary provides a "functional 'tool'" (Vygotsky, 1934/1986, p. 107) that may further support children's interests in and conversations about print as they internalize words describing written language

(e.g., *read, write, story, word, page, book, letter, capital, spell*). Children who enter formal reading instruction with limited vocabulary concerning print may be at risk for reading difficulties because this vocabulary is entrenched in formal reading instruction (van Kleeck, 1990).

What Is the Scientific Basis for Print Referencing?

A large body of empirical work provides evidence for the potential value of print referencing, making it an appropriate technique for reading teachers seeking to use evidence-based practices. These studies have provided rich qualitative descriptions of the ways adults may mediate children's interactions with print (Clay, 1991; Snow & Ninio, 1986) plus experimental investigations of how specific adult behaviors influence the amount of time children spend looking at print in books (Evans et al., 2008) or the frequency of children's responses about print (Girolametto, Weitzman, Lefebvre, & Greenberg, 2007). Studies have also used survey data to show that parental reports of how often they explicitly teach their children about print during literacy activities, including readalouds, is positively associated with their children's emergent literacy skills (Sénéchal, LeFevre, Thomas, & Daley, 1998).

Convincing evidence for the positive impact of print referencing comes from several recent studies that have sought to explicitly test whether print referencing improves children's print knowledge using experimental methods in which one group of children receives print referencing and others do not. Experimental methods that feature random assignment provide strong evidence of the causal impacts of a particular instructional approach (in this case, children's exposure to print referencing) and associated changes in child outcomes (in this case, children's print knowledge growth over time). We provide an overview of these studies, and encourage readers to review the original works for specific details.

In an initial study of print referencing, published in 2000 by Justice and Ezell, researchers randomly assigned 28 parent–child pairs (14 in an experimental group, 14 in a control group) to implement a 16-session book reading program in their homes over a four-week period. The children were 4 years old and had typically developing language ability as assessed through standardized testing. Parents received one new book per week to use in their home reading sessions. Prior to the home reading program parents in the experimental group viewed a 10-minute video that modeled for them how to integrate verbal and nonverbal references to print into reading sessions. Parents in the control group were told only to read the books as they normally would with their children. Comparison of children's gains on an emergent literacy assessment battery conducted before and after their four-week reading programs showed that children in the experimental group exhibited significantly greater growth on measures of print concepts, concept of word, and word identification.

In a related study, Justice and Ezell (2002) randomly assigned 30 children (15 in an experimental group, 15 in a control group) to complete a 24-session book reading program held over eight weeks in a preschool center. The children ranged in age from 3 to 5 years, had typically developing language ability, and were from lower income households. Each child completed small-group reading sessions, and a total of eight book titles were rotated through the reading sessions. The single difference between the reading program for the children in the experimental group and those in the control group was that the former included nine references to print in each reading session whereas the latter included nine references to pictures. Children in the experimental group showed significantly greater growth from pretest to posttest on measures of alphabet knowledge, concept of word, and word identification.

Table 1 Print Targets Addressed Through Print-Referencing Read-Alouds in Early Childhood Settings

Print Targets	Definition/Examples
Print Meaning Domain	
Print Function	The function of print is to carry meaning; some special typefaces convey meaning. Sometimes print appears in illustrations (e.g., visible sound).
	• "These are fox's words—he's talking."
	• "These words are red because he's angry."
Environmental Print	Words present in the environment are portrayed in illustrations (e.g., signs, labels, lists, calendars, recipes, etc.).
	• "This jar has the word *Cookies* on it."
	• "Let's read these traffic signs."
Concept of Reading	The function of reading is to convey information or tell a story. There are many things we do when we read.
	• "If I want to find out how they solve this problem I will have to keep reading."
	• "Who can tell me some things we do when we read?"
Book & Print Organization Domain	
Page Order	The order in which book pages are read (i.e., the physical act of manipulating a book).
	• "I read this page first and this page next."
	• "Where is the front of the book?"
Title of Book	The role of the title as a label and to convey meaning.
	• "This is the half title page. It tells us the name of the book again."
	• "The title page tells us this was published in New York."
Top and Bottom of Page	Reading in English occurs from top of the page to the bottom of the page.
	• "This is the top of the page. The writing starts here."
	• (move finger down page) "I will read this top line, then this line, and then this last line."
Print Direction	Reading in English must occur from left to right. Some text is printed with unusual orientations or shapes to convey meaning.
	• (sweep finger under print) "When I read I go this way."
	• "These words are printed at an angle so they'll look like they're splashing into the water."
Author's Role	The role of the author(s)/illustrator(s).
	• "The author is the person who wrote the words in this book."
	• "The author wrote a dedication to his mother."
Letters Domain	
Names of Letters	There are names for all 26 letters.
	• "I see a word on this page that starts with an *R!*"
	• "Who can find a letter *S*?"
Concept of Letter	The purpose of letters in forming words. The same letters can be used in many ways.
	• "I see the same letter in these two words."
	• "There are three letters in the word *cat*."
Upper and Lower Case Letters	Letters come in two forms.
	• "This is a capital *D*. Damian has a capital *D* in his name."
	• "Uppercase *S* is the same shape as lowercase *s*."
Words Domain	
Concept of Word in Print	Words are distinct units of print and are different from letters.
	• "Let's count the words on this page."
	• "Who can show me just one word?"
Words Domain	
Short vs. Long Words	Words have different structures. Some words are short, others are long.
	• "*Dinosaur* is a long word. It has lots of letters."
	• "Which word is longer—*vegetable* or *soup*?"

(continued)

Table 1 Print Targets Addressed Through Print-Referencing Read-Alouds in Early Childhood Settings *(continued)*

Print Targets	Definition/Examples
Letters vs. Words	Letters make up words. • "This is the letter *G*. It is in the word *grow* and *garden*." • "This is the word *sun*. *S-u-n* spells sun."
Word Identification	Some familiar or meaningful words can be identified. • "This is a picture of a tomato. The word *tomato* is written beside it." • "This is the word *the*. It's in this book a lot!"

Adapted from Justice, Sofka, Sutton, & Zucker. (2006). Adapted with permission.

Of particular relevance to the present audience, a recent replication involved testing the impact of print referencing when implemented by preschool teachers during whole-group, classroom read-alouds over an entire academic year. This large scale multistate study is called Project STAR (Sit Together and Read) and will ultimately involve replication tests in 90 early childhood classrooms and 90 early childhood special education classrooms. Results from an initial cohort involving 106 4-year-old children randomly sampled from 23 need-based Project STAR classrooms indicated that children who experienced daily whole-group read-alouds in which teachers used print referencing showed significantly greater gains on three measures of print knowledge (name-writing ability, alphabet knowledge, print concepts) from fall to spring compared with children who received "business-as-usual" read-alouds with the same set of books and the same schedule of reading (see Justice et al., 2009). The major difference between this study and previous experimental studies of print referencing is that this study involved implementation of print referencing by classroom teachers for an entire academic year in their whole-group read-alouds; additionally, the 106 children studied showed more diversity than prior samples with respect to cultural backgrounds and level of achievement.

Other researchers have found similar positive effects for print referencing. Notably, Lovelace and Stewart (2007) studied the effectiveness of using non-evocative print-referencing (i.e., commenting, tracking, and pointing) with preschoolers with language impairment. This study involved a single-subject research design and five 4- to 5-year-old children who participated in regular one-on-one read-alouds conducted in the classroom setting by research personnel. Children in this study made significant growth in knowledge of print concepts over the intervention period. Taken together, the convergent findings across research studies involving various implementers (e.g., parents, teachers, research personnel), various recipients (e.g., children who are developing typically, children who have developmental disabilities), and various settings (e.g., classrooms, homes, clinics) provide strong and consistent evidence that use of print referencing within the familiar contexts of read-alouds is a useful method for improving emergent readers' knowledge about print.

Suggestions for Print Referencing

Thus far we have explained the "what" and the "why" behind print referencing; that is, we have defined what techniques adults can use to reference 15 print targets (see Table 1) and we have summarized several research studies demonstrating the effectiveness of print referencing for increasing emergent readers' print knowledge. Now we turn to important questions about when, how, and with what texts print referencing should be used to derive suggestions for reading teachers and classroom teachers to effectively integrate print referencing into their larger curriculum. We offer suggestions from previous research and from our own study of transcripts of teachers who have strategically encouraged their 4-year-old students to engage with print during Project STAR read-alouds (Justice et al., 2009).

When and How Do Teachers Integrate Print Referencing?

Instructional time is a precious commodity in classrooms; accordingly, teachers want to know how to make the most of every minute. Thus, teachers may wonder how often they ought to reference print when reading. As a general guideline, our suggestion is that print referencing should be used when it seems to add value to a read-aloud experience in terms of furthering children's print knowledge. What this means is that when teachers are reading books with children with the intent of promoting their literacy development, print referencing can be incorporated. For instance, many preschool classrooms start their day with a group read-aloud that serves explicit instructional purposes relevant to the classroom curriculum or state learning standards. In such cases, this read-aloud provides an exemplary opportunity to incorporate print referencing as a means to heighten children's attention to and learning about print. Most of the available work on benefits attributable to adult use of print referencing has featured children's participation in only one read-aloud per day for three or four days per week (e.g., Justice & Ezell, 2002; Lovelace & Stewart, 2007). Consequently, it seems that in the typical preschool classroom, if children could participate in one small- or large-group read-aloud per day that involves opportunities to learn and talk about print, benefits to their print knowledge would be apparent.

Within these read-alouds, it is reasonable to ask how much attention, exactly, the teacher should direct to print. Generally, teachers must be strategic in considering how much attention to print should occur to promote children's learning about the forms and functions of print while not detracting from the reading experience or other benefits that might be gained from that experience (e.g., learning new vocabulary words, developing content knowledge). In Project STAR, teachers deliberately highlighted two specific print targets during a read-aloud (e.g., print function, page order) and addressed these using varying combinations of techniques to highlight print (e.g., commenting, tracking) and varying amounts of scaffolding to differentiate for individual students' understandings of the print target. In instances when it seems that children just do not want to talk about print, teachers can rely on nonverbal techniques to draw children's attention to interesting aspects of print within texts because adults' verbal references to print (i.e., questions and comments) and nonverbal references to print (i.e., tracking print) both increase the amount of time children spend looking at print during read-alouds (Justice et al., 2008).

Let's look at an excerpt from a read-aloud of *The Way I Feel* (Cain, 2000) that shows how a teacher leverages a combination of print referencing techniques to evoke children's attention to and consideration of print in the book. The teacher is discussing the heading on a page about feeling shy; the word *shy* is printed in a thin, pink typeface against a pastel background.

Teacher: Now you can barely see the **word** *shy*. It's in light pink. You see it right there? (Points to word)

Child: Yeah.

Teacher: (Tracks letters as she spells) **S-H-Y.** It's hiding in the page, because even the **word** is shy. (She hides her face behind the book as if she is shy.) Shy is an interesting word that we should talk about. We read a book about a shy character last week. Do you remember what we said *shy* means?

This excerpt is useful for consideration, as it illustrates how print referencing can be used alongside other techniques that can promote children's language growth within the read-aloud. There is tremendous value in read-alouds that focus on narrative events or vocabulary in the book (Sipe, 2008; Teale, 2003); teachers should ensure that inclusion of a focus on print does not preclude other opportunities for talking about interesting words, text structures, or story content.

Print referencing can be used alongside other techniques that can promote children's language growth within the read-aloud.

How Can Teachers Fully Engage Children When Using Print Referencing?

Print referencing read-alouds require teachers to pay careful attention to individual characteristics of children, including their orientation toward literacy and their desire and need for active engagement in interactions with teachers. Particularly for those at-risk for later reading difficulties, it is important to use social activities like read-alouds to foster a positive orientation to literacy. When adults embed print references into book reading, lively discussions about print unfold because young children typically find print as interesting as other text stimuli, such as illustrations; this can promote children's positive orientation toward literacy. Project STAR teachers used a variety of methods to make discussions exciting and fun. Many teachers, for example, linked the printed text to meaningful print in the children's lives. In this excerpt from a discussion of *Rumble in the Jungle* (Andreae, 1996), the teacher points to the word *tiger* and connects the print to children's own names (all names are pseudonyms).

Teacher: Look at this **word** boys and girls. This **word** begins with a **T,** like Tim's name begins with a **T.** Can you think of any other **words** that begin with **T**—like *Tim* and *tiger?*

Research has indicated that children's names constitute a unit of print that is of great interest to young children (Clay, 2000; Treiman & Broderick, 1998).

In other sections of this read-aloud this teacher demonstrates sensitivity to students' attentional focus by finding creative ways to actively engage students with print. She encouraged a kinesthetic response to print by asking students to "skywrite" the letter Z during *Rumble in the Jungle* (Andreae, 1996).

Teacher: Now who do we have?

Children: Zebras!

Teacher: The zebras. That's right. Look, here's the **letter Z.** Put your finger up and let's make the **letter Z.** (Teacher and children point their index finger in air and move their arms together, the teacher with her back to the children so as to not confuse the orientation of the letter.) Across, slant down, and then back across.

In addition, Project STAR teachers asked children to come forward and point to print or turn pages during reading, thereby actively involving children with print.

Young children will comment on or ask questions about print, particularly when print is made salient through features like speech bubbles or as environmental print embedded in illustrations (Smolkin, Conlon, & Yaden, 1988). Teachers should encourage children's spontaneous comments about print during read-alouds by spending time following a child's lead when print is discussed; this communicates that the child's point of view is valuable.

What Are Appropriate Texts for Print Referencing?

As we turn to the question of which texts are best suited to print referencing, it is important to take a step back and consider why the print itself is worthy of our attention. Sipe (2008) explained that children's picture books provide a sophisticated visual aesthetic experience that in many ways is like an art form in which print is a key aspect:

Navigating picturebooks requires that we pay attention to every feature, from the front cover and the dust jacket to the back cover . . . We should speculate (along with children) on why the illustrator, designer, or editor made these choices, communicating to children that every single detail of the book—down to the typefaces, the size and shape of the book, and the placement of the illustrations on the pages—is the result of somebody's calculated decision.

As Sipe pointed out, all elements of a book's design communicate meaning and warrant attention for reasons beyond learning how to handle a book or name its parts; there is interdependence between the printed text and the pictures in creating the full story. When considering features of print within children's books, it is often possible to see how the illustrator or author use a visual "language" through such features of typeface as colors (e.g., bright colors suggest happiness/optimism), lines (e.g., jagged fonts suggest anxiety/pressure), and orientations (e.g., horizontal is stable, whereas diagonal words suggest motion). In high print salience books, a term which describes children's books with a high frequency of interesting print features, texts and pictures are completely interdependent because print is embedded in illustrations through speech balloons, visible sounds, or environmental print labeling objects in illustrations (e.g., the word *honey* on a jar). Print salient books are particularly amenable to creating a context in which print referencing is a natural fit to the read-aloud experience.

Table 2 Print Salient Features

Print in Illustrations					Print in Body of Text	
Labels	**Environmental Print**	**Visible Speech**	**Visible Sound**	**Letters in Isolation**	**Font Changes**	**Bold or Unique Fonts**
Diagrams, figures, or photos contain a print label.	Object has a label, word, or letter on it, often on everyday objects (e.g., jar labeled "Cookies" or "Stop" sign).	Character has words or speech balloons nearby indicating it is speaking.	Character or object has a sound written nearby (e.g., /grrr/ near a tiger, "clunk" near a wheel).	Letters are printed in isolation, as may occur in an alphabet book.	Changes to font color/size/ orientation (e.g., words are written at an angle or in an arc or swirl instead of standard horizontal).	Font changes (e.g., from **serif** to **block** or artistic) including bold, italics, or underlining.

In this transcript, the teacher discusses how two different typefaces in *The Way I Feel* (Cain, 2000) carry noteworthy meaning. She discusses the heading word *silly* that is written in a rainbow of colors with a curly font that follows a wavelike orientation. The *S* and the dot of the lowercase *I* have small eyes drawn within so that they appear cross-eyed.

Teacher: Look at that **word** *Silly*. How does that **word** look?

Several children: Silly

Teacher: It looks silly! (Points to plainer typeface below) Do those **words** look the same?

Children: No.

Teacher: (Points to silly again) What do they have on these **letters?**

Children: Eyes!

Teacher: Eyes!

Child: Eyes in S.

Teacher: So the **letters** look like the **words** feel in this book . . . They look silly. That's the word *silly.*

Child: The word's silly?

Teacher: Yes, and that's the way he feels on this page.

Teachers should use print referencing with high print salience texts as well as with texts that do not have particularly interesting print features. Nonetheless, high print salience texts, like the one in this example, can provide a natural springboard for talking about print targets such as how print carries meaning or functions in the environment (Zucker, Justice, & Piasta, in press). There are many examples of high-quality children's literature that contain print salient visual aesthetic elements, including popular titles and classics; and print salient texts extend beyond the genre of alphabet books, which are also known to promote talk about print (e.g., Bradley & Jones, 2007). Table 2 provides a simplified version of a rubric we have used to analyze the occurrence of print salient features in texts, and Table 3 lists some high print salience texts coded on this rubric. It is likely that analyzing your

Table 3 Texts Containing Print Salient Features

Text (Author)	Illustrations					Text	
	Labels	**Environmental Print**	**Visible Speech**	**Visible Sound**	**Letters in Isolation**	**Font Changes**	**Bold or Unique Fonts**
Big Plans (Shea & Smith, 2008)		+				+	+
Bunny Cakes (Wells, 2000)		+				+	+
Fancy Nancy (O'Connor, 2006)		+				+	
Growing Vegetable Soup (Ehlert, 1993)	+	+					+
I Stink (McMullan, 2002)			+	+	+	+	+
Miss Bindergarten Gets Ready for Kindergarten (Slate, 1996)		+			+	+	+
The Noisy Airplane Ride (Downs, 2005)	+			+		+	+
Rumble in the Jungle (Andreae, 1996)				+		+	+
Truck (Crews, 1997)		+					
The Way I Feel (Cain, 2000)	+					+	+

library collection with an eye toward the important ways that print carries meaning will produce several titles through which meaningful discussions about print can occur.

Get More From a Read-Aloud

Daily classroom read-alouds provide an important context for supporting children's emergent literacy skills, particularly children's developing knowledge of print forms and functions. Although read-alouds are a fairly commonplace activity within most early childhood classrooms, evidence suggests that this activity is most often used as a time to discuss story meaning or comprehension skills; too often, educators do not take advantage of this activity as an opportunity to develop children's print-related skills. This article provides guidance to educators, including reading specialists, regarding how print referencing may be used to increase children's knowledge about print, and, as importantly, to support children's development of an interest in print as a salient feature of many texts.

In the present educational climate, educators are being pressed to use instructional techniques that do many things at once. Regarding emergent literacy instruction, educators are asked to use techniques that are linked to state standards of learning and that have scientific support with respect to demonstrated increases in students' learning, while simultaneously ensuring that these techniques are developmentally appropriate, engaging and motivating, and sensitive to the diverse needs of their students. These are indeed tall orders! In the present article, we discussed a simple, inexpensive, and likely high-yield technique that early educators may easily implement and that we believe achieves all of these aims. Educators can take a few small steps such as the following to get started tomorrow on making print referencing a systematic component of their literacy instruction.

- **Determine which read-aloud within your classroom will regularly involve your use of print referencing techniques.** These may be large-group or small-group sessions. Just be sure that every child in the classroom is involved!
- **Examine the 15 targets presented in Table 1. Order these over the remaining weeks of school so that one or two targets are addressed in each reading session.** There are many ways to organize the targets: you might rotate these daily (a different target each day) or by week. It's up to you—the important thing is to ensure that all of the targets receive attention during an academic year and that you revisit print targets as necessary to ensure children's understanding of print.
- **Examine your classroom library or school library to select books that feature a high level of print salience.** You might use the rubric in Table 2. Try to secure a collection of 20 or 30 books that you can read aloud repeatedly over the year to address your selected targets. You might rotate books daily or use one book for a week. Regardless, be sure that children have multiple opportunities to hear each book, as this seems an important component of most print referencing studies to date.

Note

This research was supported by Grant R305F050124 from the U.S. Department of Education, Institute of Education Sciences.

References

Adams, M.J. (1990). *Beginning to read: Thinking and learning about print*. Cambridge, MA: MIT Press.

Bradley, B.A., & Jones, J. (2007). Sharing alphabet books in early childhood classrooms. *The Reading Teacher, 60*(5), 452–463. doi:10.1598/RT.60.5.5.

Chall, J.S. (1996). *Stages of reading development* (2nd ed.). Fort Worth, TX: Harcourt Brace.

Clay, M. (2000). *Concepts about print: What have children learned about the way we print language?* Portsmouth, NH: Heinemann.

Clay, M.M. (1991). Introducing a new storybook to young readers. *The Reading Teacher, 45*(4), 264–273. doi:10.1598/RT.45.4.2.

Evans, M.A., & Saint-Aubin, J. (2005). What children are looking at during shared storybook reading: Evidence from eye movement monitoring. *American Psychological Society, 16*(11), 913–920.

Evans, M.A., Williamson, K., & Pursoo, T. (2008). Preschoolers' attention to print during shared book reading. *Scientific Studies of Reading, 12*(1), 106–129. doi:10.1080/10888430701773884.

Ezell, H.K., & Justice, L.M. (2000). Increasing the print focus of adult-child shared book reading through observational learning. *American Journal of Speech-Language Pathology, 9*(1), 36–47.

Girolametto, L., Weitzman, E., Lefebvre, P., & Greenberg, J. (2007). The effects of in-service education to promote emergent literacy in child care centers: A feasibility study. *Language, Speech, and Hearing Services in Schools, 38*(1), 72–83. doi:10.1044/01611461(2007/007).

Justice, L.M., & Ezell, H.K. (2000). Enhancing children's print and word awareness through home-based parent intervention. *American Journal of Speech-Language Pathology, 9*(3), 257–269.

Justice, L.M., & Ezell, H.K. (2002). Use of storybook reading to increase print awareness in at-risk children. *American Journal of Speech-Language Pathology, 1* (1), 17–29. doi:10.1044/10580360(2002/003).

Justice, L.M., & Ezell, H.K. (2004). Print referencing: An emergent literacy enhancement strategy and its clinical applications. *Language, Speech, and Hearing Services in Schools, 35*(2), 185–193. doi:10.1044/0161-1461(2004/018).

Justice, L.M., Kaderavek, J.N., Fan, X., Sofka, A., & Hunt, A. (2009). Accelerating preschoolers' early literacy development through classroom-based teacher–child storybook reading and explicit print referencing. *Language, Speech, and Hearing Services in Schools, 40*(1), 67–85. doi:10.1044/0161-1461(2008/07-0098).

Justice, L.M., Pullen, P.C., & Pence, K. (2008). Influence of verbal and nonverbal references to print on preschoolers' visual attention to print during storybook reading. *Developmental Psychology, 44*(3), 855–866. doi:10.1037/0012-1649.44.3.855.

Justice, L.M., Sofka, A.E., Sutton, M., & Zucker, T.A. (2006). *Project STAR: Fidelity coding checklist*. Charlottesville: Preschool Language and Literacy Lab, University of Virginia.

Lane, H.B., & Wright, T.L. (2007). Maximizing the effectiveness of reading aloud. *The Reading Teacher, 60*(7), 668–675. doi:10.1598/RT.60.7.7.

Lomax, R.G., & McGee, L.M. (1987). Young children's concepts about print and reading: Toward a model of word reading acquisition. *Reading Research Quarterly, 22*(2), 237–256. doi:10.2307/747667.

Lovelace, S., & Stewart, S.R. (2007). Increasing print awareness in preschoolers with language impairment using non-evocative print referencing. *Language, Speech, and Hearing Services in Schools, 38*(1), 16–30. doi:10.1044/0161-1461(2007/003).

Sénéchal, M., LeFevre, J., Thomas, E.M., & Daley, K.E. (1998). Differential effects of home literacy experiences on the development of oral and written language. *Reading Research Quarterly, 33*(1), 96–116. doi:10.1598/RRQ.33.1.5.

Sipe, L.R. (2008). *Storytime: Young children's literary understanding in the classroom.* New York: Teachers College Press.

Smolkin, L.B., Conlon, A., & Yaden, D.B. (1988). Print salient illustrations in children's picture books: The emergence of written language awareness. In J.E. Readence & R.S. Baldwin (Eds.), *Dialogues in literacy research* (37th yearbook of the National Reading Conference, pp. 59–68). Chicago, IL: National Reading Conference.

Snow, C.E., & Ninio, A. (1986). The contracts of literacy: What children learn from learning to read books. In W.H. Teale & E. Sulzby (Eds.), *Emergent literacy: Writing and reading* (pp. 116–137). Norwood, NJ: Ablex.

Sulzby, E., & Teale, W. (1996). Emergent literacy. In R. Barr, M.L. Kamil, P.B. Mosenthal, & P.D. Pearson (Eds.), *Handbook of reading research* (Vol. 2, pp. 727–757). Mahwah, NJ: Erlbaum.

Teale, W.H. (2003). Reading aloud to children as a classroom instructional activity: Insights from research to practice. In A. van Kleeck, A.A. Stahl, & E.B. Bauer (Eds.), *On reading books to children: Parents and teachers* (pp. 109–133). Mahwah, NJ: Erlbaum.

Treiman, R., & Broderick, V. (1998). What's in a name: Children's knowledge about the letters in their own names. *Journal of Experimental Child Psychology, 70*(2), 97–116. doi:10.1006/jecp.1998.2448.

van Kleeck, A. (1990). Emergent literacy: Learning about print before learning to read. *Topics in Language Disorders, 10*(2), 25–45.

Vygotsky, L.S. (1978). *Mind in society: The development of higher psychological processes* (M. Cole, V. John-Steiner, S. Scribner, & E. Souberman, Eds. & Trans.). Cambridge, MA: Harvard University Press.

Vygotsky, L.S. (1986). *Thought and language* (A. Kozulin, Trans.). Cambridge, MA: MIT Press. (Original work published 1934.)

What Works Clearinghouse, Institute of Education Sciences. (2007, January). *Interactive shared book reading.* Retrieved June 20, 2008, from http://ies.ed.gov/ncee/wwc/pdf/WWC _ISBR_011807.pdf.

Zucker, T.A., Justice, L.M., & Piasta, S.B. (in press). Prekindergarten teachers' verbal references to print during classroom-based large-group shared reading. *Language, Speech, and Hearing Services in Schools.*

Children's Literature Cited

Andreae, D. (1996). *Rumble in the jungle.* London: Little Tiger Press.

Cain, J. (2000). *The way I feel.* Seattle, WA: Parenting Press.

Crews, D. (1997). *Truck.* New York: HarperCollins.

Downs, M. (2005). *The noisy airplane ride.* Berkeley, CA: Tricycle Press.

Ehlert, L. (1993). *Growing vegetable soup.* San Diego: Harcourt.

McMullan, K. (2002). *I stink!* New York: HarperCollins.

O'Connor, J. (2006). *Fancy Nancy.* New York: HarperCollins.

Shea, B., & Smith, L. (2008). *Big plans.* New York: Hyperion.

Slate, J. (1996). *Miss Bindergarten gets ready for kindergarten.* New York: Dutton.

Wells, R. (2000). *Bunny cakes.* New York: Puffin.

Critical Thinking

1. You have been asked to present a brief description of print referencing for parents at the Back-to-School Night. Prepare a five-minute presentation or demonstration.

2. Find three books *not* listed by Zucker, Ward, & Justice that you could recommend to parents during your presentation at the Back-to-School Night. Prepare a table like Table 3 in the article to illustrate why your selected books are appropriate for teaching print referencing.

ZUCKER is a postdoctoral research fellow at the University of Texas Health Science Center—Houston, USA; e-mail tricia.zucker@uth.tmc.edu. **WARD** is a doctoral student at the University of Virginia, Charlottesville, USA; e-mail aew9b@virginia.edu. **JUSTICE** teaches at The Ohio State University, Columbus, USA; e-mail ljustice@ehe.osu.edu.

Supporting the Literacy Development of Children Living in Homeless Shelters

Insights into how educators can create greater classroom support for homeless children, particularly in literacy learning and development, are provided in this article.

Laurie MacGillivray, Amy Lassiter Ardell, and Margaret Sauceda Curwen

Diego was incredible. He had just come from Mexico and he had the most incredible vocabulary. Just a tremendous vocabulary. He just spoke English so beautifully . . . I asked her [Diego's mom] and she said that he had learned it watching TV and also by talking to people in the hotel that was the shelter . . . whoever he was talking to could have been a former university professor because this kid was just tremendous . . . [when] he told me [they were moving] . . . I said, "You've got to learn to read, and if you go to [another state] you won't have a chance to be here very long and I'm really worried about you because you've got to be in one place long enough to get reading. If you can get reading, and you go anywhere you want, then you're going to be OK." Well, Diego went home and he had a talk with his mom and then the mom came back and she said, "I was going to go to [another state], but we're not going to go. We're going to wait until the end of the school year and then we'll go. . . ." And it made me realize again the power of our words and the power that we have to influence and truly make a difference.

—First-grade teacher

Each night in the United States approximately 1.5 million children do not have a home to call their own (National Center on Family Homelessness, 2009). While homelessness is a huge problem, it is also true that any time labels are attached to children, there is a danger of stereotyping.

Educators don't intend to do a disservice, but in the absence of factual understandings of what students go through, filling in the blanks with assumptions is too easily done. No doubt the word *homeless* engenders fear and worry, and when coupled with children we tend to think of only the negative. As a result

of observing and interviewing many children and mothers, as well as social service workers, teachers, principals, and county office personnel in southern California and western Tennessee, we have learned much of what families experience during a challenging time of transition in their lives (see MacGillivray, 2010a; MacGillivray, Ardell, & Curwen, in press, to learn more about our work). Ultimately in this article we provide insights into how educators can create greater classroom support for this population, particularly in literacy learning and development. First, we present some background information about the most recent and influential national policy related to families who are homeless.

Federal Policy Defining Homelessness

The McKinney Homeless Assistance Act of 1987 defines a homeless person as one who (a) lacks a fixed, regular, and adequate nighttime residence or (b) lives in a shelter, an institution, or a place not designed for, or ordinarily used, as a sleeping accommodation for human beings. The Act is also meant to ensure that children of homeless families continue to have access to public schooling. The reauthorization of the McKinney Act by the federal No Child Left Behind Act of 2001 reiterates this guarantee, including children's right to remain in their school of origin with district-paid transportation. Still, the barriers to an uninterrupted school experience are monumental. Issues related to residency, guardianship, school records, immunization, and transportation, although addressed by this legislation, can still be obstacles to school attendance (Mawhinney-Rhoads & Stahler, 2006; Sinatra, 2007; Stronge, 2000). These impediments are best understood through a description of life in a homeless shelter.

What Living in a Homeless Shelter Means

In our research, we learned that families tend to use shelters when all other housing options have been exhausted. Many have lived with friends and extended family until the situation became unbearable due to strained interpersonal relations, insufficient space, or limited financial resources. Parents worry from night to night about where the family will sleep. Emergency or long-term homeless shelters may be the only option.

The term *homeless shelter* encompasses variety and diversity with respect to purpose (e.g., religious affiliation, domestic violence shelters), offerings and services (e.g., room, self-contained apartment, kitchen privileges), and rules for residency (e.g., curfews, mandatory meetings). The majority of family shelters serve only mothers and their children. This gender bias is in part explained by the fact that 84% of families experiencing homelessness are headed by women (Buron, Cortes, Culhane, Khadduri, & Poulin, 2008).

Shelters are not regulated by the government unless they are receiving federal Housing and Urban Development monies, so there are often no minimum standards or official guidelines for a homeless shelter. In our work, we visited or learned about shelters that offered families varied living arrangements ranging from apartments, a private bedroom and bath, shared sleeping space in churches, and sleeping cots assembled in an outdoor parking lot. Still, there are some general commonalities across shelters. Frequently a shelter establishes a set of rules that families must follow to maintain their residence status. Such mandates may include staying clean and sober, transferring wages or paying a nightly charge, keeping evening curfews often as early as 6:00 P.M., maintaining consistent school attendance or demonstrated job pursuit, attending mandated meetings several nights a week while children are in shelter-provided childcare, and, in some cases, staying away from the shelter when the children are in school.

Other shelter requirements affect family stability and cohesiveness. For example, 55% of the cities surveyed by the U.S. Conference of Mayors (2006) report that families may have to break up to be sheltered. With few exceptions, daughters of all ages can accompany their mothers to a shelter while sons over the age of 12 cannot. Depending on the shelter, a family's length of stay can range anywhere from six weeks to two years. Despite these variations, many goals are the same: mothers have to find a job and a safe place to live, clean up their credit, pay off utility bills, and—for some—get clean and sober. With the demand for shelter space, there is very little room for misstep on the part of families because there are always new families who will agree to abide by the shelter's expectations. Although mothers still take primary responsibility for meeting their children's needs, the shelter can also influence the types of activities available to children. These resources may include items that promote children's educational experiences such as computers and children's books.

Authors' Perspective

We examined the literacy practices of families living in homeless shelters as well as perceptions of homeless children

<table>
<tr><td>

Reflection Question

What are some of the misconceptions many people have about homeless children and their reading needs?

</td></tr>
</table>

through participant observation and interviews conducted in western Tennessee and southern California. Formal interviews took place with over 70 stakeholders including supervisors and staff at shelters for homeless families, persons related to nonprofit organizations that serve children who are homeless, principals, classroom teachers, and mothers and children staying in shelters for homeless families. Laurie (first author) also served as a participant observer in one shelter for four months, documenting informal conversations and families' interactions with text or text-related events, such as discussions about the Bible. For this article, we drew upon transcripts from the formal interviews and field notes from the observations.

Sociocultural theory framed our work and allowed us to see the critical role of context in assigning meaning to events. We used a robust definition which includes the physical, social, and geographical dimensions of context. This offered a lens to better understand literacy interactions. This is particularly true with families living in shelters because many teachers know so little about this situation. For example, when we talk about storybook reading before bedtime, we assume that children feel safe and have their own personal space to relax, but that in fact may not be the case. Our attention to larger unrelated literacy events seeks to situate reading and writing within the often looming issues of housing, employment, and health. We do not believe one's competency in literacy prevents homelessness or resolves the surrounding issues, rather we are struck by the way mothers and children take up literacy practices during a time of crisis (MacGillivray, 2010b).

Family Literacy Practices within a Shelter

Upon entering the first shelter Laurie studied, one dedicated to serving mothers and children who were victims of domestic violence, she explained to the families that she was there to document their literacy practices. The response from many families was that while they were happy to have her there, they did not believe she would see them doing anything. This reflects the prevalent misconception that only storybook reading or school-like activities count as reading and writing. Only a few weeks later, she had observed several instances within and across families of mothers and children engaging in literacy events such as passing notes across the dinner table to ensure private conversations in the large social space, studying together with flashcards at night, making Mother's Day cards, decorating their rooms with Bible verses and books from the public library, and discussing good books they had read with one another.

Awareness seemed to increase their attention to these wider practices. Mothers and children began to share with Laurie other issues that shaped their literacy practices such as how their personal collections of books were locked up in storage and how their prior journal writing practices were suspended due to the lack of privacy in the shelter. They also noted how important the public library was to them as a no-cost, safe, high-quality, family-oriented place to spend time with their children. Mothers indicated how much they relied on connections with religious institutions to help them reinvent themselves. This social connection was kept at all costs, even if it meant that they had to meet with their evening Bible study group over the phone due to nighttime curfew rules. While these examples demonstrate how life in the shelter both impedes family literacy practices and spurs families to expand upon their existing repertoire, we believe that the most significant consequence of the interaction was the value assigned to what they were doing for children in terms of modeling and facilitating literate practices.

Working with Children and Families Residing in Shelters: Five Perspectives

The daily circumstances of homelessness can easily get lost in the discussion of broad trends and generalizations. Drawing from multiple interviews and observations in southern California and western Tennessee and their surroundings areas, we selected a few key voices that offer more personal perspectives. Rather than a single in-depth case study, we decided to share five outlooks that offer an introduction to the complexity surrounding children living without homes. The voices speak of their own conditions and in that way capture how literacy can be integral to the lives of those caught in the crisis of homelessness.

In what follows, we present five points of view:

1. A director of a homeless shelter
2. A principal of a school with many students who are homeless
3. A teacher who has many students in her classroom who do not have homes
4. A parent living in a homeless shelter
5. A child living in a homeless shelter

These voices were chosen from more than 70 interviews because the individuals were articulate and brought critical issues to the forefront. In no way are they meant to be representational of the experiences found in our work; rather we hope they will nurture complex conversations about homeless children and literacy. After each perspective, we address what teachers might learn from these vignettes.

A Director of a Homeless Shelter

Laurie got to know Ms. Carpenter (all names have been changed to protect privacy) through a series of interviews. She is a director of a long-term shelter for women who are homeless, have young children, and are addicted to drugs and alcohol. During the conversations it became clear how Ms. Carpenter's identity as the director was deeply intertwined with her literate self. The quote that follows signals two key ideas. The first is Ms. Carpenter's recognition of herself as a role model. The second key point clarifies her view of how literacy could be used to equalize hierarchical relationships inherent in shelter living:

> I know that I am looked at in leadership, and they're following my lead, and I just happen to love to read, and so I bring that to the table. And I enjoy it. I love talking. I love sharing what I've found and what I'm reading, and um, and I thank God that I do model a behavior that the women like. So part of [mothers and children] interacting with me is, "Ms. Carpenter let me tell you what I read.". . . We talk about a book we love.

Evidence of Ms. Carpenter's belief in literacy's potential to uplift lives is reflected in many facets of the routines established in this shelter. There is a quiet place where women can read. Daily time is set aside for mothers to read to their children. Ms. Carpenter makes it clear that all mothers need to focus on books with their children each day. In literature discussions, the mothers talk about the Bible and other types of inspirational and motivational materials. This shelter director serves as a powerful model for how to be a literate person and a leader in scaffolding the residents' own reading practices. Importantly, Ms. Carpenter creates literacy opportunities that many families who live in more permanent houses may not have.

What we found most striking at this shelter were the ways the director used literacy to foster intimacy between a mother and child. Ms. Carpenter discovered that many mothers beginning to heal from substance abuse become aware of how their own children had been hurt in the process. Ms. Carpenter explained that this realization can sometimes make mothers hesitant to hold their children. One of the reasons she mandated daily reading time was because "it is the most powerful and effective way that we start bonding between our mothers and our children." Storybook time then serves as a back door to intimacy. As a family read storybooks together, Ms. Carpenter noticed how over time they tended to scoot closer together. Read-alouds became a way to not only strengthen literacy practices but also to nurture parent–child relationships.

What can teachers learn from this example? Homelessness does not necessarily rule out the significance that reading and writing can play in individual lives. In fact, a shelter can actually increase a family's exposure to a variety of adults who have the potential to serve as models. There are often teachers, professional or volunteer, who are present for evening tutoring. Case managers and shelter staff can be influential in creating structural changes, such as schedules and events in which literacy plays a key role. They can also engage in individual acts such as recommending a book or inquiring into a book's plot. Certainly we do not want to deny the presence of negative models in shelters, which are filled with adults and children in crisis. Nor do we want to create the sense that shelter staff members, already busy with a multitude of tasks and pressing priorities, always make literacy a top priority. But what we see here is the opportunity for adults who can act as extended and supportive forces in the lives of families in crisis. As educators, we must all first recognize the potential and possibility even in the most seemingly unlikely places.

Principal of an Elementary School

One of our more inspiring stories came from an interview with the principal of an elementary school that served a majority homeless population of students. As a result, district officials communicated with the principal that they would understand that her school's test scores might be affected by issues of poverty and transience. Determined to prove otherwise, this administrator organized an action plan that included, among other things, holding intake meetings with each new family, scheduling immediate academic assessments for each new student, fostering ties with the community to bring resources to the school site, and maintaining high academic expectations for all students. As a result of such deliberate action, her school's test scores rose and the site was granted an official recognition of excellence from the state. She explained that viewing her new students only as bright and capable, while also paying attention to their specific academic, personal, and social needs, contributed to the school's rise. For example, she pointed out that many families and children were often reluctant to identify themselves as living in a shelter. Many teachers, therefore, were not always aware which students in their class, if any, were homeless. The key in these situations was to address social issues such as homelessness within the context of the regular curriculum, to be prepared with knowledge of community resources, and to be well-informed of families' fundamental rights should children identify themselves as homeless.

What can teachers learn from this example? Individual children's needs across all areas of their life—academic, social, and emotional—are important to take into account. Immediate academic assessments helped teachers to address children's needs. Intake meetings helped school officials understand the family's unique situation, and were particularly helpful in this case because the school was so well-networked in the community. For example, the school's staff could help families instantly by providing backpacks with school supplies, assisting with paperwork associated with enrolling in free lunch programs, and arranging regular site visits of a mobile health care clinic so that children could have their health needs addressed. Because many families struggle with the stigma associated with the label of homelessness, personal relationships established during an intake meeting help them to transition to a new schooling institution quickly. Moreover, a message of respect and concern is communicated by the school.

A Classroom Teacher

A few years ago, Laurie got to know a remarkable first-grade teacher who works in a school with a high rate of children who are homeless. This educator's focus on the classroom environment reflects a deep sensitivity to the challenging lives of many of her students. Many of them are precariously housed; their day-to-day lives do not preclude sleeping in different places. In the midst of chaotic lives, this teacher considers her classroom to be an oasis. Fresh flowers are just as important as basics such as paper towels and soap, which she supplies. Her explicit intention is to make the parents and children feel that the classroom is their home and to offer a tranquil place to learn (Monkman, MacGillivray, & Leyva, 2003).

This sensitivity was also evident in her curriculum. For example, during a lesson in which the first-grade children were making three-dimensional habitats, the students started making connections to their own difficult living conditions. As Laurie and her colleagues wrote in an earlier article,

> Many of the children talked about overcrowded apartments and the homes they wished to have in the future. Through a variety of [quality children's] literature, such as *A House Is a House for Me* (Hoberman, 1978) the teacher encouraged the children to think beyond a literal notion of a house as the current place where one lives. The students were encouraged to reflect, look toward the future, and imagine possibilities. (MacGillivray, Rueda, & Martinez, 2004, p. 151)

During a lesson in which the first-grade children were making three-dimensional habitats, the students started making connections to their own difficult living conditions.

This teacher responded to the children's talk and more notably also created a space for them to address their situations in the curriculum.

What can teachers learn from this example? Our actions as teachers and the ways we think about our classrooms are critical. This teacher saw the need for her room to be a place of comfort for parents and children. To accomplish this goal she sometimes spent her own money to purchase basic materials. In the first-grade curriculum, understanding one's home and place in the surrounding community is a typical social studies theme that she seamlessly adapted to include children's background experiences. It might have been easier to quickly move to another assignment due to a discomfort in dealing with the children's realities. Instead she opened up the notion of what homes can be. She created a space for children to talk about the realities of their lives, something that is often overlooked in a crowded school day's schedule. Through re-imagining their lives, she encouraged children to look forward and to envision alternatives.

A Parent Living in a Homeless Shelter

We have met many amazing parents during our work with families who are living without homes. We selected Lacey because she is one example of a mother with literacy practices of her own and a desire for her child to be a strong reader and writer. She is a 25-year-old single mother of a 22-month-old son. She lives in a long-term shelter in which she has her own apartment.

Growing up, Lacey was one of five children and even though her mother worked steadily, sometimes holding down two jobs, they were homeless three or four times. She herself became homeless after economic and domestic stress ended her marriage. Lacey has been in this shelter for four months and has created the environment with her son in mind. She shared, "Everything that I buy him, I want it to be a learning experience from the fridgerator [sic] to the restroom to his room is a learning experience for him."

Lacey dropped out of high school in ninth grade, but she loves to read and write and has aspirations to someday start a magazine for teenagers to satisfy what she perceives as an unfilled niche in the marketplace. She describes her reading choices as, "Mostly, um, nonfiction, I got some fiction, um love novels, um it just depends on what sparks my interest. . . ." Lacey also talked about her toddler's emergent reading behaviors, "He's not even reading the book. He was like 'chum chum chum, chum chum. . . .' And that's exactly how he sounds because he, he's reading. He can't read, but he's reading like that." Lacey's family has experienced homelessness in two generations, yet this has not stripped away the importance of reading and writing. Literacy is still the warp and weft of their lives.

What can teachers learn from this example? Parents often see their children interacting with texts beginning at a very young age but may or may not understand the significance. In this example, Lacey recognizes important behavior and she might have appreciated a teacher's insights about the developmental milestone. Through parents describing their children's out-of-school behavior and teachers sharing the children's in-school behavior, a powerful partnership can be anchored in a mutual desire to support the child. As teachers we can foster a sense of community by extending parents' understanding of their children's literacy development and making them feel critical to the learning process (Walker-Dalhouse & Risko, 2008).

A Child Living in a Homeless Shelter

The most striking thing about the children we have met is their ability to survive and often thrive under very difficult conditions. We were particularly struck by the account of one near-adolescent and his perspective into how transitory residency impacted his academic performance. Twelve-year-old Leslie was in foster care between the ages of 4 and 9 and then lived in a home for three years with his mother and four of his five siblings. During that time, he was on the honor roll at his school. Most recently, they left their house due to spousal abuse and they have been homeless for five months.

The consequences of living in a homeless shelter are often visible. Leslie, a preteen, has lost his right to be alone and complained to his mother, "I'm 12. I can't even go to the bathroom without you being right outside the door." His exasperation over the lack of privacy was exacerbated by the toll that his family's high mobility was having on his academic program. When he recently received a poor report card, his mother shared his frustrated explanation,

> It's because we're moving. We've been to four schools in the last five months. How did you expect me to do? I'm

an honor roll student. I know you expect it, but you've got to get for real. It's a lot of changes. You've got to look at it from my standpoint.

Leslie elaborated on the cost of these moves, "One school is in one thing and then when you go to another school it's a whole different thing. . . . They're all easy, it's just you miss stuff. That's what makes it harder." From the child's perspective, the struggle was not about following the same curriculum. As Leslie said, "All teachers teach differently." His strong academic skills were not enough for him to weather frequent moves. The need to grasp each teacher's instructional and communicative style overrode his academic abilities.

What can teachers learn from this example? Moments of quiet time and alone time can be especially important for children living among the commotion of others' noise. Also, helping children adapt to a new school is more than providing a uniform curriculum. Classroom communities have their unique cultures with agreed upon practices, norms, and behaviors. Conversations about classroom expectations and routines are critical to help the child acclimate to a new learning community. But more than that, as teachers, we need to be aware of our own assumptions about classroom expectations that newly arrived students might not have the time to figure out. Clarifying both the rules and the norms in a nonjudgmental, matter-of-fact way can help children transition into our classrooms.

Looking across the Perspectives

As often happens, thinking about the experiences of one particular population of students helps us to be better teachers to all of our students. Hearing these five perspectives can guide us as educators to reconsider the important part we play in the lives of children, their families, and in the community as a whole. First, like the shelter director, we can be role models integrating literacy into our lives. Listening to her experience also reminds us that we must be open to the possibility that our students may already have literate role models present in their surroundings. Knowing that these powerful allies may exist allows us to see children living in difficult circumstances in a new light. Second, the principal's voice reminds us of the important stance we take as teachers: that of advocates for children. By recognizing that we may be in a position to connect families with the community at large, we can be poised to take immediate action in addressing their needs and concerns. Third, the trio of voices from the teacher, parent, and child serve as a reminder to cultivate mutual trust. Sharing our experiences with one another can help make sense of the situation at hand. Taking on this kind of responsibility—to help create a safe, stable, and meaningful classroom environment—can be powerful in the lives of all students, and particularly for this population of children.

Suggestions for Educators

Our purpose in writing this article is to provide information that may assist educators with a better understanding of how to create greater classroom support, particularly in literacy learning and development, for children and families who are homeless.

As stated previously, these different perspectives are not representative of each group but rather offer a multifaceted glimpse into homelessness—the full implications of which are difficult to grasp. Drawing from our conversations with homeless mothers, children, and other stakeholders, we would like to make the following specific suggestions for educators. Although these recommendations are targeted for a particular student population, we see these as applying universally to professional practice.

- Remember that school is often a place of refuge, comfort, and stability. For many children, especially those who move frequently from place to place, school may be the best part of their day. Welcoming strategies to help children settle in to a new school situation such as intake meetings, immediate academic assessments, and assigning peer buddies can help ease fears children may have as they encounter a new situation. Additionally, keeping the academic expectations high while also accounting for children's basic human needs, such as adequate nutrition and sleep, means that teachers have to be flexible and thoughtful in their decision making for this population of students.

- Remember that families residing in shelters have restrictions on their time. These restrictions apply to evening as well as daytime hours. To maintain their eligibility to stay at a shelter, family members may not be in a position to attend their child's teacher meetings or school events because of the shelter's competing work or schooling requirements. Rather than interpreting parental absences as a lack of commitment to their children's education, ask families what you can do to support an ongoing partnership with them in educating their children. Phone conferences might be a good alternative, or initiating an interactive journal with the parent about what's happening at school and at home could help with teacher–parent dialogue.

- Remember that children in shelters may have less time and space for homework. While some parental outreach strategies such as newsletters, learning supports, and positive notes home are valuable (Opitz & Rasinski, 1998), the unique pulls and distractions of families living in a shelter must be recognized. As teachers, we can be flexible in homework requirements, such as providing a weekly packet of work due every seven days. This may help families who do not have their weeknights free due to mandatory meetings at the shelter.

- Remember that your role in the community can make a difference for a child and his or her family. It may seem trite, but as educators, our professional expertise and our local knowledge can ease the way for new arrivals. Educate yourself on the rights of homeless families, available community resources specific to homeless children, and available community resources for children in general. This information will allow you to advocate and network to help meet students' needs. Connecting children and their families to community institutions, such as public libraries, may also be a good idea.

- Remember that literacy plays an important role for children and families. Especially in times of crisis, it can provide a bridge for individuals to find refuge in stories of others' experiences (MacGillivray, 2010b). People often use literature to make sense of their own situation, write to record their thoughts, or read to temporarily escape from the difficulties in their own lives (Noll & Watkins, 2003). Teachers can use research-based comprehension strategies such as making connections and inferences to link texts in multiple ways to children's lives (Harvey & Goudvis, 2007; Keene & Zimmermann, 2007). Instruction need not be in the context of a formal unit on homelessness per se, but instead can address universal generalizations such as the value of diversity, tolerance, and perseverance, and the importance of community.

Homelessness is caused by economic and social problems that have yet to be solved. In many ways, children without homes are more like other students than they are different. The life challenges faced by these children can be found in homes across the social strata. For example, many of our families with homes face similar situations such as divorce, mental or physical illness, substance abuse, and job loss. As educators, the soundness of our practice comes from the time we take to learn about the lives of all the children in our classroom and from our creation of spaces where they can name, discuss, and work through issues in their lives.

References

Buron, L., Cortes, A., Culhane, D.P., Khadduri, J., & Poulin, S. (2008). *The 2007 Annual Homeless Assessment Report to Congress.* Retrieved March 11, 2009, from repository.upenn.edu/cgi/viewcontent.cgi?article=1142&context=spp_papers.

Harvey, S., & Goudvis, A. (2007). *Strategies that work: Teaching comprehension for understanding and engagement* (2nd ed.). Portsmouth, NH: Heinemann.

Keene, E.O., & Zimmermann, S. (2007). *Mosaic of thought: The power of comprehension strategy instruction* (2nd ed.). Portsmouth, NH: Heinemann.

MacGillivray, L. (2010a). "Hallelujah!" Bible-based literacy practices of children living in a homeless shelter. In L. MacGillivray (Ed), *Literacy in times of crisis: Practices and perspectives* (pp. 32–46). New York: Routledge.

MacGillivray, L. (Ed). (2010b) *Literacy in times of crisis: Practices and perspectives.* New York: Routledge.

MacGillivray, L., Ardell, A.L., & Curwen, M.S. (in press). Libraries, churches and schools: Literate lives of homeless women and children. *Urban Education.*

MacGillivray, L., Rueda, R., & Martinez, A. (2004). Listening to inner city teachers of English-language learners: Differentiating literacy instruction. In F. Boyd & C.H. Brock (Eds.), *Multicultural and multilingual literacy and language practices* (pp. 144–160). New York: Guilford.

Mawhinney-Rhoads, L., & Stahler, G. (2006). Educational policy and reform for homeless students: An overview. *Education and Urban Society, 38*(3), 288–306. doi:10.1177/0013124506286943.

Monkman, K., MacGillivray, L., & Leyva, C.H. (2003). Literacy on three planes: Infusing social justice and culture into classroom instruction. *Bilingual Research Journal, 27*(2), 245–258.

National Center on Family Homelessness. (2009). *America's youngest outcasts: State report card on child homelessness.* Newton, MA: Author. Retrieved May 27, 2009, from www.homelesschildrenamerica.org/national_extent.php.

Noll, E., & Watkins, R. (2003). The impact of homelessness on children's literacy experiences. *The Reading Teacher, 57*(4), 362–371.

Opitz, M., & Rasinski, T. (1998). *Good-bye round robin: Twenty five effective oral reading strategies.* Portsmouth, NH: Heinemann.

Sinatra, R. (2007). Literacy success with homeless children. *Journal of At-Risk Issues, 13*(2), 1–9.

Stronge, J.H. (2000). Educating homeless children and youth: An introduction. In J.H. Stronge & E. Reed-Victor (Eds.), *Educating homeless students: Promising practices* (pp. 1–19). Larchmont, NY: Eye on Education.

U.S. Conference of Mayors. (2006). *Hunger and homelessness survey.* Retrieved March 11, 2009, from usmayors.org/hungersurvey/2006/report06.pdf.

Walker-Dalhouse, D., & Risko, VJ. (2008). Homelessness, poverty, and children's literacy development. *The Reading Teacher, 62*(1), 84–86. doi:10.1598/RT.62.1.11.

Critical Thinking

1. What did you learn about families who must use homeless shelters?

2. Did this differ from your perception prior to reading this article?

3. What was the concept that most changed your thinking?

4. Select one of the suggestions at the end of the article. Complete one activity that the authors suggest that you would be able to use in the future, such as researching the resources available for homeless families in your area.

Laurie MacGillivray teaches in the College of Education at The University of Memphis, Tennessee, USA; e-mail laurie.macgillivray@memphis.edu. **Amy Lassiter Ardell** just completed a Postdoctoral Research Fellowship at the University of Southern California, Los Angeles, CA, USA; e-mail amyardell@gmail.com. **Margaret Sauceda Curwen** teaches in the College of Educational Studies at Chapman University, Orange, CA, USA; e-mail mcurwen@chapman.edu.

Note—All authors contributed equally to this article.

From *The Reading Teacher,* vol. 63, no. 5, 2010, pp. 384–392. Copyright © 2010 by International Reading Association. Reprinted by permission.

Integrating Children's Books and Literacy into the Physical Education Curriculum

JOAN C. FINGON

Introduction

Since the onset of No Child Left Behind (NCLB, 2002) schools have been focusing on raising test scores in reading and mathematics, while at the same time feeling pressured to reduce subjects such as physical education and health. It seems for many educators finding time in the school day for students' physical activity has become increasingly challenging. Yet, according to Centers for Disease Control and Prevention (CDC) the academic success of America's youth is strongly linked with their health. One approach that could enhance students' learning is through integrating more physical fitness into the curriculum. Likewise, instructional time might also be increased if physical educators and classroom teachers collaborated and shared resources.

Purpose

This article evolved based on countless discussions with graduate students about the alarming number of unhealthy and overweight children in schools today. Most of these students are elementary classroom teachers who work in high-poverty, low-income urban schools. As a result of NCLB requirements, many of these schools have been designated as 'needs improvement' mainly due to students' poor test scores on standardized tests. For the most part, teachers in these schools believe they were spending too much time on basic skills and test preparation and not enough time on other subjects such as health and physical education. What was most compelling from class conversations was that almost all teachers indicated they saw benefits in academic learning when their students were healthy. They also expressed a willingness to collaborate with physical educators and support physical education programs in their schools.

Since physical educators typically have less time with students than classroom teachers, this article supports the integration of literacy learning and physical activity in helping children succeed in school. It offers a thoughtfully prepared and annotated children's book list related to health and physical education, as well as ideas for using some of these resources in the classroom. It also reinforces how physical activity can be supported in the curriculum without taking away activity time from physical education.

Importance of Physical Activity

All children should be provided with opportunities for physical activity. It contributes in their development to lead productive and healthy lives. According to the National Center for Chronic Disease Prevention and Health Promotion (CDC), physical activity helps children:

- Build and maintain healthy bones and muscles.
- Reduce the risk of developing obesity, chronic diseases, and cardiovascular disease.
- Reduce feelings of stress, depression and anxiety.
- Increase self esteem and capacity for learning.

Benefits and Uses of Children's Literature

One way schools can support students' learning is through children's literature. Children's books give students new worlds to discover that can stimulate their imaginations as well as help them learn how to relate and interact in the real world. When children at any age discover enjoyment and pleasure in books, they develop positive attitudes toward them that usually expand to a lifetime of appreciation (Norton, 2007). Children's books also present students with opportunities to explore a wide range of topics that can help them develop and acquire new knowledge. Essentially, children's literature is effective for basic operations associated with: 1) thinking, 2) observing, 3) comparing, 4) classifying, 5) hypothesizing, 6) organizing,

7) summarizing 8) applying, and 9) criticizing (Norton, 2007, p. 11). Moreover, children's books can enhance student learning by:

- Reinforcing major concepts or ideas taught in a lesson or activity.
- Defining key vocabulary or terms.
- Helping students empathize and relate to others.
- Answering student's questions to help them understand the importance of what they are learning.

There are several ways that children's books can be utilized in the classroom. For example, one strategy called a "read aloud" involves the teacher reading a story, children's picture book, or wordless book (a book with illustrations and no text) to a small group or whole class. Read alouds provide opportunities for oral and written expression as well as time for students to question, discuss, empathize, and relate their ideas to what they are learning. Children's books can also provide enjoyment, interest, relay new knowledge, or reinforce concepts through a shared learning experience (Norton, 2007). Another strategy that is effective is called a "picture walk" whereby the teacher shows the book illustrations and highlights the key concepts without reading the actual text. Essentially, once children have had opportunities to share books it can enhance their own learning experiences.

Since literature is a crucial resource there are many possibilities for sharing and integrating children's books into the physical education curriculum. For example, one way to enhance or reinforce students' interest and attitude about physical education could be piqued by allowing students to read books about real sports heroes and heroines serving as good role models. Students can also be introduced to a variety of individual and team sports, facts about food and nutrition, exercise, and the human body through listening and sharing information provided in children's books. students may also enjoy silly or humorous poems and short stories related to school health, nutrition, recess, or games in general. Children's books related to health and physical education can also be used for book reports and small group oral presentations as well as other literacy activities. Additionally, children's books can be used as a quick warm-up activity or introduction to a lesson, during a transition period between subjects or classes, or as a follow-up or cool-down activity.

Overall, the following children's book list can be used with students interchangeably by PE and classroom teachers. This book list represents a wide range of reading levels based on the following criteria: l) accuracy and quality of information (more or less didactic or informative); 2) colorful illustrations or photographs; 3) humor including jokes and riddles; 4) usefulness of additional resources (e.g., activities, experiments, games, recipes, etc.); and 5) general interest and age appropriateness for children.

- *Eat this, not that! For Kids!* written by David Zinczenko and Matt Goulding (Rodale, 2008) is a great easy-to-read resource with colorful photographs, detailed analysis, and nutritional tips on the most popular food choices for kids. It describes the best (eat this) and worst (not that) options available at most restaurants and stores, and it is the favorite among the teachers and there are other books in this series. (K–8).
- *Eat healthy, feel great* by William and Martha Sears and Christie Watts Kelly, and wonderfully illustrated by Renee Andriana (Little Brown, 2002) uses appropriate language such as 'red, yellow and green light' foods for children to associate with in making good food choices which also includes quick and easy recipes. (K–3).
- *Food hates you too and other poems* by Robert Weinstock (Hyperion Books, 2009), is a superbly illustrated book that includes 19 short and clever poems. Similar to Shel Silverstein's style, it describes all kinds of foods that children can chuckle over. (K–3).
- *Good enough to eat: A kid's guide to food and nutrition* by Lizzy Rockwell (HarperCollins, 1999) is an impressive book packed with illustrations and information presented in an effective way for younger readers to learn that eating healthy starts early in life. (Pre K–2).
- *Gregory and the terrible eater* (Scholastic, 1989) by Mitchell Sharmat is a light hearted story about Gregory the goat, a 'picky eater' who doesn't like to eat garbage like everyone else and convinces his family to eat healthy foods. (K–2).
- *Let's eat* edited by Ana Zamorano and Amy Griffin is a beautifully illustrated picture book by Julie Vivas (Scholastic, 1999) showing the importance of Hispanic families spending mealtime together and what happens when mother misses dinner to have a baby. (Pre K–3).
- *My food pyramid: Eat right, exercise, have fun* by DK publishing (2007) is a well organized and easy-to-read book describing the new USDA food guide pyramid. Informs and empowers children to think about what they eat and how to stay in shape. (Pre K–3).
- *Showdown at the food pyramid* written and brightly illustrated by Rex Barron (Putnam, 2004) is a clever and witty story using characters such as hotdogs and ice cream who take over the food pyramid. When the healthier food groups get together, they figure out a way to balance the food pyramid making everyone happy. (K–2).
- *Sword of a Champion: The story of Sharon Monplaisir (Anything You Can Do . . . New sports Heroes for Girls)* by Doreen and Michael Greenberg illustrated by Phil Velikan (Wish Publishing, 2000) is a compelling adventure story about fencing Olympic champion Sharon Monplaisir. Excellent book for integration of English, Social Studies, physical education and technology. Nancy Lieberman-Cline is also featured in the series. (4–8).

- *The busy body book; A kid's guide to fitness* by Lizzy Rockwell (Crown Books, 2004) contains clear and inviting information about how the body functions in a way that youngsters can readily understand. (Pre K–3).
- *My amazing body: A first look at health and fitness* is another easy to read picture book written by Pat Thomas and illustrated by Lesley Harker (Barron's Education Series, 2001) that lists the basics of health and physical fitness including advice for parents and teachers. (K–2).
- *The monster health book: A guide to eating healthy, being active and feeling great for monsters and kids!* by Edward Miller (Holiday House, 2008) is a substantial teacher resource packed with information and jokes children can relate to about exercise and eating healthy. (2–5).
- *The race against junk food* (*Adventures in Good Nutrition*) by Anthony Buono and Roy Nemerson (HCOM, 1997) is a story about a boy named Tommy who travels down the 'vitamin highway' learning fun and interesting facts about food and nutrition. (3–6).
- *Spriggles motivational books for children: Health and nutrition* (No. 2) by Jeff and Martha Gottlieb (Mountain Watch Press, 2002) is a story written in short rhymes about a charming little seal who eats all the right foods. (Pre K–2).
- Another book by Jeff and Martha Gottlieb and illustrated by Alexander Gottlieb, *Spriggles motivational books for children: Activity and exercise* (No. 3) (Mountain Watch Press, 2001) describes adorable characters like 'Freddie the Frog' doing a variety of exercises told in rhyme format. (Pre K–2).
- *I.Q. gets fit* written by Mary Ann Fraser (Walker, 2007) is a delightful little tale about a weakly little mouse who decides to change his ways and get into shape and stop eating junk food. (Pre K–2).
- *Healthy me: Fun ways to develop good health and safety habits* by Michele O'Brien-Palmer (Chicago Press, 1999) is a hands-on science-related book with basic information about nutrition and exercise filled with games, recipes, and experiments for young children. (K–3).
- *Food and nutrition for every kid: Easy activities that make learning science fun* by Janice Van Cleave (Wiley & Sons, 1999) is a well organized teacher resource packed with information about how children can make wise food choices for good health including experiments they can do in school and at home. (3–6).
- Sharon Gordon's *Exercise* (Children's Press, 2003) is a Rookie Read-About Health book with colorful photographs that present information for young readers about the importance of exercise. (Pre K–2).

For further convenience, these books are arranged in alphabetical order by author, including title, grade level, illustrations, topic, didactics (content), humor, games, recipes, or activities in Figure 1.

Other Connections

There are other ways that health, physical activity, and literacy learning can be supported in the elementary school curriculum. For example, physical educators can provide leadership and support by:

- Collaborating with the school librarian in selecting high quality health/PE children's books for students' school wide use. (Refer to the book list provided elsewhere in this article to use as a model.)
- Sharing children's books and other print resources with classroom teachers that support the health and PE curriculum.
- Joining the school wide literacy or reading committee.
- Encouraging nutrition school programs such as 'Harvest of the Month' which provides materials and resources to support healthy food choices through increased access and consumption of fruits and vegetables as well as encourage daily physical activity (www.Harvestofthemonth.com).
- Communicating with classroom teachers to reinforce physical activity and literacy skills whenever possible.

Future Implications

Most educators would acknowledge American students could be in better physical shape and eating healthier foods. While it is critical that all students learn to read and write, they also need a well balanced curriculum. No Child Left Behind legislation has been one of the reasons why school leaders seem to be in a quandary over what subjects should be taught in the school curriculum (Pellegrini & Bohn, 2005). However, regardless of the amount of time schools have for health and physical education most would agree that finding more ways to combine literacy with physical education could benefit students. One idea that can help schools reinforce students' literacy skills and healthy living is through integrating high quality physical education and health children's books into the classroom. According to Rudman and Pearce (1988) children's books can serve as minors for children, reflecting their appearance, their relationships, their feelings and thoughts in their immediate environment (p. 159). In addition, no matter what students are learning they need opportunities to apply skills, concepts, information, or ideas in books (Norton, 2007). While much can be gained from these ideas and resources, clearly, they are no substitute for acquiring highly qualified physical educators and maintaining quality physical education programs. As the current NCLB legislation goes under reauthorization, students' health and well being should be top priority.

Children's Book Author/Title	Grade level	Color Illus.	Health/ Nutrit	PE	More didactic	Less didactic	Humor	Games, recipes, activities
Barron/Showdown at the Food Pyramid	K–2	X	X			X	X	
Buono/Race Against Junk Food	3–6	X	X		X			
DK/My Food Pyramid	PreK–3	X	X		X			X
Fraser/ I.Q. Gets Fit	PreK–2	X		X		X	X	
Greenberg/Sword of a Champion	4–8			X	X			X
Gordon/Exercise	PreK–2	X		X		X		
Gottlieb/Spriggles Motivational: Activity & Exercise	PreK–2	X		X			X	
Gottlieb/Spriggles Motivational: Health & Nutrition	PreK–2	X	X			X	X	
Miller/The Monster Health Book	2–5 TR	X	X		X		X	X
O'Brien-Palmer/Healthy Me	K–3	X	X	X	X			X
Rockwell/Good Enough to Eat	PreK–3	X	X		X			X
Rockwell/The Busy Body Book	PreK–3	X	X			X		
Sears/Eat Healthy, Feel Great	K–3	X	X	X				
Sharmat/Gregory the Terrible Eater	K–2	X	X			X	X	
Thomas/My Amazing Body	K–2	X	X	X	X			
VanCleave/Food & Nutrition	3–6 TR		X		X			X
Weinstock/Food Hates You Too	K–3	X				X	X	
Zamorano/Let's Eat	PreK–3	X				X		
Zinczenko/Eat This Not That!	K–8 TR	X	X		X			X

TR = Teacher Resource

Figure 1 Health and Physical Education Children's Books by Author, Title, Grade Level, Illustration, Topic, Didactics, Humor, Games, Recipes, or Activities

References

Centers for Disease Control and Prevention. Healthy Schools Healthy Youth. Student Health and Academic Achievement. Childhood Obesity, available at www.cdc.gov/healthyyouth.

No Child Left Behind Act of 2001, Pub. L. No. 107-110, 115 Stat. 1425. (2002).

Norton, D. E. (2007). Through the eyes of a child: An introduction to children's literature. Pearson Education Inc.: New Jersey.

Pellegrini, A. D. & Bohn, R. (2005). Recess: Its roles in education and development. Developing Mind Series. Mahwah: New Jersey: L. Erlbaum Associates.

Rudman, M. Kabakow, & Pearce, A. Markus. (1988). For love of reading: A parent's guide to encouraging young readers from infancy through age 5. Mount Vernon: NY: Consumer Union.

Children's Book References

Barron, R. (2004). Showdown at the food pyramid. New York: Putnam.

Buono, A., & Nemerson, R. (1997). The race against junk food. HCOM. Inc.

Fraser, M.A. (2007). I.Q. gets fit. New York: Walker.

Greenberg, D., & Greenberg, M. (2000). Sword of a champion: The story of Sharon Monplaisir (Anything You Can Do . . . New Sports for Girls). Wish Publishing.

Gottlieb J., & Gottlieb, M. (2002). Spriggles motivational books for children: Health and nutrition. Mountain Watch Press.

——. (2001). Spriggles motivational books for children: Activity and exercise. Mountain Watch Press.

Miller, E. (2008). The monster health book: A guide to eating healthy, being active and feeling great for monsters and kids! New York: Holiday House.

My food pyramid: Eat right, exercise, have fun. (2007). New York: DK Publishing.

O'Brien-Palmer, M. (1999). Healthy me: Fun ways to develop good health and safety habits. Chicago Press.

Rockwell, L. (2004). The busy body book. Crown Publishing.

——. (1999). Good enough to eat: A kid's guide to food and nutrition. New York: HarperCollins.

Sharmart, M. (1998). Gregory the terrible eater. Scholastic.

Sears, W., Sears, M., & Watts Kelly, C. (2002). Eat healthy, feel great. Little, Brown.

Thomas, P. (2001). My amazing body: A first look at health and Fitness. Barrons Education Series.

Van Cleave, J. (1999). Food and nutrition for every kid: Easy activities that make science fun. Wiley & Sons, Inc.

Weinstock, R. Food hates you too and other poems. (2009). Hyperion Books.

Zamorano, A. (1991). Let's eat. Scholastic.

Zinczenko, D, & Goulding, M. (2008). Eat this, not that! For Kids! Rodale Inc.

Critical Thinking

1. What are the motivations of this author for using children's literature in a physical education classroom?

2. Many of the books listed in the article are for very young children. Do you think this is an activity that is best for K–2 classes or can it be used at higher levels? Justify your answer.

3. Do you think this idea could generalize to other content areas such as art and music? What topics could be covered with books about art and music?

JOAN C. FINGON is a professor of education and reading ot California State University of Los Angeles.

"Integrating Children's Literature in the Physical Education Curriculum" was just published in Strategies: A Journal for Physical and Sports Educators (March/April, 2011). 24(4). p. 10–13.

You Gotta See It to Believe It: Teaching Visual Literacy in the English Classroom

By teaching students how to read and view all texts critically, not just the traditional print texts, teachers can build upon the skills students need to read and write, increasing their literacy levels in all areas.

ROBYN SEGLEM AND SHELBIE WITTE

Clarisse: What do the instructions mean when they ask "what the painting says"?

Daniel: You've got to be able to read the picture.

Clarisse: Easy. It says "Lift Thine Eyes."

Daniel: Duh. Not just the words, you gotta be able to read the entire picture, like it has words on it. Like, look at all the people looking down. What do you think that means or what it's sayin'?

Clarisse: That people aren't paying attention?

Daniel: Right, that people are too caught up in their lives to see what's happening.

Clarisse: To stop and smell the roses? Whatever that means, I've heard my mom say it.

Daniel: Yeah, I think that's right. That sometimes we don't pay attention to life and it just goes on without us.

This discussion of Norman Rockwell's painting "Lift Up Thine Eyes" illustrates a student's discovery of a different way of reading (all student names used are pseudonyms). More than ever in the history of education, the demands placed upon students in the realm of literacy are becoming more stringent. No longer are the abilities to read and write in a linear, left-to-right fashion the sole indicators of successful communications. Rather, the world is made up of visual symbols that require more complex thinking skills than traditional literacy requires.

Today, the concept of literacy has ceased to be narrowly defined. Literacy is now a fluid concept determined by cultural context (Williams, 2004). From this necessity and with this fluidity in mind, students need instruction in analyzing and creating a variety of texts in new ways (Alvermann, 2002). If educators want students to perform well in both the world and on new assessments, students need a critical understanding of print and nonprint texts in relationship to themselves as readers and viewers within different social, cultural, and historical contexts (Alvermann & Hagood, 2000). Incorporating visual literacy into the curriculum is vital for student success.

Why Visual Literacy?

While many agree that visual literacy should be included in the educational arena, there has been great debate among researchers as to what the term actually encompasses. Visual literacy was originally recognized as the ability for someone to discriminate and interpret the visuals encountered in the environment as fundamental to learning (Debes, 1969). Critics of that original interpretation of visual literacy feel it is too broadly stated, failing to narrow the concept to what visual literacy allows people to do or how symbols work within its context (Avgerinou & Ericson, 1997). During the 1980s and early 1990s, three major categories emerged to refer to visual literacy: human abilities, the promotion of ideas, and teaching strategies (Avgerinou & Ericson, 1997). With these three categories in mind, perhaps the best definition for visual literacy is a simple one, such as the one Braden and Hortin (1982) proposed: "Visual literacy is the ability to understand and use images, including the ability to think, learn and express oneself in terms of images".

Because using visuals is a powerful instructional tool, and because students receive information in a variety of formats, literacy must be expanded beyond traditional reading and writing to include the visual arts as one of the ways in which we communicate (Flood & Lapp, 1997/1998). According to Flood and Lapp (1997/1998), the best reason most teachers give for not including visual arts within the classroom is their fear that it would take time away from traditional reading and writing skills. Their view, while legitimate, denies students the experience of the layered information in the real world and reflects the unsupported view that traditional literacy is the only literacy. This article seeks to explore the issues encompassing visual literacies as well as to provide ideas for teachers on how to begin working with them in the classroom.

Visual Literacy at Work

Including visualization in the classroom cannot be a one-shot activity. Rather, it must be woven into the regular classroom curriculum. Following Eisner's (1992) philosophy that imagination and reading ability are closely interwoven, it is important to understand the diverse ways in which students imagine or visualize. Instantaneously, students can receive imagery and information from television shows and movies, cartoons, websites, and advertisements. Helping students to understand the diversity of print and non-print texts as well as the visual connections that can be made between them is a practical way to connect the concrete and abstract thinking of students who struggle to make meaning from text. While many students automatically interpret print text into nonprint visual images, some students struggle with making the leap from words to images.

Visualization—the ability to build mental pictures or images while reading—partnered with a reader's prior background knowledge and level of engagement in the reading topic greatly affects the reader's understanding of the text (Keene & Zimmermann, 1997). Visualization allows students the ability to become more engaged in their reading and use their imagery to draw conclusions, create interpretations of the text, and recall details and elements from the text (Keene & Zimmermann, 1997). Struggling students' ability to monitor and evaluate their own comprehension is enhanced by mental imagery (Gambrell & Bales, 1986). When a breakdown in comprehension occurs, and a mental image cannot be visualized, students will become aware of the need for a corrective strategy.

Creating visual images or mind movies while one reads is an essential element of engagement with the text, comprehension, and reflection (Wilhelm, 2004). Visualization and the creation of visuals allow students ways to read, respond, analyze, organize, and represent the learning that is taking place. Visualization strategies (Gambrell & Koskinen, 2002; Keene & Zimmermann, 1997; Wilhelm, 1995) can do the following:

- Heighten motivation, engagement, and enjoyment of reading
- Immerse students in rich details of the text
- Improve literal comprehension of texts
- Build background knowledge
- Aid in identifying important details to form inferences, elaborations, and patterns across multiple texts
- Help in solving spatial and verbal problems
- Improve a reader's ability to share, critique, and revise what has been learned with others

Through emphasizing and modeling visualization with students, teachers show how effortlessly connections between text and media can be made. Bridging visualization to the world of multiliteracies allows students to compose and explore ideas through "democratic avenues of meaning making" (Wilhelm, 2004).

Tattoos

Visual media are not confined to glossy pages or computer screens. Perhaps one of the most fascinating forms to today's youth are the colorful images that span the bicep or peek over the top of a sock. Like a modern-day coat-of-arms, tattoos have burst into the popular culture of the United States in a powerful way. Tattoos, once viewed as taboo, are seen in a variety of environments. Celebrities such as Angelina Jolie famously bare their tattoos for tabloids, while networks develop reality shows depicting the journeys of tattoo artists, shops, and the background stories about the individuals who patronize them (e.g., *Inked, Miami Ink, L.A. Ink*). This fascination can be translated into an introduction to visual media.

To accomplish this, we introduced our ninth-grade students to the Norman Rockwell painting "Tattoo Artist." Rockwell illustrates a scene in which a Navy sailor chooses to have a tattoo applied, signaling his newest relationship with Betty, while above the chosen spot, viewers can see that this arm has chronicled all his past relationships, a single line struck through each name to signify the end of the relationship. Typically, the students picked up on the irony of the painting immediately and make the connection to their own relationship pasts. Many students cringed when thinking what their arms might look like had they tattooed each former flame on their arms.

To encourage students to move beyond their initial reactions, we also prompted them to think of Rockwell's painting as a scene from a movie, predicting what each character is thinking in this snapshot of a scene. This required students to pay close attention to the details presented in the painting. They had to read every nuance to frame a narrative that explores each character's motivation and reactions. This attention to detail also highlights that the growing list of names, like tattoos, cannot be undone with a simple change of mind.

Once students realized the permanence of tattoos as depicted in Rockwell's painting, we provided articles related to the health risks and issues surrounding tattoos. We then asked students to design personal tattoos that symbolized an important life event. Although the tattoo designs were not applied as actual tattoos, designing hypothetical personal tattoos gave students the opportunity to express themselves and their experiences through color and images. Knowing that tattoos are essentially permanent, the students were asked to keep this permanence in mind as they designed their tattoos.

Megan, a student reluctant to write in class, created a tree tattoo to symbolize her complicated family history. Because we asked students to write about the tattoo's symbolism Megan wrote at length about the impact of her family history on her life:

My family tree is complicated, so complicated that to explain it at length wouldn't really matter. What matters is my life is a tree unlike any other . . . not straight and tall like a redwood or well-rounded and full like an evergreen. My tree is broken and jagged and yet, it springs a newness when I least expect it.

Megan was also able to verbalize the impact that this visual image would have on others as they view it. "When others see my tattoo, I don't want them to feel sorry for me or focus on all of the dead branches. I want them to focus on the hope that there will be more leaves if I'm given the chance."

Once students had an opportunity to explore how their own histories would shape their tattoos, they were then asked to apply the tattoo activity to a character from Shakespeare's *Romeo and Juliet*. Creating a tattoo to represent the character traits of one of Shakespeare's memorable characters allowed the students to better examine the play as well as understand how precisely a visual image can be used to represent their comprehension. Kevin chose to create a tattoo for the character of Friar Lawrence. In his explanation of the tattoo, Kevin wrote about the importance of Friar Lawrence:

Some people think that Friar Lawrence wasn't an important character in the play, but I disagree. I think that he was really important because not only does he marry Romeo and Juliet in secret, but he also spends the rest of the play trying to cover up his mistakes as they snowball. The scales for the Montague and Capulet families represent his efforts to balance the destruction that will follow.

Kevin went on to analyze the ethical repercussions of Friar Lawrence's actions, explaining that "the serpent in the tattoo represents the sin that rears its head in his actions and intertwines itself so closely to him that he has difficulty determining the difference between right and wrong."

More than an art activity, creating tattoos to represent literary characters challenges students to think beyond the written text. By representing their personal journeys as well as fictional characters in texts, students weave together their exposure to print and nonprint texts through a layering of mental, emotional, and physical learning activities (Bloom, 1969; Krathwohl, Bloom, & Masia, 1964; Simpson, 1972).

Collages

Including visuals is sometimes as simple as reexamining how we accomplish routine classroom assignments. Take research, for example. The traditional approach to teaching students how to research and paraphrase sources tends to be rather linear. Students find information on their topics, write down their sources, and then attempt to put what they found in their own words. Unfortunately, this often leads to hours of frustration as teachers discover paper after paper that simply lifted information from the original sources. Angered, the teacher returns to the classroom, scolding the class for their laziness. Then, when the next group of papers comes in, the process repeats itself, leaving the teacher even more upset. Plagiarism is an issue that English teachers across the country battle on a regular basis, particularly with the advent of the Internet. Some students very

consciously choose to follow that easy route, anxious to get their papers turned in and out of the way. But for others, plagiarism occurs because they cannot figure out how to avoid doing it. For these students, the linear path leads to a direct transfer of information, resulting in papers that sound almost identical to the original sources.

Brock was one such student. When we asked him to research his idol, Jackie Robinson, Brock followed the traditional research route. He combed the Internet looking for sources and even brought in a book from home. And when the time came for him to turn in his paper, it reflected none of Brock's admiration. Rather, the paper was a re-creation of his three sources, albeit rearranged with words changed here and there. When we approached him, it became obvious that Brock had not purposefully cheated on the assignment. Tears filled his eyes as he promised he had not cheated. He had, he said, simply read through the information and then written it down on his note cards. Brock had such a memory for written text that even when he was not looking at the screen, he recalled most of what he had read, and because he knew he needed to get the information down, he wrote what he remembered. Brock needed something to break the linear path. Fortunately, incorporating visuals into the research process can do just that.

As one way to break the linear path and to incorporate visuals into the research process, we asked students to select a topic, searching for information just as they had always done. Instead of taking notes on the information they discovered, however, students began flipping through magazines, seeking out images to represent the key facts. This forced students to activate their background knowledge as they worked to build connections between the images in the magazines and the information they needed to convey. More often than not, students had to be creative in their illustrations because the likelihood of finding a picture of Jackie Robinson playing baseball or a Holocaust victim working behind barbed wire was slim. Then, on note cards or half sheets of paper, they would affix their pictures. Each collage represented a single idea or fact. After creating the collage, our students turned their papers over, and, using the images as a guide, they wrote one to two sentences explaining the images and citing the original source. The process required them to focus on the ideas and facts represented in their sources and not on a word-for-word replay. Most important, it broke the linear path between the written text in their sources and the written text of their papers. By taking the time to work with the information in a visual format, students were able to separate themselves from the language of the source, which resulted in language of their own. By the time they finished with the process, they had a collection of images they could arrange and rearrange as they began organizing their ideas for their papers.

Paintings

While creating collages provides an effective avenue for teaching students to paraphrase by using visual images, it can still be a challenge to some students. So what other forms can visualizing take? Anyone wandering into our classrooms might find students sketching out their preliminary ideas or sweeping broad strokes of color onto white canvases. In fact, outsiders might mistake our English class for an art class as students work to create symbolic representations of novels in the form of 11" × 14" paintings. For some, this task provides an avenue to explore their ideas and interpretations in a creative way or allows them to showcase their artistic talents in a forum that usually focuses on written language. For others, just getting started is a struggle because the novel's meaning and messages continue to elude them. Take Jake, for example. A sophomore, Jake simply did not see himself as a successful student. He struggled to keep up with reading expectations and rarely completed a writing assignment. When asked to visualize what he read, his first reaction was to throw up his hands in defeat. He simply did not know how to complete this task. Yet, he wanted to. All around him, he watched his classmates laughing as they set to work, stopping from time to time to ask their peers to read their pictures or to share their visions with us. This, he recognized, was not the typical English assignment, and he wanted to experience it just like everyone else.

To begin the assignment, we asked the class to free write on a series of guiding questions: When you think of your book, what is the overall feeling you walk away with? Which scenes in the book are attributed to this feeling? What is the overall theme or message of the book? We talked about symbolism and how to use concrete symbols to represent the abstract ideas presented in the books. The students spent an entire class period writing and sketching their ideas. When Jake left the classroom that day, his page was blank. Although he had completed his book, *I Know What You Did Last Summer* by Lois Duncan, he could not see how our class discussions could apply to this teen suspense novel. His understanding of the book was superficial. He could recite the basics of the plot but could not move his comprehension to a deeper thinking level. Thus began a series of conversations between us.

We started with what Jake did know. The book, he explained, was about four teens who had been involved in an accident the previous summer, which resulted in the death of a young boy. Months later, each of the teens was reminded of this crime as an unknown figure stalked them, sending them alarming messages. We talked about the setting of the book, pointing out that while the bulk of the book takes place during the time of the stalking, the past has a significant impact on its events. We talked about how the characters felt about what they had done, as well as about what was happening to them. We talked about the significant objects in the book that helped relay the tone and message in the book. And then we gave Jake time to think, to imagine how these elements could all come together in a single visual image. While a cohesive picture did not emerge all at once, Jake had progressed at each check. The first image he settled on became the centerpiece of his entire painting. On a sheet of paper, he had sketched a large rectangle across the top third of the page. This, he explained, was a rearview mirror. It represented the actual accident because it had been a hit-and-run, but he chose the mirror rather than another part of the car because the characters were being forced to look back on what they had done. Already, Jake was demonstrating that he had moved to a deeper understanding of the book.

His face lit up when praised about his progress, and he eagerly turned back to his sketch when presented with more questions to consider. We repeated this process as Jake worked on his confidence as a reader. By the time he had completed his painting, he had obviously made great progress in his visualization skills, resulting in a deeper understanding of the book itself. The rearview mirror reflected details like a noose, signaling the threats of the stalker, next to a set of child's clothing hanging on a clothesline. From the mirror hung the traditional evergreen air freshener, but this one was covered in blood, symbolizing how sour everything had gone, Jake explained. Through the process, Jake had learned to use the details from the book, as well as his own detailed interpretations, leaving him with a much stronger understanding of what he had read than he had possessed before.

Persuasive Narratives: J. Peterman Catalog

As big fans of *Seinfeld* in the 1990s, we believed the J. Peterman Company featured on the show was fictional. Elaine, one of the show's main characters, worked at J. Peterman in a variety of capacities; most memorably, she wrote advertisements for the catalog's eclectic collection of clothing and accessories. The persuasive advertisements were long passages of description embedded within narrative, intended to bring the item to life through an adventurous story. We were thrilled to discover that the company actually existed, and we quickly ordered the catalog to use in our classrooms as examples of how writing can create visual images in a real-world medium.

To begin the activity, we showed a series of short clips from *Seinfeld* in which J. Peterman was depicted or in which the characters were working on the catalog. Although several of our students had seen *Seinfeld* in syndication, we felt it was important for all of the students to see how stories about the merchandise were developed and depicted in popular culture. Also, to help our students understand what made the catalog so unique, we surveyed a variety of catalogs from department stores to discover the ways in which items were displayed and described. Students quickly noted the differences in catalogs and the unique characteristics of J. Peterman's catalog.

To practice using the detailed narrative style, students cut out pictures of clothing and accessories from fashion and sports magazines to create parody advertisements in the J. Peterman style. Clarisse, a fashionista at heart, took great care to describe the boots in her parody ad:

> Life gets hard on the road, but that's not an excuse to not look my best. Confident and determined, I travel from city to city, state to state, meeting to meeting, with a strong walk and an even stronger mind. It's all about the impression you give, my dad would say. I'm proud to be following in his footsteps, his bootsteps. I wouldn't travel anywhere without my suede leather boots, No. 5446, in sizes 6–10, colors brown, black, and purple. $599.00.

Daniel, an unlikely catalog or mall shopper, was also inspired by the assignment and wanted to write about his mother's U.S. Army uniform:

This uniform is not for the timid or meek, nor is it for the lazy or those known to be cowards. This uniform is for those who sacrifice their lives in more ways than one. It is not a costume for your Halloween party, nor is it a piece of clothing that should be put on as carelessly as a white t-shirt while running to the store. This uniform deserves your respect. It is bravery, pride, and tradition. It is freedom. Army Dress Uniform, No. 111, in sizes 2–14, standard issue color. PRICELESS.

Clarisse and Daniel wove their narrative storylines into persuasive advertisements, including the description of the items, targeting specific audiences. This activity also prepared the students to think about objects in a personified way and to think about purpose and audience in their writing.

Our next step in the activity transitioned to writing about iconic symbols in young adult literature. Students worked collaboratively to create J. Peterman catalogs for the texts they were reading in their literature circle/book study groups. Students created catalogs for Laurie Halse Anderson's *Speak,* Walter Dean Myers's *Monster,* and Ben Mikaelsen's *Touching Spirit Bear.* The *Touching Spirit Bear* book club created an advertisement for many important objects and events in the text, most notably, the Ancestor Rock:

In a place where cold, salty water sweeps onto the rocky shore of a long forgotten island, Tlingit elders chisel away at a mountainside, freeing away tools for their tribal rituals. The Ancestor Rock is more than rock; it is truth, introspection, and justice. While pushing it up steep hillsides, the Ancestor Rock serves as a mentor and protector. And yet, when it is let go, to fall quickly down the hill it had recently climbed, it is forgiveness. Ancestor Rock, No. 232, One size fits all, Colors will vary. $199.00

Not only did the activity emphasize purpose and audience in writing, but it also demonstrated how written texts do not always need to be created in isolation. Persuasive, descriptive, and narrative texts can be interwoven to create a powerful companion to visual images. Through the development of their book club catalogs, the students touched on the important themes of each novel as well as described specific setting details and character traits of important characters. Collaboratively, the students created meaning from the text and worked together to create a project with print and nonprint texts that symbolized their collective understanding of the novel.

Gee (2000) stated that when creating meaning from texts, the human mind is social. Additionally, as the mind engages in thinking, it distributes information "across other people and various symbols, tools, objects and technologies" (para. 6). If the culture teens are immersed in revolves around the visual and the media, their minds recognize the patterns created by these images, creating a persuasive argument for incorporating these patterns within the classroom. Gee wrote that "Thinking and using language is an active matter of assembling the situated meanings that you need for action in the world" (para. 12). Taking these meanings and showing students how to apply

them both inside and outside the classroom can be an effective instructional tool.

> **If the culture teens are immersed in revolves around the visual and the media, their minds recognize the patterns created by these images, creating a persuasive argument for incorporating these patterns within the classroom.**

A study by Pompe (1996) about popular culture's influence on young consumers upheld her convictions as to why it is so influential on students. She found that the pleasures provided by these visually oriented texts were deep in nature, rather than superficial; that consumers' desires were powerful influences on what the popular media produced; that viewers and listeners of audiovisual texts just as actively made meaning as readers of print text; and that teachers and students could satisfy their own desires while they were learning about the desires of others. It is this powerful influence that makes popular media texts important additions to the classroom. By including elements of popular culture, teachers can tap into the patterns students' minds already recognize, which makes transitioning them to more traditional texts much more effective.

Poetry Comics

Graphic novels are more popular in our culture than ever before. Whether they are in the form of the traditional Japanese art (manga) or the more popular Americanized version of graphic illustrations such as the *Bone* novels by Jeff Smith, these books often sit atop a pile of students' chosen books. Canon classics and new young adult literature are even being reformatted to appeal to a new generation of graphic novel readers. Much more than comic strips, today's graphic novels are complex and mature, capturing an intellectual readership looking for more visual stimulation from their reading experiences.

There are two reasons teachers should be drawn to the manga genre: first, the popularity of the genre, measured by sales and distribution, and second, the unique multimodal reading that manga demands (Schwartz & Rubinstein-Ávila, 2006). Fortunately, it is possible to marry students' outside interests with those of traditional academia. An example of this would be tackling complicated texts in the classroom using poetry comics. Poetry comics illustrate poetry in the form of a comic strip. The text of the comic strip is the text of the poem, with illustrations inspired by the text. To begin this activity with our eighth-grade students, we introduced Langston Hughes's "A Dream Deferred," and after reading it as a class, we presented a poetry comic based on Hughes's poem (see Morice, 2002). A comparison of the two emphasizes the ways in which poetry can be interpreted and illustrated differently by each reader.

Once students had a clear understanding of poetry comics, we asked them to read two complex poems, Walt Whitman's "O Captain! My Captain" and T.S. Eliot's "The Naming of Cats," and demonstrate their understanding through poetry comics. Jasmine tackled Eliot and illustrated the poem with her understanding of the text. Ordered in a traditional comic strip format, Jasmine also added personalized touches outside of the borders. Jasmine incorporated the entire poem in its traditional form, while giving the narrator a cat personality.

Kaitlin approached Whitman in a different comic format. Instead of the traditional squares in a linear sequence, Kaitlin opted for ships to anchor each stanza, with characters quoting lines from the poem. Kaitlin understood the poem to be about President Abraham Lincoln's death and chose to depict the country metaphorically as the ship Whitman speaks of in the poem.

Much more than a superficial illustration of poetry, these poetry comics allow for students to experiment with narrator voice, setting, and literal and metaphorical meanings. Layering complex literary analysis skills with visual representations allows students to practice visualizing the texts that they read. Graphic representations of popular texts provide a contemporary canvas for authors to share their stories using a fresh, relevant approach. Educators, librarians, and bookstores that have embraced this new genre of literature have difficulty keeping titles on their shelves. Further, they are pleased to see more young people choosing books at a time when video games and the Internet seem to take up so much attention. With the growing demand for and popularity of graphic novels, the integration of the genre with traditional English language arts practices should continue to be explored (Schwartz & Rubinstein-Ávila, 2006).

Final Thoughts

Just as the classrooms and students of the 21st century look very different than those of centuries before, so too must the curriculum change. Teachers can prepare students for today's changing world by introducing texts of all types into the learning environment.

By teaching students how to critically read and view all texts, not just the traditional print texts, teachers can build upon the skills needed to read and write, increasing students' literacy levels in all areas. And perhaps even more important, as O'Brien (2001) pointed out, the study of visual symbols can reach those students who have been burned by print. Ultimately, however, visual literacy must be included within all school curricula if teachers want to adequately prepare students for a world that is surrounded by and driven by images.

References

Alvermann, D.E. (2002). Effective literacy instruction for adolescents. *Journal of Literacy Research, 34*(2), 189–208. doi:10.1207/s15548430jlr3402_4.

Alvermann, D.E., & Hagood, M.C. (2000). Critical media literacy: Research, theory, and the practice in "new times." *The Journal of Educational Research, 93*(3), 193–206.

Avgerinou, M., & Ericson, J. (1997). A review of the concept of visual literacy. *British Journal of Educational Technology, 28*(4), 280–291. doi:10.1111/1467-8535.00035.

Bloom, B.S. (Ed.). (1969). *Taxonomy of educational objectives: The classification of educational goals* (Handbook I: The cognitive domain). New York: David McKay.

Braden, R.A., & Hortin, J.A. (1982). Identifying the theoretical foundations of visual literacy. *Journal of Visual/Verbal Languaging, 2*(2), 37–42.

Debes, J.L. (1969). The loom of visual literacy—An overview. *Audio Visual Instruction, 14*(8), 25–27.

Eisner, E.W. (1992). The misunderstood role of the arts in human development. *Phi Delta Kappan, 73*(8), 591–595.

Flood, J., & Lapp, D. (1997/1998). Broadening conceptualizations of literacy: The visual and communicative arts. *The Reading Teacher, 51*(4), 342–344.

Gambrell, L.B., & Bales, R.J. (1986). Mental imagery and the comprehension-monitoring performance of fourth- and fifth-grade poor readers. *Reading Research Quarterly, 21*(4), 454–464. doi:10.2307/747616.

Gambrell, L.B., & Koskinen, P.S. (2002). Imagery: A strategy for enhancing comprehension. In C.C. Block & M. Pressley (Eds.), *Comprehension instruction: Research-based best practices* (pp. 305–318). New York: Guilford.

Gee, J.P. (2000, September). Discourse and sociocultural studies in reading. *Reading Online, 4*(3). Retrieved October 18, 2008, from www.readingonline.org/articles/art_index.asp?HREF=/articles/handbook/gee/index.html.

Keene, E.O., & Zimmermann, S. (1997). *Mosaic of thought: Teaching comprehension in a reader's workshop.* Portsmouth, NH: Heinemann.

Krathwohl, D.R., Bloom, B.S., & Masia, B.B. (1964). *Taxonomy of educational objectives: The classification of educational goals* (Handbook II: Affective domain). New York: David McKay.

Morice, D. (2002). *Poetry comics: An animated anthology.* New York: T&W Books.

O'Brien, D. (2001, June). "At-risk" adolescents: Redefining competence through the multiliteracies of intermediality, visual arts, and representation. *Reading Online, 4*(11). Available: www.readingonline.org/newliteracies/lit_index.asp?HREF=/newliteracies/obrien/index.html.

Pompe, C. (1996). "But they're pink!"—"Who cares!" Popular culture in the primary years. In M. Hilton (Ed.), *Potent fictions: Children's literacy and the challenge of popular culture* (pp. 92–125). London: Routledge.

Schwartz, A., & Rubinstein-Ávila, E. (2006). Understanding the manga hype: Uncovering the multimodality of comic-book literacies. *Journal of Adolescent & Adult Literacy, 50*(1), 40–49. doi:10.1598/JAAL.50.1.5.

Simpson, E.J. (1972). *The classification of educational objectives in the psychomotor domain.* Washington, DC: Gryphon House.

Wilhelm, J.D. (1995). Reading is seeing: Using visual response to improve the literary reading of reluctant readers. *Journal of Reading Behavior, 27*(4), 467–503.

Wilhelm, J. (2004). *Reading is seeing: Learning to visualize scenes, characters, ideas, and text worlds to improve comprehension and reflective reading.* New York: Scholastic.

Williams, B.T. (2004). "A puzzle to the rest of us": Who is a "reader" anyway? *Journal of Adolescent & Adult Literacy, 47*(8). Retrieved October 18, 2008, from www.readingonline .org/newliteracies/lit_index.asp?HREF=/newliteracies/jaal /5-04_column_lit/index.html.

Critical Thinking

1. Make a table or graphic organizer to compare and contrast visual literacy and print referencing.

2. Tell why visual literacy could be important to the grade or content you will teach.

3. Provide examples of visuals you might use to enrich students' ability to learn your subject matter.

ROBYN SEGLEM is a National Board Certified Teacher and an assistant professor at Illinois State University, Normal, USA; e-mail rseglem@ ilstu.edu. SHELBIE WITTE is a National Board Certified Teacher and an assistant professor at Florida State University, Tallahassee, USA; e-mail switte@fsu.edu.

From *Journal of Adolescent & Adult Literacy,* November 2009, pp. 216–226. Copyright © 2009 by International Reading Association. Reprinted by permission via Copyright Clearance Center.

Strategies for Teaching Algebra to Students with Learning Disabilities: Making Research to Practice Connections

Tricia K. Strickland and Paula Maccini

To help students with learning disabilities (LD) meet the algebra requirements necessary for high school graduation and prepare for postsecondary education and occupational opportunities, teachers look to research for effective strategies to successfully instruct these students (The Access Center, 2004). In a previous review of algebra interventions for secondary students with LD published from 1970 to 1996, Maccini, McNaughton, and Ruhl (1999) determined that certain strategies improve students' performance in algebra, including the use of (a) general problem-solving strategies in problem representation and problem solution, (b) self-monitoring strategies, (c) the concrete-representation-abstract instructional sequence, and (d) teaching prerequisite skills. This article summarizes the research on a set of complementary strategies and approaches for teaching algebra. Explicit instruction, graduated instructional sequence, technology, and graphic organizers are discussed as strategies for boosting student ability in algebra.

Explicit Instruction
Definition
Explicit instruction is a method of teacher-directed instruction that incorporates the following teaching functions: an advanced organizer, teacher demonstration, guided practice, independent practice, cumulative practice, and curriculum-based assessment to provide data to drive instructional planning. As shown in Figure 1, Maccini, Strickland, Gagnon, and Malmgren (2008) summarized

the explicit instructional cycle as described by Hudson and Miller (2006). Explicit instruction incorporates the components of direct instruction, which has 30 years of empirical support as an effective method of teaching students with LD (Rosenshine & Stevens, 1986). Additionally, the National Mathematics Advisory Panel (2008) recommended that students with LD receive explicit instruction on a regular basis.

Summary of the Research and Instructional Implications
Mayfield and Glenn (2008) examined the effects of five intervention phases (i.e., cumulative practice, tiered feedback, feedback plus solution sequence instruction, review practice, and transfer training) on student performance in multiplying and dividing variables with coefficients and exponents and solving linear equations. Limited improvements were noted for cumulative practice (i.e., practicing

Table 1   Transfer Training

Example of transfer training	
Steps for implementation	**Example**
Step 1: Problem-solving task is broken into target skills.	$3x^6 \times 6x^8$
	$\dfrac{18x^{14}}{9x^7}$
Step 2: Original problem-solving task provided.	$\dfrac{3x^6 \times 6x^8}{9x^7}$

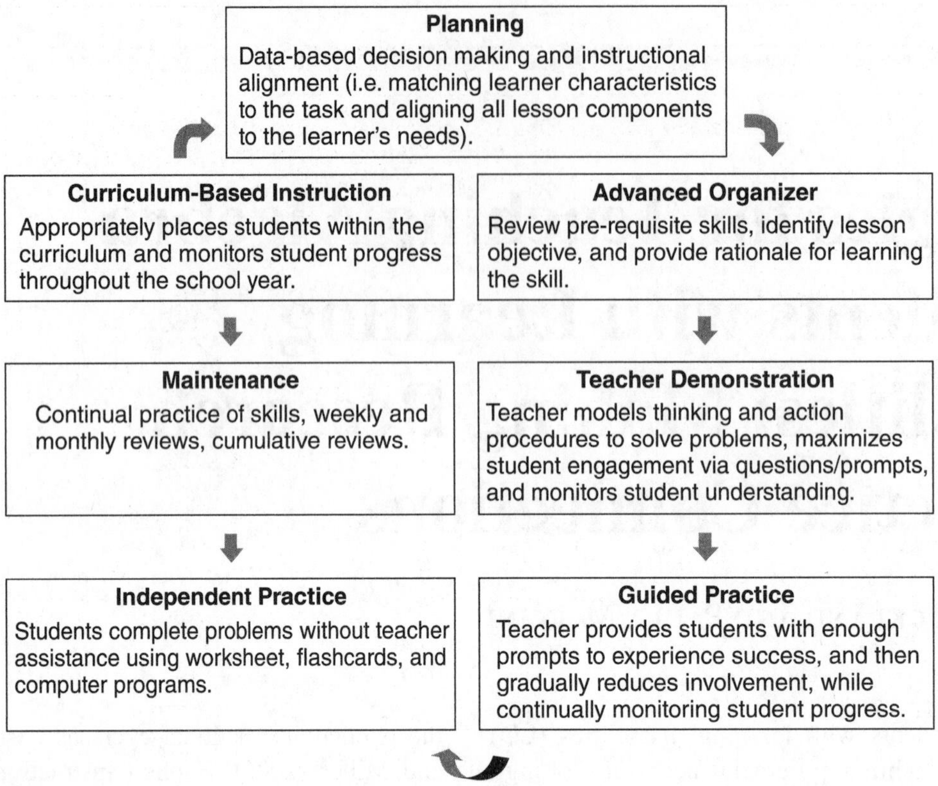

Figure 1 Explicit teaching cycle

Note. From "Accessing the General Education Math Curriculum for Secondary Students with High Incidence Disabilities," by P. Maccini, T. Strickland, J. C. Gagnon, and K. Malmgren, 2008, Focus on Exceptional Children, 40(8), p. 6. Copyright 2008 by Love Publishing. Reprinted with permission.

targeted skills necessary to complete novel problems) and feedback plus solution sequence instruction (i.e., providing writing prompts that are faded over time). However, they found that transfer training (i.e., presenting a novel problem as a series of steps) produced consistent improvements in students' performance. Specifically, transfer training is similar to performing a task analysis, in which a complex task is taught as a series of sequential target tasks. Mastery of target tasks transfers to the completion of the complex task. This is an important area of research given that many students with LD experience difficulty generalizing learned material to novel situations (Bley & Thorton, 2001; Gagnon & Maccini, 2001; Kroesbergen & Van Luit, 2003).

An example of transfer training is provided in Table 1. In order for students to solve the original problem,

$$\frac{3x^6 \times 6x^8}{9x^7},$$

the teacher first presents the problem as two target skills,

$$3x^6 \times 6x^8 \text{ and } \frac{18x^{14}}{9x^7}.$$

After successfully solving the target skills, the teacher then provides the entire problem for the students to solve.

Graduated Instructional Sequence
Definition

The graduated instructional sequence involves a three-stage process in which students begin instruction at the concrete level, proceed to a semiconcrete or representational stage, and end with abstract notation. Physical manipulatives commonly used at the concrete level include counters, blocks, algebra tiles, and geoboards. Drawings, pictures, and virtual manipulatives are tools used at the semiconcrete or representational stage. At the abstract level, students use mathematical notation (i.e., numbers, symbols, and variables). Students must successfully solve problems using physical objects prior to advancing to the semiconcrete or representational stage, and then successfully solve problems using pictorial representations prior to advancing to the abstract stage (Witzel, Mercer, & Miller, 2003). The terms *concrete-semiconcrete-abstract* (CSA) and *concrete-representational-abstract* (CRA) are used synonymously to refer to this teaching continuum that involves a multisensory approach to learning (Witzel, 2005).

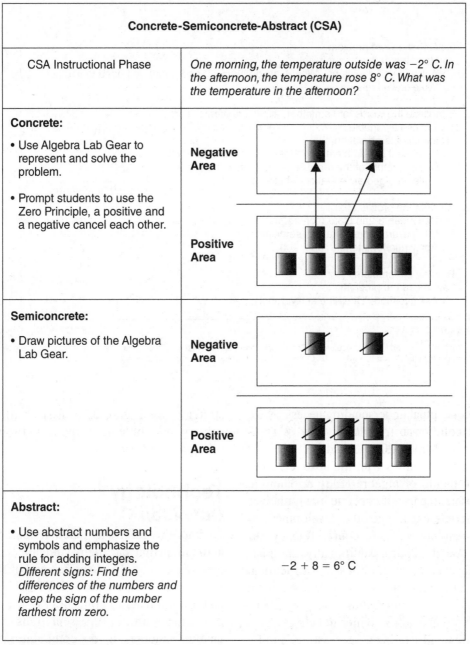

Concrete-Semiconcrete-Abstract (CSA)

CSA Instructional Phase	*One morning, the temperature outside was −2° C. In the afternoon, the temperature rose 8° C. What was the temperature in the afternoon?*
Concrete: • Use Algebra Lab Gear to represent and solve the problem. • Prompt students to use the Zero Principle, a positive and a negative cancel each other.	**Negative Area** **Positive Area**
Semiconcrete: • Draw pictures of the Algebra Lab Gear.	**Negative Area** **Positive Area**
Abstract: • Use abstract numbers and symbols and emphasize the rule for adding integers. *Different signs: Find the differences of the numbers and keep the sign of the number farthest from zero.*	$-2 + 8 = 6° C$

Figure 2   Concrete-semiconcrete-abstract example

Summary of the Research and Instructional Implications

Three studies (Maccini & Hughes, 2000; Maccini & Ruhl, 2000; Witzel et al., 2003) investigated the effects of the graduated instructional sequence. In a comparison study, Witzel et al. (2003) found that the use of the CRA sequence was a more effective intervention than traditional teaching using abstract notation only on the solution of multistep linear equations. Although the CRA group outperformed the abstract-only group to a statistically significant level, the CRA group did not perform to

mastery level, indicated by low mean scores on posttest and follow-up measures (27% and 25%, respectively). Maccini and Hughes (2000) and Maccini and Ruhl (2000) also studied the effects of the graduated instructional sequence on the representation and solution of contextualized word problems involving integers. In both of these studies, students reached criterion level of 80% accuracy or greater on two consecutive probes.

The use of concrete manipulatives and visual representations is a recommended instructional strategy across age bands and mathematical domains, including algebra,

---

STAR Strategy

1. **S** earch the word problem.
   a. Read the problem carefully.
   b. Ask yourself questions: "What facts do I know?" and "What do I need to find out?"
   c. Write down facts.

2. **T** ranslate the words into a mathematical equation.
   a. Choose a variable.
   b. Identify the operation(s).
   c. Represent the problem with Algebra Lab Gear (concrete).
      Draw a picture of the representation (semiconcrete).
      Write an algebraic equation (abstract).

3. **A** nswer the problem.
   Use Algebra Lab Gear (concrete).
   Use picture representation (semiconcrete).
   Apply rule for integers (abstract).

4. **R** eview the problem.
   a. Reread the problem.
   b. Ask question, "Does the answer make sense? Why?"

Figure 3 STAR strategy

Note. From "Accessing the General Education Math Curriculum for Secondary Students with High Incidence Disabilities," by P. Maccini, T. Strickland, J. C. Gagnon, and K. Malmgren, 2008, *Focus on Exceptional Children*, 40(8), p. 19. Copyright 2008 by Love Publishing. Reprinted with permission.

as it develops the conceptual understanding necessary for success at the symbolic or abstract level (Bley & Thorton, 2001; Hudson & Miller, 2006). Students with LD may have significant difficulties with the abstract, complex, and intuitive nature of algebra (Bley & Thorten, 2001). To compensate, the use of concrete manipulatives and hands-on materials encourages the development of conceptual understanding and procedural fluency for students with LD (Witzel, 2005). Additionally, the graduated instructional sequence exemplifies an instructional approach that incorporates the goals of the National Council of Teachers of Mathematics (NCTM; 2000) standards with use of hands-on activities to help students explore mathematics and has been successfully implemented with components of explicit instruction (Hudson, Miller, & Butler, 2006).

Figure 2 provides an example of the implementation of the CSA sequence. During the concrete phase, students use Algebra Lab Gear (Picciotto, 1990) to represent and solve contextualized problems containing positive and negative integers. In the semiconcrete phase, students draw pictures of the manipulatives to represent and solve the problems. In the abstract phase, students represent and solve the problems by using numerical symbols. Instruction includes teacher modeling, guided practice, independent work, and corrective feedback. Additionally, students follow the STAR strategy (see Figure 3) to assist with representing and solving the problems correctly and self-monitoring their academic performance.

Technology
Definition

Technology refers to calculators, computer systems, and video that can help students learn and do mathematics and is an essential and influential principle for school mathematics (NCTM, 2000). Technology enables students to conceptually learn mathematics by providing multiple representations of the concept and enables students to do computations and procedures that may be laborious without the use of technology (NCTM, 2000).

Summary of the Research and Implications for Practice

Three studies (Bottge, Heinrichs, Chan, & Serlin, 2001; Bottge, Rueda, LaRoque, Serlin, & Kwon. 2007; Bottge, Rueda, Serlin, Hung, & Kwon, 2007) investigated the use of video-based instruction entitled *enhanced anchored instruction* (EAI) on students' algebra performance with linear functions, lines of best fit, variables, and slope. EAI is specifically designed to improve the mathematics and

Table 2 Implementing Enhanced Anchored Instruction (EAI) in the Classroom

	Implementation of *Kim's Komet* video-based anchor
Purchasing	*Kim's Komet* is one episode in a series called *The New Adventures of Jasper Woodbury.* • The *Kim's Komet* videodisc can be ordered from ThinkLink Learning. The website address is www.thinklinklearning.com/sol_jasper.php.
Lesson plan overview	The teacher facilitates and asks guiding and prompting questions as needed to allow students to find the solutions to the math problems or "challenges" embedded within the video episode. • Students view an 8-minute video, which has a time display for returning and fast forwarding to different parts of the video. • Students may work in small groups to solve the problems.
First challenge	Students identify the three fastest cars. • Times and distances are given but distances vary.
Second challenge	Students construct the "line of best fit" on a graph to predict the speed of cars that have been released from various heights on a ramp. • Students use their own stop watches to clock times. • The videodisc allows students to choose various heights on the ramp to release the car.
Grand pentathlon event	Video-based event in which Kim's car travels on five trick ramps attached to the end of the original straight ramp. • Students are provided with the speed needed for the successful completion of each trick. • Students choose the release point. • Kim's car will either successfully complete the trick, if released from the correct height, or crash. • Students may earn points for successful tricks.
Application of problems	Students participate in their own model car soapbox derby. • Build model ramps, perhaps with the assistance of technology education teachers and parent volunteers. • Students build and decorate their own model cars. • Model cars timed using an infrared detector. • Students solve problems similar to those on video.

problem-solving performance of secondary students with LD and involves the use of video-based problems and hands-on activities with group activities. The researchers determined that students with disabilities improved their problem-solving skills when provided EAI, although outcomes on computational skills were mixed, with students frequently performing worse on computational posttests. The performance of students with LD receiving EAI in an inclusive classroom matched or exceeded the performance of their nondisabled peers on problem-solving measures (Bottge et al., 2001; Bottge, Rueda, Serlin, et al., 2007).

Enhanced Anchored Instruction is a promising intervention for teaching problem-solving skills to secondary students with disabilities in self-contained special education classrooms (Bottge, Rueda, LaRoque, et al., 2007) and in inclusive classrooms (Bottge et al., 2001; Bottge, Rueda, Serlin, et al., 2007). Additionally, EAI incorporates several NCTM process standards, as real-world problems encourage problem solving, mathematical connections, mathematical communication, and mathematical reasoning (Hudson, Miller, & Butler, 2006). The use of technology such as EAI provides students with LD access to a wide range of algebra tasks that previously were unattainable due to learning deficits (i.e., poor recall of math facts, difficulty with algorithms, poor sequential memory, difficulty understanding abstract concepts). Students with LD also commonly use calculators to address deficits in arithmetic and may use computer algebra systems (CAS) to support conceptual and procedural understanding of more difficult algebra tasks, such as multiplying binomials and factoring trinomials (Kieran & Saldanha, 2005).

Virtual manipulatives, such as those found at the National Library of Virtual Manipulatives website (http://nlvm.usa.edu/en/nav/vLibrary.html), also provide multiple practice opportunities involving algebra tasks, such as functions, equations, multiplying and factoring expressions, and graphing. Additionally, the NCTM website, Illuminations (http://illuminations.nctm.org), provides a wide variety of online mathematics activities, many with accompanying lesson plans.

Guidelines for implementing EAI in the algebra classroom for secondary students with LD are presented in Table 2. For example, teachers can incorporate the use of EAI with use of a digital video titled *Kim's Komet*. In the video, students solve problems, including determining the fastest model car and constructing a graph to predict the speed of a car at the end of a straightaway when released from any height on a soapbox derby ramp. Students can build model cars to release on a ramp and solve additional problems similar to those in the video.

Graphic Organizers
Definition

Graphic organizers, such as diagrams and charts, are visual representations that depict the relationship between facts or ideas within a learning task (Hall & Strangman, 2002). Graphic organizers help arrange information in an orderly manner, which may assist students with LD who have deficits involving the language of mathematics and working memory deficits that may interfere with solving multistep problems associated with algebra.

Summary of the Research and Instructional Implications

Ives (2007) explored the use of a graphic organizer as a tool for solving systems of linear equations in two related studies. The first study addressed the effects of a graphic organizer on the solution of systems of two linear equations in two variables. The researcher found no significant difference in solving for the solution of systems of equations between groups of students instructed in the use of the graphic organizer and students who did not have access to the graphic organizer. Both groups performed with approximately 40% accuracy. When the graphic organizer was extended to the solution of three linear equations in three variables, participants who used the graphic organizer demonstrated greater gains, significantly outperforming the comparison group (i.e., 61% to 42%).

The use of a graphic organizer to solve systems of linear equations is a potentially effective tool for students with LD. This may be especially beneficial for students with LD who have deficits related to semantic memory, which is characterized by difficulties in retrieving basic facts and procedures and is associated with language deficits and reading disabilities (Geary, 2004). Teachers can develop a variety of graphic organizers to assist students with numerous algebraic tasks. For example, a graphic organizer for solving quadratic equations is illustrated in Figure 4. Students are instructed to (a) start with the quadratic equation in the top block, (b) follow the arrows and factor the quadratic to represent two new equations, and (c) solve each equation.

Summary

Overall, promising interventions for teaching algebra to students with LD include components of explicit instruction (i.e., cumulative practice, feedback plus solution sequence instruction, and transfer training), use of the graduated instructional sequence, enhanced anchored instruction, and graphic organizers. As more students with LD are participating in general education classrooms with rigorous mathematics standards, there is a critical need to incorporate research-supported

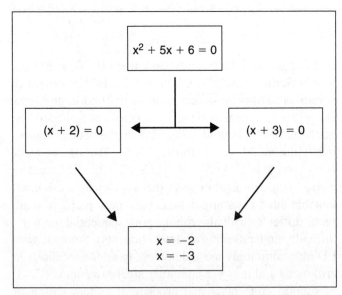

Figure 4 Graphic organizer for solving a quadratic equation

practices for all learners to successfully access an age-appropriate mathematics curriculum (Individuals With Disabilities Education Act, 1997; No Child Left Behind, 2002).

Declaration of Conficting Interests

The author(s) declared no conflicts of interest with respect to the authorship and/or publication of this article.

Funding

The author(s) received no financial support for the research and/or authorship of this article.

References

The Access Center. (2004). *Using peer tutoring to facilitate access.* Washington, DC: Author. Retrieved September 10, 2009, from www.k8accesscenter.org/training_resources/documents /PeerTutoringFinal.pdf.

Bley, N. S., & Thorton, C. A. (2001). *Teaching mathematics to students with learning disabilities* (4th ed.). Austin, TX: PRO-ED.

Bottge, B. A., Heinrichs, M., Chan, S., & Serlin, R. C. (2001). Anchoring adolescents' understanding of math concepts in rich problem-solving environments. *Remedial and Special Education. 22,* 299–341.

Bottge, B. A., Rueda, E., LaRoque, P. T., Serlin, R. C., & Kwon, J. (2007). Integrating reform-oriented math instruction in special education settings. *Learning Disabilities Research & Practice, 22,* 96–109.

Bottge, B. A., Rueda, E., Serlin, R. C., Hung, Y., & Kwon, J. M. (2007). Shrinking achievement differences with anchored math problems: Challenges and possibilities. *Journal of Special Education, 41,* 31–49.

Gagnon, J. C., & Maccini, P. (2001). Preparing students with disabilities for algebra. *Teaching Exceptional Children, 34*(1), 8–15.

Geary, D. C. (2004). Mathematics and learning disabilities. *Journal of Learning Disabilities, 37*(1), 4–15.

Hall, T., & Strangman, N. (2002). *Graphic organizers.* Wakefield, MA: National Center on Accessing the General Curriculum. Retrieved September 9, 2009, from www.cast.org/publications /ncac/ncac_go.html.

Hudson, P., & Miller, S. P. (2006). *Designing and implementing mathematics instruction for students with diverse learning needs.* Boston: Pearson Education.

Hudson, P., Miller, S. P., & Butler, F. (2006). Adapting and merging explicit instruction within reform based mathematics classrooms. *American Secondary Education, 35*(1), 19–32.

Individuals With Disabilities Education Act of 1990, 20 U.S.C. § 1400 *et seq.* (1990) (amended 1997).

Ives, B. (2007). Graphic organizers applied to secondary algebra instruction for students with learning disabilities. *Learning Disabilities Research & Practice, 22*(2), 110–118.

Kieran, C., & Saldanha, L. (2005). Computer algebra systems (CAS) tools for coaxing the emergence of reasoning about equivalence of algebraic expressions. In H. L. Chick & J. L. Vincent (Eds.), *Proceedings of the 29th Conference of the International Group for the Psychology of Mathematics Education* (Vol. 3, pp. 193–200), Melbourne, Australia: PME.

Kroesbergen, E. H., & Van Luit, J. E. H. (2003). Mathematics interventions for children with special education needs: A meta-analysis. *Remedial and Special Education, 24*(2) 97–114.

Maccini, P., & Hughes, C. A. (2000). Effects of a problem-solving strategy on the introductory algebra performance of secondary students with learning disabilities. *Learning Disabilities Research & Practice, 15*(1), 10–21.

Maccini, P., McNaughton, D., & Ruhl, K. L. (1999). Algebra instruction for students with learning disabilities: Implications from a research review. *Learning Disabilities Quarterly, 22,* 113–126.

Maccini, P., & Ruhl, K. L. (2000). Effects of a graduated instructional sequence on the algebraic subtraction of integers by secondary students with learning disabilities. *Education and Treatment of Children, 23,* 465–489.

Maccini, P., Strickland, T., Gagnon, J. C., & Malmgren, K. (2008). Accessing the general education curriculum for secondary students with high-incidence disabilities. *Focus on Exceptional Children, 40*(8), 1–32.

Mayfield, K. H., & Glenn, I. M. (2008). An evaluation of interventions to facilitate algebra problem solving. *Journal of Behavioral Education, 17,* 278–302.

National Council of Teachers of Mathematics. (2000). *Principle and standards for school mathematics.* Reston, VA: Author.

National Mathematics Advisory Panel. (2008). *Foundations for success: The final report of the national advisory panel.* Washington, DC: U.S. Department of Education.

No Child Left Behind Act of 2001, 20 U.S.C. 70 § 6301 *et seq.* (2002).

Picciotto, H. (1990). *The algebra lab.* Sunnyvale, CA: Creative Publications.

Rosenshine, B., & Stevens, R. (1986). Teaching functions. In M. C. Wittrock (Ed.), *Handbook of research on teaching* (3rd ed., pp. 376–391). New York: Macmillan.

Witzel, B. (2005). Using CRA to teach algebra to students with math difficulties in inclusive settings. *Learning Disabilities: A Contemporary Journal, 3*(2), 49–60.

Witzel, B., Mercer, C. D., & Miller, M. D. (2003). Teaching algebra to students with learning difficulties: An investigation of an explicit instruction model. *Learning Disabilities Research & Practice, 18*(2), 121–131.

Critical Thinking

1. Why did the authors select these four teaching strategies to share?

2. Review each strategy to determine which group of students might benefit from using each strategy, in addition to those with learning disabilities. Explain why you think a particular strategy would be useful for a specific group of students.

3. Could these strategies be used in other areas of mathematics? Which ones? How?

4. If you teach a content area other than algebra, how might you use these strategies in your content area? Select a specific teaching or learning activity for each strategy.

TRICIA K. STRICKLAND is a doctoral candidate at the University of Maryland, College Park. Her research interests include mathematics for secondary students with learning disabilities. **PAULA MACCINI** is an associate professor at the University of Maryland, College Park. Her research interests involve mathematics interventions for secondary students with high-incidence disabilities.

From *Intervention in School and Clinic,* vol. 46, no. 1, 2010, pp. 38–45. Copyright © 2010 by Pro-Ed, Inc. Reprinted by permission via Copyright Clearance Center.

Do Girls Learn Math Fear from Teachers?

Washington (AP)—Little girls may learn to fear math from the women who are their earliest teachers.

Despite gains in recent years, women still trail men in some areas of math achievement, and the question of why has provoked controversy. Now, a study of first- and second-graders suggests what may be part of the answer: Female elementary school teachers who are concerned about their own math skills could be passing that along to the little girls they teach.

Young students tend to model themselves after adults of the same sex, and having a female teacher who is anxious about math may reinforce the stereotype that boys are better at math than girls, explained Sian L. Beilock, an associate professor in psychology at the University of Chicago.

Beilock and colleagues studied 52 boys and 65 girls in classes taught by 17 different teachers. Ninety percent of U.S. elementary school teachers are women, as were all of those in this study.

Student math ability was not related to teacher math anxiety at the start of the school year, the researchers report in today's edition of Proceedings of the National Academy of Sciences.

But by the end of the year, the more anxious teachers were about their own math skills, the more likely their female students—but not the boys—were to agree that "boys are good at math and girls are good at reading."

In addition, the girls who answered that way scored lower on math tests than either the classes' boys or the girls who had not developed a belief in the stereotype, the researchers found.

"It's actually surprising in a way, and not. People have had a hunch that teachers could impact the students in this way, but didn't know how it might do so in gender-specific fashion," Beilock said in a telephone interview.

Beilock, who studies how anxieties and stress can affect people's performance, noted that other research has indicated that elementary education majors at the college level have the highest levels of math anxiety of any college major.

"We wanted to see how that impacted their performance," she said.

After seeing the results, the researchers recommended that the math requirements for obtaining an elementary education teaching degree be rethought.

"If the next generation of teachers—especially elementary school teachers—is going to teach their students effectively, more care needs to be taken to develop both strong math skills and positive math attitudes in these educators," the researchers wrote.

Janet S. Hyde, a professor in the Department of Psychology at the University of Wisconsin-Madison, called the study a "great paper, very clever research."

"It squares with an impression I've had for a long time," said Hyde, who was not part of the research team.

Hyde was lead author of a 2008 study showing women gaining on men in math skills but still lagging significantly in areas such as physics and engineering.

Girls who grow up believing females lack math skills wind up avoiding harder math classes, Hyde noted.

"It keeps girls and women out of a lot of careers, particularly high-prestige, lucrative careers in science and technology," she said.

Beilock did note that not all of the girls in classrooms with math-anxious teachers fell prey to the stereotype, but "teachers are one source," she said.

Teacher math anxiety was measured on a 25-question test about situations that made them anxious, such as reading a cash register receipt or studying for a math test. A separate test checked the math skills of the teachers, who worked in a large Midwestern urban school district.

Student math skills were tested in the first three months of the school year and again in the last two months of the year.

The research was funded by the National Science Foundation.

Critical Thinking

1. Where did you learn to love or fear mathematics?

2. Describe what the teacher or other person did to cause this love/fear you felt for mathematics.

3. With a small group of peers, make a list of ways that teachers can encourage all students to love and learn math.

UNIT 4

Creating Caring Communities of Learners

Unit Selections

Learning Outcomes

After reading this unit, you will be able to:

- Design a plan for establishing positive relationships with and among your students.

- State reasons why involving parents in your classroom is important to student learning.

- Describe how you will make and maintain a relationship with families of your students or future students.

- Share your rationale for or against using tangible rewards for learning.

- Prepare a plan for using rewards to motivate reluctant students to become lifelong learners.

- Explain how to find the appropriate classroom currency to motivate reluctant learners.

- Outline the steps effective principals take to ensure that all students learn.

- Describe what a highly effective teacher does to help students achieve.

- Hypothesize why bullying is so difficult to stop.

Student Website

www.mhhe.com/cls

Internet References

American School Board Journal
www.asbj.com/TopicsArchive/Bullying/default.aspx

Teacher Vision
www.teachervision.fen.com/education-and-parents/resource/3730.html

Coalition of Essential Schools
www.essentialschools.org

The National Coalition for Parent Involvement in Education (NCPIE)
www.ncpie.org

Office of Safe and Drug-Free Schools
www2.ed.gov/about/offices/list/osdfs/index.html

GLSEN: Gay, Lesbian and Straight Education Network
www.glsen.org/cgi-bin/iowa/all/home/index.html

All of us are situated in social, political, and economic circumstances, which inform and develop our values. Our values are usually derived from principles of conduct that we learn in each of our histories of interaction with ourselves (as they form) and in interaction with others. This is to say that societal values develop in a cultural context. Teachers cannot hide all of their moral preferences. They can, however, learn to conduct just and open discussions of moral topics without succumbing to the temptation to indoctrinate students with their own views. In democratic societies, such as the United States, alternative sets of values and morals co-exist. What teachers perceive to be worthwhile and defensible behavior informs our reflections on what we as educators should teach. We are immediately conscious of some of the values that affect our behavior, but we may not be as aware of what informs our preferences. Values that we hold without being conscious of them are referred to as tacit values: these are values derived indirectly after reasoned reflection on our thoughts about teaching and learning. Much of our knowledge about teaching is tacit knowledge, which we need to bring into conscious cognition by analyzing the concepts that drive our practice. We need to acknowledge how all our values inform, and influence, our thoughts about teaching. Teachers grapple with the dilemma of their own values versus the values of their students.

Students need to develop a sense of genuine caring both for themselves and others. Teacher must model and teach students how to be a caring community of learners by building positive relationships with the students, their parents, and the community outside the school. The articles in this unit offer practices and suggestions to help teachers. Brown states that some discount the importance of establishing relationships with students in middle and secondary classes, but the proven connection between positive relationships and school achievement is strong. She discusses seven opportunities for establishing positive relationships with middle schoolers, however, these can be used at any grade level. All students want and appreciate a teacher who cares and values them. Schools have an obligation to individual students and to their families as well. Sometimes teachers engage in the classist idea that families are uncaring, uninformed, distracted, or too disorganized to offer educational and behavioral support to their children. What may be missing is a teacher who knows and understands that caregivers may have valid reasons for their lack of involvement. We have long-standing research that says when parents are involved in schools, their child's achievement improves.

How can a teacher connect with all parents? Kersey and Masterson offer practical suggestions for building bridges and strong ties to families; including suggestions to overcome parent reluctance, share information, and maintain parent involvement throughout the year. Another concept that is essential to building a caring community is a student who believes that her efforts will make a difference and that the future holds promise for her life. Motivated students believe in the future. These students believe that investing in today will bring a positive payoff in the future. How do we motivate students to be intrinsically motivated? Blackburn and Armstrong offer suggestions for connecting

© Corbis/SuperStock

learning to successful completion of activities that will motivate the most hard-hearted student. Furthermore, Jackson asserts that every classroom has its own currency that is a medium of exchange and a driving force in the classroom. This currency is the behavior (or motivational thoughts) students engage in to learn knowledge and skills in the class. She describes the conflict that results when the currency desired by students is not acknowledged and used by the teacher. The suggestion in this article will help teachers support English Language Learners (ELL) as well as invest all students in creating an inclusive classroom culture. However, establishing positive relationships and making sure that we use the appropriate currency to motivate students does not mean we are "fluffy" or "soft" in our attention to the real work of schools, making sure that students achieve. In the article, "She's Strict for a Good Reason," researchers share the stories of 31 teachers whose students are high achievers in low-performing, high-poverty, and high-minority schools. How do they do it when others around them are failing? The researchers found these teachers had common behaviors in the classroom and held similar beliefs about their responsibility as teachers. Likewise, Chenoweth found the important commonly held insights about teaching and leading that principals of high-performing, high-poverty, and high-minority schools learned as they turned around their previously low achieving schools. For example, school leaders must be guardians of their students' future, not of their staff members' happiness. What does that mean?

Creating caring communities of learners seems impossible if we look carefully at the high numbers of bullying cases that are on the nightly news. Even television programs such as GLEE have recurring cases of bullying with no evidence of adult intervention. Graham defines bullying, common myths, and shares interventions teachers and school leaders can use.

The role of a teacher goes well beyond the image of a stern-faced person standing at the front of a room, where rows and rows of quiet robot-like students churn out page after page of perfect papers written in error-free standard English. We are so much more than that made-for-TV movie trailer.

The Power of Positive Relationships

TARA BROWN

The research is clear: humans are literally "hard-wired" with the desire and need to connect. We are social beings who thrive on healthy relationships. And yet, the importance of positive relationships in our schools is often overlooked.

Despite the proven connection between positive relationships and student achievement, some discount relationship building in middle grades and high schools as a bunch of "fluff" more appropriate for the elementary school.

For middle grades kids who are trying to gain some independence and figure out which way is up, relationships with classmates and teachers are crucial to success. I offer seven relationship-based strategies that can transform your classroom into a positive learning environment.

1. Be the CEO of Your Classroom.

Students look for reasons to respect and follow you. You must send the message from Day One that you are in control and worthy of their respect.

This message, however, should not convey an overbearing, authoritarian, inflexible approach. Striking the right balance between being approachable without being their friend is the challenge and art of teaching.

Communicate to your students your absolutes. Establish the boundaries and don't move them. Because conflict is a part of growing up, they will test those lines. Be firm.

Still, keep rules to a minimum. Review and practice these rules the first weeks of school. Don't make the false assumption that students know what you want from them. Simply stating rules and putting them on the wall is not sufficient. Discussing, practicing, and reinforcing your rules are crucial to ensuring all students thoroughly understand your expectations.

2. Embrace Their Individuality.

If we are honest with ourselves, we must admit that embracing students for who they are is likely one of the toughest challenges for educators. Young adolescents are trying to sort out who they are and how to "show up" in life; sagging pants or piercings don't tell the whole story. You can give them a gift by embracing them for their individuality and uniqueness rather than giving in to stereotyping and judging.

At the beginning of the year, pass out a student profile form. Ask about hobbies, family, goals, dreams, talents, interests, likes, dislikes, and favorite things. Spend time reading these profiles and using the information to connect with your students in casual conversation.

Taking an interest in their lives, their quirks, and their desire to dance to their own beat is often the most powerful strategy you can use to open that door and reach a child.

3. Create a Community within the Classroom.

Help students get to know each other. The sooner you are able to help students realize that there are more similarities than differences among them, the more comfortable they will be in the class. You can do this in several ways.

- Pair up students and give them three minutes to find as many similarities between themselves as possible, such as love baseball, play the guitar, been to Canada, have two brothers. Then combine pairs so four people are trying to find similarities in three minutes. When they realize how much they have in common, they'll help you build a more productive learning environment.

- Give students two or three minutes to share their life highlights with a partner, who then shares this information with the class. Reverse roles and do it again. This activity will quickly get everyone talking and learning something about everyone else.

- Get a large 12-month wall calendar that you can write on with dry erase markers. Let students mark their birthday on the calendar. They will find even more similarities among themselves as they see who has birthdays close to theirs or are the same zodiac sign. You could even designate someone to compile a list of all birthdays that fall in each month of the year and come up with a unique way to celebrate each month's birthdays.

4. Let Them Get to Know a Part of You.

Some educators really struggle with this concept because they fear familiarity might create a more undisciplined atmosphere in the classroom. The fact is, the more comfortable your students are with you, the more relaxed and receptive they will be.

Have students submit questions they would like to ask you about yourself. Designate time at the end of class on random days and just pull out questions and answer them. You can have a lot of fun with this, and it will help your students begin seeing you as a real person.

Another strategy is to share hobbies, favorite sports teams, pets, talents, books, movies, and music. I've known educators who brought in tomato plants and let their students help grow them, or who incorporated juggling or singing or their love of sports into lessons and dialogue.

One colleague met with several students before school and during lunch to work on guitar riffs together. One of those students told me that playing guitar with that teacher was the only thing that kept him coming to school.

Don't be afraid to let your hair down and have a little F-U-N with your students.

5. Learn All Students' Names within 48 Hours.

Many students feel invisible as they walk down hallways and can literally go the entire day without talking to anyone. When you address your students by name, you are showing them respect. It sends the message that they are important enough for you to take the time to learn and use their names. Acknowledging an individual creates a connection.

After you learn their names, use them everywhere: in the class, in the hallway, and in the cafeteria. Some students will be shocked that you addressed them by their name after only two days, and it will have an impact.

Nicknames can be even more powerful because of the uniqueness to that individual. When I was 13, my middle school principal nicknamed me "Slim," and years later, when I saw him in town, he still called me "Slim." Even as an adult, that made me smile and I felt the same feeling that I did when I was 13: special.

6. Examine and Improve Nonverbal Communication.

We all know how dreadful speeches and presentations can be when the speaker is unenthusiastic and disconnected from the audience. It's all about effective communication.

Are you connecting with your students and presenting yourself and the material in a way that gives them a reason to get excited, to sit up and pay attention? Do your body language, voice inflection, volume, and facial expressions convey a sense of high energy, excitement, and relevance?

Do you smile at your students? I've worked with teachers who wouldn't smile if you paid them. SMILE! It is welcoming, inviting, high energy. Students (and even more so, students from poverty) rely heavily on nonverbal communication and are always watching those around them for their nonverbal cues.

Ask a trusted colleague to observe you and take notes about your nonverbal communication for a class period. Honest assessment and feedback are crucial, and helpful to making positive changes. Or, set up a video camera in the back of the room, turn it on, and press record. When you review the tape, it will serve as a powerful reminder of those things you do that are surprising, distracting, repetitive, annoying, boring, or irritating. This one painful exercise can fast forward improvement in your nonverbal communication and your overall presentations.

We are all lifetime learners. You can't improve if you don't know what to work on. Be brave—take the plunge! Your students will thank you.

7. Treat All Students with Dignity and Respect at All Times.

What if all the teachers in your school embraced the concept that their classroom would be a Yell Free Zone? What if every administrator could say to every parent in the community, "My personal pledge to you is that your child will never be yelled at by any adult in this building"? How would that transform the culture and climate within the school? Within your classroom? Within the community?

As adults, we may be the only positive role models in many of our students' lives. As frustrated as we get at times, we should never yell at or demean a student. When we incorporate good manners in our classrooms and maintain a consistent demeanor, we show respect and help our students understand and learn the power of positive, healthy interaction.

Sometimes we lose our temper, overreact, or respond negatively toward a student because of something that's going on in our own lives. My plea to every educator is to maintain a personal routine of exercise and healthy nutrition to decrease stress, increase energy, and help maintain a positive attitude toward every student.

All about Relationships

Positive relationships truly have the ability and the power to unleash untapped potential in our students. While many teachers may not think they have the time to spend building relationships, I suggest that we don't have the time not to. Relationships and instruction are not an either–or proposition, but are rather an incredible combination. Research tells us this combination will increase engagement, motivation, test scores, and grade point averages while decreasing absenteeism, dropout rates, and discipline issues.

Begin to unleash the power of positive relationships in your classroom.

Critical Thinking

1. Think back to your K–12 school experiences. Can you remember the teacher who made a connection to you or taught the class you couldn't wait to get to each day? What did that teacher do that made her memorable? Compare her strategies to the strategies offered by Brown.

2. Brown proposes seven ways to establish positive relationships in your classroom. What do each of these mean to you, personally? Create one or two activities for each of the seven strategies, in addition to those in the article, that you will be able to use in your classroom.

3. We have all heard about the mentor teacher who told the student teacher, "Don't smile until Christmas." What would you say to that mentor to change his mind?

TARA BROWN, an NMSA member, is an educator, speaker, trainer, and author of *Different Cultures—Common Ground: 85 Proven Strategies to Connect in the Classroom.* E-mail: tbrown@leadersedgeconsulting .org.

Teachers Connecting with Families— In the Best Interest of Children

Katharine C. Kersey and Marie L. Masterson

When parents are involved in school, their children's achievement improves. Children make friends more easily and are more successful learners (NCPIE, 2006).Children whose families participate in school activities stay in school longer and take more advanced classes (Bamard 2004). But the greatest benefit to children of a successful home-school partnership is that children are more motivated to succeed (Hoover-Dempsey et al. 2005).

To connect parents with school, teachers need to learn the best ways to share information and thereby build bridges and strong ties with families. They need to find ways to establish positive relationships by shifting from a focus on children's problems to affirming children's strengths. Such approaches can improve classroom-home communications and encourage all families to become involved.

Knowing and Understanding Families

Most parents can remember what it felt like to take their child to school for the first time. Those hours seemed endless. Was she OK—smiling, crying, or hurt? Could you hardly wait to see her? What positive things did her teacher have to say when you picked up your child after her first day at kindergarten? If you waited to learn what she did on her first day and the teacher didn't say anything at all, were you crushed? Had you hoped that she would tell you what a nice little girl you had (in other words, that you'd done a good job)?

There are reasons a parent might feel intimidated by a teacher or hesitant to come to a conference. One parent expressed frustration that he left a meeting at work and drove 45 minutes during the worst traffic of the day, only to have 10 or 15 minutes with his child's teacher! Other parents say that they did not feel welcome at their children's school. Sometimes, parents can feel a teacher is questioning their competence, and so when they come for a meeting, they are defensive. Parents could be anticipating bad news. They

may be surprised if the teacher has something nice to say. Teachers need to build parents' confidence that their school encounters will result in positive interactions and success for their child.

At times, when parents hesitate to become involved, it may be because they feel inadequate in terms of their education or perhaps are unable to read. Teachers may use language a parent doesn't understand or describe a child's progress in educational jargon, which the parent is reluctant to admit confuses him. Parents may cringe at the thought of being asked questions they can't answer. And most of all, parents don't want to feel judged for their child's problems, behaviors, or poor progress.

Distrust and uncertainty work both ways. Teachers themselves can feel intimated by parents. In some cases, a parent's strong personality comes across as demanding or accusatory, Teachers may worry about being caught off guard or asked a question not easily handled. They too could fear being judged or embarrassed. One teacher said that at the end of a parent teacher conference, she experienced an awkward moment when she tried to shake hands with the parent, a practice she didn't know was considered disrespectful in the family's culture. She now takes the time to learn about the cultures of the children in her class. Setting parents at ease and helping them know that as teachers we want the same things they want for their children is well worth the time and energy it takes.

Sharing Information with Families

The positive interactions teachers use to create connections with parents are in the best interest of the child (Hamre & Pianta 2005). Successful teachers make it their business to connect with families and plan ways to build strong relationships with children and parents. Setting up an open and positive system of teacher availability supports cooperative and productive teacher-parent relationships.

The following suggestions illustrate some specific ways to build bridges and strengthen the bond between teacher and parent. Using strategies such as these can ensure that when challenges come, a strong foundation is already in place .

Before School Starts

- **Send a personalized postcard** to every child saying " See you soon at school You'll make friends and enjoy learning!"
- **Make a phone call** to each child: "I am calling to talk to Maria. I am your new teacher, and I look forward to seeing you."
- **Have an open house** for children and families as an orientation to school. Let the children explore the room so they will feel safe. Join the children at their level when you talk to set them at ease. Introduce children and families with common interests.
- **When the school year begins,** hold a Welcome Parents meeting [AQ3a Indicate when this takes place.] to show families that you care about their ideas and interests. Ask each family to complete a questionnaire to help you learn children's interests, strengths, pets, and hobbies. Ask for information about allergies and special concerns.

Begin the meeting with a Family Introduction Circle: "Whose mom or dad are you?" "Tell us something about _____ [child's name]." "What would you like everyone to know?" "Do you have something you would like to share with the children about your job, hobby, or a special interest?" Hand out copies of daily schedules, menus, and other items. Provide copies in the home languages of the families in the group. Plan time for a group of parents to get to know each other, and help them find ways to connect.

Make and share a "Me Bag." Bring special items that show and tell about you personally. Let families get to know you and about the things you love. You can share the same Me Bag with the children when school begins, and let the children bring in their Me Bags as well.

Throughout the Year

- **Call children at home.** Leave a message on the home answering machine during the school day. "Jamal, I am calling to say I noticed you help Brandon on the playground. He seemed grateful for your help." It takes 15 seconds, and Jamal may never want to erase it. Set aside a time each week to make these calls, and keep a list to make sure to include every child.

- **Send home a Great Moments! Certificate.** Attach a digital photo to the certificate and highlight a special contribution, a kind gesture, or clever words a child has used. Send three to five certificates each day to ensure each child receives one during the week.
- **Use the phone to share news.** Ask parents to let you know when they are available, and then set up a schedule so they can look forward to hearing from you. Be available for parents to call you at a set time if they have questions or want to talk. When a child is sick, it is appropriate to call her home to let her know she is missed.
- **Send e-mail communications.** "Today we had a picnic. We went outside under a tree. Ask Carmen to tell you what she did." Do this frequently so parents come to associate e-mails with memories of their children's experiences.
- **Say at least one positive thing each** time you see a parent. "Danny has such a wonderful sense of humor." "Teresa told me about your camping trip." Run after a parent to say, "I want to tell you . . . !" Parents will enjoy hearing about interesting things their child has done and learned.
- **Record the positive things children do.** Place them on 3 × 5 cards in a notebook you can share each time you see a parent—another opportunity to connect. Focus on conveying the message, "I notice your child!"
- **Encourage parent volunteers.** Any time you invite a parent to class, the child will feel excited and special. Encourage parents to read, share some expertise, or tell about a special interest. Let the parent's child help. Find creative ways for parents to make meaningful contributions to the classroom that can fit in their schedules (organizing child portfolios, photo copying, planning parties, or preparing for an art, music, or dramatics activity).
- **Send home weekend project packs** with activities parents and children can do together. An example could be a class mascot—a stuffed animal that takes turns going home with the children and have the families keep a diary of his activities. Children will take pride in bringing home the pet and then sharing their diary entry with classmates when the mascot returns to school.

During Parent Conferences

- **Focus on a child's natural strengths.** Affirm the child. Share special traits and unique capabilities. "Judy's block buildings are complex and inventive." "Joey shows compassion to his peers." "Jasmine enjoys exploring new aft materials." A teacher can help parents see the potential in their child and encourage them to support and nurture the child's gifts at home.

- **Always get the parent to talk first.** Say, "Tell me about your child?" The parent may ask, "What do you want to know?" You can respond, "Anything you want to tell me." Such an approach lets parents take the lead and feel relaxed and open to a conversation.

- **Ask parents for their perspectives.** Parents are experts about their child and may describe a child's strength or need. When they mention a strength, ask, "How do you support her at home?" When they tell you about a problem, ask, "How do you deal with that?"

- **Ask for help!** If the child is experiencing difficulty at school and you think the parent needs to get involved, you might introduce your concern by saying, "There is something I'd like your help with."

- **Focus on one important issue.** When you have concerns, choose one that you think can be helped or fixed. First, identify it, and then brainstorm some solutions. Together with the family you can agree to a plan. "I will work on this at school, while you work on it at home. Let's set an appointment to get together again in two weeks." This tells parents that by working together you can help the child succeed.

- **Start and end on positive notes.** Tell something good first. It lets the parents relax and know you notice special things about their child. Make sure to end with a commitment. "I appreciate and value the time that I share with your child, and I want to help her develop and learn."

- **Send a reminder.** Call or send an e-mail the day before to confirm the next appointment. "If you can't come that day, when is it convenient for you to come?"

When Parents Are Not Able to Come to School

- **Share successes immediately.** With parental permission, allow a child to call a parent during the day to tell about something great he just did. You can call also: "I want you to know that Joshua counted to six in Spanish today!"

- **Videotape children's activities,** presentations, and special accomplishments. Send the tape home on loan for parents to appreciate what they see their child learning and doing. Or upload the video to the school or classroom website.

- **Send home daily sheets.** Use photos and descriptions to show parents the activities and learning in which the children are engaged.

- **Fill a class newsletter with highlights** of community activities, parenting and positive guidance tips, and information about the class curriculum. Children can help write the news for this newsletter!

Use Affirmations to Connect with Families

With parents, use every opportunity to connect positively: "I can't wait to see you and tell you all of the wonderful things your child is doing!" When a teacher adopts this attitude in her interactions with parents, they will eagerly join in to support school and classroom activities for their child. Tell parents what the child is learning about himself, new friends, the world, and the outdoors. Parents need to hear what children are learning socially and how they are becoming successful. It is our job as teachers to help each child navigate the world successfully. We can give parents hope and confidence that their child is well on his way to achieving that goal.

It is always in the best interest of the child to connect with parents. When teachers and parents build connections and work together, children are more successful—both academically and socially. The relationships teachers form early with parents help children become socially and emotionally competent and do better in school (Walker et al. 2005). As a result, children have fewer behavior problems both at school and at home (NCPIE 2006). Family connections built, when children are young pay off in a lifetime of rich dividends for the child.

Teachers can tell families, "I hear about you all the time. I heard what a great thing you all did together last night." These positive affirmations make a parent feel relaxed and stand up tall. You're the teacher, are building bridges. You have a lasting impact on parents when you share your values and your goals for their children. You empower parents to be more successful in their parenting role when you connect them positively to their child's teacher and to school.

Once families feel comfortable and understand how important they are to their child's success, a strong relationship begins. The partnership strengthens as school and teacher become a source for positive information. Through this approach to building connections, teachers create authentic, caring relationships with families, and parents become active participants in their child's success.

References

Barnard, W.M. 2004. Parent involvement in elementary school and educational attainment. *Children and Youth Services Review* 26 ( ): 39–62.

Gladwell, M. 2005. Blink: *The power of thinking without thinking.* New York: Little, Brown.

Hamre, B., & R. Pianta. 2005. Can instructional and emotional support in the first-grade classroom make a difference for children at risk of school failure? *Child Development* 76 (5): 949–67.

Hoover-Dempsey, K., M. Walker, H. Sandler, D. Whetsel, C. Green, A. Wilkins, & K. Closson. 2005. Why do parents become involved? Research findings and implications. *Elementary School Journal* 2 (106): 105–30.

NCPIE (National Coalition for Parent Involvement in Education). 2006. What's Happening. *A new wave of evidence: The impact of school, family and community connections on student achievement.* www.ncpie.ore/WhatsHappening /researchJanuary2006.html

Walker, J.M., A.S. Wilkins, J.R. Dallaire, H.M. Sandler, & K.V. Hoover-Dempsey. 2005. Parental involvement: Model revision through scale development. *The Elementary School Journal* 106 (2): 85–104.

Critical Thinking

1. Give three reasons why involving parents in your classroom is important to your teaching and to student learning. Cite information from articles in this unit.

2. Which of the authors' suggestions for connecting with parents will you adopt? Share your reasons.

3. In the next two articles, you will read about motivating students and about understanding the currency that will help you connect. After you have read those articles, summarize what you have learned about motivating students and their families.

KATHARINE C. KERSEY, EdD, is professor of early childhood, an educator, and the director emeritus of the Child Study Center, Old Dominion University (ODU), in Norfolk, Virginia. She is the former chair of ODU's Department of Early Childhood, Speech Pathology, and Special Education and is a child behavior expert, TV consultant, teacher and parent educator, author, and speaker. kkersev@odu.edu

MARIE L. MASTERSON, PhD, is the early childhood specialist for the Virginia Department of Education and adjunct professor of early childhood education at Old Dominion University. She is coordinator of the ODU Director's Institute and an educational researcher, child behavior consultant, and speaker. mmasters@odu.edu

Motivation: It's All About Me

Students who see value in work and experience success are more likely to be motivated.

BARBARA R. BLACKBURN AND ABBIGAIL ARMSTRONG

Do you teach students who are intrinsically motivated? Intrinsic motivation comes from within. It's the sense of working toward something simply because we want to or because we see value in the accomplishment, and it is relatively easy to know when a student is intrinsically motivated.

However, in schools, often we focus much of our time and attention on extrinsic rewards such as points and prizes because they are so much easier and they do motivate many students, particularly for the short term. Intrinsic motivation seems to be harder for us. After all, how do you motivate someone to be self-motivated? There are two key elements to intrinsic motivation: value and success. If we tap into students' perceptions of value and feelings of success, we can help them be more motivated.

> **Often we focus much of our time and attention on extrinsic rewards such as points and prizes because they are so much easier and they do motivate many students, particularly for the short term. Intrinsic motivation seems to be harder for us.**

Seeing the Value of Learning

First, students are more motivated when they see the value of learning. When students ask, "Why do we need to learn this?" they are looking for value. There are several ways to help students see the value of specific learning. In an English class, you might ask students to research authors or poets. As a part of the project, ask students to identify commonalities between themselves and their subject. As one student commented, "I had to work hard, but it was fun to find out how I was similar to Emily Dickinson!"

A science teacher in the South asked her students to "cloud watch" so they could predict weather fronts. Her students were excited, because they learned how to predict a possible snowstorm. In that region, snow meant a day off school, so students loved learning to figure out when it was likely to snow.

A third way to incorporate value is to ask students to interview family members.

If you are talking about a recent historical event, they can ask different people what they remember about it. Or, if you are discussing school rules, they can talk to their family members about school rules when the adults were students. Both ideas help students connect the learning to their own personal situations.

Success Motivates

Students also are more motivated when they experience success. This can happen when they make connections, know the answer to a question or understand new knowledge. It's important to build opportunities for success into lessons.

For example, before students give an oral presentation in class, give them opportunities to share with some of their classmates first. Students gain confidence if the peer responses are appropriate; if they are not, their peers can help them fix the problem before a classroom response is given.

You even can do this with simple answers to questions you ask. Ask students to turn to a partner and answer the question you asked. As you walk around and monitor the class, preselect some of your reluctant students to share, by saying to them, "Wow, you are exactly right! I want you to share that with everyone, so I'll be calling on you in a few minutes." Then, when you ask them to share with the class, they are confident they are correct.

Self-reflection is another way that students can experience success. Students have an opportunity to reflect on their progress and can share this progress with the classroom teacher in a non-threatening environment. For example, use feedback cards (see [sample feedback card]). At the end of class, ask students to complete the card about the lesson. Then, at the start of your lesson the next day, use the anonymous feedback forms to review learning. One of the benefits of this is that Jonathan learns the information, but isn't embarrassed that everyone in

---

Ways I am Like Langston Hughes

We are both guys.
We are both African-American.
We have both been to Mexico.
He graduated from college and I will too!

Ways I am Different from Langston Hughes

He's dead and I'm not.
He was really old and I'm young.
He has been to Europe and I have not.
His parents were divorced, my parents are married.
He has a street named for him, and I do not.

Today, I understood _____
_____
_____

I wish I knew _____
_____

I also want to tell you _____
_____
_____

---

class knows that he doesn't understand. Through careful guidance, students will learn to think about their own learning on a regular basis.

Teachers also should help students celebrate their success. For students who are struggling, even small successes should be celebrated in the classroom. One teacher created a "Student Progress" bulletin board. She decorated it with butterflies and each student in the class was able to post work they had done. The only criterion was that the work should be something the student was proud of. The weekly process of changing the board required students to focus on what they were doing well.

Applications for Working with Adults

Understanding the aspects of intrinsic motivation also is applicable for working with adults. Consider attempting to communicate with distraught parents. It's helpful to remember that they also are viewing events through the lenses of value and success. For example, their concern over a son or daughter's low grade may be compounded by their concern over a loss of a college scholarship. Or, they may view the grade as a reflection of their parental ability. As one parent said, "I thought I had helped my son get ready for the test. I don't know what I did wrong."

In these cases, it's important to recognize their concerns and address them. Tell them, "One low grade does not necessarily impact the overall grade. If your son continues to work hard, he can improve for the grading period. I know that you are helping your son, and you are doing a good job. Sometimes, you can do your best and students still make a poor grade. At home, please

continue to reinforce and check homework, encourage reading and follow-up with me regularly."

Success Provides Opportunities for Further Successes

Students who see value in work and experience success are more likely to be motivated. There are simple ways you can build these aspects into your daily instruction. Then, as you and your students experience success, you will be motivated to try other techniques that will increase student and parent motivation and provide opportunities for success.

Critical Thinking

1. Think about your personal experience as a student. What motivated you as a middle or secondary student?

2. Were your motivators intrinsic or extrinsic?

3. Do you think your motivators would work with students you are likely to find in your classroom? Explain.

4. Review the strategies for connecting with families or caregivers suggested in the Kersey and Masterson article. Which of those strategies support positive motivation in adults? If you think they do not motivate families, revise at least two of those strategies to motivate parents in a positive way.

BARBARA R. BLACKBURN is an internationally bestselling author with Eye on Education, and actively consults with school systems regarding student motivation, student engagement and increasing rigor. She can be reached at www.barbarablackburnonline.com. ABBIGAIL ARMSTRONG is an assistant professor in the Richard W. Riley College of Education at Winthrop University in Rock Hill, South Carolina, specializing in preparing future teachers and working with at-risk students (sarmstrong@winthrop.edu).

Start Where Your Students Are

Robyn R. Jackson

Good grades. A quiet classroom. These are often what teachers value. But, what if students come to class looking for something else?

Cynthia quickly moved through the classroom, collecting the previous evening's homework assignment. While her back was to the door, Jason hurried in and slid into his seat. Without turning around, Cynthia said, "I saw that, Jason."

The class erupted in laughter as Jason blushed. "Take out your homework, and I'll be around in a second to deal with you," Cynthia instructed.

When Cynthia reached his chair and noticed that Jason did not have any work out, she moved past and finished collecting the other papers. She got the class started on a warm-up exercise and called Jason to her desk.

"Where's your homework?" she asked.

"I forgot to do it," Jason muttered.

"So you're not only late to class, but you also don't have your homework? Hmm, this is serious," Cynthia said. "Do you know what you owe me?"

"Detention?" Jason guessed.

Cynthia shook her head. "No indeed. You need to make things right with me. Tomorrow when you come to class, you need to be here early with your homework—*and* a Snickers bar. And it better be fresh!"

Jason looked up, startled, then smiled widely. He went back to his seat and got to work. The next morning, he arrived at Cynthia's class with not one but two Snickers bars and cheerfully handed in his missing homework assignment.

When Cynthia first told me this story, I have to admit that I was shocked. It seemed that she was letting Jason off the hook. "Cynthia, please tell me you aren't shaking kids down for candy," I mocked.

She laughed and then explained that too often, we make too big a deal of it when students make mistakes. We treat their mistakes as personal affronts and, as a result, kids are afraid to mess up—afraid that if they do, there is no road back. Over the years, Jason had adopted a cavalier attitude because he believed that once he made a mistake—and he made them all the time— he had ruined the entire school year. By having him give her a Snickers bar, Cynthia showed him a pathway to redemption.

"It isn't about the Snickers bar," she explained. "It's about giving kids a tangible way of redeeming themselves and recovering from their mistakes."

Cynthia is starting where her students are.

The Currency of the Classroom

Currency is a medium of exchange. Any behavior that students use to acquire the knowledge and skills important to your class functions as currency. For instance, if we teachers value student engagement, we take time and expend effort to make our lessons interesting to students. In exchange for our efforts, students give us their attention, curiosity, and participation. If students value adult approval, they work hard to abide by classroom rules and do well on assignments. In exchange for their efforts, we show them our approval in the form of praise, special classroom assignments, and attention.

But sometimes students come to school with currencies we find problematic. For instance, a student might use sarcasm as a way of earning the respect of his peers because it shows how clever and funny he is. However, teachers don't usually welcome sarcasm in their classrooms because they see it as a sign of disrespect; instead of gaining their admiration, it usually incurs their censure. If students don't feel that we understand or value their currencies, they often assume that there is no place for them in the classroom—and they opt out. What's worse, sometimes students *do* carry the preferred currency but resist spending it in the classroom because they resent the fact that it is the only currency we accept.

Currencies even influence the way students acquire the curriculum. The explicit curriculum is the stated objectives, content, and skills that students are expected to acquire. But to access that curriculum, students need to understand and possess certain underlying knowledge and skills.

For example, the explicit curriculum may require that students multiply fractions correctly or explain how geographic features affect migration patterns. But for students to do this, they need to have the right currencies. They need to know how to take effective notes, study from these notes, independently practice applying their skills, learn from their errors and self-correct, pay attention in class, monitor their comprehension, and ask for help when they do not understand.

To demonstrate that they have mastered the material, students need to understand how to write an essay or solve a certain number of math problems correctly under timed conditions. Many students struggle in school not because they can't learn the explicit curriculum, but because they don't have the currencies needed to access this curriculum.

These types of exchanges happen all the time in the classroom. As teachers, we communicate which currencies we require and accept in our classrooms; our students do their best to acquire and trade in our accepted form of currency. When they already possess—or can obtain and effectively use—our accepted form of currency, they thrive. When they can't, they flounder. In fact, most conflicts in the classroom are the result of a breakdown in the currency exchange.

A Winning Strategy

When we don't understand the concept of currencies, we often attempt to mitigate classroom problems by attempting to connect with our students through their interests or to backfill any learning gaps we discover. We may even try to reward students in ways that make sense to us but that are inconsistent with what they value. When we focus on superficial traits without also paying attention to students' currencies, we miss important information about what students can do and what they value—and even our noblest attempts to connect with them can backfire.

When I first started teaching advanced placement (AP) English, I attempted to get my students to sign up to take the AP exam by telling them how much it would help them in college. I explained the importance of having a capstone event that would really test how well they had achieved the course's objectives, and I showed them statistics on how much better students did in college after having taken the exam. I even broke down the economic advantages of having earned college credit in high school and the effect that doing so would have on their overall college costs.

Nothing worked. They didn't sign up for the test. It wasn't that they didn't see the benefit of taking the test. They knew it was important. But I realized that I wasn't starting where they were. I was trying to motivate them using *my* preferred currencies, not theirs.

So I changed my tack. I started a competition among my three AP classes to see which class would have the greatest percentage of test takers. All of a sudden, students were racing to sign up for the test. Within a week, 95 percent of my students had signed up. Although my students could intellectually see the value of taking the test, it wasn't until I connected signing up for the test to something they valued—in this case, it was competition and the camaraderie of affiliation with the "winning" class—that they actually signed up.

Starting where your students are goes beyond playing getting-to-know-you games to understand their likes and dislikes, their interests and hobbies. Such efforts can quickly become superficial. Can you really effectively get to know all 20–35 students in your classroom or make a personal connection with each one fast enough or deeply enough to help each student find a way to access the curriculum? Even if you could, can you really make logical connections between the curriculum and their lives every single lesson, every single day? Our students may be amused by our attempts to discuss with them hip-hop artist Jay Z's latest hit or the plot of an episode of the TV show *Gossip Girl*. However, will doing so really help them connect with the curriculum in a way that enables them to leverage their skills and talents to meet or exceed the objectives—especially when that curriculum is not always immediately relevant to their worlds or when we don't understand their worlds well enough to make a plausible connection?

Instead of forging superficial connections, starting where your students are is about showing kids how to learn in ways that work best for them. It's about creating spaces in the classroom where our students can feel comfortable being who they are rather than conforming to who we think they should be. It's about helping kids feel safe enough to bring with them their skills, strengths, culture, and background knowledge—and showing them how to use these to acquire the curriculum.

Getting Started

If we want to start where our students are, we have to understand how currencies are negotiated and traded in the classroom. The first step is to clarify the currencies we value. What do we consider to be a good student? How do we reward students for doing well? What do we think should motivate students?

When we understand our own currencies and recognize that they may be different from those our students value, we open ourselves to recognizing alternative currencies. For instance, earning good grades is a currency we may recognize. Maybe your students are not motivated by grades but really want the approval of their friends. When you recognize that being motivated by grades is really your preferred currency and that approval from friends isn't good or bad, that it's simply an alternate form of currency, you can find ways to leverage this currency to help students learn. Thus, you may stop trying so hard to get students to value grades and instead set up a classroom culture in which students push one another to do their very best. Understanding your currencies helps you withhold judgment and abandon the idea that your preferred currency is more valuable than those of your students.

Next, we need to unpack our curriculum so we have a better idea of the underlying skills—particularly the soft skills—that students need to be successful. For example, I once worked with a school whose students were struggling. The teachers complained that the students never did their homework. We sat down as a group and examined the homework assignments. One teacher assigned students to read a chapter of the textbook and take notes in preparation for a class discussion the following day. When we unpacked the assignment, we realized that to complete it, students would have to spend about two hours reading the densely written 19 pages, take 25 pages of notes using Cornell note-taking sheets, and look up 10 vocabulary words. Students would also have to organize their notes in such a way that they could refer to them quickly as support for any arguments they wanted to develop as they participated in the discussion. Now we understood why so many students were not completing their homework.

Once you understand the soft skills that are implied by the curriculum, the next step is to determine which of these soft skills your students already possess and which ones they will need to acquire. You can accomplish this through a quick pre-assessment or by observing how students interact with the material and with one another.

Or you can ask them directly. I often conduct focus groups with the students in the schools with which I work. I show them a list of the soft skills they will need to be successful in a particular class and ask them whether they know how to do these things. On the basis of their feedback, their teachers and I can determine what we need to preteach students to help them successfully tackle a particular lesson.

Our students often carry currencies that can help them learn, but we don't recognize that these currencies are valuable because they don't look like the ones we value. For instance, a student may have a different organizational system for his notebook that works better for the way he thinks, or a student may process information better by talking about it rather than writing about it, or a student may have a method for solving mathematical equations that differs drastically from the one you taught, but that is equally sound.

I once coached a teacher who was having difficulty with a student who interrupted her while she was teaching to ask questions and offer comments of his own. He wasn't intentionally being disrespectful, but it drove her crazy. After meeting with the student and his parents during parent/teacher conferences, she noticed that the family all talked at once. It was how they processed information. They thought aloud. At the same time. Loudly.

Once she recognized that his interruptions were not because he couldn't control himself, that they were just how he processed information, she no longer saw them as annoying, but as evidence that he was thinking and eager to share his thinking with the class. She then was able to figure out a way to help him process the information without disrupting the class. She showed him how to keep a journal during class discussions to write down his thoughts as they came to him and to select one or two comments to share. Eventually he learned how to participate in class discussions without the journal and to share his thinking appropriately.

Yes, But . . .

When I tell the Cynthia story in the workshops I give, many teachers become dismayed. Although they enjoy hearing about Cynthia's Snickers bar strategy it doesn't feel comfortable to them. It's a great story but what about those of us who are uncomfortable with forging a connection over candy?

I once coached a teacher who was having difficulty with her 6th graders. Whenever she gave them an assignment, they would spend the period talking to one another, finding any excuse to get out of their seats. No matter how often she threatened them, she couldn't keep them focused. I offered to observe her classroom and provide her with some feedback, but after being in her classroom for 30 minutes, I didn't see any gross misbehavior. The students were squirrelly but most of their talking was about the work. After school let out for the day, I met with her to discuss what I saw. Before I could begin, she said, "Do you see what I have to deal with? I'm exhausted. They just won't behave!"

"What would your class look like if your students were all well-behaved?" I asked.

"They'd all be in their seats quietly working," she said. "They'd raise their hands and ask permission before they got up to do anything, and they would also raise their hands before talking so that everyone can be heard."

I listened to her list and realized that she was talking about her currencies. She valued a quiet classroom and thought that was how students learned best. However, her students valued being able to discuss what they were learning with their classmates and getting up and moving once in a while. That was how they learned best. I explained to the teacher the concept of currency and then asked, "If you were sure that your students were talking about the lesson, would you allow them to talk quietly in class as they were working?"

She thought for a moment; I could tell she was uncomfortable with the idea. Finally she said, "I suppose so, but I'm afraid it might get out of hand."

We finally figured out a way for her to structure the students' conversations so that she could still feel that the class was orderly and productive. She decided to pause during the lesson and allow students time to turn to their neighbors and discuss the information before moving on in the lesson. That way, students had a chance to process the information during the lesson and were less likely to talk about it later on. She found a way to acknowledge their currencies while honoring her own.

Finding Common Ground

When you recognize and honor students' currencies, you don't abandon your own. Rather, you find a common currency that you both carry. This creates a safe place for both you and your students to be who you are. In Cynthia's case, she wanted Jason to acknowledge his mistake and correct it; Jason wanted a chance to do so without feeling like a failure or a bad person. The candy bar provided the common ground. Had Cynthia asked for an apology or demanded that Jason redeem himself by staying after school and repaying her the time he missed in class by being late, she might have alienated him. But by finding a common currency, she was able to quickly get Jason back on track.

For you, that common ground might be something less tangible. Maybe you are more comfortable lecturing, but your students are not good note takers. So you provide them with a note-taking sheet that helps them learn in the way that you are most comfortable teaching. Or perhaps you don't like lavishing verbal praise on your students, but verbal praise is their preferred form of currency. So you develop a set of code words you can use with students that signal to them that they have done a good job.

When you start where your students are, when you find that common currency you both carry, you communicate to students that it's OK to be exactly who they are. You create spaces for students to leverage who they are and what they know, to access the curriculum.

Critical Thinking

1. Think back to your days in public school; pick any grade or content area. What was the primary currency that got you motivated to do well in that class?

2. Do you think the currency that worked for you will work with the students you may be teaching? Support the reasons in your answer with information from the articles in this unit.

ROBYN R. JACKSON is President of Mindsteps and author of *Never Work Harder Than Your Students* and *Other Principles of Great Teaching* (ASCD, 2009); robyn@mindstepsinc.com.

From *Educational Leadership,* February 2010, pp. 6–11. Copyright © 2010 by ASCD. Reprinted by permission. The Association for Supervision and Curriculum Development is a worldwide community of educators advocating sound policies and sharing best practices to achieve the success of each learner. To learn more, visit ASCD at www.ascd.org.

Leaving Nothing to Chance

Principals from high-performing, high-poverty, and high-minority schools discuss what it takes to ensure that all students achieve.

KARIN CHENOWETH

A myth plagues the United States that low-income students and students of color arrive at school so damaged that schools cannot be expected to help them achieve at high levels. Early this year, the lieutenant governor of South Carolina gave voice to this myth: "You show me the school that has the highest free and reduced [-price] lunch," he said, "and I'll show you the worst test scores."

Certainly it's true that, *in general,* high-poverty and high-minority schools are low achieving. However, some schools with what are called "challenging" student bodies excel at helping their students achieve. These schools offer hope that all is not lost in the essential bargain that the United States offers its citizens: a fair start for all children.

Doing Everything Right

I have spent the last six years identifying and visiting almost two dozen high-performing high-poverty and high-minority schools across the United States to try to figure out what makes them more successful than ordinary schools. My theory is that if we fully understood what they do, more schools could follow in their footsteps. The schools I'm drawing on here all won the Education Trust's Dispelling the Myth award for educating low-income and minority students to high academic levels.

The schools I studied

- Had substantial enrollment of low-income students and students of color
- Had high absolute achievement (nearly all students met or exceeded state standards).
- Had high relative achievement (larger percentages of low-income students and students of color met or exceeded standards than in other schools in their respective states).
- Did not have entrance standards for students (that is, no magnet schools or schools requiring entrance exams or teacher recommendations were included).
- For the most part, were regular neighborhood schools.

These schools succeed by doing just about everything right, from classroom management to curriculum to assessment to discipline.

It isn't easy to do everything right. But the educators in these schools know that their students are particularly vulnerable to sloppy or inadequate instruction in a way that many middle-class children are not. As a result, they operate on a higher plane than many middle-class schools that can count on their students' families to make up for deficiencies in teaching or curriculum.

Five Insights for Success

It will come as no surprise that each of these schools has a leader with valuable, hard-won knowledge. Five insights emerged from extensive interviews with these leaders.

1. It's Everyone's Job to Run the School.

Asked how she could focus on student achievement when a crisis erupted in the lunchroom or a bathroom ceiling collapsed, Elain Thompson, who led enormous improvement at P.S. 124 in Queens, New York, replied that it wasn't up to her alone. Addressing the lunchroom crisis or seeing that the ceiling got fixed "was someone else's job." Every problem in the school fell under the purview of a staff member. It was Thompson's job to make sure there was a capable adult who could solve the problem. This is how she was able to keep her focus on student achievement rather than on the daily crises that often consume principals.

Another high-achieving principal—Sharon Brittingham, who led the transformation of Frankford Elementary School in rural Delaware from a low-performing school to one of the top-performing schools in the state—says that many principals find it easier to stay mired in day-to-day crises. By solving all the problems that emerge—the lunchroom runs out of French fries or the 6th grade field trip's charter buses are late—principals experience quick successes and get staff members' approbation.

Now a principal coach throughout the state, Brittingham calls that approach "majoring in the minors." She notes that it's difficult for principals to leave the day-to-day issues in someone else's hands in order to focus on the major issues of improving instruction. But keeping a laserlike focus on instruction is the only way for schools to improve.

Because this approach requires competence at every level, principals bring rigor to hiring decisions. Each new teacher and staff member must be part of a team that is continually improving. The interview process for new teachers takes "a long time," said Molly Bensinger-Lacy, former principal of Graham Road Elementary, which she led from being one of the lowest-performing schools in Fairfax County, Virginia, in 2004 to one of the highest-performing schools in the state four years later.

Bensinger-Lacy's expectations for teachers included the following:

- Participating in professional learning communities.
- Teaching during at least one of the intersessions in what was then a year-round school.
- Participating in after-school classes in reading and math.
- Taking on extra responsibilities beyond classroom instruction, such as sponsoring a club or helping lead a professional development session.
- Keeping up with professional literature and research.

Laying out these expectations in detail—in addition to gauging prospective teachers' willingness to collaborate closely with colleagues on mapping out curriculum, planning lessons, developing formative assessments, and studying data in detail—is part of what made the interview process so lengthy. With few exceptions, this approach ensured that schools like Graham Road hired the right teachers.

These principals also take tenure decisions seriously. In too many schools, teachers receive their third or fourth contract without serious evaluation, meaning that they drift into tenure protections. The New Teacher Project found that only 1 percent of teachers had had 60 minutes or more of observation before their final evaluation.[1] In contrast, teachers who earn tenure protection in the schools I studied have demonstrated not only competence and caring, but also an ability and willingness to keep honing their skills. Administrators frequently observe in their classrooms. In addition, because teachers are part of active professional communities such as grade-level teams and vertical articulation teams (across grade levels), they don't teach in isolation.

Ultimately, this mandate for excellence holds for everyone in the building, from the school secretaries who must efficiently process paperwork and welcome parents and visitors, to the cafeteria workers who must provide nutritious food in a welcoming atmosphere, to the paraprofessionals who support instruction. They are all part of creating a school with high student achievement.

Agnes "Terri" Tomlinson, principal of George Hall Elementary School, which went from being one of the lowest-performing schools in Mobile, Alabama, in 2004, to achieving recognition as a top Alabama school in 2008, said, "Most principals don't realize that support staff can be your undertakers—they will bury you."

The correlate of making sure that "the right people are on the bus," as Jim Collins put it in *Good to Great* (HarperBusiness, 2001), is that each staff member has an opportunity to help make significant decisions within his or her purview of responsibility. Principals might, for example, encourage teachers to make important decisions related to classroom instruction, such as what phonics program to use or how to use Title I dollars.

2. Inspect What You Expect—and Expect That All Students Will Meet or Exceed Standards.

Valarie Lewis, who followed Elain Thompson as principal of P.S. 124 in Queens, explains one of the keys to her success: verifying that everyone in the building is doing his or her job. "Inspect what you expect," she says.

According to Lewis and her peers, it is not enough for principals to simply set clear expectations that all students will succeed. They must provide the critical eye, the evaluative sense, that ensures that all educators in the school continually monitor their own results against their goals so they can improve.

For example, these school leaders may leave the question of which phonics program to adopt to the kindergarten and 1st grade teachers. But they continually look at reading assessment data and watch classrooms to see whether the program is doing what it's supposed to do: help all students learn to decode. If some students still falter, it's the principal's job to monitor their progress and ask what other interventions the teachers are introducing. If teachers pool their knowledge and still come up short, it's up to the principal to know what training would help the teachers better do their jobs and then make sure they get it, whether it's bringing in an expert on vocabulary acquisition or sending teachers to a conference focused on differentiating instruction or improving reading fluency.

Dannette Collins, a teacher at George Hall Elementary in Mobile, Alabama, says that what she most values about her principal is that she "makes sure everyone does their work." In other schools where she has taught, Collins said, the principals didn't bother noticing whether teachers who agreed to take on a responsibility, such as developing materials for a commonly taught lesson, actually fulfilled it. She and other conscientious teachers were left feeling overwhelmed; not only did they have to do their own jobs, but they also had to pick up the slack of others who didn't—or risk harming students. This sense of being among the few people who actually do their jobs contributes to teacher burnout.

But exactly how do principals in these schools hold people accountable? Too often in U.S. schools, the only choice has seemed to be between zero accountability and a harsh, martinet-like system of control where people are told what to do and are punished if they don't follow orders. The school leaders described here have developed a different approach that may lie at the heart of what distinguishes them from other, less successful principals. It could be called . . .

3. Be Relentlessly Respectful—and Respectfully Relentless.

Despite their distinctive styles, all these school leaders consciously attempt to model for their teachers and students the way free citizens should treat one another in a democracy—with tolerance, respect, and high expectations. Take, for example, Deb Gustafson, who in 2001 took over as principal of Ware Elementary, the first school in Kansas to be put "on improvement" because of its low achievement. The school she inherited had an atmosphere of disrespect, and student suspensions and teacher grievances were commonplace.

That fall, when teachers arrived for work, Gustafson began to transform the negative tone. "I told the teachers that I would never reprimand them for anything except speaking to children inappropriately," she remembers. "This is how you will talk to kids, I told them, no matter how disrespectfully they speak to you." When teachers responded that they were only reacting to students' disrespectful remarks, Gustafson said that it's grown-ups, not students, who are responsible for setting the tone of schools. To help teachers understand what she expected, she led a book study of *Teaching with Love and Logic: Taking Control in the Classroom* (Love and Logic Press, 1995) by Jim Fay and David Funk.

This respect carries over to dealing with teachers. Gustafson assumes that all teachers want to be successful. That's easy enough when teachers *are* successful. The test comes when they're not. At Ware, if specific teachers struggle, Gustafson or her assistant principal talks with them at length about their plans to succeed with each student and how they might improve their knowledge and skills. It can be a difficult conversation that involves reviewing each student's achievement data and noting that, for example, a student who did well the previous year with another teacher is now faltering in the new classroom.

In this conversation, respectful relentlessness means that school leaders establish the professional expectation that every student will meet or exceed state standards and that those students who surpass the standards need further intellectual challenges, such as reading more complicated books or writing in-depth term papers. Their relentless respect means that they assume that teachers want to be successful, so teachers whose students fail to meet or exceed standards receive support. Those who don't improve face other tough conversations, such as whether they think they would be more successful in another field; several teachers who concluded that they would be more successful elsewhere have left the profession.

In Michigan's Godwin Heights, assistant superintendent Arelis Diaz formally evaluates each lagging teacher every year. "The union asks me, 'When are you going to stop evaluating?' and I say, 'When [the teacher] can show me achievement results.'"

The leaders in these schools bring urgency to such discussions. They understand that if their students do not have a good education, they may face lives of poverty and dependence. They know that school leaders must be guardians of their students' futures, not of their staff members' happiness. "It's the job of a principal to make a marginal teacher uncomfortable," says one principal. Another says, "No one has the right to waste a day in the life of a child."

But high-performing principals also know they must support teachers. In the observation system that principal Diane Scricca instituted at Long Island's Elmont Memorial Junior-Senior High School, whenever a teacher is observed—seven times a year for new teachers and a minimum of two times a year for veterans—the observer gives many "commendations." These consist of specific things that the teacher is doing right, from establishing a good rapport with students to leading a strong opening activity. The evaluator then gives one or two "recommendations" that the teacher is expected to work on before the next observation, with concrete ideas about how to proceed. If the teacher needs to improve the kinds of questions he or she asks, for example, that teacher might be steered to the classrooms of veteran teachers who excel in their questioning techniques. If the teacher makes no effort to improve and doesn't visit the recommended classrooms, then the hard conversation begins.

No one has the right to waste a day in the life of a child.

School leaders must be guardians of their students' future, not of their staff members' happiness.

As part of their "relentless respect" for staff members, effective principals steer clear of arbitrary decisions based on personal preference. For example, the principal of George Hall Elementary School said that although she prefers orderly classrooms, she recognizes that some teachers can succeed in more relaxed environments. So, despite her personal preference, she does not criticize teachers because their chairs are not in straight rows and their binders are askew—as long as their students are learning.

4. Use Student Achievement Data to Evaluate Decisions.

These schools use student achievement data to either confirm or reconsider decisions. For example, several years ago, Capitol View Elementary in Atlanta, Georgia, decided to tackle its students' relatively low performance on state tests of science knowledge. The team members in charge of spending the school's federal Title I dollars decided that in addition to buying lab tables, stools, and microscopes, they would hire a science teacher to do laboratory experiments with the students. The following year, the staff members looked at the students' higher science scores as evidence that they had made the right decision. If they had seen little or no improvement, they would have rethought their approach and adjusted their program.

Because this practice has not been the norm for educators in the past, it often falls to the principal to help teachers learn to sift through student data without feeling defensive and under attack. When Bensinger-Lacy first became principal of Graham

Road Elementary, she led teachers in examining classroom data, searching for patterns of success and failure. For example, she helped teachers find which of their peers excelled with helping their students add three-digit numbers and which had the most success teaching students to write essays. She then made sure that the less successful teachers had opportunities to learn from their more successful peers. Similarly, after one midyear kindergarten data meeting that recognized a teacher for her expertise in teaching students all their letters, this teacher did a workshop for her fellow teachers—complete with shaving cream and modeling clay—to demonstrate how she taught this skill.

It took a while for teachers to realize that the point was not to find fault but to establish the professional expectation that every student will achieve and, when students fail, to pinpoint ways to improve.

5. Do Whatever It Takes to Make Sure Students Learn.

One final lesson that many of the highly successful leaders talk about is to do whatever it takes.

When Agnes Tomlinson took over George Hall Elementary in 2004 after the Mobile Public School System reconstituted the school—meaning that all staff members had to reapply for their jobs—she found that some disgruntled former employees had trashed the building. With the help of her assistant principal and a maintenance worker, she spent the summer clearing the school of debris.

In the middle of a difficult transition, Tomlinson couldn't do what she was able to do later on: rely on other staff members to do their jobs. In a completely broken school, she found herself, literally, doing the repair work needed to create the right environment for teaching and learning.

Their Best Hope

The leaders in these schools know it's up to them to create the conditions under which their kids will learn. "We become students' advocates," said one principal, "because they have no one else to demand the best from them."

Note

1. See *The Widget Effect,* by the New Teacher Project, 2009. Available: http://widgeteffect.org.

Critical Thinking

1. Chenoweth states "School leaders must be the guardians of their students' future, not of their staff members' happiness." What does this mean to teachers in that principal's school? As a teacher (or future teacher) would you agree that this is how it should be?

2. Review the five insights for success explained in this article. For each of the five, suggest two actions you would take, as a teacher or principal, to make that strategy a reality.

3. Chenoweth did not discuss families in the article. Based on what you have read in the previous articles, how might you involve family members in *leaving nothing to chance*?

KARIN CHENOWETH is senior writer with the Education Trust and author of *It's Being Done: Academic Success in Unexpected Schools* (Harvard Education Press, 2007) and *How It's Being Done: Urgent Lessons from Unexpected Schools* (Harvard Education Press, 2009); kchenoweth@edtrust.org.

Author's note—This article was adapted from a forthcoming paper on leadership to be published by the Education Trust. The Wallace Foundation has supported the Education Trust's leadership work; this paper, however, does not necessarily represent the foundation's views.

She's Strict for a Good Reason

Highly Effective Teachers in Low-Performing Urban Schools

Studying the work of highly effective teachers can help us better understand what really works to improve student learning and help us avoid practices that are complicated, trendy, and expensive.

For four years, we studied 31 highly effective teachers in nine low-performing urban schools in some of the most economically depressed neighborhoods in Los Angeles County, Calif. The first thing that struck us was how strict the teachers were. But it was a strictness that always was inseparable from a grander purpose, even in students' minds. For example, a 2nd grader admitted, "Ms. G kept me in the classroom to do my work. She is good-hearted to me." A high school math student wrote, "I think Mrs. E is such an effective teacher because of her discipline. People might think she is mean, but she is really not. She is strict. There is a difference. She believes every student can learn."

MARY POPLIN ET AL.

The teachers we studied had the highest percentage of students moving up a level on the English/language arts or math subtests of the California Standards Test (CST) for two to three years. Toward the end of the school year, we asked their students why they thought their teacher taught them so much. One Latino 4th grader summed up much of what we discovered: "When I was in 1st grade and 2nd grade and 3rd grade, when I cried, my teachers coddled me. But when I got to Mrs. T's room, she said, 'Suck it up and get to work.' I think she's right. I need to work harder."

We began our study with three questions: Are there highly effective teachers in low-performing urban schools? If so, what instructional strategies do they use? And what are their personal characteristics?

Are there highly effective teachers in low-performing urban schools?

If so, what instructional strategies do they use?

What are their personal characteristics?

There are highly effective teachers in these schools, and we chose 31 of them for our study. They included 24 women and seven men; 24 taught English/language arts, and seven taught math; 11 taught in elementary schools, nine in middle schools, and 11 in high schools. In the year they were observed, these teachers' CST data revealed that 51% of their students moved up a level, 34% maintained their levels, and only 15% dropped a level.

These results were very different from those of their peers teaching in the same schools. For example, in three high schools, we calculated every teacher's achievement and found disheartening data. Fifty percent of the English teachers and 60% of the math teachers had between 30% and 75% of their students dropping a level in a single year. Sixty-five percent of the English teachers and 68% of the math teachers had the same number or more students going down a level as going up.

Clearly, the highly effective teachers were different. What was happening in their classrooms? Who were these high performers?

The Classroom

Strictness. These teachers believed their strictness was necessary for effective teaching and learning and for safety and respect. Students also saw their teacher's strictness as serving larger purposes. Students explained that their teacher was strict "because she doesn't want us to get ripped off in life," "because she wants us to go to college," "because she wants us to be at the top of 2nd grade," "because she wants us to be winners and not losers," and "because he has faith in us to succeed."

Instructional intensity. The second most obvious characteristic was the intensity of academic work. There was rarely a time when instruction wasn't going on. Our first visit to the only elementary teacher identified for mathematics gains found Ms. N marching her 1st graders to the playground as they chanted, "3, 6, 9, 12, 15 . . . 30" As the year progressed, they learned to march by 2s through 9s; by May her "almost 2nd graders" could multiply. She told us that she appreciated the standards as guides —"to know what I'm responsible for teaching"—and that she always tried to "push the students just a little bit into 2nd grade."

The teachers transitioned from one activity to another quickly and easily. Many of them used timers, and students often were reminded of the time remaining for a particular activity. At one school, teachers met students in the hallway during the passing periods and talked with them. When the final bell rang, these teachers instructed students on exactly what should be on their desk when they sat down: "When you get inside the door, take your jackets off; get out your book, pencil, and notebooks; then put everything else in your backpack and under your desks." As students entered, conversations ended and students prepared for work.

Most teachers began with an overview of the day. In some cases, students were required to copy the daily agenda in their notebooks—"In case your parents ask you what you learned today, I want you to be able to tell them."

Movement. Perhaps the single most productive practice of most of these teachers was their frequent movement around the classroom to assist individual students. The time spent at students' desks provided feedback on the effectiveness of their instruction, kept students on track and focused, offered individual students extra instruction and encouragement, and even allowed for brief personal interactions between teachers and students. This simple, almost instinctive activity of walking around accomplished scores of purposes *naturally*—individualized and differentiated instruction, informal assessments, teacher reflection, teacher/student relationships, response to intervention (RTI), and classroom management. By walking around, teachers came to know their students. For example, Mrs. M asked a middle school student whose head was on his desk what was wrong. He replied, "I don't feel so good." She headed toward him, proclaiming, "Remember what I always tell you, you'll feel much better when you get your work done. Here, let me help you." She stayed by his side until he had a good start on his work. We rarely knew which students were classified as special education or English language learners because teachers' personal assistance helped mask this.

The single most productive practice of most of these teachers was their frequent movement around the classroom to assist individual students.

Traditional instruction. Traditional, explicit, teacher-directed instruction was by far the most dominant instructional practice. We were constantly reminded of Madeline Hunter's sequences—anticipatory set, input, modeling, checking for understanding, guided practice, monitoring, closure, independent practice, and review. Instruction was, for the most part, unabashedly and unapologetically from the state standards and official curriculum materials. Ms. N told us, "Open Court is very helpful and gives you good pacing." This surprised the team, as there had been a good deal of contention in Los Angeles over requiring this series.

Typically, following energetic content presentations and demonstrations, teachers entered into whole-class discussions. Students were called on randomly and had to use full sentences and high-level vocabulary. Teachers always *pushed* students (a term used by teachers and students). Ms. P said to one young girl, "That is absolutely correct! Now, can you say that like a 5th grader?" At one elementary school, teachers required students to reference the previous student's comment before offering their own; this encouraged students to pay attention to one another. Teachers followed instruction and discussion with independent practice. At this stage, they began moving around. One teacher said, "If I see two or three having trouble, I stop, go back, and teach it another way."

What we saw *least* was also instructive. There were very few constructivist projects in their classrooms. The ones we saw were short-lived, and they often appeared to be used more as practice or a reward for learning than as a route to it. Cooperative and collaborative learning activities were also limited except in two classes. Most cooperative activities were brief pair-shares. Some of our teachers were adamantly opposed to it. High school teacher Mr. Mc told us, "In school, I helped 500 students get a better grade, 495 of whom learned nothing from the experience." His counterpart, Mr. T, said, "It's not realistic." From the back of the room, the team often observed that even the best cooperative activities allowed for a good deal of irrelevant socializing.

When we asked teachers to describe their classrooms to a stranger, not one of the 31 used race, class, or ethnic terms.

Though the teachers were from a variety of ethnic groups, we saw very little evidence of overtly planned activities that directly addressed culture unless it was built into curriculum materials. Cloetta Veney (2008) studied two of our elementary schools' classrooms and concluded that they resembled those in the effective classroom literature of the 1980s more than today's cultural proficiency models. When we asked teachers to describe their classrooms to a stranger, not one of the 31 used race, class, or ethnic terms.

Pat Pawlak (2009) found that the students of these teachers said—60% more frequently than any other comment—that their teacher helped them because he or she *explained things over and over*. We consistently found that students expressed appreciation for explicit instruction with patience.

Exhorting virtues. Every few minutes, these teachers encouraged students to think about their future and to practice particular virtues. The top virtues were respecting self and others, working hard, being responsible, never giving up, doing excellent work, trying their best, being hopeful, thinking critically, being honest, and considering consequences. Respect was paramount, and even a small infraction drew quick rebuke and consequences.

Teachers always linked doing well in school to going to college and getting good jobs so that they could someday support their families and own houses and cars. Mrs. C told her students how missing one word on a spelling test lost her a job she desperately wanted and needed. Ms. P told of problems she had experienced in her life. One of her students told us, "She has passed through some trouble in her life and does not want that to happen to us. So, she is preparing us for troubles and telling us what is the best choice."

These teachers focused less on making the work immediately relevant than on making the link to their futures. Even 2nd graders knew this—"Ms. G is weird, strict, mean, and crazy. This classroom is smart and nerdy because she wants you to go to college."

Strong and respectful relationships. The teachers had a profound respect for students. There was a sense that teachers were genuinely optimistic for their students' futures. Teachers often provided students with a vision of their best selves. Middle school teacher Ms. P told us, "All students need to know that you respect them and care for them. Fortunately, that is very easy. I try to make sure every so often that I have said something personal to each of them." She bent down at a student's desk and said, "Alejandro, I can see

you are very good at math. I look forward to seeing what you will do in your life." Now, Alejandro has heard from a respected adult outside his family that his math skills may play into his future.

Teachers often provided students with a vision of their best selves.

Respect for students is a more accurate description of what we saw than simply caring for the students. The teachers did not need the students to love them; they needed to see their students achieve. Ms. B said, "I'm hard on my students, but at the same time, they know it is out of love. I've had to fail some students. . . . When I see them in the hall, they still greet me. They tell me they wish they were back in my class—they say they know why they failed my class."

The High-Performing Teachers

Though they shared common strategies, the teachers were quite diverse—11 were black, nine white, seven Latino, three Middle Eastern Americans, and one Asian-American. Their ages ranged from 27 to 60, and years of experience from three to 33. Two-thirds of the teachers (23) were educated in nontraditional teacher education programs—teaching before they finished their credentials. Nearly half (14) were career changers. Almost one-third (9) were first-generation immigrants. While they were all highly effective, few fit the definitions of highly qualified in terms of National Board certifications and degrees.

The teachers were strong, no-nonsense, make-it-happen people who were optimistic for students' futures, responsible, hard working, emotionally stable, organized, and disciplined. They were also energetic, fit, trim, and appeared in good health. They were comfortable in their own skins and humorous. Ms. M told her high school students, "If you develop multiple personalities, you better assign one to do your homework."

What do they believe? Their most central beliefs include:

1. Every one of my students has much more potential than they use;
2. They have not been pushed to use it;
3. It is my responsibility to turn this situation around;
4. I am able; and
5. I want to do this for them.

Ms. M said simply, "They can do and be so much more."
Teachers didn't use the students' backgrounds as an excuse for not learning, and yet they were not naive about

the challenges facing some students. They had confidence that what they did in the classroom would truly help students.

Teachers had a pragmatic attitude about testing. "It's required all your life," Mr. T told us. Mrs. C said of the district assessments, "I really like them, I like them a lot. I've been embarrassed by them a few times, but I am all for them." Ms. K said, "When students don't do well, I take it personally. I know I shouldn't, but I think that that bothers me." These teachers neither taught to the tests nor ignored them; tests were simply another resource.

Several additional incidents were instructive for those of us who work in teacher development, supervision, and evaluation. First, not one of our teachers had any idea that they were more successful than their colleagues teaching similar students. The student achievement data that was available to them did not allow for such comparisons.

Second, in a couple of cases, the principals were resistant to a teacher who emerged from the data, urging us to observe a different teacher. However, none of the nominated teachers made the cut when we rechecked the data. To be honest, when we first entered their classrooms, we also were surprised because of our preconceptions about what effective instruction should and shouldn't look like.

An incident is instructive here: One day, Ms. N was visibly shaken after a visit from a district teacher development specialist. She told our team member that she must be a terrible teacher and didn't think that she should be in the study. The researcher told her that she certainly wasn't a bad teacher but, if she liked, the researcher could come back another day. This demonstrates the importance of knowing the achievement data before we target teachers for intervention. Many teachers in that school needed instructional interventions, but it is counter-productive to take a veteran teacher of 33 years who is highly effective year after year and to shake her confidence in order to make her use preferred strategies. Teachers who have demonstrated results should be granted considerable freedom in determining their classroom instruction.

The teachers respected their principals. The teachers were the authority in their classrooms, and their principals were their authorities. However, they did not seem to be particularly close to their principals because the teachers were more focused on the inside of their classrooms than on networking with administrators. One teacher summed up their relationships when she said, "We get along."

Conclusion

Our concerns about the limitations of traditional, explicit instruction may be unfounded. What we found were happy and engaged students obviously learning from committed, optimistic, disciplined teachers. These teachers were realistic; they did not set their goals too broadly (saving children) or too narrowly (passing the test). Their students were being taught that mathematics, reading, speaking, listening, writing, and the formation of character are necessary for life beyond their neighborhoods.

We need to be cautious about adopting complicated, trendy, and expensive practices. We need to re-evaluate our affection for cooperative/collaborative learning, extensive technology, project-based learning, and constructivism, as well as our disaffection with explicit direct instruction and strict discipline. These teachers were direct, strict, deeply committed, and respectful to students. Their students, in turn, respected them. Mr. L's math students said it best: "It takes a certain integrity to teach. Mr. L possesses that integrity." "One thing for sure, his attitude is always up. He never brings us down, but we all know he has faith in us to learn and succeed."

References

Pawlak, Pat. "Common Characteristics and Classroom Practices of Effective Teachers of High-Poverty and Diverse Students." Doctoral dissertation, Claremont Graduate University, 2009.

Veney, Cloetta. "The Multicultural Practices of Highly Effective Teachers of African American and Latino Students in Urban Schools." Doctoral dissertation, Claremont Graduate University, 2008.

Critical Thinking

1. Make a list of all the actions taken by highly effective teachers in the classroom section of the article. As a student, have you been in classrooms where teachers practiced those strategies? What do you remember most about that classroom or teacher?

2. Who are these highly effective teachers? Describe the characteristics of these teachers. Any surprises for you in those characteristics?

3. Are you surprised by their attitudes toward standardized testing? Why do you think it is not a serious concern for them?

4. The researchers said, "To be honest, when we first entered their classrooms, we also were surprised because of our perceptions about what effective instruction should and shouldn't look like." What did they see that they were not expecting? What was missing from the classroom that they thought would be there?

5. If you could talk to these teachers, what would you say? What questions would you ask?

MARY POPLIN is a professor of education at Claremont Graduate University, Claremont, Calif. **JOHN RIVERA** is a professor and special projects assistant to the president, San Diego City College, San Diego, Calif., and the study's policy director. **Dena Durish** is coordinator for alternative routes to licensure programs for Clark County School District, Las Vegas, Nev. **Linda Hoff** is director of teacher education at Fresno Pacific University, Fresno, Calif. **Susan Kawell** is an instructor at California State University, Los Angeles, Calif. **Pat Pawlak** is a program administrator in instructional services at Pomona Unified School District, Pomona, Calif. **Ivannia Soto Hinman** is an assistant professor of education at Whittier College, Whittier, Calif. **Laura Straus** is an instructor at the University of Montana Western, Dillon, Mont. **Cloetta Veney** is an administrative director at Azusa Pacific University, Azusa.

From *Phi Delta Kappan,* by Poplin et. al., Mary, vol. 92, no. 5, 2011, pp. 39–43. Reprinted with permission of Phi Delta Kappa International, www.pdkintl.org, 2009. All rights reserved.

What Educators Need to Know about Bullying Behaviors

Sandra Graham

Peer victimization—also commonly labeled *harassment* or *bullying*—is not a new problem in American schools, though it appears to have taken on more epic proportions in recent years. Survey data indicate that anywhere from 30% to 80% of school-age youth report that they have personally experienced victimization from peers, and 10% to 15% may be chronic victims (e.g., Card and Hodges 2008). A generation ago, if we had asked children what they worry most about at school, they probably would have said, "Passing exams and being promoted to the next grade." Today, students' school concerns often revolve around safety as much as achievement, as the perpetrators of peer harassment are perceived as more aggressive and the victims of their abuse report feeling more vulnerable.

In the past 10 years—perhaps in response to students' growing concerns—there has been a proliferation of new studies on school bullying. For example, a search of the psychology (Psyc INFO) and Educational Resources Information Center (ERIC) databases using the key words *peer victimization, peer harassment,* and *school bullying* uncovered 10 times more studies from 2000 to 2010 than during the previous decade (about 800 versus 80).

Even though the empirical base has increased dramatically during these past 10 years, many widespread beliefs about school bullying are more myth than fact. I label these beliefs as myths because researchers who study bullies and victims of many different ages and in many different contexts have not found them to be true.

I define peer victimization as physical, verbal, or psychological abuse that occurs in and around school, especially where adult supervision is minimal. The critical features that distinguish victimization from simple conflict between peers are the intent to cause harm and an imbalance of power between perpetrator and victim. This intended harm can be either direct, entailing face-to-face confrontation; indirect, involving a third party and some form of social ostracism; or even "cyberbullying." Taunting, name-calling, racial slurs, hitting, spreading rumors, and social exclusion by powerful others are all examples of behaviors that constitute peer victimization. My definition doesn't include the more lethal types of peer hostility, such as those seen in the widely publicized school shootings; although some of those shootings may have been precipitated by a history of peer abuse, they remain rare events. My definition emphasizes more prevalent forms of harassment that affect the lives of many youth and that the American Medical Association has labeled a public health concern.

Six myths cloud our understanding of bullying behavior in schools and prevent us from addressing the issue effectively.

Myth #1: Bullies Have Low Self-Esteem and Are Rejected By Their Peers.

A portion of this myth has its roots in the widely and uncritically accepted view that people who bully others act that way because they think poorly of themselves. Recall the self-esteem movement of the 1980s whose advocates proposed that raising self-esteem was the key to improving the outcomes of children with academic and social problems. Yet there is little evidence in peer research to support the notion that bullies suffer from low self-esteem. To the contrary, many studies report that bullies perceive themselves in a positive light, often displaying inflated self-views (Baumeister et al. 2003).

Many people also believe that everybody dislikes the class bully. In truth, research shows that many bullies have high status in the classroom and have many friends. Some bullies are quite popular among classmates, which may in part account for their relatively high self-esteem. In our research with middle school students, we have found that others perceive bullies as especially "cool," where coolness implies both popularity and possession of desired traits (Juvonen, Graham, and Schuster 2003). As young teens test their need to be more independent, bullies sometimes enjoy a new kind of notoriety among classmates who admire their toughness and may even try to imitate them.

Myth #2: Getting Bullied Is a Natural Part of Growing Up.

One misconception about victims is that bullying is a normal part of childhood and that the experience builds character. In contrast, research quite clearly shows that bullying experiences increase the vulnerabilities of children, rather than making them more resilient. Victims are often disliked or rejected by their peers and feel depressed, anxious, and lonely (Card and Hodges 2008). Part of this psychological distress may revolve around how victims think about the reasons for their plight. For example, repeated encounters with peer hostility, or even an isolated yet especially painful experience, might lead that victim to ask, "Why me?" Such an individual might come to blame the predicament on personal shortcomings, concluding, "I'm someone who deserves to be picked on," which can increase depressive affect (Graham, Bellmore, and Mize 2006). Some victimized youth also have elevated levels of physical symptoms, leading to frequent visits to the nurse as well as school absenteeism. It is not difficult to imagine the chronic victim who becomes so anxious about going to school that she or he tries to avoid it at all costs. Nothing is character building about such experiences.

Bullying experiences make children more vulnerable, not more resilient.

Myth #3: Once a Victim, Always a Victim.

Although there is good reason to be concerned about the long-term consequences of bullying, research remains inconclusive about the stability of victim status. In fact, there is much more discontinuity than continuity in victim trajectories. In our research, only about a third of students who had reputations as victims in the fall of 6th grade maintained that reputation at the end of the school year and, by the end of 8th grade, the number of victims had dropped to less than 10% (Nylund, Nishina, Bellmore, and Graham 2007). Although certain personality characteristics, such as shyness, place children at higher risk for being bullied, there are also a host of changing situational factors, such as transitioning to a new school or delayed pubertal development, that affect the likelihood of a child continuing to get bullied. These situational factors explain why there are more temporary than chronic victims of bullying.

Myth #4: Boys Are Physical and Girls Are Relational Victims and Bullies.

The gender myth emerges in discussions that distinguish between physical and psychological victimization. The psychological type, often called "relational bullying," usually involves social ostracism or attempts to damage the reputation of the victim. Some research has suggested that girls are more likely to be both perpetrator and target of the relational type (for example, Crick and Grotpeter 1996). Because a whole popular culture has emerged around relationally aggressive girls (so-called *queen bees* or *alpha girls*) and their victims, putting these gender findings in proper perspective is important. In many studies, physical and relational victimization tend to be correlated, suggesting that the victim of relational harassment is also the victim of physical harassment. Moreover, if relational victimization is more prevalent in girls than boys (and the results are mixed), this gender difference is most likely confined to middle childhood and early adolescence (Archer and Coyne 2005). By middle adolescence, relational victimization becomes the norm for both genders as it becomes less socially accepted for individuals to be physically aggressive against peers. Relational victimization is a particularly insidious type of peer abuse because it inflicts psychological pain and is often difficult for others to detect. However, it's probably a less gendered subtype than previously thought.

Myth #5: Zero Tolerance Policies Reduce Bullying.

Zero tolerance approaches, which advocate suspending or expelling bullies, are sometimes preferred because they presumably send a message to the student body that bullying won't be tolerated. However, research suggests that these policies often don't work as intended and can sometimes backfire, leading

---

Resources

Teaching Tolerance, a project of the Southern Poverty Law Center

Dedicated to reducing prejudice, improving intergroup relations, and supporting equitable school experiences for children. Teaching Tolerance provides free educational materials to teachers. The organization's magazine, *Teaching Tolerance,* is also available free to educators.
www.tolerance.org

Office of Safe and Drug-Free Schools

Provides in-depth, online workshops focused on bullying prevention: "Exploring the Nature and Prevention of Bullying." Materials from that workshop are available online.
www2.ed.gov/admins/lead/safety/training/bullying/index.html

In addition, clicking on the link for "Resources and Links" will connect you with a lengthy list of relevant organizations, books, web sites, and videos.

Gay, Lesbian and Straight Education Network (GLSEN)

Provides resources and support for schools to implement effective and age-appropriate antibullying programs to improve school climate for all students.
www.glsen.org

to increases in antisocial behavior (APA Zero Tolerance Task Force 2008). Moreover, black youth are disproportionately the targets of suspension and expulsion, resulting in a racial discipline gap that mirrors the well-documented racial achievement gap (Gregory, Skiba, and Noguera 2010). Before deciding on a discipline strategy, school administrators must consider the scope of the problem, who will be affected, the fairness of the strategy, and what messages are communicated to students.

Zero tolerance policies often don't work as intended and can sometimes backfire, leading to increases in antisocial behavior.

Myth #6: Bullying Involves Only a Perpetrator and a Victim.

Many parents, teachers, and students view bullying as a problem that's limited to bullies and victims. Yet, much research shows that bullying involves more than the bully-victim dyad (Salmivalli 2001). For example, bullying incidents are typically public events that have witnesses. Studies based on playground observations have found that in most bullying incidents, at least four other peers were present as either bystanders, assistants to bullies, reinforcers, or defenders of victims. Assistants take part in ridiculing or intimidating a schoolmate, and reinforcers encourage the bully by showing their approval. However, those who come to aid the victim are rare. Unfortunately, many bystanders believe victims of harassment are responsible for their plight and bring problems on themselves.

Thoughts on Interventions

Educators who want to better understand the dynamics of school bullying will need to learn that the problems of victims and bullies aren't the same. Interventions for bullies don't need to focus on self-esteem; rather, bullies need to learn strategies to control their anger and their tendency to blame others for their problems. Victims, on the other hand, need interventions that help them develop more positive self-views, and that teach them not to blame themselves for the harassment. And peers need to learn that as witnesses to bullying, their responses aren't neutral and either support or oppose bullying behaviors.

Most bullying interventions are schoolwide approaches that target all students, parents, and adults in the school. They operate under the belief that bullying is a systemic problem and that finding a solution is the collective responsibility of everyone in the school. Two recent meta-analyses of research on antibullying programs suggest that the effects are modest at best (Merrell et al. 2008; Smith et al. 2004). Only about a third of the school-based interventions included in the analyses showed any positive effects as measured by fewer reported incidents of bullying; a few even revealed increased bullying, suggesting interventions may have backfired. These findings don't mean schools should abandon whole-school interventions that

have a research base. Instead, the modest results remind us that schools are complex systems and what works in one context may not be easily portable to other contexts with very different organizational structures, student demographics, and staff buy-in. Research on decision making about program adoption reveals that many teachers are reluctant to wholly embrace bullying interventions because they either believe the curriculum doesn't provide enough time and space to integrate such policies or that parents are responsible for developing antibullying attitudes (Cunningham et al. 2009).

Although obvious gains from systemwide interventions may be modest, teachers can take steps on an individual and daily basis to address bullying. First, teachers should never ignore a bullying incident. Because most bullying occurs in "un-owned spaces" like hallways and restrooms where adult supervision is minimal, teachers should respond to all bullying incidents that they witness. A response by a teacher communicates to perpetrators that their actions are not acceptable and helps victims feel less powerless about their predicament. This is especially important because students often perceive school staff as unresponsive to students' experiences of bullying.

Second, when possible, adults can use witnessed bullying incidents as "teachable moments," situations that open the door for conversations with students about difficult topics. For example, teachers may intervene to confront students directly about why many youth play bystander roles and are unwilling to come to the aid of victims, or how social ostracism can be a particularly painful form of peer abuse. At times, engaging in such difficult dialogues may be a more useful teacher response than quick and harsh punishment of perpetrators.

Finally, one meaningful factor that consistently predicts victimization is an individual's differences from the larger peer group. Thus, having a physical or mental handicap or being highly gifted in a regular school setting, being a member of an ethnic or linguistic minority group, suffering from obesity, or being gay or lesbian are all risk factors for bullying because individuals who have these characteristics are often perceived to deviate from the normative standards of the larger peer group. Students also tend to favor the in-group (those who are similar to them) and to derogate the out-group (those who are different). A strong antidote to this tendency is to teach tolerance for differences, an appreciation of diversity, and the value of multiple social norms and social identities co-habiting the same school environment. The effects of teaching tolerance may last a lifetime.

How Can Schools and Teachers Respond to Bullying?

Adults should intervene whenever they witness a bullying incident. Use bullying incidents as teachable moments to stimulate conversations, not merely as opportunities to punish the perpetrator. Teach tolerance for differences and an appreciation of diversity.

References

American Psychological Association Zero Tolerance Task Force. "Are Zero Tolerance Policies Effective in the Schools? Evidentiary Review and Recommendations." *American Psychologist* 63 (December 2008): 852–862.

Archer, John, and Sarah Coyne. "An Integrated Review of Indirect, Relational, and Social Aggression." *Personality and Social Psychology Review* 9, no. 3 (2005): 212–230.

Baumeister, Roy F., Jennifer D. Campbell, Joachim I. Krueger, and Kathleen D. Vohs. "Does High Self-Esteem Cause Better Performance, Interpersonal Success, Happiness, or Healthier Lifestyles?" *Psychological Science in the Public Interest* 4 (May 2003): 1–44.

Card, Noel, and Ernest V. Hodges. "Peer Victimization Among Schoolchildren: Correlates, Causes, Consequences, and Considerations in Assessment and Intervention." *School Psychology Quarterly* 23, no. 4 (December 2008): 451–461.

Crick, Nicki, and Jennifer Grotpeter. "Children's Treatment by Peers: Victims of Relational and Overt Aggression." *Development and Psychopathology* 8, no. 2 (1996): 367–380.

Cunningham, Charles E., Tracy Vaillancourt, Heather Rimas, Ken Deal, Lesley Cunningham, Kathy Short, and Yvonne Chen. "Modeling the Bullying Prevention Program Preferences of Educators: A Discrete Choice Conjoint Experiment." *Journal of Abnormal Child Psychology* 37, no. 7 (October 2009): 929–943.

Graham, Sandra, Amy Bellmore, and J. Mize. "Aggression, Victimization, and Their Co-Occurrence in Middle School." *Journal of Abnormal Child Psychology* 34 (2006): 363–378.

Gregory, Anne, Russell Skiba, and Pedro Noguera. "The Achievement Gap and the Discipline Gap: Two Sides of the Same Coin?" *Educational Researcher* 39, no. 1 (January 2010): 59–68.

Juvonen, Jaana, Sandra Graham, and Mark A. Schuster. "Bullying Among Young Adolescents: The Strong, the Weak, and the Troubled." *Pediatrics* 112 (December 2003): 1231–1237.

Merrell, Kenneth W., Barbara Gueldner, Scott Ross, and Duane Isava. "How Effective Are School Bullying Intervention Programs? A Meta-Analysis of Intervention Research." *School Psychology Quarterly* 23, no. 1 (March 2008): 26–42.

Nylund, Karen, Adrienne Nishina, Amy Bellmore, and Sandra Graham. "Subtypes, Severity, and Structural Stability of Peer Victimization: What Does Latent Class Analysis Say?" *Child Development* 78, no. 6 (2007): 1706–1722.

Salmivalli, Christina. "Group view on Victimization: Empirical Findings and Their Implications." In *Peer Harassment in School: The Plight of the Vulnerable and Victimized*, ed. Jaana Juvonen and Sandra Graham: 39-420. New York: Guilford, 2001.

Smith, J. David, Barry Schneider, Peter Smith, and Katerina Ananiadou. "The Effectiveness of Whole-School Anti-Bullying Programs: A Synthesis of Evaluation Research." *School Psychology Review* 33, no. 4 (2004): 547–560.

Critical Thinking

1. Bullying continues to be a serious problem in all schools. Did you experience bullying—as a bully, victim, or by-stander—when you were in school?

2. What are the lasting effects of bullying in your case?

3. Of the six most common myths about bullying, which one do you think most contributes to the continuance of bullying?

4. What do you think we could do to change the perceptions of school personnel?

SANDRA GRAHAM is a professor of education in the Graduate School of Education and Information Studies, University of California, Los Angeles.

UNIT 5

Addressing Diversity in Your School

Unit Selections

Learning Outcomes

After reading this unit, you will be able to:

- Restate the issues and concerns regarding the academic outcomes of Latino students.

- Select strategies that would be helpful in your local school district's efforts to support Latino students.

- Explain the importance of knowing the academic language skills of the students who are ELL in your classroom.

- Consider which effective teaching practices suggested by Gandara would also be helpful for all students.

- Determine appropriate teaching methods to use in teaching content to students who are ELL.

- Apply appropriate support materials to lesson plans for students who are ELL.

- Outline appropriate ways to include multicultural activities into content area lessons.

- Design guided notes for lectures and activities in your grade level or content area.

- Determine strategies to use in secondary content area classrooms to increase student achievement.

- Apply appropriate strategies to avoid conflict when collaborating with others.

Student Website

www.mhhe.com/cls

Internet References

The Literacy Web
www.literacy.uconn.edu/index.htm

New Horizons for Learning
www.newhorizons.org

National Association for Multicultural Education (NAME)
www.nameorg.org

Everything ESL
www.everythingesl.net

The Center for Comprehensive School Reform and Improvement
Center's Home page: www.centerforcsri.org
Center's link for resources on English Language Learners and Diverse Students: www.centerforcsri.org/index .php?option=com_content&task=view&id=678&Itemid=126

The Power of Two
www.powerof2.org

The concepts of culture and diversity encompass all the life ways, customs, traditions, and institutions that people develop as they create and experience their history and identity as a community. In the United States, very different cultures coexist within the civic framework of a shared constitutional tradition that guarantees equality before the law. So, many people are united as one nation by our constitutional heritage. Some of us are proud to say that we are a nation of immigrants. We are becoming more multicultural with every passing decade. As educators we have a unique opportunity. We are given the role to encourage and educate our diverse learners. The articles in this unit reflect upon all the concerns mentioned above. At this point you might want to return to Unit 2 to review the data in article 9: *Who Are America's Poor Children?* You can establish a classroom that is a place of care and nurture for your students, is multicultural-friendly, equitable, and free from bigotry, where diverse students are not just tolerated but are wanted, welcomed, and accepted. Respect for all children and their capacity is the baseline for good teaching. Students must feel significant and cared for by all members of the classroom. Our diverse children should be exposed to an academically challenging curriculum that expects much from them and equips them for the real world.

On average, Latino students never perform as well as other students, not even in kindergarten. In some states the Latino school-age population has nearly doubled since 1987, and is approaching one-half of all students. Unfortunately these students are more likely to attend a hypersegregated school, where the population is 90–100 percent minority, and less likely to read or do math at grade level or earn a college degree. In fact, they drop out of high school at higher rates than all other categories of the student population. After presenting these sad data, Gándara discusses ways in which this trend can be changed. In the end, she remarks that it is in our best interest to take action to help these students. Perhaps one reason Latinos are experiencing difficulty in our schools is that we do not have enough teachers trained to help ELLs. Included in this unit, Coleman and Goldenberg discuss the research on academic language proficiency. Learning academic language takes several years longer than conversational language; however, sometimes teachers confuse the use of social or conversational language and assume that a student should be able to learn in English. Understanding this and what to do about teaching students who do not have strong academic English will help teachers know how to help ELLs in their classes. Teachers have concerns about trying to teach students who are ELL and integrated into the general education classroom. How can they teach the content while also teaching the students to speak English? Those two tasks seem mutually exclusive at first consideration. Tissington and LaCour offer six strategies that have proven successful with struggling students and suggest these strategies will work for language learners of all types. They offer a list of story books that promote language building and a rubric for assessment of progress. Piper and Shaw selected a specific content unit, Photosynthesis, to illustrate how a general education teacher can incorporate specific content, teaching strategies, and assessment techniques that

© Comstock/PictureQuest

are helpful to ELLs as well as being useful with other students. The article contains a chart of fluency levels that is particularly helpful for teachers. Both of these articles contain specific information, illustrations, and detailed plans for teaching and implementing their suggestions.

As teachers work to address diversity, Noftle and Pacino suggest that all students should be provided with opportunities to experience cultures different from their own. In fact, for students who live in regions of the county where there is little diversity these experiences and exposure to other cultures is especially important. Their primary concern is that we should not send graduates into the twenty-first century without an understanding of non-Western mode of discourse or lacking in literacy skills for the digital age. Konrad, Joseph, and Itoi suggest that taking notes during lectures, class discussion, and reading texts is challenging for many students. Further, teaching all students to use guided notes can be helpful to both ELLs and those with learning and language disabilities. There are examples of guided notes across several grade levels and content areas.

Meeting Students Where They Are: The Latino Education Crisis

Patricia Gándara

They're the fastest-growing ethnic group but the most poorly educated. Do we have what it takes to close the gap?

From their first day of kindergarten to their last day of school, Latinos, on average, perform far below most of their peers. They now constitute the largest minority group in the United States and the fastest growing segment of its school-age population. As such, they are inextricably bound up with the nation's future.

The Latino public school population nearly doubled between 1987 and 2007, increasing from 11 to 21 percent of all U.S. students (National Center for Education Statistics [NCES], 2009b). The U.S. Census Bureau predicts that by 2021, one of four U.S. students will be Latino. In key states in the U.S. Southwest, such as Texas and California, the Latino school-age population is already approaching one-half of all students. In these states, the future is already here.

But it's a troubling picture. Latinos are the least educated of all major ethnic groups (see Figure 1). Although a large gap exists between the college completion rates of whites and blacks, both groups show steady growth. However, the growth in college degrees for Latinos is almost flat. The failure over more than three decades to make any progress in moving more Latino students successfully through college suggests that what we have been doing to close achievement gaps is not working. This fact has enormous consequences for the United States, as the job market continues to demand more education and Latinos continue to make up a larger and larger portion of the workforce.

Behind at the Start

Can schools close these gaps? It is instructive to look back to the first days of schooling to see the differences that exist at that point. Data from the 1998 Early Childhood Longitudinal Study show that only one-half as many Latino children as white children fall into the highest quartile of math and reading skills at the *beginning* of kindergarten, and more than twice as many fall into the lowest quartile. The gap is even wider between Latino and Asian students (see Figure. 2).

Figure 1 Bachelor's Degree Completion by Ethnicity

	Year				
Ethnicity	1975	1985	1995	2005	2008
White	24	24	29	34	37
Black	11	12	15	18	21
Latino	9	11	9	11	12

The figures represent the percentage of 25- to 29-year-olds in the United States who completed a bachelor's degree or higher.

Source: *Current Population Survey (CPS), Annual Social and Economic Study Supplement*, 1971–2005, previously unpublished tabulation, November 2005, and *American Community Survey 2008*, by U.S. Census Bureau, Washington, DC: U.S. Department of Commerce.

Figure 2 Percentage of Kindergartners Scoring at Highest and Lowest Quartiles, on the 1998 Early Childhood Longitudinal Study

	Reading		Math	
Ethnic Group	Highest Quartile	Lowest Quartile	Highest Quartile	Lowest Quartile
White	30	18	32	18
Asian	39	13	38	13
Black	15	34	10	39
Latino	15	42	14	40
Native American	9	57	9	50

Source: *America's Kindergartners: Findings from the Early Childhood Longitudinal Study*, by J. West, K. Denton, and E. Germino-Hausken, 2000, Washington, DC: National Center for Education Statistics.

Access to preschool education, of which Latino children have less than any other major group (NCES, 2009a), contributes to some of this early gap, but it cannot account for all of it. The evidence shows that poverty is the culprit. Young Latino children are more than twice as likely to be poor as white children and are even more likely to be among the poorest of the poor. At least one-third of Latino families lack health insurance; many Latino children rarely see a doctor, dentist, or optometrist, and so they often go to school with toothaches, uncorrected vision problems, and untreated chronic health problems (Berliner, 2009). Many also go to school hungry. These all constitute serious impediments to learning that schools are often poorly equipped to address.

Latino students are many more times as likely as students from other ethnic groups to come from homes where parents do not speak English well—or at all—and where parental education is low. More than 40 percent of Latina mothers lack even a high school diploma, compared with only 6 percent of white mothers; and only about 10 percent of Latina mothers have a college degree or higher, compared with almost one-third of white mothers (see Figure 3). Although Latino students may come from loving homes, limited education and resources do affect their education outcomes. There is no better predictor of how well children will fare in school than parents' education attainment (Murnane, Maynard, & Ohls, 1981).

It is difficult for parents to impart to their children experiences and knowledge that they do not have. Many studies have shown that school benefits poor children more than middle-class children (Alexander, Entwisle, & Olsen, 1997; Coleman, 1966); in the case of poor children, schools offer what parents cannot, whereas for middle-class children, school supplements what the home and community routinely offer. Under the right conditions, schools could conceivably close the gaps for Latino children, but the schools that serve most Latino students today have not met those conditions.

Figure 3 Mother's Education Level by Ethnicity

Ethnicity	Less than High School	High School	Bachelor's Degree or Higher
Latino	41.3%	28.6%	9.9%
White	5.9%	29.0%	31.7%
Black	18.2%	34.4%	15.3%
Asian	16%	22.2%	44.7%

Asian percentages were based on a small sample, so they may not be entirely representative.

Source: *Current Population Survey (CPS), Annual Social and Economic Study Supplement, 1971–2005,* previously unpublished tabulation, by U.S. Census Bureau, 2005, Washington, DC: U.S. Department of Commerce. Available: http://nces.ed.gov/pubs2007/minoritytrends/tables/table_5.asp

Segregated from the Mainstream

In the United States as a whole, Latinos are slightly more likely than black students (39.5 percent vs. 38.3 percent) to attend hypersegregated schools—those that are 90 to 100 percent nonwhite. In the large central cities in the west, more than 60 percent of Latinos attend hypersegregated schools (Orfield & Frankenberg, 2008).

This means that many Latino students lack access to peers from the mainstream U.S. culture, which inhibits their understanding of the norms, standards, and expectations of the broader society. For example, these students may rarely come into contact with anyone who has gone to college or who intends to go, so the aspirations and knowledge about getting to college never develop. It also means that Latino students are likely to attend underresourced schools with poorer facilities and less-qualified teachers than mainstream students experience.

The Need for Comprehensive Support

Factors like health care; intense neighborhood segregation (which results in school segregation); and the language and resources of the family may seem beyond the scope of what most schools can reasonably address. But other factors—such as teacher quality, school facilities and resources, and a rich curriculum—are very much within the purview of schools.

One key to successfully meeting Latino students' needs is to conceptualize our efforts as a *continuum* of interventions rather than discrete interventions; according to the literature, the effect of a single intervention tends to fade in the absence of sustained supportive environments. Preschool won't, on its own, permanently narrow or close achievement gaps, just as the effects of an intervention in elementary school will probably not last through high school.

The evidence suggests that a continuing net of support for disadvantaged students is likely to significantly improve their academic outcomes and reduce the wide gaps in achievement that now exist. It follows that under these conditions, students will be more likely to graduate from high school and successfully prepare for college.

A Focus on Early Childhood

If Latino children are going to catch up with their more-advantaged peers, they must have access to high-quality preschool. We have never been successful in closing these achievement gaps after students are in elementary school.

A number of studies have demonstrated the effectiveness of high-quality Head Start–type programs that provide comprehensive services to students and their families.

The research on Head Start has demonstrated "moderate effects on pre-academic skills, greater parental awareness of the needs of their children and increased skills in meeting those needs, and provision of health and nutrition services and information" (Gándara & Contreras, 2009, p. 259). Of course, once children leave Head Start, they also lose the health and family support services that are so important for many low-income Latino students.

In his study of Oklahoma's universal preschool program, Gormley (2008) documented that Latino students benefited more than any other category of student from attending preschool. In both reading and math readiness, the Latinos in the program performed approximately one year above those Latino students who did not attend preschool. Students in full-day kindergarten also outperformed those who attended a half-day program. The researchers attributed the score gains to the policy of hiring fully credentialed teachers and paying them at the same salary level as other teachers. The teachers not only were competent, but also were likely to stay and build strong programs at the center over time. Other researchers have found similar gains for low-income preschool students in high-quality programs (Karoly et al., 1998).

The single biggest argument against providing universal preschool—apart from its cost—is that research has shown that the positive effects are not sustained for many students; students show an initial rise in test scores that seems to disappear after one or two years of school (Currie & Thomas, 1995). However, researchers have argued that this is probably because the schools these students attend are too weak to sustain the positive effects of preschool. Research has also shown that students' environments outside school probably contribute more to schooling outcomes than in-school factors do. Compared with all other developed nations of the world, the United States provides the weakest safety net for its low-income students and their families (Rainwater & Smeeding, 2005). This surely contributes to the erosion of positive effects of schooling interventions.

A Focus on K–12 Supports

To sustain the effects of early interventions, it is crucial to strengthen the capacity of K–12 schools to monitor and support students once they arrive at school. Some programs, such as Project GRAD (www.projectgrad.org), have attempted to bundle research-based interventions that follow students as a cohort through their K–12 years. These include well-established programs, such as the University of Chicago School Mathematics Project (http://ucsmp.uchicago.edu) and Success for All (www.successforall.net). In fact, consistent with other studies, the Success for All researchers found good outcomes for Spanish-speaking students in their regular English curriculum but superior outcomes using their bilingual curriculum (Slavin & Cheung, 2005).

Although Project GRAD takes a whole-school reform approach, it also monitors students and their progress. Recent findings indicate that students who stay in the program longer appear to benefit the most and that careful monitoring of individual students is central to the effectiveness of education interventions (Gándara & Bial, 2001).

Dual-Language and Two-Way Immersion Programs

Programs promoting bilingualism have been found to produce superior academic outcomes for both Latino students whose first language is Spanish and for non-Spanish speakers, while also developing a strong competence in a second language (see Genesee, Lindholm-Leary, Saunders, & Christian, 2006). Such programs, whose goal is to transform monolingual speakers of either English or Spanish into fully bilingual and biliterate students, have mushroomed in recent years. Because the programs give equal status to both languages and typically enroll Latino students alongside non-Latino students, they have the additional advantage of fostering positive intergroup relations and increasing Latino students' social capital, as the Latino students are fully integrated with their middle-class peers (Morales & Aldana, 2010). These programs usually have long waiting lists.

Magnet Schools

Magnet schools often specialize in a specific field, such as medicine, the arts, or science. A number of studies have shown that in addition to benefitting from a more desegregated schooling experience, magnet school students tend to outperform students in regular public and private schools in both reading and math scores on standardized tests (Frankenberg & Seigel-Hawley, 2008).

Dropout Prevention and College-Going Programs

High school programs that focus on immediate issues such as dropout prevention and college-going tend to be more successful for Latino youth than those with less focused goals. Effective programs tend to share five components (Gándara & Bial, 2001). They (1) provide at least one key person whose job it is to know, connect with, and monitor the progress of each student; (2) structure a supportive peer group that reinforces program goals; (3) provide access to strong curriculum that leads to college preparation; (4) attend to students' cultural backgrounds; and (5) show students how they can finance their education, providing scholarships when possible.

One high school program that focuses specifically on preparing Latino students for college is the Puente Project, which is active in 36 California high schools. Through a school support team, the program provides a net of services: two years of intensive college-preparatory English, focusing on writing skills and incorporating Latino literature;

intensive college counseling; and a mentor from the community who acts as a guide and role model. The program has doubled the college-going of participating students and has motivated them to attend more selective schools. This is important because Latino students tend to enroll in less selective colleges than they qualify for (Fry, 2004), and students who attend more selective schools tend to have higher graduation rates (Sigal & Tienda, 2005). Key to the success of the program is its strong adult-student connections and the availability of a counselor to advocate for the students.

School Attachment and Belonging

Latino students' extraordinarily high dropout rate is related, in part, to their lack of attachment to school and a sense of not belonging. A crucial means by which students attach to school and form supportive friendship groups is through extracurricular activities—sports, band, newspaper, and other clubs. Unfortunately, Latino students are less likely to participate in these activities, either because they perceive the club to be exclusive or because of logistical problems, like needing to work or help out at home after school or not having transportation or the money required for the activity. Latino students' absence from these activities is also related to their lack of access to the same social circles as their middle-class peers, reducing their chances of being invited into these activities.

Schools that effectively address this issue find ways to incorporate clubs, sports, and other activities into school routines and bring the benefits of these activities into the classroom. For example, some schools mix students in heterogeneous classes and create conditions for students from different groups to interact in conditions in which they are more equal in status (see Gibson, Gándara, & Koyama, 2004).

How School-Community Partnerships Can Help

Schools alone cannot close the yawning gaps in achievement. But schools can partner with other institutions to help narrow those gaps. Collaboration in the following three areas can make a significant difference for many Latino students.

- *Create magnet schools that appeal to middle-class parents.* Some interventions are not costly in terms of dollars but require spending political capital. For example, in gentrifying areas of the inner cities, we could attack the problem of neighborhood and school segregation through thoughtful and progressive planning. The apartments that have sprung up in formerly downtrodden areas typically market to professional single people and young couples without children—the assumption being

that young families do not want to live in the city center. We need to create attractive options by offering desegregated, high-quality schools adjacent to open spaces that could serve both the families of young professionals and inner-city residents. Because dual-language programs often appeal to middle-class parents, it would make sense to include such programs as features of new inner-city magnet schools.

- *Work with health and social service agencies.* Because access to health care and social services is an acute problem for Latino families, schools should be the primary contact for these kinds of services for youth. The Center for Health and Health Care in Schools (n.d.) reports that in 2006, there were more than 1,800 school-based health centers around the United States, providing care for children who might otherwise not have been able to access it. Although this is an encouraging number, it represents a small fraction of U.S. schools that serve low-income students and Latinos.

An evaluation of California's Healthy Start Program, which provides integrated services primarily to Latino children and families, showed that it reduced needs for food, clothing, transportation, and medical and dental care; improved clients' emotional health and family functioning; reduced teen risk behaviors; modestly improved grade point averages; and reduced student mobility (Wagner & Golan, 1996). Nevertheless, the program has progressively lost funding. One study found that such programs are difficult to operate because of the need to integrate many services that compete with one another for dollars (Romualdi, 2000). However, if we can stabilize funding, these programs can make a big difference in the lives of Latino children. Placing medical, dental, and social services in an accessible, safe place makes sense if the goal is to help schools do their job of teaching these students. Critics have argued against the "effectiveness" of these centers, in part because research has failed to show that they significantly raise standardized test scores. But children who arrive at school with basic health, emotional, and nutritional needs unmet are not ready to learn. It only makes sense to evaluate the centers on their primary mission—healthier developmental outcomes for children that ultimately lead to better opportunities to learn. Moreover, if such programs can create family attachments to a school, thereby reducing student mobility, this could result in long-term benefits for Latino students.

- *Reach out to parents in culturally appropriate ways.* Many studies have shown that a primary reason that

Latino students do not complete college degrees is because they don't understand how to prepare for college or even why they should attend. Their parents, who have often not completed high school in the United States, are even less familiar with these issues.

However, given the opportunity, most parents are eager to help their children succeed in school. One example of an effective program designed specifically for Latino immigrant parents is the Parent Institute for Quality Education (PIQE). Founded in San Diego, California, in 1987 but now operating in both Washington, D.C., and Texas, PIQE teaches parents, in nine weekly evening sessions, how to monitor their children's progress, advocate on their behalf, and prepare them for college. Many of the staff members who run the program were once parent participants. One evaluation of the program found that participating parents read more with their children and understood more about how they could support their children's education (Chrispeels, Wang, & Rivero, 2000).

Doing Whatever It Takes

No silver bullet or single program can close the enormous gap between Latino students and their peers with respect to academic achievement and attainment. But it's in all of our interests to find ways to begin the process of narrowing those gaps. This will require the collaborative efforts of both schools and social service agencies. It will also take the political courage to acknowledge that schools cannot do this alone—and that the rest of society will need to step up to the challenge.

References

Alexander, K., Entwisle, D., & Olsen, L. (1997). *Children, schools, and inequality.* Boulder, CO: Westview Press.

Berliner, D. (2009). *Poverty and potential: Out-of-school factors and school success.* Boulder, CO, and Tempe, AZ: Education and the Public Interest Center.

Center for Health and Health Care in Schools. (n.d.). *Health services.* Available: www.healthinschools.org/Health-in-Schools/Health -Services.aspx.

Chrispeels, J., Wang, J., & Rivero, E. (2000). *Evaluation summary of the impact of the Parent Institute for Quality Education on parent's engagement with their children's schooling.* Available: www.piqe.org/Assets/Home/ChrispeelEvaluation.htm.

Coleman, J. (1966). *Equality of educational opportunity.* Washington, DC: U.S. Government Printing Office.

Currie, J., & Thomas, D. (1995). Does Head Start make a difference? *American Economic Review, 85,* 341–364.

Frankenberg, E., & Seigel-Hawley, G. (2008). *Rethinking magnet schools in a changing landscape.* Los Angeles: Civil Rights Project/Proyecto Derechos Civiles.

Fry, R. (2004). *Latino youth finishing college: The role of selective pathways.* Washington, DC: Pew Hispanic Center. Available: http://pewhispanic.org/reports/report.php?ReportID=30.

Gándara, P., & Bial, D. (2001). *Paving the way to postsecondary education.* Washington DC: National Center for Education Statistics.

Gándara P., & Contreras, F. (2009). *The Latino education crisis: The consequences of failed social policies.* Cambridge, MA: Harvard University Press.

Genesee, F., Lindholm-Leary, K., Saunders, W., & Christian, D. (2006). *Educating English language learners: A synthesis of research evidence.* New York: Cambridge University Press.

Gibson, M., Gándara, P., & Koyama, J. (Eds.). (2004). *School connections: U.S. Mexican youth, peers, and school achievement.* New York: Teachers College Press.

Gormley, W. (2008). The effects of Oklahoma's pre-K program on Hispanic children. *Social Science Quarterly, 89,* 916–936.

Karoly, L. A., Greenwood, P. W., Everingham, S. S., Hoube, J., Kilburn, M. R., Rydell, C. P., Sanders, M., et al.(1998). *Investing in our children: What we know and don't know about the costs and benefits of early childhood interventions.* Santa Monica, CA: RAND.

Morales, P. Z., & Aldana, U. (2010). Learning in two languages: Programs with political promise. In P. Gándara & M. Hopkins (Eds.), *Forbidden language: English learners and restrictive language policies.* New York: Teachers College Press.

Murnane, R., Maynard, R., & Ohls, J. (1981). Home resources and children's achievement. *The Review of Economics and Statistics, 63*(3), 369–377.

National Center for Education Statistics. (2009a). *The condition of education.* Washington, DC: U.S. Department of Education.

National Center for Education Statistics. (2009b). Racial/ ethnic enrollment in public schools. Indicator 7. In *The condition of education.* Washington, DC: U.S. Department of Education.

Orfield, G., & Frankenberg, E. (2008). *The last have become first: Rural and small town America lead the way of desegregation.* Los Angeles: UCLA Civil Rights Project/Proyecto Derechez Civiles.

Rainwater, L., & Smeeding, T. (2005). *Poor kids in a rich country: America's children in comparative perspective.* New York: Russell Sage.

Romualdi, E. V. (2000). Shared dream: A case study of the implementation of Healthy Start (California). (Doctoral dissertation, University of California, Davis). *Dissertation Abstracts International, 61*(09). (UMI No. 9315947).

Sigal, A., & Tienda, M. (2005). Assessing the mismatch hypothesis: Differentials in college graduation rates by institutional selectivity. *Sociology of Education, 78*(4), 294–315.

Slavin, R., & Cheung, A. (2005). A synthesis of research on language of reading instruction for English language learners. *Review of Educational Research, 75,* 247–284.

Wagner, M., & Golan, S. (1996). *California's Healthy Start school-linked services initiative: Summary of evaluation findings.* Menlo Park, CA: SRI International.

Critical Thinking

1. What is the crisis? How will this crisis impact the communities with high Latino populations?

2. What are the potential social and educational implications of the high dropout rates for Latino students?

3. Which of the strategies mentioned by Gándara do you think would be most effective in your community?

Explain your choice and why you think it is best for your community.

PATRICIA GÁNDARA is Professor of Education at University of California, Los Angeles, and Codirector of the Civil Rights Project. She is the coauthor, with Frances Contreras, of *The Latino Education Crisis: The Consequences of Failed Social Policies* (Harvard University Press, 2009).

From *Educational Leadership,* February 2010, pp. 24–30. Copyright © 2010 by ASCD. Reprinted by permission. The Association for Supervision and Curriculum Development is a worldwide community of educators advocating sound policies and sharing best practices to achieve the success of each learner. To learn more, visit ASCD at www.ascd.org.

What Does Research Say about Effective Practices for English Learners?

PART II: Academic Language Proficiency.

RHODA COLEMAN AND CLAUDE GOLDENBERG

U sing strategies and techniques that make academic content more accessible, classroom teachers can help ELL students keep pace academically.

This is the second in a four-part series written exclusively for the Kappa Delta Pi Record. Each article summarizes what research says about effective practices for ELL. The authors draw on several recent reviews of the research (August and Shanahan 2006; Genesee et al. 2006; Goldenberg 2008; Saunders and Goldenberg, in press). The fust article in the series (which appeared in the Fall 2009 Record) covered research on English oral language instruction. This, the second article, deals with academic language and literacy in English. Article three Record Spring 2010) takes this research into practice by describing an observation tool (the CQeII) that is useful for planning and coaching teachers who want to implement effective strategies in their classrooms. The final article (Record Summer 2010) is about school and district reform and offers practical recommendations for administrators and teacher leaders so that the research can more readily translate into practice.

Academic language is a vital part of content-area instruction and is one of the most pressing needs faced by English Language Learners (ELLs). The fundamental challenge ELLs in all-English instruction face is learning academic content while simultaneously becoming proficient in English. Because of this challenge, we, as educators, do not know to what extent ELLs can keep pace academically with English speakers; nonetheless, our goal should be to make academic content as accessible as possible for these students and promote English language development as students learn academic content.

Academic language differs from everyday language and knowing the differences is important for effective academic instruction. Academic language refers to the sort of language competence required for students to gain access to content taught in English and, more generally, for success in school and any career where mastering large and complex bodies of information and concepts is needed (Fillmore and Snow 2000). Academic language, the language of texts and formal writing, is different from everyday speech and conversation, what Cummins (1984) has referred to as Basic Interpersonal Communication Skills (BICS). BICS, in general, is language used for communication skills in everyday social interactions. In contrast, Cognitive Academic Language Proficiency (CALP) is the oral and written language related to literacy and academic achievement (Cummins 1984).

The terms BICS and CALP have somewhat fallen out of favor, in part because they imply a hard dichotomy that might be misleading. There is likely to be a great deal of grey area, where language has both conversational and academic elements. Nonetheless, BICS and CALP identify a useful distinction between (a) language that is relatively informal, contextualized, cognitively less demanding, used in most social interactions, and generally learned more easily; and (b) language that is more formal, abstract, used in academic and explicit teaching/learning situations, more demanding cognitively, and more challenging to learn.

Fluency in academic language is especially critical for academic achievement. Knowledge of academic disciplines—science, social studies, history, mathematics—is, of course, the primary objective of content-area instruction. Just as important is the language needed to learn about and discuss academic content. Most ELLs eventually acquire adequate conversational language skills, but they often lack the academic language skills that are essential for high levels of achievement in the content areas.

Educators must focus on the academic language needed for academic achievement. Yet, we are lacking a solid research base that identifies effective techniques and approaches. There are, however, promising directions—e.g., Dutro and Moran (2003), Schleppegrell (2001); Lyster (2007), and Zwiers (2008). Educators are strongly encouraged to learn about them, implement them in their classrooms, and try to determine which best meet the needs of English learners.

For both oral and academic language, students need to be taught expressive as well as receptive language.

Using sheltered instruction strategies makes grade-level academic content comprehensible; that is, students develop receptive language in order to comprehend or, at least, get the gist of a lesson. From this type of instruction, students do not necessarily develop expressive language so that they can speak and write in the language. Students need to be taught expressive language—"comprehensible output" (Swain 1985)—so that they can answer questions, participate in discussions, and be successful at showing what they know on assessments.

Because content instruction may be an excellent opportunity to teach language skills in a meaningful context, teachers may integrate both types of instruction throughout the day. There is no reason to believe these types of instruction are mutually exclusive. This support for ELLs in the general classroom may be offered in addition to a separate English Language Development (ELD) block.

Academic and conversational English are different . . . and similar!

It is important to note that there is a connection between conversational and academic language; they are not completely distinct from each other. Using students' everyday experiences can help students learn academic language. That is, if students are familiar with a task in a social context, they may be able to adopt appropriate language from that task and transfer it to school-based tasks.

For example, a student might know how to retell what happened on a favorite television show or present an argument for why he should be able to go out and play basketball at the park. Accordingly, that student may be able to transfer the language he or she uses to express cause and effect regarding behavior and consequences to a science experiment, an if-then hypothesis structure, or a historical sequence of causally linked events. If a student can compare and contrast dogs and cats, this same structure applies to comparing and contrasting two systems of government. To help students make these language connections, teachers should bring this skill to a conscious level. Though students may be able to make comparisons in their everyday life, they may need to learn how these structures are transferable to school-based situations. There is not a clear line separating conversational from academic language. describes the differences between conversational and academic language and also shows the grey area where the two overlap. Categories used in the table are based on Goldenberg and Coleman (in press).

Academic language instruction should include not only the vocabulary of the content subjects, but also the syntax and text structures. Schleppegrell (2001) distinguished between academic language and everyday speech and explained how academic language is about so much more than learning content-specific, or technical, vocabulary. Students may know the meanings of individual content-specific words, yet still not be able to understand the larger meaning when reading them in a sentence or be able to combine them to write a sentence.

Academic language and curriculum content are closely intertwined. It is not sufficient for a student to comprehend only text and teacher-talk well—that is, to have receptive understanding. The student also must be able to express his or her complete thoughts orally and in writing using academic language. For example, students need to understand how to construct a sentence or paragraph (orally and in writing) that expresses compare/contrast or cause and effect (Dutro and Moran 2003).

Language development and sheltering techniques should be incorporated into content instruction.

Sheltered instruction strategies, or SDAIE (Specially Designed Academic Instruction in English), provide comprehensible input for any content area. The term comprehensible input refers to strategies that enable ELLs to understand the essence of a lesson by means of context or visual cues, clarification, and building background knowledge that draws on students' experiences (Krashen and Tenell 1983).

What is often overlooked is that sheltered instruction calls for all lessons to have clearly stated language objectives in addition to providing comprehensible input. Short (1994) discussed the importance of explicit language instruction along with content-area instruction. She advocated developing language objectives in addition to content-area objectives for ELLs to provide them access to the core curriculum. The SIOP model for making content comprehensible to English Learners also emphasizes the need for a language objective along with a content objective (Echevarria, Vogt, and Short 2008) and suggests the language goals be adjusted for the students' proficiency levels (Genesee et al. 2006, 191).

For example, students studying how the saguaro cactus survives in the desert in science (content objective) have a language objective of writing cause-and-effect sentences using signal words "because" and "as a result of." For example, "Because its accordian skin holds water, the saguaro cactus can survive in the desert." and "As a result of its shallow roots, which capture surface water, the saguaro cactus can survive in the desert." A social studies teacher having students interview a grandparent or other elder to learn about the past can instruct students on how to correctly phrase interview questions (language objective). An English teacher having students write about setting (content objective) can use this as an opportunity to teach a lesson on adjectives (language objective). However, the language objectives, like the content objectives, should not be chosen randomly. They should be selected based on the proficiency level and grade level standards appropriate to the students.

Educators must take care that ELD does not displace instruction in academic content. Content-based ELD, which is driven by the ELD standards, does not replace content instruction driven by the content standards. In other words, just because an ELD lesson is about a science topic does not mean it meets the requirements for standards-based science instruction in that grade level. A sheltered lesson makes standards-based content instruction accessible. A content-based ELD lesson has language as a focus, but uses a content area as the medium. This type of lesson is not the same as standards-based content instruction.

Closing Thoughts

Most ELLs take years to develop the level of academic English proficiency required for full participation in all English classrooms (Genesee et al. 2006). It does not take much imagination to conclude that if (a) students are functioning at less than high levels of English proficiency; and (b) instruction is offered only in mainstream academic English, these students will not have access to the core academic curriculum. They will have virtually no chance of performing at a level similar to that of their English speaking peers. Whether students are in primary language (that is, "bilingual") or English-only programs, educators must focus intensively on providing them with the academic language skills in English they will need to succeed in school and beyond.

To move this discussion from research to practice, let's take a look at a scenario that incorporates some of these recommendations. This is an actual lesson taught by a 5th-grade teacher.

Elementary Academic Instruction

Mrs. C is teaching a 5th grade social studies lesson on immigration. ELD levels range from early intermediate to fluent English. The language objective is for students to write cause-and-effect sentences about the immigrant experience—e.g., "Because we wanted a better life, my family immigrated to the United States" or "My family immigrated to the United States because we wanted a better life." This lesson is designed to motivate interest in and build background for a chapter on immigration in the history textbook that students will read later.

Before students read the state-adopted history textbook, Mrs. C looks for key passages. She analyzes them for any words, phrases, or concepts that may need clarification and any concepts for which she may need to build background knowledge. She also looks for supportive visuals in the textbook, such as charts, graphs, maps, and photos.

Mrs. C begins the lesson by sharing pictures of her family members who were immigrants. Next she puts on a babushka (Russian for scarf) and a long skirt and becomes her own immigrant grandmother. Speaking in the first person, she tells the story of when, how, and why she came to America. She points to Russia on a map. As she tells her story, "grandmother" holds up vocabulary cards with the words immigrant, motivation, perspective, ancestor, and descendant, and she uses each word in context. For example, "I am an immigrant from Russia. I used to live in Russia, but I came to live in America. My motivation or reason for coming to America was . . ."

Students are then invited to interview her—that is, ask her questions—in preparation for their assignment to interview an immigrant. The person can be a family member or, if that is not practical, a neighbor or teacher. The students and Mrs. C. discuss possible interview questions, using the target vocabulary words, and decide: "From what country did you immigrate to the United States? When did you arrive? What are some things you remember about that experience? What was your motivation for coming/leaving? What was your perspective, or how did you feel about immigrating?" When the students return with their interview responses, Mrs. C records them on a graphic organizer with these headings: Person, Country, Motivation for Immigrating, and Perspective.

Mrs. C models how to turn the answers into cause-and-effect statements, using sentence frames:

_____ because _____.

Because _____, _____.

Students respond with sentences orally and in writing—such as.

My great-grandmother immigrated to the United States from Russia in 1903 because she wanted religious freedom. My grandmother likes it here because she can attend a synagogue.

Because of the potato famine, my ancestors immigrated to the United States from Ireland. They were sad because they had to leave some family members behind.

References

August, D., and T. Shanahan, eds. 2006. Developing literacy in second-language learners: Report of the National Literacy Panel on Language Minority Children and Youth. Mahwah, NJ: Erlbaum.

Cummins, J. I 984. Wanted: A theoretical framework for relating language proficiency to academic achievement among bilingual students. In Language proficiency and academic achievement, ed. C. Rivera, 2–I9. Clevedon, Avon, England: Multilingual Matters.

Dutro, S. 2005. A focused approach to frontloading English language instruction for Houghton Mifflin reading, K-6, 4th ed., Califomia Reading St Literature Project. Santa Cruz, CA: ToucanEd.

Dutro, S., and C. Moran. 2003. Rethinking English language instruction: An architectural approach. In English learners: Reaching the highest level of English literacy, ed. G. C. Garcia, 227–58. Newark, DE: International Reading Association.

Echevarra, J., M. Vogt, and D. Short. 2008. Making content comprehensible for English Leamers: The SIOP* model, 3rd ed. Needham Heights, MA: Allyn St Bacon.

Fillmore, L. W., and C. E. Snow. 2000. What teachers need to know about language. In What teachers need to know about language, ed. C. T. Adger, C. E. Snow, and D. Christian, 7–53. Washington, DC: Center for Applied Linguistics.

Genesee, F., K. Lindholm-Leary, W. M. Saunders, and D. Christian. 2006. Educating English Language Learners. New York: Cambridge University Press.

Goldenberg, C. 2008. Teaching English Language Leamers: What the research does- and does not- say. American Educator 32(2): 8–23, 42–44.

Goldenberg, C, and R. Coleman. In press. Promoting academic achievement among English learners. Thousand Oaks, CA: Corwin.

Krashen, S. D., and T. D. Terrell. 1983. The natural approach: Language acquisition in the classroom. Hayward, CA: Alemany Press.

Lyster, R. 2007. Learning and teaching languages through content: A counterbalanced approach. Philadelphia, PA: John Benjamins Pub.

Saunders, W. M., and C. Goldenberg, C. in press. Research to guide English Language Development instruction. In Improving education for English Learners: Research-based approaches, ed. D. Dolson and L. Burnham-Massey. Sacramento, CA: CDE Press.

Schleppegrell, M. J. 2001. Linguistic features of the language of schooling. Linguistics and Education 12(4): 431–59.

Short, D. J. 1994. Expanding middle school horizons: Integrating language, culture, and social studies. TESOL Quarterly 28(3): 581–608.

Swain M. 1985. Communicative competence: Some roles of comprehensible input and comprehensible output in its development. In Input in second language acquisition, ed. S. M. Gass and C. G. Madden, 235–56. Rowley, MA: Newberry House Publishers.

Zwiers, J. 2008. Building academic language: Essential practices for content classrooms, grades S-1 2. San Francisco, CA: Jossey-Bass.

Rhoda Coleman is Research Fellow at The Center for Language Minority Education and Research at California State University, Long Beach, where she also teaches in the College of Education. She was a California State Teacher of the Year and Milken recipient.

Claude Coldenberg is Professor of Education at Stanford University. His research focuses on academic achievement among English learners. He was on the Committee for the Prevention of Early Reading Difficulties in Young Children and the National Literacy Panel.

Portions of this article are based on the authors' forthcoming book Promoting Academic Achievement among English Learners, to be published by Corwin Press in 2011, and are used with permission.

Critical Thinking

1. Summarize the research presented in this article.

2. Create a resource file of teaching strategies or methods and materials that you can use to teach linguistically or culturally diverse students.

3. What are the positive effects of diversity in our schools? Provide rationales for your challenges based on the articles in this unit.

RHODA COLEMAN, *"What Does Research Say about Effective Practices for ENGLISH LEARNERS?"*. Kappa Delta Pi Record. Find-Articles.com. 30 Mar, 2010. http://findarticles.com/p/articles /mi_qa4009/is_201001/ai_n45882227

Strategies and Content Areas for Teaching English Language Learners

Dr. Laura Tissington and Dr. Misty LaCour

Introduction

Language and literacy education for students who are English language learners (ELLs) has been well cited in the research as a current hot topic (Anthony, 2008). However, educators and other school professionals often disagree on the best way to teach ELLs. Moreover, programs to address the needs of ELLs vary greatly. The child's first experience with school, both positive and negative, has shown to have a lasting effect. Therefore, in order to meet the needs of ELLs, educators must provide the most conducive environment for learning as possible.

Getting Started

English language learners (ELLs) are one of the largest groups to struggle with literacy (Hickman, Pollard-Durodola, & Vaughn, 2004). Because of this, focus of instruction should be placed on the learner's ability to comprehend the lesson content and not on the learner's language proficiency (Myburgh, Poggenpoel, & Rensburg, 2004). Moreover, research has indicated that ELLs benefit from the same explicit, systematic instruction proven to be effective for native English speakers (Mathes, Pollard-Durodola, Cardenas-Hagen, Linan-Thompson, and Vaughn, 2007). Teachers of ELLs should employ strategies in their classrooms to benefit all of their students. See Table 1 for six strategies and content areas for teaching English language learners.

The Six Strategies and Content Areas

Drama and Movement

Incorporating physical experiences such as drama and movement in reading instruction has shown to be fun for children. For ELLs especially, drama and movement has been shown to help with decoding, fluency, and vocabulary (Sun, 2003). Moreover, good teaching pedagogy should not be limited strictly to reading instruction. Early childhood teachers often use play and drama for learning experiences as appropriate for that stage and age of development for various content areas (Royka, 2002).

Reig & Paquette (2009) suggested the use of games to aid ELLs in classroom instruction. For example, We're Movement Machines was a game to mimic machines in motion. Falling Rain Dance to imitate weather in movement was another such teaching and learning game. Another game, Strike up the Gadget Band, to explore sounds and actions of ordinary kitchen gadgets, was also shown to benefit learners, especially ELLs.

Math

Classroom teachers must employ strategies to help ELLs with basic mathematics concepts. Furthermore, mathematic concepts can be taught kinesthetically. An example would be for students to measure items using their body parts such as arms, legs, or hands. Math concepts such as rhythms and patterns can also be taught kinesthetically (Church, 2001). For example, teaching aides such as Counting 1 to 20 by Jack Hartman, Everything Has a Shape by Hap Palmer, and Shapes All Around Us by Music Movement & Magnetism were methods in which ELLs mastered mathematics concepts.

Music

In addition to movement strategies, music can also be used to motivate and stimulate ELLs who are struggling with language development (Abril, 2003). Basic music concepts can be taught through games such as Musical Follow the Leader. Another strategy to help ELLs learn through music were activities which actively engaged them with instruments, such as drums or Orff instruments.

Vocabulary for basic music concepts, as with other content areas, can be taught with hand signs or gestures (Abril, 2003). Word play, chants, and songs are other examples for teaching music to ELLs. Another example of a teaching tool for ELLs was to use music with repetition, even silly songs (Abril, 2003).

Science

Pray & Monhardt (2009) proposed a process for teaching science to ELLs as follows: a) determine appropriate skills and concepts, b) determine specific activities, c) include students' background knowledge, and d) appropriately assess student learning. Other teaching strategies, such as providing stimulating environments

Table 1 Six Selected Strategies and Content
for Teaching English Language Learners

Strategy/Content	Description	Examples
Drama and Movement	Vocabulary	Acting out a story which includes new vocabulary words.
	Reader's Theatre	Read and dramatize a short script.
	Games	Play movement games to mimic actions, sounds, and concepts.
Math	Basic concepts	Measure with body
	Rhythms	Clap to poems or songs
	Patterns	Kinesthetic movement
Music	Culture	Motivate and stimulate
	Home Language	Word play, chants, songs, repetition
	Instrumentation	Drums or Orff instruments
	Vocabulary	Hand signs or gestures
Science	Environment	Experiences with various environments
	Vocabulary	Experiments
	Involvement	"I Spy" walks
Social Studies	Navigation	Role play, Four Corners game
	Shared	Field trips, guest speakers, experiences
	Graphic	Venn diagrams, series of events chains,
	Organizers	compare and contrast matrices, T-charts
	Collaboration	Small peer groups, lively discussion
Storybook Reading	Vocabulary	Storybooks, experience with words
	Comprehension	Explicit print referencing
	Overall Literacy	Scaffolding
	development	Dialogic reading
		Word elaboration
		Scripted lessons
		Initial sounds

such as oceans, swamps, or parks in science instruction, provided necessary shared learning experiences (Rillero, 2005). In addition, taking "I Spy" walks (Rosenow, 2008) and using science experiments (Rivkin, 2005) to promote vocabulary were also important strategies for teaching ELLs.

Social Studies

Role play and the Four Corners game for navigational words and skills have been suggested by Rieg & Paquette (2009) to teach social studies. Tompkins (2009) cautioned to include shared language experiences to read, talk, listen, or write about social studies content for ELLs. Further, content related field trips and invited guest speakers were ways to include shared language experiences. Another strategy was the use of graphic organizers such as Venn diagrams, series of events chains, compare and contrast matrices, and T-charts to reinforce the language (Weisman, E.M. & Hansen, L.E., 2007).

An example of peer collaboration in social studies classrooms to include ELLs was to make charts to compare and contrast geographic regions throughout the United States. Further, students may work in small groups for rich discussion, and then write graphic organizers to summarize main points to reduce language (Weisman, E.M. & Hansen, L.E., 2007).

Storybook Reading

Research argued that vocabulary which affected reading fluency as well as comprehension for ELLs can be predicted by a student's level of vocabulary knowledge (Grabe, 1991; McLaughlin, 1987). Moreover, vocabulary can be enhanced by learning words in context and providing opportunities for oral response (Hickman, Pollard-Durodola, & Vaughn, 2004). In addition, differentiating between important and non-important text, and engaging in peer conversations about the text were shown to be important indicators of success in comprehension strategies. See Table 2 for suggested storybooks aligned specifically to suggested strategies for effective teaching to ELLs.

Table 2   Suggested Storybooks and Strategies for Teaching ELLs

Strategy/Content Area	Storybook	Author
Vocabulary	A Letter to Amy	Keats, E.J.
	The Wind Blew	Hutchins, P.
	The Ugly Vegetables	Lin, G.
Comprehension	Jump, Frog, Jump!	Kalan, R.
	Good Night, Gorilla	Rathmann, P.
	Chugga-Chugga, Choo-Choo	Lewis, K.
Scaffolding/Dialogue:	Corduroy	Freeman, D.
building overall early	Big Red Barn	Brown, M.W.
literacy development	Jesse Bear, What Will You Wear?	Carlstrom, N.W.
	Noisy Nora	Wells, R.
	One Dark Night	Wheeler, L.

Table 3   Sample Rubric for Inquiry-Based Science Lesson on Magnets

English Language Ability

	Excellent	Revise
Beginning	Demonstrates or presents findings with one or two word descriptors and/or pictures with the use of "helper sentence starters." Each presentation contains a question, a plan for investigation, a description of the data, and conclusions.	Demonstrates findings with one or two word descriptors and/or pictures. However, the presentation omits one or more key features and does not thoroughly describe the key features.
Intermediate	Presents findings using sentence descriptors and/or pictures. Each presentation contains a question, a plan for investigation, description of the data, and conclusions.	Presents findings using Sentence descriptors and/or pictures. However, the presentation omits one or more of the key features and does not thoroughly describe the key feature.
Advanced	Presents findings using paragraph descriptors and/or pictures. Each presentation contains a question, a plan for investigation, a description of the data, and conclusions.	Presents findings using paragraph findings and/or pictures. However, the presentation omits one or more of the key features and does not thoroughly Describe the key features.

Note: National Research Council (1996). *National science education standards*. Washington, D.C.: National Academy Press.

Assessment

As with any assessment, the primary purpose has been to evaluate whether the student has met the desired learning objectives. When creating assessments, teachers should include accommodations for language ability (Pray & Monhardt, 2009). For example, the use of one or two word descriptors to describe concepts after the vocabulary has been taught has shown to be useful for ELLs. Further, assignments as well as assessments should include language reduced proficiency. See Table 3 for a sample rubric for an inquiry-based science lesson on magnets.

Conclusion

Strategies employed to aide any struggling learners were shown to be equally, if not more, effective for teaching ELLs. Several classroom strategies and content area suggestions were made in this article, but it is certainly not an exhaustive list. Good teaching strategies for all students have been proven as good teaching strategies for ELLs. Good strategies that work for any struggling learners may also benefit ELLs. Because of this, all students, including English language learners, will have a better chance at proficiency when presented with these strategies.

References

Abril, C.R. (2003). No hablo ingles: Breaking the language barrier in music instruction. *Music Educator's Journal, 89*(5), 38–43.

Anthony, A.R. (2008). Output strategies for English-language learners: Theory to practice. *The Reading Teacher, 61*(6), 472–482.

Church, E.B. (2001). The math in music and movement. *Early Childhood Today, 15*(4), 38–45.

Hickman, P., Pollard-Durodola, S., & Vaughn, S. (2004). Storybook reading: Improving vocabulary and comprehension for English-language learners. *The Reading Teacher, 57*(8), 720–730.

Mathes, P.G., Pollard-Durodola, S.D., Cardenas-Hagen, E., Linan-Thompson, S., and Vaughn, S. (2007). Teaching struggling readers who are native-Spanish speakers: What do we know? *Language, Speech, and Hearing Services in Schools, 38*(3), 260–271.

Myburgh, O., Poggenpoel, M., & Van Rensburg, W. (2004). Learners' experience of teaching and learning in a second and third language. *Education, 124*(3), 573–84.

Pray, L., & Monhardt, R. (2009). Sheltered instruction techniques for ELLs. *Science and Children, 46*(7), 34–38.

Rillero, P. (2005). Exploring science with young children. *Early Childhood Today, 19*(6), 8–11.

Reig & Paquette (2009). Using drama and movement to enhance English language learners' literacy development. *Journal of Instructional Psychology, 36*(2), 148–154.

Rivkin, J.G. (2005). Building teamwork through science. *Early Childhood Today, (19)*6, 36–42.

Rosenow, N. (2008). Teaching and learning about the natural world: Learning to love the earth and each other. *Young Children, 63*(1), 10–14.

Royka, J.G. (2002). Overcoming the fear of using drama in English language teaching. *The Internet TESL Journal, (8)*6.

Sun, P. (2003). Using drama and theatre to promote literacy development: Some basic classroom applications. *The Clearinghouse on Reading, English, and Communication Digest (187)*.

Tompkins, G. (2009). Language Arts Patterns of Practice (7 Ed.) Upper Saddle River, NJ: Pearson.

Weisman, E.M. & Hansen, L.E. (2007). Strategies for teaching social studies to English-language learners at the elementary level. *The Social Studies, 98*(5), 180–184.

Critical Thinking

1. What did you learn from reading this article? How might this information be useful to you or other teachers?

2. Create an activity that is developmentally appropriate for your content area and uses one of the strategies found in Table 1.

3. Review the list of books in Table 2. Why are these especially good for novice readers who are ELL? What other group of students would benefit from using these books to develop language skills?

4. Create a list of books that would be appropriate for older readers in upper elementary or middle schools and would also meet the unique needs of readers who struggle with English.

Teaching Photosynthesis with ELL Students

SUSAN PIPER AND EDWARD LEWIS SHAW JR.

Although many educators may recognize the need to go beyond rote memorization techniques in order to achieve high academic outcomes with English language learners (ELLs), many also need help designing the classroom environment so that neither language acquisition nor content literacy learning is impeded by linguistic obstacles (Wong Fillmore and Snow 2000). ELLs do not come to us as blank slates. Difficulties ELLs experience may not be a matter of lack of content knowledge, but rather a lack of linguistic complexity in English.

The challenge lies in creating activities that promote the academic course of study while advancing English language fluency. One approach in planning instruction is to consider what students can do with support at their various fluency levels to demonstrate understanding of content. The National Science Education Standards (NSES; National Research Council [NRC] 1996, 32) Standard B states, "Teachers of science guide and facilitate learning. In doing this, teachers recognize and respond to student diversity and encourage all students to participate fully in science learning." All science teachers should provide access to good science instruction, regardless of what type learner is in their class (ibid.).

Background

Teachers of English for Speakers of Other Languages (TESOL), the international organization for promoting the needs and language development of ELLs, adopted a framework of standards developed by the World-Class Instructional Design and Assessment (WIDA) consortium of states. This framework offers a comprehensive understanding of English linguistic fluency, as well as academic proficiency in content areas for English language learners. Using this resource as a guide enables content area teachers to have a better understanding of not only what their ELLs can do at their given fluency levels, but also what they may do to advance ELLs to the next fluency level. Table 1 is the framework used for planning this lesson. It includes the stages of language development as well as the corresponding federal classifications for ELLs as a frame of reference. The characteristics and expectations outlined in the framework are taken from the WIDA Can Do Standards for ELLs.

The activities and accommodations represent those items in the following lesson that fulfill both the expectations of students at each fluency level and the NSES standards for teaching photosynthesis.

In my third-grade classroom, students were preparing to learn about photosynthesis.[1] Of the 18 students in the classroom, three spoke Spanish as their primary language, four students spoke Korean at home, and one student spoke German. One student in the class was born in China but moved to the United States in kindergarten and primarily spoke English, although she could still communicate in Chinese. Not only did I have a large number of ELLs in my classroom, but they spanned all fluency levels. It was therefore important that I planned instruction to address the needs of students at each level.

I realized that the day's lesson on photosynthesis would require that I provide a variety of activities for varying linguistic needs. Based on the information I had been given about each of my ELLs, I knew their approximate proficiency levels and was, therefore, able to make accommodations to my basic lesson without compromising the academic integrity of the content. Based on the TESOL and WIDA standards and my state course of study for third-grade science, I developed activities that benefitted not only ELLs, but also students whose primary language was English.

Photosynthesis Activity
Materials

- WIDA's Can Do descriptors for the levels of English Language Proficiency, PreK–12
- Various art supplies
- Small, live, potted plants
- Watering pitcher
- Bilingual dictionaries
- Safety goggles

Procedure

It is important to maintain the focus of learning objectives when making accommodations for English language learners in order to maintain the academic integrity of the content. After considering what students may produce in terms of linguistic complexity, you may better plan the accommodations for your lesson. In my lesson on photosynthesis I wanted the students to understand the basic overview of the process and then to move them into a more content-oriented understanding.

There are many ways to introduce the process of photosynthesis. We began our journey in a wooded area behind the school. Because this activity involved physical movement and observation, it was one in which all students could easily participate—a starting point where all could feel successful. Before beginning this activity, I inspected the area to ensure the safety of all my students. I also checked for any medical emergency procedures. Students were asked to sit on the ground, put on their safety goggles, and observe the area around them. As they looked around, I said the following, using gestures:

> We eat food *(make eating gesture)* and breathe in air *(inhale deeply)* to live. Have you ever thought about how plants live? Do plants eat food in the same way we do *(make an eating gesture toward a plant)*? No *(shake head).* They don't eat in the same way, do they? How do plants eat? *(Gently remove the plant or plants from the pot. I recommend trying this prior to meeting with the students to ensure ease of removal without damaging the plant.)* Plants have roots. Do you see the roots? I am going to pass the plant so that each of you can touch it and see the roots. *(Pass it around the group. This tangible contact with the plant will help students remember the lesson.)* The roots on the plant receive water from rain or from us if the plants live in our homes *(water plant with watering can to simulate rain).* Is that all plants need? What do you think? Do you need more than water to live? We breathe. That helps us live *(inhale deeply and hold it as you talk).* Did you know that we help plants breathe and they help us breathe *(exhale dramatically onto the plant)*? When we exhale *(exhale again for emphasis),* plants use that to help them live. They produce oxygen to help us breathe *(inhale dramatically).* But plants need one more thing to live and make food. Do you know what they need? They need sunlight *(point to the sun).*

At this point, I called students to stand by me and show the class how plants eat and live. The great thing about an activity like this is that students can feel successful by merely gesturing. It does not require linguistic complexity in the target language, and, therefore, students can feel success early in the lesson. Note that I had not yet used any scientific language.

We returned to the classroom to capture what we had learned in a visual way for display. Based on the language proficiency standards about linguistic fluency, I knew that I could expect certain things of my students at various levels. At the most basic level, I wanted all my students to sketch what they understood about what we had just discussed. All students were able to do so, regardless of their fluency levels.

In order to help students understand that photosynthesis is a process and a word used to describe the process by which plants make food, I started with a simple drawing for reinforcement.

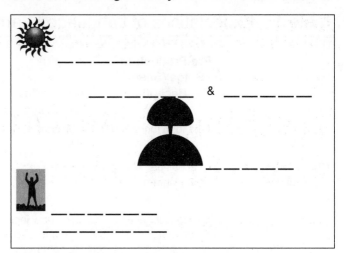

Figure 1   Completely blank diagram.

I wanted them to make the connection between what they had learned and what they had observed firsthand by being able to communicate their scientifically correct drawings to other classmates. I knew that many English language learners had arrived from other countries with mathematical understandings that we might consider advanced for a particular grade level. For example, some of the students from South Korea made the connection between what we had discussed thus far and the chemical equation for photosynthesis. Some of them were trying to remember the equation by writing it on their papers. For those students I included the chemical equation in the sketch of the photosynthetic process. I wanted students to know that during daylight plants consume carbon dioxide and water, with oxygen being a byproduct. In the absence of sunlight, oxygen is not created, but respiration continues and produces carbon dioxide.

On the second day of the lesson, students in groups containing both native and nonnative speakers of English traveled through centers related to the process to further emphasize the concepts of photosynthesis. These centers, although beneficial (and observably enjoyable) to all members of the class, were particularly designed to promote the linguistic fluency of the ELLs in the class. Note that the centers offered activities that achieved the same assessment goals at varying levels of linguistic complexity.

Center 1: Label the Diagram
Materials

- Blank diagram about photosynthesis
- Diagram with some of the letters entered
- Diagram with all letters entered

Procedures

Students were provided with a blank diagram and asked to label the photosynthetic process. There were three levels of diagrams at the station. One was completely blank (see Figure 1), challenging the student to produce the names of the parts of the process. Another option was a diagram with a word bank that allowed students to see the word in its entirety before filling

Table 1 Expectations of Language Learners Corresponding with Fluency Levels

	Pre-Production Stage (Silent or Receptive Period)	Early Produc-tion Stage	Speech Emer-gence Stage	Intermediate Language Proficiency Stage	Advanced Language Profi-ciency Stage
Length	10 hs for 6 months	An additional 6 months	An additional year	An additional year	5–7 years
Characteristics and expectations	Label objects, pic-tures, diagrams	Make lists	Reproduce bare-bones expository or narrative texts	Summarize infor-mation from graph-ics or notes	Apply information to new contexts
	Draw in response to a prompt	Produces drawings, phrases, short sen-tences, notes	Compare and con-trast information	Edit and revise writing	React to mul-tiple genres and discourses
	Produce icons, symbols, words, phrases to convey messages	Give information requested from oral or written directions	Describe events, people, processes, procedures	Create original ideas or detailed responses	Author multiple forms or genres of writing
Activities and accommodations	Draw or illustrate the process of photosynthesis	Draw or illus-trate and label the process of photosynthesis	Describe the process of pho-tosynthesis using simple phrases and sentences	Describe the pro-cess of photosyn-thesis in paragraph form	Describe the pro-cess of photosyn-thesis and explain how environmental conditions can both enhance and hin-der the process
Corresponding state or federal classification	NEP, (1) Non English Proficient ENTERING	LEP, (2) Limited English Proficient BEGINNING	LEP, (3) Limited English Proficient DEVELOPING	LEP, (3–4) Limited English Proficient EXPANDING	FLEP, (5–6) Fluent English Proficient BRIDGING

Source: Adapted by Susan Piper from WIDA designations, TESOL designations, NSES standards, and federal fluency designations for use in training classroom teachers to make accommodations for English language learners.

in the blanks on the diagram (see Figure 2). A third option for those who were not yet ready to label the parts without a guide was a diagram with blanks with some of the letters entered (see Figure 3). Students were allowed to choose which diagram to complete, as this was an activity to challenge or reinforce the photosynthesis concept. Early finishers were encouraged to help guide other group members in completing their work.

Also in this center was a large blank felt diagram containing words with Velcro attached. Students were able to practice and check each other using this model before putting their answers on paper. Many ELLs are intimidated by the thought of put-ting an incorrect answer into print. This strategy allowed them appropriate practice and aid in becoming comfortable with the learning process.

Center 2: Writing about Photosynthesis
Materials

- Cloze passages with word bank
- Cloze passages without word bank

Procedure
Students were prompted to explain the process of photosyn-thesis. Students could attempt to write about photosynthesis without the aid of a scaffold. Also available in this center were cloze passages (see Figure 4) of two levels: one with a word bank and one without. The idea of cloze passages is to allow students to demonstrate their understanding without penalizing them for their level of linguistic fluency. Cloze passages serve an additional purpose: allowing students to see and participate in academically structured writing.

Center 3: Webquest + PowerPoint

Materials

- Computer with Internet access and PowerPoint program
- Various Web sites

Procedure
Students were sent to several Web sites (note that availability of Web sites may be subject to district policy for Internet access).

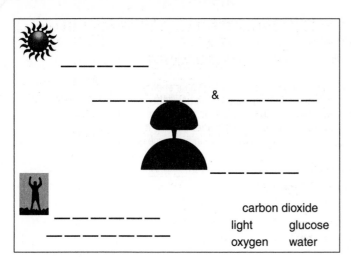

Figure 2 Diagram with word bank.

carbon dioxide

light   glucose

oxygen   water

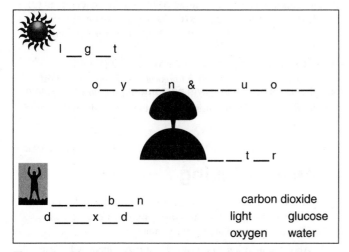

Figure 3 Diagram with word bank and some letters entered.

carbon dioxide

light   glucose

oxygen   water

Using information they gathered from the Web sites, students created PowerPoint presentations to explain aspects of photosynthesis they had not learned in the previous lesson. These were presented to their classmates. The PowerPoint presentations were evaluated on their scientific accuracy. Some sites to which I sent students were the following:

- What Is Photosynthesis? is a site that has a drawing of a plant and what is produced during photosynthesis (www.emc.maricopa.edu/faculty/farabee/BIOBK /BioBookPS.html).
- *NOVA*'s Illuminating Photosynthesis is an excellent review with a lot of animation and minimal use of words or symbols (www.pbs.org/wgbh/nova/methuselah /photosynthesis.html).
- Cell Biology Animation offers an animated outline of photosynthesis that requires a greater mastery of English and chemical equations (www.johnkyrk.com /photosynthesis.html).
- A Virginia Tech College of Natural Resources photosynthesis and respiration site allows you to select the languages of your students. There are activities,

labs, and links that teachers can use for their ELL and English-speaking students (www.fw.vt.edu/dendro /forestbiology/photosynthesis.swf).

- Biology4kids has some drawings but is heavy on reading (www.biology4kids.com/files/plants _photosynthesis.html).
- A short video by Peter Weatherall on Totlol has an oral description of photosynthesis followed by an animation of the process. It is good for introduction or review for ELL as well as English-speaking students (www.totlol.com/ watch/vTx9XHMG68Q /Photosynthesis-Video-By-Peter-Weatherall/0).

I also used Google language tools, which can be accessed on the right side of the Google search screen. Although this tool does not offer perfect translation into other languages, many students have reported using the tool to assist in understanding Web sites and other documents. The tool basically transforms a Web site into the same site in another language. Such tools can be helpful, but keep in mind that this is an electronic, word-to-word translator and, therefore, not as reliable as a human translator.

Center 4: Photosynthesis Dictionary
Materials

- Mini-dictionary example
- Bilingual dictionaries
- Paper
- Pencils
- Stapler

Procedure

At this center, students make a mini-dictionary (one is provided as an example for them). Basically, they are replicating the dictionary provided as an example, but they may keep and use it as a study tool. At this center, students used bilingual dictionaries when they desired. They illustrated the words in their own dictionary to help them master this process. In order to promote a sense of cultural understanding and awareness, speakers of English as their primary language were encouraged to create bilingual dictionaries using the primary languages of the other group members.

Assessment

In assessing ELLs, I have found that the most important thing I can do for them is allow them to demonstrate their understanding of the content without penalizing them for their limited English linguistic knowledge. Using an alternative assessment is one way to determine whether students understand the content. To do this while still maintaining high content standards, look back at the course of study to see precisely what your students are expected to know. When I did this, I found that I had been

---

Photosynthesis

Directions: Use the words in the box below to help you finish the story about photosynthesis.

Every living thing needs energy to live. We eat feed to help keep us healthy and give us energy
_____ is the way plants make food. To make energy-producing food, plants use light,
_____, and _____. This produces the food plants needs to live. Plants also
help us breath by producing _____, which we take into our bodies to keep the
blood in our bodies healthy. We breathe out _____, which plants use in the process
of making food.

---

carbon dioxide	glucose	water	light
oxygen	photosynthesis		

Figure 4   Photosynthesis cloze passage with word bank.

using forms of assessment (essays, true/false, multiple choice) that relied on linguistic knowledge but did not necessarily rely on their content knowledge. Using assessments similar to those in the centers can help determine how well students mastered the content goals without penalizing them for language barriers.

Conclusion

The possibility of having ELLs in your class increases every year. Your modeling of good science teaching, emphasis on mastery of content, and inclusion of all students in class discussions and activities can provide all students a chance for scientific literacy. These activities provide a bridge for ELL students to be successful in their science class without complete mastery of the English language. For ELL students to be successful in the classroom and in life despite their language challenges, changes to traditional instruction must be made.

Note

1. Throughout the lesson description "I" refers to the first author, Susan Piper.

References

National Research Council (NRC). 1996. *National science education standards*. Washington, DC: National Academy Press.

Teachers of English for Speakers of Other Languages (TESOL). 1997. *ESL standards for pre-K–12 students*. Alexandria, VA: TESOL.

Wong Fillmore, L., and C. Snow. 2000. What teachers need to know about language. *ERIC Clearinghouse on Language and Linguistics*. Washington, DC: Center for Applied Linguistics.

World Class Instructional Design in Assessment (WIDA) Consortium. 2007. *English language proficiency standards and resource guide: Prekindergarten through grade twelve*. Madison, WI: Board of Regents of the University of Wisconsin System.

Critical Thinking

1. While this teacher had a diverse classroom that many of us may not experience, what is one lesson we can take away from her lesson planning discussion?

2. About an hour ago you learned that two students who just arrived from France will join your class on Monday. They speak some conversational English learned mostly from watching television shows and movies from the United States. Review Table 1 with those new students in mind. What are three implications for teaching you content or grade level?

3. Examine the ways that Piper assessed student learning across the unit on photosynthesis. How did she assess knowledge and avoid penalizing students for lack of language skills? What other activities or ways could she assess students in her class without penalizing students whose language skills lag behind their content knowledge?

Literacy and Literature for 21st Century Global Citizenship

JAMES NOFTLE AND MARIA A. PACINO

While the student population is dramatically changing, Shure (2001) reports that minority students make up approximately 40% of the student population throughout the United States, with approximately 69% of the student population in urban school districts, the implications for the classroom teacher are significant. However, according to the National Collaborative on Diversity in the Teaching Force (2004), as of 2003, 90% of public school teachers were White, 6% were African American, and fewer than 5% were of other racial/ethnic backgrounds.

According to the Cooperative Children's Book Center (CCBC), as cited by Stewart (2008), of the 2,800 books reviewed by CCBC, only 75 were authored by African American authors, 149 were about Africans or African-Americans; four were written [by] American Indians, 34 were about American Indians, 60 were written by Asian Pacifics/Asian Pacific Americans, 64 were written about Asian Pacifics/Asian Pacific Americans; and 50 were written by Latinos and 76 were written about Latinos. While these figures are disheartening, they demonstrate the lack of balance among minority authors.

Preparing individuals for twenty-first century citizenship for pluralist, global democracies means redefining literacy and acquiring skills that go beyond reading and writing, especially in the digital age. Western notions of literacy have been primarily text based and tend to devalue and exclude cultures which emphasize oral tradition, observational skills, and non Western modes of discourse, often characteristic of immigrant populations. Since schooling is the primary vehicle for literacy development, educators must find ways to create meaningful literacy environments that connect theoretical foundations of literacy to life experiences that allow learners to discover meaning.

Beyond reading and writing skills, representative types of literacy include print and non print materials, academic ability in numeracy, quantitative and qualitative research, information access and management, science, economics, computer and digital technology, social media interaction, critical thinking, cultural awareness, cross cultural-communication, including bilingual and/or multilingual expertise, analysis of issues from multiple perspectives, understanding of families and communities in the world, character development, conflict resolution, and moral/ethical decision making for participatory democracy. Schooling is the primary vehicle for literacy development. Consequently, our classrooms should provide a balance of literacy types to promote the literacy development.

> Whether we call it literacy for learning or learning how to learn, whether it involves traditional texts . . . or non traditional formats involving representational or tool literacies teachers can do much to help students acquire the skills necessary not only to survive, but also to thrive . . . in the millennium. (Rafferty, 1999, p. 25)

Multicultural literature, especially personal narratives of people from diverse backgrounds and experiences, provide an opportunity for individuals to understand the world, to self reflect, and to define themselves. Immigrant stories are powerful because they portray the pain and sacrifice of acculturation while providing immigrant students with encouragement and hope for success in the future. When selecting multicultural books (and other materials), educators need to follow selection criteria which focus on anti-bias curriculum and enables learners to understand, value, and prize diverse cultures.

Multicultural literature is a powerful medium that can foster within students the ability to construct a variety of perspectives about other cultures, roles within that society, an understanding of traditions, beliefs, customs, and values. Furthermore, multicultural literature allows students to explore distant continents they may not otherwise experience. A teacher's classroom library collection should "represent the perspectives of a range of cultures and serve as a form of advocacy on behalf of students from minority backgrounds by making them feel included in classrooms and school environments" (Agosto, 2007; p. 27). A well-balanced classroom library encourages students to value diverse perspectives while acknowledging the significance of other cultures. The integration of multicultural resources within the literacy domain promotes a sense of belonging amongst immigrant and minority youth, thus facilitating student learning while fostering acceptance of individual differences. Furthermore, our youth need to be informed, engaged, and possess the cognitive skills to function in a pluralistic world. Today's classroom must provide opportunities for students to synthesize their moral, ethical, familial and political beliefs regarding local, regional, and national understandings and have the ability to express those ideologies (Stewart, 2008).

According to Nieto and Bode (2008), multicultural education not only leads to greater empathy and understanding, but more importantly, it addresses four areas of potential conflict: racism and discrimination, structural conditions that may limit learning, the impact of culture on learning, and language diversity. The inclusion of multicultural literature in the classroom permits students to conceptualize human atrocities, and develop an understanding of how some groups/cultures have been marginalized throughout history. In addition, multicultural literature embodies a more productive school climate, fosters a deeper awareness of the role of culture and language, identifies major contributions of various cultures, while instilling an appreciation of how others live and work together.

Furthermore, the inclusion of multicultural literature can assist students with the demands of adjusting to a new community and school. Given the large influx of new immigrants and the few support services to prepare newcomers, one viable resource for the classroom teacher is the facilitation of appropriate literature to open dialogue and promote greater acceptance with a multicultural perspective. Classroom teachers must make a concerted effort to build relationships that promote, support, and sustain diverse communities of learners. A deliberate anti-bias approach through the use of children's literature can assist students to develop a better understanding of diverse families, gender differences, human differences, ethnicity, and social class. According to Delpit (2006), "When teachers do not understand the potential of the students they teach, they will underteach them no matter what the methodology" (p. 175).

Delpit (2006) presents a strong argument for multicultural literature when she states, "If we are to survive as a species on this plan[e]t we must certainly create multicultural curricula that educate our children to the differing perspectives of our diverse population. Our children of color need to see the brilliance of their legacy, too" (p. 177). However, many children enter school having spent their early years in a monocultural environment that reflects the beliefs and attitudes of their environment. Unfortunately, their perceptions of others are formed from a mirage of stereotypes influenced by the television, videogames, movies, and other for various available media (Lowery & Sabis-Burns, 2007). Children subsequently develop a skewed and myopic view of society, one that does not accurately represent the world in which we live. Since many students lack an understanding of cultures different from their own, the preconceptions about diverse groups and the negative internalization in which people of different cultures are treated, the problem becomes compounded. Nonetheless, it becomes the responsibility of the classroom teacher to present curriculum and literacy strategies that focus on other cultures, thus broadening cultural exposure.

Multicultural literature provides learners opportunities to engage in effective reading strategies which promote literacy development. A variety of effective reading strategies will not only foster in students the ability to read strategically, but will facilitate the importance of discovering human values universal to all cultures and identities, as well as cultural values that are distinctive. The following is a suggested list of useful strategies to engage learners with multicultural narratives. All learners should have the opportunity to:

- identify elements of plot where character development may have been the same or different in another cultural setting, or based on different cultural values
- form text-to-text generalizations that allow students to transmit learning from one piece of literature to understand another piece of literature
- relate literature to personal lives based on the literary characters
- assess points of view; importance of characters, traits, values, impact of events on plot and story development
- develop an appreciation of human nature and the universal human condition common across all cultures
- identify with characters whether the same or a different social class and/or condition, gender, religious affiliation, or disability
- develop an appreciation of struggles and sacrifices of oppressed groups or cultures
- respond to literature via dramatic play, art, writing, music, or dance with props or manipulatives
- become inspired to learn more, or connect with other cultures
- participate in group discussions to simulate thinking, consider another perspective, and develop an appreciation for social learning and collective efforts
- engage in role playing for students to trade places with a character; enables students to examine attitudes, beliefs, and feelings, regarding prejudice and discrimination; poetry, biographies, and fictional stories are powerful sources of discussion and role playing
- justify opinions, events, and relationships across cultures
- identify stereotypes with regard to prejudice or discrimination in literary works
- analyze various types of text, both print and non-print in a global society
- understand the power of storytelling and how legends are passed down from generation to generation within cultures
- analyze the role of conflict resolution across cultures
- examine diverse issues with regard to race, class, gender, and other cultural perspectives
- develop skills for effective communication in cross-cultural settings
- become familiar with bilingual texts and narratives
- have opportunities for involvement in cross-cultural community service

- reflect on one's cultural heritage to gain insight into family history and origin
- utilize multicultural literature to facilitate the acculturation process of immigrant children
- use critical thinking skills to reflect on social justice and equity in global societies
- engage in understanding biographical narratives from the perspective of moral development
- examine and affirm one's own cultural identity
- analyze the value and role of women and minority groups in society
- utilize tools for evaluating social media
- become ethically responsive consumers of information in a digital world
- develop appropriate skills for online learning, responding, and engaging in online learning
- examine the role of globalization in a multicultural world

Preparing citizens for a global, digital age means that we must find new ways of teaching in a world of digital, multimedia literacy. The University of Southern California (USC) created an Institute of Multimedia Literacy to assist faculty and students in acquiring new ways of thinking in a digital age. The following captures the essence of their philosophy:

> Its purpose is not to teach about the tools of multimedia but rather to focus on new expressive practices enabled by these tools. For example, we all know how to make arguments in text, but how should we make an argument visually? More generally, how can we communicate effectively using image, text, sound, movement, sequence, and interactivity? (Brown, 2006; p. 21)

The proliferation of social media networks requires learners to become savvy consumers of technology. Critical thinking skills must be implemented in an effort to examine and assess various media environments in terms of the reliability and validity of information, as well as the ethical implications of a digital world. Furthermore, distance learning, especially online education, has become increasingly more popular as a means of reaching a larger number of students across the globe. In virtual classrooms, learners must follow effective, intercultural communication protocols in responding to threaded discussions, use email appropriately, develop classroom projects individually or collaboratively, and utilize various multimedia platforms.

As educators, we have a responsibility to find effective ways of preparing students for twenty-first century citizenship in pluralistic democracies in the digital age. We must expose learners to meaningful literacy experiences that teach about responsible citizenship in terms of equity, diversity, and social justice. One of the most effective means of teaching about these issues is through multicultural literature. Multicultural literature liberates students to explore their own heritage and

world consciousness, moving them to action. As we attempt to redefine literacy for the twenty-first century, schools, teachers, and parents must develop a partnership in assisting students to become lifelong learners who engage critical inquiry as consumers of information/knowledge delivered through many print and non-print formats and who are able to use this information/knowledge to make ethical decisions in a global democracy.

References

Agosto, D. E. (2007). Building a multicultural school library: Issues and challenges. *Teacher Library, 34*(3), 27–30.

Brown, J. S. (2006, September/October). New learning environments for the 21st century: Exploring the edge. *Change 38,* 18–24.

Delpit, L. (2006). *Other People's Children: Cultural conflict in the Classroom,* 3rd Ed. The New Press, New York, NY.

Lowery, R. M. & Sabis-Burns, D. (2007). From borders to bridges: Making cross-cultural connections through multicultural literature. *Multicultural Education,* 14(4), 50–54.

National Collaborative on Diversity in the Teaching Force, *Assessment of Diversity in America's Teaching Force: A Call to Action* (Washington, D.C., October, 2004).

Nieto, S. & Bode, P. (2008). *Affirming Diversity: A Sociopolitical Context of Multicultural Education,* 5th Ed. Allyn and Bacon, Boston, MA.

Rafferty, C. D. (1999). *Literacy in the information age. Educational Leadership, 57,* 22–25.

Stewart, L. S. (2008): Beyond borders: Reading "other" places in children's literature. *Children's Literature in Education. 39,* 95–105.

Shure, J. (2001). Minority teachers are few and far between. *Techniques: Connecting education and careers,* 76(5), 32.

Critical Thinking

1. Noftle and Pacino suggest that teachers should include multicultural literature as part of a multicultural curriculum. What are the primary reasons they are advocating for a more multicultural curriculum?

2. The authors offer a list of opportunities that all students should have. Review the list to find opportunities that you think could be included in your content area or grade level. Share these with other members of the class and explain why you chose them.

3. According to these authors, digital literacy should be part of preparing K–12 students for global citizenship in the twenty-first century by helping students become critical consumers of information delivered in print and nonprint formats. Reflect on how teachers might accomplish this task.

JAMES NOFTLE, Azusa Pacific University, CA, USA. **MARIA A. PACINO,** Azusa Pacific University, CA, USA.

Using Guided Notes to Enhance Instruction for All Students

Moira Konrad, Laurice M. Joseph, and Madoka Itoi

- Pay special attention to this main idea
- Engage in a written reflection
- Put down your pencil and listen to a story
- Try a challenge problem

Instructional time constraints and increased accountability require teachers to accomplish more in less time. All students are expected to make academic gains each year (i.e., adequate yearly progress); thus, teachers need to increase their instructional efficiency. One way to increase efficiency is to teach new skills and content directly through lecture (Heward, 2001). During teacher-directed lectures, students are expected to take notes to help them obtain important information.

However, for many students, taking notes from lectures or reading material can be challenging, especially for those who have learning disabilities (Hughes & Suritsky, 1994). These students often perceive traditional note-taking as labor-intensive and frustrating due to difficulties in deciphering relevant information during lectures (Barbetta & Skaruppa, 1995; Stringfellow & Miller, 2005). Additionally, listening to a lecture and taking notes at the same time poses a real challenge (Barbetta & Skaruppa, 1995). Therefore, students may choose not to take notes during lectures and play a more passive role during classroom instruction.

An alternative to traditional note-taking is a method called *guided notes*. Guided notes are "teacher-prepared handouts that 'guide' a student through a lecture with standard cues and prepared space in which to write the key facts, concepts, and/or relationships" (Heward, 1994, p. 304). Research has demonstrated that guided notes improve outcomes for students with a range of ages, skills, and abilities (Konrad, Joseph, & Eveleigh, 2009). Specifically, guided notes increase active student responding (Austin, Lee, Thibeault, Carr, & Bailey, 2002; Blackwell & McLaughlin, 2005; Heward, 1994), improve the accuracy of students' notes (Sweeney et al., 1999), and improve students' quiz and test performance (Patterson, 2005). Additionally, research has revealed that students prefer to use guided notes over taking their own notes (Konrad et al., 2009) or using preprinted notes (Neef, McCord, & Ferreri, 2006). Not only do guided notes help students attend to lectures better, this form of note taking serves as a model for helping students learn how to take better notes on their own.

Developing Guided Notes

According to Heward (2001), guided notes are created by first developing an outline of the lecture using presentation software such as PowerPoint or overhead transparencies, focusing on the most important concepts that students need to learn. A handout consisting of blanks where important information (e.g., content that will be included on follow-up assessments) is omitted accompanies the teacher's lecture notes (see Figure 1 for a sample page from a set of guided notes). The students fill in the blanks with key concepts as they listen to the lecture. An adequate number of blanks is distributed throughout the handout to encourage active engagement, and each blank should contain enough space so students can record all essential information. In general, each blank on the guided notes should require students to record one to three words (Sweeney et al., 1999), but varying the length may help students attend to the lecture. Consider including in the guided notes one-word, two-word, or three-word responses (and occasionally four- or five-word responses for older students) in an unpredictable pattern to help keep students alert and on their toes.

For students who have difficulties with fine motor tasks, teachers can modify guided notes by (a) making the blanks shorter (i.e., requiring the students to write fewer words), (b) giving the students choices to circle, (c) allowing students to select and paste (e.g., with hook-and-loop fasteners or stickers) the correct responses, or (d) using assistive technology (e.g., computer software or adaptive assistive devices) to permit students to select correct responses.

In addition to the blanks, which serve as cues to prompt students to write information provided during the lecture, teachers can use symbols to help students anticipate what to expect (Heward, 2001). For example, consider using a star symbol to indicate main ideas so students know which information is most important and will likely appear on upcoming tests. See Table 1 for several examples of symbols teachers can use to cue students. Start with just two or three symbols; use them consistently; and as students get more comfortable and proficient with guided notes, you can gradually add other cues.

A lecture does not need to be a dry, monotonous delivery of material, and teachers who use guided notes do not have to forgo their personal teaching styles. Teachers can keep lectures interesting by interspersing stories, examples, and personal

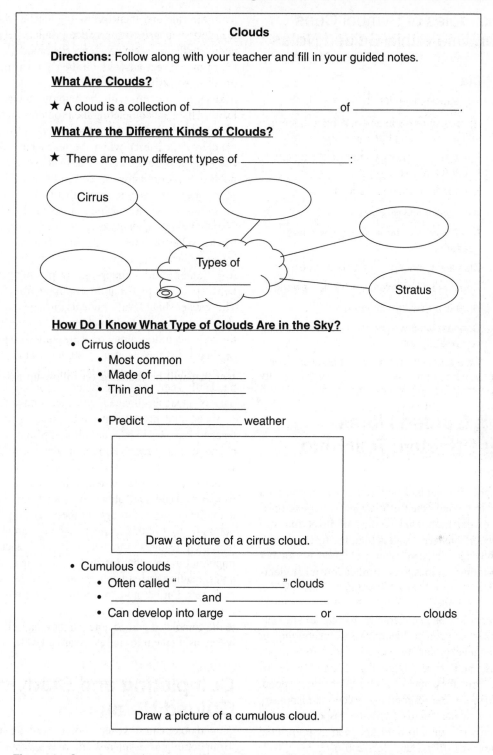

Figure 1 Sample page from a set of guided notes with embedded graphic organizers

experiences (Konrad et al., 2009). One way to do this might be to include cues in the guided notes (perhaps indicated by a specific symbol; see Table 1) that signal students to listen to a supplemental story. It is important that the anecdotes are relevant, purposeful, and strategically integrated into the lecture and that students know what they should take away from these stories.

Distinguishing essential from nonessential content during a lecture is challenging for many students (Stringfellow & Miller, 2005). This may especially be the case for students whose native language is not English. Guided notes may be a less cumbersome way of helping English language learners (ELL) take notes while simultaneously attending to the language as well as the relevant content conveyed during the lecture (Tam & Scott, 1996). Teachers may want to work with ELL specialists and/or translators to include, within the guided notes, translations of key words and phrases in the students' native language(s).

Table 1 Examples of Symbol Cues Teachers Can Use within Guided Notes

Symbol	Cue
★	Pay special attention to this main idea
ⓘ	Here is some supplemental information that is interesting but will not be tested
✑	Put down your pencil and listen to a story or anecdote
✐	Engage in a written reflection
?	Try a challenge problem
📖	Read from your book and answer these questions
🗨	Discuss a concept with a classmate
📓	Complete these exercises for homework
✄	Here is a new tool for learning
⇄	Connect what we just learned to something you already knew
❑	Stop and self-monitor your behavior; have you been on-task?

Combining Guided Notes with Other Effective Teaching Strategies

Guided notes should be combined with other evidence-based teaching strategies to increase their effectiveness. For example, as an alternative to the traditional method of involving students in class question–answer sessions (i.e., the teacher poses a question and calls on a student who has raised his or her hand), choral responding and response cards allow all students to respond in unison (Heward, 1994; Randolph, 2007). When teachers lecture using guided notes, they can stop at strategic points to review what has been covered by having all students respond to questions or prompts using choral responding or response cards. The teacher simply asks a question, provides a brief thinking pause, and gives a signal (e.g., a snap or a verbal cue such as "class" or "show me") for all students to respond. On the signal, students either respond orally (choral response), by writing on small white boards (write-on response cards); or by selecting cards or items to hold up, such as preprinted response cards (Heward, 1994; Randolph, 2007).

Partially completed graphic organizers, such as story or geography maps, word webs, and Venn diagrams, may be embedded into guided notes to aid in labeling essential elements and gaining an understanding about relationships among concepts (Dye, 2000). See Figure 1 for an example of how a graphic organizer can be embedded into guided notes.

The teacher can also create worksheets that follow a *model-lead-test* teaching sequence and then have the students complete it along with the teacher. For example, when teaching an algorithm to solve equations, students can complete guided notes to learn the rule and then follow the teacher through the model-lead-test sequence with practice problems. The teacher should complete the first few problems (i.e., model) while the students fill in the correct answers on their guided notes (i.e., teacher-directed worksheets). The teacher should then complete the next set of problems with the help of students in the class (i.e., lead) as they are completing the problems on their guided notes. Finally, students should complete the last few problems independently (i.e., test), while the teacher monitors. The teacher can then provide the correct answers on the overhead for students to self-correct or can collect the notes and use the last set of problems as a way to assess that lesson's objective(s).

Similarly, when teaching a spelling rule (e.g., the first doubling rule), students can complete guided notes while the teacher states (and writes) the rule. The rule should be followed by examples (e.g., hop + ing = hopping) and nonexamples (e.g., jump + ing ≠ jumpping) for practice with discriminating between words that require doubling from those that do not. The teacher should walk students through the first example(s) to show them how and when to apply the rule (i.e., model), while the students follow along on their guided notes. The teacher can gradually fade assistance as students practice with additional examples (i.e., lead) until they are able to apply the rule independently (i.e., test). See Figure 2 for an example of the first page of a teacher-directed worksheet on the first doubling rule.

When students are expected to read material independently, teachers can provide them with guided notes to prompt them to attend to main ideas and important details, reflect on content, and check for understanding. For instance, when students are reading a chapter in a history textbook, they can record key concepts as well as stop and think about how events are related at certain signal points inserted throughout their guided notes. When guided notes are used in this manner, students can receive guidance on the salient features of text without direct teacher assistance. It is important to note that for students to benefit from using guided notes, reading assignments should be at their independent reading levels. Furthermore, once students have finished reading and filling in the guided notes independently, they should have access to the completed guided notes so they can self-correct their notes before using them to study (Lazarus, 1993).

Completing and Studying Guided Notes

Guided notes can serve as a tool to facilitate students' preparing for upcoming assessments, and one advantage of using guided notes is that students are more likely to leave class with a complete and accurate set of notes (Konrad et al., 2009) from which to study. However, some students may need close monitoring as they complete the guided notes, particularly when they are first learning how to use them. Monitoring student use of guided notes may be easily accomplished in an inclusive classroom where team-teaching occurs (Konrad et al., 2009). For instance, while one teacher is lecturing to the class, the other can assist by monitoring and providing feedback to all students on the accuracy of their guided notes. Furthermore, some students

Teacher-directed Worksheet on the First Doubling Rule
(I–I–I Rule)

- Today's rule is called the "First _____ Rule" or the _____ Rule.
- Here's the rule:
  - ○ In words with
    - _____ _____,
    - ending in _____ _____,
    - after _____ vowel,
    - double the final consonant before adding a vowel suffix.
  - ○ Why's this rule called the I–I–I rule? (Let's circle all the Is in the rule.)

Examples

- Watch Me:
  - ○ The word is **hop** and I want to add the suffix–ing
    - Is the word one syllable? _____
    - Does the word end in one consonant? _____
    - Does that consonant come after one vowel? _____
    - So, do we follow the I–I–I rule? _____
    - Double the final consonant before adding the vowel suffix: hop + ing = _____
- Let's Try One Together:
  - ○ The word is **sit** and I want to add the suffix –ing
    - Is the word one syllable? _____
    - Does the word end in one consonant? _____
    - Does that consonant come after one vowel? _____
    - So, do we follow the I–I–I rule? _____
    - Double the final consonant before adding the vowel suffix: sit + ing = _____
- Your Turn:
  - ○ The word is **run** and I want to add the suffix –ing
    - Is the word one syllable? _____
    - Does the word end in one consonant? _____
    - Does that consonant come after one vowel? _____
    - So, do we follow the I–I–I rule? _____
    - Double the final consonant before adding the vowel suffix: run + ing = _____

Non-Examples

- Watch Me:
  - ○ The word is **play** and I want to add the suffix –ing
    - Is the word one syllable? _____
    - Does the word end in one consonant? _____
    - Does that consonant come after one vowel?
    - So, do we follow the I–I–I rule? _____
    - Just add the vowel suffix: play + ing = _____

Figure 2   Sample page from a teacher-directed worksheet

may need additional contingencies to use guided notes. For example, teachers can award bonus points for complete and accurate notes. If teachers collect guided notes on an unpredictable schedule, students know that they should be ready to turn them in at any time. This also makes monitoring student note-taking and delivering contingent reinforcement less cumbersome to manage on a day-to-day basis. Another way to motivate students to complete guided notes is to give in-class, open-note quizzes immediately following lectures. Teachers should design these quizzes so that students with complete guided notes will be able to do well.

Even when students are absent, they should be held accountable for learning the content that was covered during their absence. Teachers can leave a blank copy of the guided notes along with a copy of the completed notes in a "While You Were Out" folder. Students can then learn to complete the guided notes from the missed lecture(s) upon their return. This way, students who are not at school can still have opportunities for active responding.

Once students have a set of accurate lecture notes, they should be taught and encouraged to use those notes to study for upcoming quizzes and exams. To promote active studying,

Characters in *The Giver* by Lois Lowry (1993)

Directions: Follow along with your teacher and classmates as you learn about and discuss the characters in the novel. Once you have completed the guided notes, fold the page in half to quiz yourself. Be sure to quiz yourself from left to right **AND** from right to left. You can also pair up with a classmate and quiz each other. When you quiz each other, be sure to mix up the order in which you ask the questions.

Characteristics	Character
1. Who is the main character in the novel?	**1.** _____
2. Write three adjectives that describe the main character.	**2.** a. _____ b. _____ c. _____
3. Which character is pale-eye, bearded, and tired?	**3.** _____
4. What is Jonas' mother's profession?	**4.** _____
5. What is Jonas' father's profession?	**5.** _____
6. Write three adjectives that describe Asher.	**6.** a. _____ b. _____ c. _____
7. Write three adjectives that describe Lily.	**7.** a. _____ b. _____ c. _____
8. Write three adjectives that describe Fiona.	**8.** a. _____ b. _____ c. _____
9. Which character receives the assignment to become Caretaker of the Old?	**9.** _____
10. Which character has the most honored profession/assignment in the Community?	**10.** _____

Figure 3 Sample page from columnar guided notes

instructors can format guided notes in columns with questions, prompts, or main ideas on the left side and answers or supporting details on the right side (see Figure 3) (Weishaar & Boyle, 1999). Students can then learn to fold the paper down the middle to quiz themselves. This format may also serve as a model for students learning to take their own notes.

Additionally, teachers can help students create study cards (Itoi, 2004; Wood, 2005) by printing their guided notes on both sides of a sheet so that one side allows students to take notes, whereas the other side consists of questions relevant to the information on the guided notes side of the card. Figures 4 and 5 illustrate how a set of guided note study cards should be formatted. Specifically, the completed guided notes become the backs of the study cards (i.e., answers); and the questions,

which are printed on the back of the original set of guided notes, become the front sides. With this format, students can simply cut out the notes to create a set of flashcards. Teachers should lead structured review sessions to show students how to study with flash-cards and should emphasize repeated practice in which students read the question to themselves, say the answer, and check the answer by referring back to the information recorded on the guided notes.

When instructors combine guided notes with in-class review time, learning outcomes are enhanced (Lazarus, 1993). A review session using a set of guided notes study cards easily can take place in a peer-tutoring context, in which students teach one another under the direction of a teacher (e.g., Veerkamp, Kamps, & Cooper, 2007). Teachers should simply

Guided Notes: Parts of Speech

Name _____

Date _____

Directions: These guided notes will be the backs of your study cards. Complete them with the teacher and wait for instructions on how to cut them into cards and use them to study.

1 (back)

_____ is used to name a person, animal, place, thing, and abstract idea. Examples:

_____

_____

2 (back)

_____ tells you the action or the state of being. Examples:

_____

_____

3 (back)

_____ tells you something extra about the person or objects. Examples:

_____

_____

4 (back)

_____ tells you something extra about the verb, an adjective, or another adverb by answering questions such as "how" "when" or "how much." Examples:

_____

_____

5 (back)

_____ is always used with a noun and tells you something extra about a noun. There are only three of them:

_____

_____

6 (back)

Figure 4   Sample back page from a set of guided notes study cards

divide students into pairs and provide each student with a peer-tutoring folder (Heward, 2006), which contains the guided notes study cards in a "Go" pocket. Students take turns reading the questions and answering them by saying aloud the words in the blanks from the guided notes. Once students master a card, it can be moved into a different pocket in the folder (e.g., mastered).

Promoting Higher Order Thinking

In addition to assisting students with studying for exams, guided notes can also be used to promote higher order thinking. For example, teachers can encourage students to reflect on the lecture by including within the guided notes stopping points for students to pause and think critically, ask questions, connect with personal experience, relate to prior knowledge, and generate new ideas.

Reciprocal teaching may also be implemented during a class lecture similar to the way in which this method is implemented in a reading group (Palinscar & Brown, 1984; van Garderen, 2004). After the teacher has created and modeled a lecture using guided notes, students in the class can take turns creating guided notes and leading the class through a minilecture using

their prepared guided notes. Students who lead the class need to be well prepared so that they can respond to questions and clarify responses made by their classmates. The instructor may ask two students to cocreate and colead a lecture using guided notes. Students will need structure and guidance throughout this process, and teachers will need to use their best judgment in determining if this form of reciprocal teaching is appropriate for their classroom given the diverse characteristics and needs of their students.

Conclusion

With so much material to cover in so little time, guided notes can be helpful for teachers in holding themselves accountable for reaching daily objectives. Teachers may want to create a packet of guided notes that corresponds to an instructional unit and decide (ahead of time) which pages will be covered on which days. This can help the teacher strategically plan ahead and stay on task during lectures rather than straying off topic. Teachers should design assessments (e.g., quizzes, exams) that are direct measures of mastery of material covered within the guided notes. They should use the data from

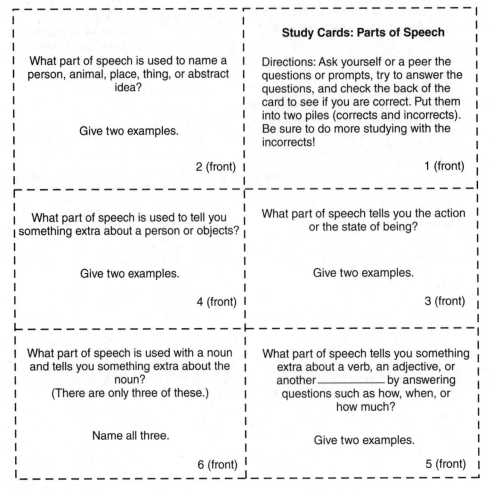

Study Cards: Parts of Speech

Directions: Ask yourself or a peer the questions or prompts, try to answer the questions, and check the back of the card to see if you are correct. Put them into two piles (corrects and incorrects). Be sure to do more studying with the incorrects!

1 (front)

What part of speech is used to name a person, animal, place, thing, or abstract idea?

Give two examples.

2 (front)

What part of speech tells you the action or the state of being?

Give two examples.

3 (front)

What part of speech is used to tell you something extra about a person or objects?

Give two examples.

4 (front)

What part of speech tells you something extra about a verb, an adjective, or another _____ by answering questions such as how, when, or how much?

Give two examples.

5 (front)

What part of speech is used with a noun and tells you something extra about the noun?
(There are only three of these.)

Name all three.

6 (front)

Figure 5   Sample front page from a set of guided notes study cards

these assessments to evaluate the effectiveness of their lessons and make appropriate instructional adjustments as needed.

The suggestions offered here are not exhaustive of all possible ways guided notes can be implemented. This versatile tool not only facilitates students' attention to lecture, ease in studying for exams, and improved test performance, it helps teachers organize and pace their delivery of lecture content.

References

Austin, J. L., Lee, M. G., Thibeault, M. D., Carr, J. E., & Bailey, J. S. (2002). Effects of guided notes on university students' responding and recall of information. *Journal of Behavioral Education, 11,* 243–254.

Barbetta, F. M., & Skaruppa, C. L. (1995). Looking for a way to improve your behavior analysis lectures? Try guided notes. *The Behavior Analyst, 18,* 155–160.

Blackwell, A. J., & McLaughlin, T. F. (2005). Using guided notes, choral responding, and response cards to increase student performance. *International Journal of Special Education, 20,* 1–5.

Dye, G. A. (2000). Graphic organizers to the rescue! Helping students link—and remember—information. *TEACHING Exceptional Children, 32*(3), 72–76.

Heward, W. L. (1994). Three "low-tech" strategies for increasing the frequency of active student response during group instruction. In R. Gardner, D. M. Sainato, J. O. Cooper, T. E. Heron, W. L. Heward, J. Eshleman, & T. A. Grossi (Eds.), *Behavior analysis in education: Focus on measurably superior instruction* (pp. 283–320). Monterey, CA: Brooks/Cole.

Heward, W. L. (2001). *Guided notes: Improving the effectiveness of your lectures.* Columbus: Ohio State University Partnership Grant for Improving the Quality of Education for Students With Disabilities.

Heward, W. L. (2006). *Exceptional children: An introduction to special education.* Upper Saddle River, NJ: Prentice Hall.

Hughes, C. A., & Suritsky, S. K. (1994). Note-taking skills of university students with and without learning disabilities. *Journal of Learning Disabilities, 27,* 20–24.

Itoi, M. (2004). *Effects of guided notes study cards on the accuracy of lecture notes and next-day quiz scores of students in a 7th grade social studies classroom.* Unpublished master's thesis, Ohio State University, Columbus.

Konrad, M., Joseph, L. M., & Eveleigh, E. (2009). A meta-analytic review of guided notes. *Education & Treatment of Children, 32,* 421–444.

Lazarus, B. D. (1993). Guided notes: Effects with secondary and post secondary students with mild disabilities. *Education and Treatment of Children, 16,* 272–289.

Lowry, L. (1993). *The giver.* New York, NY: Dell Laurel-Leaf.

Neef, N. A., McCord, B. E., & Ferreri, S. J. (2006). Effects of guided notes versus completed notes during lectures on college students' quiz performance. *Journal of Applied Behavior Analysis, 39,* 123–130.

Palinscar, A. S., & Brown, A. L. (1984). Reciprocal teaching of comprehension fostering and comprehension monitoring activities. *Cognition and Instruction, 1,* 117–175.

Patterson, K. B. (2005). Increasing positive outcomes for African American males in special education with the use of guided notes. *Journal of Negro Education, 74,* 311–320.

Randolph, J. J. (2007). Meta-analysis of the effects of response cards on student achievement, participation, and intervals of off-task behavior. *Journal of Positive Behavior Interventions, 9,* 113–128.

Stringfellow, J. L., & Miller, S. P. (2005). Enhancing student performance in secondary classrooms while providing access to the general education curriculum using lecture format. *TEACHING Exceptional Children Plus, 1*(6), 2–16.

Sweeney, W. J., Ehrhardt, A. M., Gardner, R., Jones, L., Greenfield, R., & Fribley, S. (1999). Using guided notes with academically at-risk high school students during a remedial summer social studies class. *Psychology in the Schools, 36,* 305–318.

Tam, B. K. Y., & Scott, M. L. (1996). Three group instructional strategies for students with limited English proficiency in vocational education. *Journal of Vocational Special Needs Education, 19*(1), 31–36.

van Garderen, D. (2004). Reciprocal teaching as a comprehension strategy for understanding mathematical word problems. *Reading & Writing Quarterly, 20,* 225–229.

Veerkamp, M. B., Kamps, D. M., & Cooper, L. (2007). The effects of classwide peer tutoring on the reading achievement of urban middle school students. *Education and Treatment of Children, 30,* 21–51.

Weishaar, M. K., & Boyle, J. R. (1999). Note-taking strategies for students with disabilities. *Clearing House, 72,* 392–395.

Wood, C. L. (2005). *Effects of random study checks and guided notes study cards on middle school special education students' notetaking accuracy and science vocabulary quiz scores.* Retrieved from OhioLINK Electronic Thesis and Dissertations Center.

Critical Thinking

1. Guided notes can be helpful to students with learning disabilities; however, there are several other types of students who could benefit. Who are these students and why would guided notes be useful for them?

2. While guided notes are generally used for taking notes during a lecture in class, how else might teachers use this strategy to provide equitable access to the curriculum and support student learning?

3. Find a lesson plan or activity that you have taught or find one from another source. Now prepare guided notes to support a student who has difficulty writing or using standard English in a classroom setting.

4. Some teachers consider providing notes of any kind to students as coddling or enabling helplessness. However, after reading this article you have determined that you will use this strategy. What would you say to relieve the concerns some teachers have about enabling?

MOIRA KONRAD, PhD, is an assistant professor of special education at Ohio State University. Her current interests include self-determination and literacy development for youth with disabilities. **LAURICE M. JOSEPH, PhD,** is an associate professor of school psychology at Ohio State University. Her current interests include academic interventions, students with disabilities, and applied behavior analysis. **MADOKA ITOI, PhD,** is a senior clinician at Spectrum Center. Her current interests include analyzing intervention efficiency and effectiveness for students with disabilities in the educational context.

Declaration of Conflicting Interest—The author(s) declared no conflicts of interest with respect to the authorship and/or publication of this article.

Funding—The author(s) received no financial support for the research and/or authorship of this article.

Strategies for Every Teacher's Toolbox

When students with learning disabilities enter secondary school, they may not have the skills or preparation to meet the academic requirements. Similarly, secondary level teachers may not be prepared to meet struggling learners' needs in their general education classrooms.

FRANK DYKES AND SUZANNE THOMAS

A h, the adolescent years. Those of us who have taught or are teaching in middle and high schools can identify with the behavioral, social, psychological, and cognitive changes that occur between the twilight of childhood and the dawning of approaching adulthood. "With emotions and hormones running rampant, and society, family, and educational systems simultaneously pulling them in different directions, it is no wonder that adolescence continues to be considered as a difficult period in the life cycle" (Sabornie & deBettencourt, 2004, p. 56). Now add learning challenges to this mix. Students who have learning challenges have the same characteristics and needs as other students, including the need for peer acceptance and peer interaction (Repetto, Webb, Neubert, & Curran, 2006).

For all students, the academic demands of secondary school are numerous. Students must be able to read and write in a variety of content areas; determine the importance of what is being said by the instructor; take notes in a format that can be used later for review; and keep track of their materials, class requirements, and daily schedules. Most students have difficulty adjusting to the demands of secondary education, but students with learning challenges have greater difficulty, perhaps because they lack certain skills, such as the ability to think critically or problem solve, or haven't been adequately prepared for the instructional changes that occur between elementary and secondary education (Sabornie & deBettencourt, 2004).

Mercer (1997) found that adolescent students with learning challenges often display the following common characteristics:

- Academic deficits
- Cognitive deficits in memory and planning
- Social skill deficits
- Study skill deficits and lack of metacognitive strategies
- Motivational problems.

These problems often become apparent at the secondary level because of the focus on content-area materials, the pace at which the material is delivered, and the short instructional time frames. Educators must be well versed in appropriate intervention strategies to help students overcome these difficulties and meet the increasing curricular demands.

Strategies for Success

As the instructional leader of a school, the principal is the "master craftsman" who is responsible for providing the resources, the materials, and the blueprint required for building the academic performance of students. Frequently this process requires a "reconceptualization of teaching at the secondary level that encompasses both content and strategy instruction" (Anderson, Yilmaz, & Wasburn-Moses, 2004). Word walls, guided notes, graphic organizers, and mnemonics are four research-based strategies that the principal can share with classroom teachers to increase all students' academic success, especially students with learning challenges.

> **As the instructional leader of a school, the principal is the "master craftsman" who is responsible for providing the resources, the materials, and the blueprint required for building the academic performance of students.**

Word Walls

One way to showcase significant vocabulary words that are related to a current topic of study is through a systematically organized collection of words that are displayed in large letters on a wall in the classroom (Wagstaff, 1999). Often educators relegate the use of word walls to the elementary classroom, but Routman (2003) noted that word walls can effectively anchor words in adolescent students' long-term memory. Word walls help students learn to use words to construct knowledge in conversation and activities; they also are a visual record of skills taught and content studied.

Word walls can be adapted for different subjects and classrooms. For example, English teachers may display words that are frequently misspelled. Mathematics teachers may use word walls to illustrate mathematical symbols and formulas and history teachers may categorize historical terms and time lines. Roaming teachers who don't have classrooms of their own can construct word walls on poster board.

When used effectively, word walls are a powerful tool for supporting the instructional program. Studies link print-rich environments to increased student achievement (McGill-Franzen, Allington, Yokoi, & Brooks, 1999). Principals can introduce the use of word walls to teachers during department meetings so that they can discuss how word walls might be used with specific content. In fact, giving each teacher an example of a word wall and a set of word cards for an upcoming unit of study is an excellent method to encourage the use of word walls.

Principals can introduce four intervention strategies—word walls, guided notes, graphic organizers, and mnemonics—to help teachers support students.

Guided Notes

One of the most common characteristics of students with learning problems is a deficit in processing skills (Salend, 2005). Some students lack visual and auditory processing skills, thereby compromising their ability to process information presented in class. Secondary teachers often assume that all students have the skills they need to be independent learners, but many students with learning challenges have trouble listening and taking notes and need an intermediate step to learn how to do it.

Guided notes are an excellent bridge to help students develop note-taking skills because they are "teacher prepared handouts that provide an outline of the lecture, which students complete during class by writing in key facts, concepts and/or relationships" (Heward, 2006, p. 203). Guided notes are a content enhancement (Bergerud, Lovett, & Horton, 1988) that can improve the organization and delivery of content so that students are better able to process, comprehend, and retain information. Students who use guided notes must actively respond during the lecture, which improves the accuracy of note taking and increases the retention of the content.

Experimental studies have indicated that students at all achievement levels consistently earn higher test scores and daily grades if they use guided notes (Austin, Lee, Thibeault, Carr, & Bailey, 2002; Hamilton, Seibert, Gardner, & Talbert-Johnson, 2000). Guided notes are a great adjunct to PowerPoint presentations and can easily be constructed using existing slide handouts. Principals can introduce secondary teachers to the use of guided notes during a faculty meeting by passing out a set of guided notes with blanks, matching items, and short-answer items that relate to the meeting's content.

Graphic Organizers

Levine (2002) said that the best way to learn is to transform the information in some manner: "if it is verbal, create a diagram or picture of it" (p. 119). One way to create a picture of information is to use a graphic organizer that depicts the relationships between facts, terms, and ideas within a learning task (Hall & Strangman, 2002). Other tools that are associated with graphic organizers include knowledge maps, concept maps, story maps, advance organizers, and concept diagrams. Ausubel (1963) originally rationalized the use of graphic organizers by speculating that a learner's existing knowledge greatly influences his or her learning. The key to using graphic organizers effectively lies in consistency, coherency, and creativity of use (Baxendell, 2003).

Possible uses for graphic organizers include illustrations of science concepts, time lines for important dates in history, Venn diagrams to compare pieces of literature, and advance organizers to preteach mathematical concepts (Dye, 2000). A study conducted by Kim, Vaughn, Wanzek, and Wei (2004) linked improved reading comprehension with the use of graphic organizers at both the elementary and secondary level. The principal can introduce graphic organizers in campus meetings by showing teachers how the general content of the meeting could be illustrated using the various organizers.

Mnemonics

Do you remember the little ditty, ROY G BIV? If you do, your teacher taught you the colors in the rainbow—red, orange, yellow, green, blue, indigo, violet—using a mnemonic. According to Scruggs and Mastropieri (1990), a mnemonic is "a specific reconstruction of target content that is intended to tie new information to the learner's existing knowledge base, and therefore, facilitate retrieval" (p. 271). Mnemonics is solidly grounded in the psychological literature about associative learning. An empirical study conducted by Mastropieri and Scruggs (1998) revealed that mnemonic strategies can enhance students' abilities to encode and recall factual information, thereby improving their performance on classroom and standardized tests.

Mnemonic techniques can be effective for both immediate and delayed recall and can facilitate performance on tasks that go beyond recall. Further, mnemonics can improve students' memory for terms that were previously unfamiliar to them (Carney & Levin, 2008). For example, science teachers could have students memorize elements in the periodic table by generating sentences with the first letter of each word representing terms in sequence (Steele, 2007). Principals could introduce mnemonics in faculty correspondence or in a faculty meeting by using a mnemonic for building procedures, such as "COPS" for the "campus operating procedures system."

Conclusion

Often, secondary school teachers have not received training in a variety of instructional strategies that will enable them to meet the needs of a diverse student body. Principals must therefore have a toolbox of strategies at their disposal to help teachers meet the needs of all kinds of learners in the general education classroom. By introducing and supporting those strategies, principals can enhance the academic achievement of all secondary students—particularly those who need additional support in the classroom.

References

Anderson, S., Yilmaz, O., & Wasburn-Moses, L. (2004). Middle and high school students with learning disabilities: Practical academic interventions for general education teachers—A review of the literature. *American Secondary Education, 32,* 19–38.

Austin, J. L., Lee, M. G., Thibeault, M. D., Carr, J. E., & Bailey, J. S. (2002). Effects of guided notes on university students' responding and recall of information. *Journal of Behavioral Education, 11*(4), 243–254.

Ausubel, D. P. (1963). *The psychology of meaningful verbal learning.* New York, NY: Grune & Straton.

Baxendell, B. W. (2003). Consistent, coherent, creative: The 3 c's of graphic organizers. *Teaching Exceptional Children, 35*(3), 46–53.

Bergerud, D., Lovitt, T., & Horton, S. (1988). The effectiveness of textbook adaptations in life science for high school students with learning disabilities. *Journal of Learning Disabilities, 21*(2), 70–76.

Carney, R. N., & Levin, J. R. (2008). Conquering mnemonophobia, with help from three practical measures of memory and application. *Teaching of Psychology, 35,* 176–183.

Dye, G. A. (2000). Graphic organizers to the rescue! *Teaching Exceptional Children, 32*(3), 72–76.

Hall, T., & Strangman, N. (2002). Graphic organizers. Retrieved from the CAST Web site: www.cast.org/system/galleries/download/ncac/NCACgo.pdf.

Hamilton, S. L., Seibert, M. A., Gardner, R., & Talbert-Johnson, C. (2000). Using guided notes to improve the academic achievement of incarcerated adolescents with learning and behavior problems. *Remedial and Special Education, 21*(3), 133–170.

Heward, W. L. (2006). *Exceptional children: An introduction to special education.* Upper Saddle River, NJ: Pearson.

Kim, A., Vaughn, S., Wanzek, J., & Wei, S. (2004). Graphic organizers and their effects on the reading comprehension of students with LD: A synthesis of the research. *Journal of Learning Disabilities, 37*(2), 105–118.

Levine, M. (2002). *A mind at a time.* New York, NY: Simon & Schuster.

Critical Thinking

1. Does it surpise you that this article was printed in a journal for principals? Why or why not?

2. Why is it important for educational leaders, like principals, to know and understand strategies that can be used in secondary classrooms? What might you say to a principal about using these strategies only for students with learning disabilities?

3. These strategies are generally well-known and used in elementary classrooms. Why do you think this article is written specifically for secondary principals and teachers?

4. Use a Google search to find other strategies that you might use at the secondary level in your content area.

Methods for Addressing Conflict in Cotaught Classrooms

GREG CONDERMAN[1]

Based only on their schedule and availability, Marci and Craig's high school assistant principal assigned them to coteach two sections of biology. Their personalities and teaching styles could not be more different. Marci is outgoing, fun, and spontaneous, whereas Craig is quiet, predictable, cautious, and serious. At the middle school, Esther and Margaret coteach sixth-grade language arts. Esther believes that students at this level need to explore to create meaning in the curriculum, whereas Margaret is a firm believer in explicit instruction and scripted lessons. Finally, Inge and Zack coteach second grade. Neither really understands his or her coteaching role, and Inge feels Zack is invading her space. These three teams, representing various subjects and grade levels, illustrate issues between coteachers that potentially could cause conflict. Without professionally addressing the issues, these teachers (all names are pseudonyms)—and the students they serve—may not experience the true benefits and intended outcomes of effective coteaching.

Coteaching represents one approach for supporting students with disabilities in the general education classroom. Friend and Cook (2010) defined coteaching as a "service delivery option for providing special education or related services to students with disabilities or other special needs while they remain in the general education classroom" (p. 109). They also emphasized that coteaching involves two or more professionals who jointly deliver instruction to a diverse group of students within a shared classroom space. Coteaching also assumes that teachers display mutual respect for each other, assume roles with parity, collectively develop specific mutual goals, assume accountability for outcomes, share resources, and communicate in ways their partner understands (Conderman, Bresnahan, & Pedersen, 2009). Therefore, effective coteaching depends, in part, on each teacher's interpersonal skills, willingness and ability to work collaboratively, and skills in successfully handling conflict.

These skills are critical because coteaching is a highly interactive endeavor that brings together two individuals with different professional backgrounds, beliefs, expertise, strengths, and needs. Although blending contrasting profiles can result in professional satisfaction and growth for coteachers and increased student academic performance (Villa, Thousand, & Nevin, 2008), coteachers are also likely to face more opportunities for potential conflict than when teaching on their own. When professionals from different disciplines with different frames of reference make decisions about student needs, they are likely to disagree about desired outcomes (Behfar, Peterson, Mannix, & Trochin, 2008). Clearly, when two or more people are together for any length of time, they will experience some conflict (Bolton, 1979).

Addressing conflict may actually produce positive outcomes. For example, appropriately addressing conflict may clarify each partner's issues, increase each person's involvement in the process and outcomes, promote professional and personal growth, strengthen interpersonal relationships, rebuild organizational systems, foster problem solving, promote flexible thinking and creativity, prevent stagnation, and encourage fun (Bolton, 1979; Dettmer, Thurston, Knackendoffel, & Dyck, 2009; Villa et al., 2008). Furthermore, addressing conflict allows partners to become aware of issues in the relationship, causes future decisions to be made more carefully, and clears the air of unexpressed resentments (Falikowski, 2007).

Despite these advantages of addressing conflict, several reasons explain why teachers may be ill equipped to address conflict. First, many special education teacher preparation programs inadequately prepare teachers for addressing conflict. Special education teachers indicate that much of their day is spent navigating adult-to-adult interactions, for which they feel ill prepared. Few authentic early clinical or student teaching opportunities are available for preservice candidates to gain such experiences before their first teaching position (Conderman, Morin, & Stephens, 2005). Similarly, many enter coteaching with minimal training in this area (Conderman, Bresnahan, et al., 2009). Consequently, coteachers may not know what to expect or how to begin their coteaching situation, which may lead to resistance, stress, and uncertainty. Traditionally, school professionals have been uncomfortable addressing conflict (Friend & Cook, 2010), thereby providing few good models for beginning, or even experienced, teachers. Collectively, these factors may contribute to coteaching partners feeling ill prepared to address and negotiate critical issues. Because of the unique structure of coteaching and its potential for conflict, this

---

[1]Northern Illinois University, DeKalb, IL, USA

article focuses on conflict within the context of coteaching by providing background on conflict, indicating possible reasons and sources for coteaching conflict, and describing ways to professionally address such conflict.

The Nature and Sources of Conflict

Defining Conflict

One general definition is that conflict occurs when individuals experience unresolved differences in terms of needs, values, goals, and/or personalities (Dettmer et al., 2009). At times, coteachers may have opposing (a) needs in terms of their contributions to the classroom, classroom organization, and/or student expectations; (b) values regarding critical student academic and social outcomes, the role of family members, and/or student responsibilities; (c) goals for themselves, each other, and/or their class; and (d) personalities such as their sense of humor, frames of reference, ways they deal with conflict, and the amount of energy and enthusiasm they portray during instruction. Villa et al. (2008) used the term *controversy* to describe situations in which coteachers have incompatible ideas (e.g., using two totally different approaches to introduce a math concept) and must reach an agreement. Friend and Cook (2010) defined conflict as a type of struggle in which individuals perceive that others are interfering with their ability to attain goals. These authors also noted that conflict can occur (a) between individuals with the same goals (e.g., both coteachers agree that coplanning is important but disagree on their approach) and (b) because of power or perceived power (e.g., the more experienced teacher assumes he or she has more decision-making authority). Moore (1996) listed five different types of conflicts:

1. value-based conflicts (caused by different goals, ways of life, or ideology),
2. structural conflicts (caused by negative patterns of behavior or interaction or by unequal power, control, or resources),
3. relationship conflicts (caused by poor communication or miscommunication),
4. data-based conflicts (caused by lack of information, misinformation, different views on what is relevant, or different interpretations of data), and
5. interest-based conflicts (caused by different procedural, psychological, or substantive interests).

These various definitions and examples provide a framework for understanding some of the unique circumstances surrounding coteaching conflict.

Sources of Coteaching Conflict

Because coteaching involves working very closely with another professional through coplanning, coinstructing, and coassessing (Muraski & Boyer, 2008), opportunities for conflict are inevitable during any or all of these coteaching components. Figure 1 lists potential sources of conflict associated with coplanning, coinstructing, and coassessing. Coteaching teams can use Figure 1 as a checklist to assess potential sources of conflict by noting areas of concern and later planning ways to address identified concerns.

As noted in Figure 1, some teachers, perhaps those who have taught the same grade level or subject for multiple years, may not share the same need for coplanning as their novice coteacher, one who is new to the content area, or a partner whose planning style is very deliberate and detailed. Admittedly, teachers approach their lessons in various ways, so finding a suitable planning time and process may take time and effort. Similarly, differences in coinstructing may emerge as teachers reveal their preferences for certain coteaching models, strategies, materials, acceptable classroom noise levels, need for structure, and instructional role of each coteacher. Finally, coteachers may differ on their beliefs and practices regarding assessment. For example, some teachers believe grades motivate students, and they value frequent student monitoring and data collection as a way to indicate student growth and inform instruction. In contrast, others view grades as tools that reduce student creativity, or they rely on end-of-semester projects or tests as major indicators of student learning. Therefore, during coplanning, coinstructing, and coassessing, coteachers should expect differences of opinion and the need for dialogue to understand their partner.

In addition to potential sources of conflict related to coplanning, coinstructing, and coassessing, other circumstances may affect the coteaching partnership and cause conflict. Personality issues may result in conflict or, at the very least, make coteaching less desirable and less enjoyable than teaching solo. Teachers who were good colleagues may not always make the best coteachers, especially if personality differences affect teaching expectations or cause one coteacher to feel unequal or disrespected, or if one coteacher uses a personality trait or strength to gain student or parent support or popularity and isolate the coteaching partner. A coteacher with a dominant or outgoing personality should not be allowed to manipulate a quiet individual, as this may lead to feelings of resentment. Unclear or different expectations of coteaching, a sense of invading one's territory, and lack of content knowledge can cause conflict. Outside sources, such as jealousies from other coworkers, misunderstandings from colleagues that coteaching is easy, pressure to raise student test scores from the cotaught class, and unclear systems of teaching evaluations are additional sources of conflict unique to some cotaught classrooms. Finally, issues related to unprofessionalism (e.g., one coteacher who does not maintain confidentialities, independently changes student grades or scores, or says negative comments about the partner to others) are quite serious, undermine the coteaching relationship, and often require administrator intervention. All of these issues illustrate potential sources of conflict unique to coteaching.

Figure 1   Checklist of potential sources of coteaching conflict

	Coplanning
	The team has not received training on coplanning
	The team does not have a common planning time
	One coteacher did not attend scheduled coplanning meeting(s)
	One or both coteachers were unprepared for coplanning meeting(s)
	Coteachers have different approaches to planning (e.g., detailed and sequential v. holistic or written v. verbal)
	Coteachers disagree on instructional sequence
	Coteachers disagree on coplanning format or form
	One or both coteachers are hesitant using a new planning approach
	One coteacher has little opportunity to contribute meaningfully to coplanning
	Coteachers assume same coplanning role (e.g., only special educator suggests accommodations) even when both could have contributed
	Other (list)
	Coinstructing
	One or both coteachers were unprepared for coinstructing
	Coteachers have different views/philosophies on teaching, learning, role of teacher, role of students, classroom management, etc.
	One coteacher always assumes lead role
	One coteacher always assumes support role
	One coteacher lacks content knowledge to deliver, support, or modify instruction
	Students view one coteacher as assistant, rather than teacher
	One coteacher feels more like assistant, rather than teacher
	One coteacher did not follow established plan
	One coteacher was not flexible with lesson when a change was needed
	Coteachers do not use parity in instruction, language, signals, and/or materials
	Other (list)
	Coassessing
	Coteachers only use types of assessments used in previous semesters
	Coteachers have different philosophies regarding grading
	Coteachers have different views on the role of assessment
	One coteacher changed the assessment without notifying the partner
	Teams rely on subjective feelings rather than objective data for making instructional decisions and student evaluations
	Only one teacher has access to student grades
	Only one teacher communicates with parents regarding student progress
	Coteachers did not reflect on lesson
	Coteachers blame each other for poor lesson delivery or inadequate student growth
	Coteachers always assume same role in assessment (e.g., only special educator makes assessment accommodations or modifications)
	Other (list)

Coteaching conflict may be especially evident with poorly matched teachers (such as Marci and Craig from our opening scenario), those who view teaching and learning in significantly different ways (such as Esther and Margaret), and those who are uncertain about their coteaching roles (such as Inge and Zack). These teams are especially likely to experience discord (Dettmer et al., 2009). When not addressed, such discord is likely to negatively interfere with the relationship between coteachers, the classroom climate, teaching skills, and student learning.

Proactive Strategies

Several proactive strategies, implemented by coteachers, can minimize the likelihood of conflict damaging the relationship. Although their implementation does not guarantee that conflict will not occur, the following strategies, based on research from business management, organizational behavior, and social and behavioral psychology (Song, Dyer, & Thieme, 2006), offer structure and support to teams and increase the likelihood that coteaching endeavors will run more smoothly.

Several resources also offer proactive support for coteaching teams (see Table 1). Coteachers are encouraged to consult such sources and complete the discussion activities or assessments with their coteacher before they enter their coteaching relationship. Completing informal assessments individually and then discussing results as a coteaching team clarifies each person's approach to addressing conflict and offers insight for partners to comfortably approach each other when conflict arises. Six specific proactive strategies follow.

1. *Discuss instructional-related issues before you begin.* Before coteaching, spend considerable time thoroughly discussing any and all issues that may impact the teaching relationship. Being honest with your partner about your teaching style; educational philosophies; views on classroom management; and thoughts on grading; as well as your teaching strengths, challenges, and goals, helps create a foundation with which to build a trusting and safe coteaching relationship. Your coteacher cannot read your mind. Being vulnerable may

be scary, but sharing ideas early avoids later surprises. Taking notes while your coteacher shares shows interest and provides a record of your discussion. Realize that ongoing discussion of these topics is critical to understanding your partner's perspectives.

2. *Ask your coteacher how he or she wants to address conflict.* Based on life experiences, gender, culture, frame of reference, and perceptions of how conflict resolution was modeled, individuals display predispositions when faced with conflict. An individual's conflict style is a behavioral orientation of how to approach and handle conflict (Falikowski, 2007). Therefore, seek to understand your coteacher's views and methods of handling conflict and how he or she wishes to be treated when you have constructive criticism to share. Specifically, ask how your coteacher wishes you to address issues, and then make a commitment to respect those wishes. Some teachers desire direct feedback (e.g., "Just tell me"), whereas others prefer a softer approach (e.g., "Gradually prepare me for your concern"). Be sure to ask your coteacher what would upset him or her in the cotaught classroom, so you can avoid embarrassment or conflict. In short, clearly stated policies and procedures that have the understanding and support of both parties create orderly processes that mitigate unnecessary conflict (Bolton, 1979). Similarly, recognizing different individuals' communication or conflict resolution styles leads to understanding and can also maximize the group's

Table 1   Resources for Coteachers

Resource	Brief description
Allesandra (2007)	Free 18-question online inventory (Platinum Rule.com) that provides information about one's interpersonal style, including preferences for handing conflict
Conderman, Bresnahan, et al. (2009)	Book that includes discussion questions and forms to guide coteachers, especially during the beginning coteaching stage
Dettmer et al. (2009)	Book that includes communication and conflict checklists and practice activities, tips for communicating effectively, and discussion questions for coteaching teams
Dieker (2006)	Coplanning book that includes a side-by-side view of each teacher's lesson contribution, with space to document interventions and student progress toward goals
Friend and Cook (2010)	Book that provides a 12-question conflict management-style survey with scoring directions which indicates a person's preference to control, compromise, build consensus, accommodate, or avoid conflict
Karten (2010)	Coplanning book with weekly/quarterly lesson plan formats, assessment, monitoring, record-keeping forms, and inclusive strategies
Miscisin (2007)	Short, free, online assessment (Truecolors.com) that provides information about one's approach to work
Murawski and Dieker (2004)	Article that offers numerous coteaching resources and questions/forms to use to prepare to coteach, clarify coteaching expectations, and promote instructional parity
Trent and Cox (2006)	Comprehensive, inexpensive, online inventory that analyzes how individuals solve problems, process information, manage change, and face risk, which includes a comprehensive report of one's profile
Villa et al. (2008)	Book that offers discussion questions and forms to guide coteachers, self-assessments, answers to frequently asked questions, and tips for promoting cooperation in cotaught classrooms

problem-solving effectiveness (Broome, DeTurk, Kristjansdottir, Kanata, & Ganesan, 2002).

3. *Put plans in writing.* Coteachers who just discuss upcoming lessons are probably more likely to forget some of the details, materials, or assigned tasks, which can cause conflict. A written lesson plan that outlines each coteacher's roles and responsibilities helps document parity. Writing lesson plans also helps teachers reflect more accurately after the lesson. Similarly, teams can return to their written plan to verify their original intent. Coteachers can use published lesson plan books or develop their own lesson plan format detailing the responsibilities of each coteacher during specified lesson segments.

4. *Address issues early.* Do not allow a concern to fester. Most likely, the issue will not go away, and in fact, given additional time, it may bother you even more. Covert conflicts need to be made overt and resolved, or they will fester and destroy the potential for a positive coteaching relationship (Villa et al., 2008). Decide if the issue is worth addressing, and if so, share your concern privately with your coteacher using a preferred method of addressing conflict. Because body language and voice intonation play an important role in communicating, issues are best discussed through face-to-face discussions rather than shared through e-mail or other written exchanges (Conderman, Johnston-Rodriguez, & Hartman, 2009). Similarly, phone exchanges should be short and to the point (Turnbull & Turnbull, 2001).

5. *Use effective communication skills.* Because coteaching is a relationship, and relationships are built on communication, take time to study effective communication skills. Most important, listen to your coteacher to find out what is important to him or her. Ask questions. Also, when you are feeling upset, calm yourself down before addressing your coteacher, so you do not respond in anger. Some effective communication skills (Conderman, Bresnahan, et al., 2009; Conderman, Johnston-Rodreguez, et al., 2009) include the following:

   a. Open-ended questions that seek information, such as, "How do you feel about doing a jigsaw activity tomorrow for social studies?"

   b. "I" messages that share how you feel about an event, such as, "I am concerned that students felt rushed to get through the jigsaw activity today."

   c. Paraphrasing or summarizing, which provides a short or longer summary of the topic of discussion as a way to check for communication accuracy and understanding, such as, "So, before we go, let's make sure we are on the same page regarding our lesson introduction tomorrow. We agreed to both introduce the lesson tomorrow with our role play. Then you will verbally describe the steps of the new math skill while I model, on the smart board. Did I miss anything?"

   d. Response to affect, which shows empathy by using a feeling word to indicate how you think someone else feels, such as, "I would be frustrated, too, if Myrna yelled at me."

   e. The sandwich technique, in which a concern is shared between two neutral statements, such as, "Willemetta, there is something I need to share with you. Remember, we agreed to come to one another if something was upsetting us. Well, I heard from another teacher that you said I have poor control of the class. This hurts me and violates our promise of confidentiality. I value our professional relationship, so I wonder how we can ensure this will not happen again." Even though using these kinds of effective communication skills may feel artificial, when used sincerely, they clarify issues and intents, thus acting as a proactive conflict intervention.

6. *Do not expect perfection.* Each of you will make mistakes, especially in the beginning of the cotaught relationship. Expect some bumps in the road. Allow yourself and your partner some grace and breathing room. Forgiveness goes a long way. Humble yourself when you make an error and be willing to forgive your partner.

Conflict Approaches

Proactive strategies will reduce potential for conflict, but most likely they will not eliminate the conflict entirely. Therefore, coteachers need to be aware of ways of approaching conflict when proactive strategies are insufficient in addressing the issue. Generally, the education and business literature indicates five main approaches to handling conflict (Copley, 2008). These include avoiding, accommodating, compromising, collaborating, and dominating. Table 2 reviews these five approaches or styles along with considerations and a coteaching example. Although a teacher's use of any of these approaches is dependent upon the situation and her or his partner, teachers should be skilled in all five strategies (Johnson, 2008). Gross and Guerrero (2000) discovered that colleagues generally view a collaborative style, with its emphasis on being polite, prosocial, and adaptive, as most appropriate and effective. In contrast, colleagues perceived the accommodating and compromising styles as neutral and the dominating and avoiding styles as less appropriate. Individuals tend to choose a conflict approach based on the importance of the issue and the consequences to the relationship (Johnson, 2008).

The Five Conflict Approaches

An *avoiding* style indicates low concern for self and others (Copley, 2008). Individuals who avoid conflict may be afraid to discuss the issue with their partner, lack effective conflict resolution skills, or think that discussing the issue may make matters worse. However, the situation is unlikely to change unless or until coteachers communicate. Therefore, teachers should first decide if the issue really bothers them. If it does not, then avoiding may be an appropriate choice.

Table 2 Common Ways of Addressing Conflict with Definitions and Examples

Approach	Considerations	Coteaching example
Avoiding	Reflect on the consequences of avoidance and decide whether you can live with the result Use avoiding when the issue is trivial, stakes are not high, confrontation will hurt a working relationship, or others can more effectively resolve the conflict (Falikowski, 2007)	Erika frequently joked with students during the first few minutes of class, which upset Woody, who perceived this behavior as unnecessary and a complete waste of time. After reflecting on Erika's behavior, Woody realized that joking with students actually produced a positive classroom environment and that the payoff was worth a few minutes of silliness.
Accommodating	If the same teacher always accommodates, an uneven power situation may emerge Accommodate when maintaining the relationship outweighs other considerations, the issue is not critical, time is limited, or interpersonal harmony and stability are valued more than the issue (Falikowski, 2007)	Even though Paula wanted to start class with a video clip, she agreed with Laura's idea of starting class with a role-play; similarly, even though Laura wanted to use an anticipation guide, she agreed to use guided notes, which was Paula's suggestion.
Compromising	Although commonly used, compromise is often a lose–lose situation as neither teacher gets what she or he really wants Compromise when individuals are equal in power and have strong interests in different solutions (Afzalur et al., 1992) or when important issues have no clear or simple solutions (Falikowski, 2007)	Because she wanted to assess students' ability to apply their newly learned essay-writing strategy, Julie wanted to develop an essay test, but Greg wanted to use a multiple choice test to save time on grading because grades were due Friday. The team agreed to a test containing multiple choice items and one short answer question in which students could apply part of their writing strategy.
Collaborating	This can be a win–win situation, especially if both teachers openly express their needs and are willing to be creative (Copley, 2008) Collaborate when maintaining the relationship is important, time is not a concern, or when it is important to merge differing perspectives (Falikowski, 2007)	Jeff wanted to use a class period to teach students how to use their homework planner, but Sarah thought this was not an effective use of instructional time. The team decided to develop an instructional video clip on using planners, place the clip on their website, and have students study the clip as a homework assignment.
Forcing	Seldom effective in coteaching but may be needed if multiple reminders have been unsuccessful, or if student achievement or behavior is deteriorating Use forcing cautiously and only when personal differences are difficult to change, fostering supportive relationships is not critical, the partner may take advantage of noncompetitive behavior, a decision must be made, or unpopular decisions need to be implemented (Falikowski, 2007)	Toni stopped attending agreed upon coplanning meetings with Lynette, even when Lynette agreed to meet at other times and use other coplanning formats that Toni suggested. Finally, Lynette e-mailed Toni (and copied the administrator) and indicated that the lesson plan would be submitted on time to the administrator with or without Toni's contribution.

This style is often appropriate when individuals are dealing with perceived tactical or minor issues (Afzalur, Garrett, & Buntzman, 1992).

An *accommodating* style involves low concern for self and high concern for others (Copley, 2008). Coteachers who accommodate attempt to diminish differences and emphasize commonalities to satisfy their partner's needs (Copley, 2008). This approach is also appropriate when the issue is not critical and/or when a partner feels he or she may be wrong. However, if one teacher habitually accommodates the other, resentment may occur (Bolton, 1979).

Coteachers may *compromise,* or meet in the middle, when their initial ideas or views are quite different, or when both parties are equally powerful. Compromising is associated with an intermediate level of concern for both self and others (Copley, 2008). This give-and-take style means that neither partner really has his or her needs met as each side gives up something to end the conflict or solve the problem.

Collaborating requires that coteachers rethink the situation with a different frame of reference and implement a third option they had not previously considered. This style is characterized by a high regard for self and others (Copley, 2008). Collaborating is associated with problem solving and generating multiple solutions and is appropriate for dealing with issues related to policies and long-range planning (Afzalur et al., 1992).

Finally, *dominating* involves imposing a solution on someone else and thus is associated with a win-lose perspective and a high concern for self and low concern for others. This

Table 3 Dos and Don'ts for Handling Coteaching Conflict

Do	Don't
Reflect on why the issue bothers you before you talk to your coteacher (Friend & Cook, 2010)	Act impulsively or when angry
Pick the right time and place to talk to your coteacher (Conderman, Johnston-Rodriguez, et al., 2009)	Share confidentialities with others, gossip, or speak unprofessionally about your partner
Use effective communication skills to share your concern (Conderman, Johnston-Rodriguez, et al., 2009b)	Blame your coteacher, offer advice, or lecture (Dettmer et al., 2009)
Focus on the issue (Bolton, 1979)	Focus on personalities, the past, or other nonrelated issues
Choose the most appropriate conflict approach for the situation and the style and needs of your partner (Conderman, Johnston-Rodriguez, et al., 2009)	Avoid all conflict or use the same approach for every situation
Listen and use a calm voice when someone shares a concern with you and acknowledge what has been said (Dettmer et al., 2009)	Get defensive when someone shares their concerns with you; say "Calm down"; tell the person how they should behave or feel (Dettmer et al., 2009)
Ask, "How can we resolve this?" (Dettmer et al., 2009)	Exit the situation without closure
Be willing to make a list of results that you consider acceptable solutions (Dettmer et al., 2009)	Be unwilling to compromise
When feelings are strong, deal with the emotional aspects of conflict first (Bolton, 1979)	Ignore the feelings of your partner and rush to a solution
Select solutions that will best meet both teacher's needs (Bolton, 1979)	Quickly and forcefully note the personal advantages of your suggestions
Agree on a written plan with outcomes and dates for accountability (Friend & Cook, 2010)	Rely on your memory for details of the plan
Evaluate the plan (Friend & Cook, 2010)	Be satisfied with sharing your feelings and discussing options
Thank your partner for coming to you with his or her concern	Take issues personally (Dettmer et al., 2009)

approach may be used when a quick decision is required or when an unpopular course of action must be implemented (Afzalur et al., 1992).

An additional option if coteachers are at an impasse is to seek counsel from an administrator, experienced teacher, or mentor. Sometimes an impartial colleague can consider issues more objectively and guide mutual brainstorming efforts. If this option is chosen, both coteachers need to agree on whom to consult, when to collectively meet with that person, and that they will agree to solutions generated.

Dos and Don'ts

Regardless of which conflict approach is used, coteachers may find the general *dos* and *don'ts* guidelines in Table 3 helpful as they discuss issues. Often, in the heat of an argument or disagreement, emotions run high, people feel threatened and defensive, and they may say or do something that they will regret later. These are exactly the occasions when teachers need to stop and think about whether their verbal and nonverbal behavior is fueling the conflict, or if their approach or reaction to their partner can support a healthy discussion of the issue. Coteachers can acknowledge interest in the partner's views through nodding, maintaining eye contact, leaning toward the person, and asking

nonthreatening questions. Several additional suggestions in Table 3 emphasize the importance of listening carefully to your partner because in conflict resolution the first goal is to deal constructively with emotions (Bolton, 1979). One specific tip for understanding your partner is that you should speak for yourself only after you have first restated the ideas and feelings of your partner accurately and to your partner's satisfaction (Bolton, 1979). This step helps teachers clarify and process both feelings and accuracy of information before generating a plan. Making a plan validates the partner's concern, and taking notes allows partners to check for understanding. Respecting your partner's feelings and indicating a willingness to make changes helps repair conflict. Remembering that the coteacher probably did not intentionally mean to cause conflict reduces defensiveness and tempers the discussion.

Conclusion

Conflict is an inevitable part of life, and teachers are likely to experience more conflict with the rise of collaborative school-based practices such as coteaching. Addressing conflict is critical for the success of coteaching teams, so both teachers are empowered and feel a sense of parity. Coteachers need to be aware of conflict when it exists, diagnose its nature, and employ an appropriate problem-solving method that achieves the goals of both parties while maintaining the professional relationship (Dettmer et al., 2009). This may be difficult for some coteachers based on their frame of reference, past experiences with conflict, the school culture, or feelings of inferiority or intimidation. To support this process, coteachers are advised to be proactive by assessing how they typically address conflict; discussing ground rules for dealing with difficult issues, so that an agreed-upon system is in place; practicing effective communication skills; and acknowledging that neither partner is perfect. When conflict arises, teachers can also reflect upon which of the five approaches of dealing with conflict is most appropriate to use, given the importance of the issue and the effect that choice may have on the coteaching relationship. Coteachers who address conflict professionally by carefully listening to their partner and considering alternative solutions are more likely to experience the personal and professional rewards associated with coteaching, which include expanding their professional repertoire of knowledge and skills, creating respectful classrooms where each teacher's strengths are honored, and fostering a safe and productive learning atmosphere where all students learn.

References

Afzalur, R. M., Garrett, J. E., & Buntzman, G. F. (1992). Ethics of managing interpersonal conflict in organizations. *Journal of Business Ethics, 11*(5), 423–432.

Alessandra, T. (2007). *The platinum rule.* Retrieved May 19, 2010, from www.platinumrule.com/free-assessment.asp.

Behfar, K., Peterson, R. S., Mannix, E. A., & Trochin, W. M. K. (2008). The critical role of conflict resolution in teams: A closer look at the links between conflict type, conflict management strategies and team outcomes. *Journal of Applied Psychology, 93,* 170–188.

Bolton, R. (1979). *People skills: How to assert yourself listen to others, and resolve conflicts.* New York, NY: Simon & Schuster.

Broome, B. J., DeTurk, S., Kristjansdottir, E. S., Kanata, T., & Ganesan, P. (2002). Giving voice to diversity: An interactive approach to conflict management and decision-making in culturally diverse work environments. *Journal of Business and Management, 8*(3), 239–264.

Conderman, G., Bresnahan, V., & Pedersen, T. (2009). *Purposeful co-teaching: Real cases and effective strategies.* Thousand Oaks, CA: Corwin.

Conderman, G., Johnston-Rodriguez, S., & Hartman, P. (2009). Communicating and collaborating in co-taught classrooms. *TEACHING Exceptional Children Plus, 5*(5), Article 3. Retrieved June 6, 2010, from http://escholarship.bc.edu/education/tecplus/vol5/iss5/art3.

Conderman, G., Morin, J., & Stephens, J. T. (2005). Special education student teaching practices. *Preventing School Failure, 49*(3), 5–10.

Copley, L. (2008). *Conflict management styles: A predictor of likability and perceived effectiveness among subordinates.* Unpublished master's thesis, Indiana University, Indianapolis.

Dettmer, P., Thurston, L., Knackendoffel, A., & Dyck, N. (2009). *Collaboration, consultation, and teamwork for students with special needs* (6th ed.). Columbus, OH: Pearson.

Dieker, L. (2006). *The co-teaching lesson plan book: Academic year version.* Whitefish Bay, WI: Knowledge by Design.

Falikowski, A. (2007). *Mastering human relations* (4th ed.). Toronto: Pearson Education Canada.

Friend, M., & Cook, L. (2010). *Interactions: Collaborative skills for school professionals* (6th ed.). Boston, MA: Pearson.

Gross, M. A., & Guerrero, L. K. (2000). Managing conflict appropriately and effectively: An application of the competence model to Rahim's organizational conflict styles. *International Journal of Conflict Management, 11*(3), 200–226.

Johnson, D. W. (2008). *Reaching out. Interpersonal effectiveness and self-actualization* (10th ed.). Boston, MA: Allyn & Bacon.

Karten, T. (2010). *Inclusion lesson plan book for the 21st century.* Port Chester, NY: Dude Publishing.

Miscisin, M. (2007). *The true colors test.* Retrieved May 20, 2010, from www.true_colors_test.com.

Moore, C. (1996). *The mediation process: Practical strategies for resolving conflict.* San Francisco, CA: Jossey-Bass.

Murawski, W., & Boyer, L. (2008, November). *What is really happening in cotaught classes? One state knows!* Paper presented at the Teacher Education Division of the Council for Exceptional Children Conference, Dallas, TX.

Murawski, W., & Dieker, L. (2004). Tips and strategies for co-teaching at the secondary level. *TEACHING Exceptional Children, 36*(5), 52–58.

Song, M., Dyer, B., & Thieme, R. J. (2006). Conflict management and innovation performance: An integrated contingency perspective. *Journal of the Academy of Marketing Science, 34*(3), 341–356.

Trent, J., & Cox, R. (2006). *Leading from your strengths.* Scottsdale, AZ: Ministry Insights Intl.

Turnbull, A., & Turnbull, R. (2001). *Families, professionals, and exceptionality: Collaborating for empowerment* (4th ed.). Upper Saddle River, NJ: Pearson.

Villa, R. A., Thousand, J. A., & Nevin, A. I. (2008). *A guide to co-teaching: Practical tips for facilitating student learning.* Thousand Oaks, CA: Corwin.

Critical Thinking

1. Think about all of the times that you have collaborated with a peer or even with a person who was a supervisor. Now pick one experience that was especially memorable. What was best about that collaboration? What was unpleasant about that collaboration?

2. Have you ever tried to co-teach? Share your story about that event.

3. Even the best of collaborators with similar goals and ideals occasionally have conflict, particularly when the stakes are high, such as in a teaching situation. Why does this happen?

4. Table 2 lists common ways that collaborators address conflict. Which of these have you used to get out of a sticky situation? Why did you choose to use that method?

GREG CONDERMAN, EdD, is an associate professor of special education at Northern Illinois University. His research interests include coteaching and instructional methods for students with mild disabilities.

Declaration of Conflicting Interest—The author(s) declared no conflicts of interest with respect to the authorship and/or publication of this article.

Funding—The author(s) received no financial support for the research and/or authorship of this article.

UNIT 6

Technology: Are We Effectively Using Its Potential in Our Schools?

Unit Selections

Learning Outcomes

After reading this unit, you will be able to:

- Consider the ways that technology can and will change schooling.
- Examine trends in technology that will allow blended learning as well as fully online learning.
- Identify the challenges that schools will face in the near future.
- Explain how a gaming device can be used to help struggling elementary readers.
- Describe how technology can be used to meet the principles of Universal Design for Learning for differentiated instruction.
- Evaluate the methods used by schools to use technology to meet individual learning needs.
- Explain why E-books and digital readers may be the next big idea in schools.
- Compose an answer for parents who have concerns about the time their child spends playing video games.
- Determine how gaming technology might be used for other educational purposes.

Student Website

www.mhhe.com/cls

Internet References

Educational Technology
www.edtech.sandi.net

Center for Applied Special Technology
http://cast.org

Curriculum Connections
www.edtech.sandi.net/old305/handouts/digitalclassroom/curriculumconnections.html

Open Thinking Wiki
http://couros.wikispaces.com/TechAndMediaLiteracyVids

No limits 2 learning: Celebrating human potential through assistive technology
www.nolimitstolearning.blogspot.com

Quest Garden
www.questgarden.com

Go2web20
www.go2web20.net

Technology has been a change agent in education. After experiencing early motion pictures in 1913, Thomas Edison declared that books would become obsolete in schools because we would be able to learn everything from movies. Most recently we have heard similar claims about digital books from advocates of Kindle, Nook, iPad, and other e-readers and sellers of audio books. What is really happening in our schools? Are textbooks disappearing? Is everyone connected? Are our students sitting all day laboring over a keyboard and staring at a screen? In this unit we will explore both the potential of the digital technology and the challenges of using this technology for teaching and learning.

There are significant trends noted by Bitter and Pierson (2002) that are important to this discussion. The first is the shift in demographics within our student population of increased numbers of students who do not live in traditional family structures, who have special needs at both the high and low ends of achievement, who are English Language Learners, or who live in poverty. For many of these students the ability to access sophisticated technology may not exist in their homes or neighborhoods. Hence, schools are the only place where they can be exposed to and made to learn about the usage of technology. These students, many of whom will need technology to access the curriculum, will pose a considerable challenge to public schools. An additional challenge, according to Bitter and Pierson, will be the acceleration of technological change that correspondingly increases the pace of change in our knowledge base. Keeping up in one's field of expertise or areas of interest has become a full-time job of its own.

In most schools, regardless of where the school is regionally or economically, most teachers who use computers do so because computers make their jobs easier and help them complete tasks more efficiently. The computer can do things the teacher cannot or is unwilling to do. We use them to keep digital grade books that will correctly calculate final grades in a flash; search for information to use in lectures; create photos and clip art to illustrate our PowerPoints; obtain lesson plans to meet state standards; and communicate with peers down the hall, the principal, and even with parents. But too often our computer may be the only computer in a classroom, or in a classroom with a LCD projector and white board. There may be a computer lab down the hall or a few computers in the media center, but very few schools have laptops or handheld devices for all students. So almost 100 years ago, Thomas Edison may have been a bit hasty to declare books a thing of the past. In fact, recently we published an article, *The Silicon Classroom* by Kaplan and Rogers (1996), in the *Education 98/99,* in which they declared that schools were rushing to spend billions on computers without a clue on what to do with them. In this issue, we are publishing an article that outlines the challenges that schools face today in implementing computer use in the classroom. Why haven't we seen greater strides made to bring every school into the digital age. We hope the articles presented in this unit will challenge you to consider how you should and will use technology to provide access to information within your content area curriculum.

The first article is meant to provide a glimpse of what is possible and what challenges still remain. Bonk notes that schooling and learning did not stop in the aftermath of hurricanes Katrina and Rita, but instead took on a new configuration. He suggests this is a model we should strive to attain in all schools. Discussions in five of the articles in this unit provide information about digital tools

© Ariel Skelley/Blend Images/Getty Images

that will help many students access the curriculum. Zascavage and Winterman explore the use of Universal Design for Learning (UDL) with assistive technology as the primary tool for differentiation. Schools have serious concerns about the costs of assistive technology that might be used by only one student. However, using UDL guidelines for making the curriculum accessible to a majority of students demonstrates that many types of technology may be considered assistive to a larger range of students.

We have examples of interesting technology use described by Ash in *Tech Tool Targets Elementary Readers.* Companies are working to develop low-cost devices that will put digital technologies into the hands of every student in a school district. Larson discusses the educational use of the increasingly popular digital readers. This technology has been available for 20 years, but is not being used widely by schools. This study demonstrates the Kindle, used by two second graders, promoted new literacy skills. Manzo found teachers using digital tools to individualize education plans for every student, regardless of ability. For example, Manzo describes a middle school that provides customized math lessons to every student every day using face-to-face instruction, software-based activities, and online lessons. Differentiation becomes less costly with Web 2.0 applications. These provide free and low-cost solutions to replace expensive technology and narrow the digital divide caused by budget constraints and poverty. We have heard in the mainstream media that playing video games is not good for children for any number of reasons. But where was the data? It is here in the article by Weis and Cerankosky describing their naturalistic research study of 64 boys, ages 6–9. They studied the effects of playing games on development of reading and writing skills. The results are what you might expect, but the reasons may be quite different. It seems that we are faced with two possibilities, being wrong in our predictions or being irrelevant luddites. It might be best if schools were somewhere along that continuum, but not at either extreme.

Reference

Bitter, G. & M. Pierson. 2002. *Using Technology in the Classroom.* Boston, MA: Allyn and Bacon.

"For Openers: How Technology Is Changing School"

Whether you're sailing around the world, homebound with the flu, or just in the market for more flexible learning, thanks to the Internet, schooling never stops.

Curtis J. Bonk

Sometimes it takes a major catastrophe to transform how we deliver schooling. In 2005, in the aftermath of Hurricanes Katrina and Rita, websites went up in Louisiana, Texas, and Mississippi to help educators, students, families, and school districts deal with the crisis. The Mississippi Department of Education (2005) announced free online courses at the high school level, and institutions from 38 states provided more than 1,300 free online courses to college students whose campuses had been affected by the hurricanes (Sloan-C, 2006).

Health emergencies in recent years have also caused educators to ponder the benefits of the Web. In 2003, during the SARS epidemic in China, government officials decided to loosen restrictions on online and blended learning (Huang & Zhou, 2006). More recently, as concerns about the H1N1 virus mounted, many U.S. schools piloted new educational delivery options, such as free online lessons from Curriki (www.curriki.org) and Smithsonian Education (www.smithsonianeducation.org). Microsoft has even offered its Microsoft Office Live free of charge to educators dealing with H1N1. The software enables teachers to share content, lesson plans, and other curriculum components, while students access the virtual classroom workspace, chat with one another on discussion topics, and attend virtual presentations.

Blended Learning Is Here

The focus today is on continuity of learning, whether learning is disrupted because of a hurricane or the flu—or because of other factors entirely. Schools may have difficulty serving students who live in rural areas; reduced budgets may limit the range of learning that a school can offer; people young and old involved in serious scholarly, artistic, or athletic pursuits may find it difficult to adhere to the traditional school structure.

In light of these developments, some school districts are resorting to blended learning options. They are using tools like Tegrity (www.tegrity.com); Elluminate (www.elluminate.com); and Adobe Connect Pro (www.Adobe.com/products/acrobatconnectpro) to provide online lectures. Many are developing procedures for posting course content and homework online. Some are trying phone conferencing with Skype (www.skype.com) or Google Talk (www.google.com/talk). Others are evaluating digital textbooks and study guides. Still others are sharing online videos from places like Link TV (www.linktv.org); FORA, tv (http://fora.tv); or TeacherTube (www.teachertube.com), with teachers often asking students to post their reflections in blogs or online discussion forums. Many schools have begun to foster teamwork by using Google Docs (http://docs.google.com) and wikis. Although some schools use e-mail to communicate messages district-wide, others are experimenting with text messaging or Twitter (http://twitter.com).

The wealth of information available online is also changing teaching practices. Teachers can access free online reference material, podcasts, wikis, and blogs, as well as thousands of free learning portals, such as the Periodic Table of Videos (www.periodicvideos.com) for chemistry courses and the Encyclopedia of Life (www.eol.org) for biology. Science teachers can use portals devoted to Einstein (www.alberteinstein.info); Darwin (www.darwin-online.org.uk); or Goodall (www.janegoodall.org). English teachers can find similar content repositories on Poe (www.eapoe.org); Shakespeare (http://shakespeare.mit.edu); and Austen (www.janeausten.org), to name just a few.

High School—Online

Tools like these enable great flexibility in learning. When I take a break from work and jog across my campus, smack in the middle of it I come to Owen Hall, home of the Indiana University High School (http://iuhighschool.iu.edu). Indiana University High School (IUHS) students can take their courses online or through correspondence or some combination of the two. Students range from those who live in rural settings to those who are homebound, homeschooled, pregnant, or gifted. Some are Americans living in other countries; some are natives of other countries whose parents want them to have a U.S. education. Some are dropouts or students academically at risk. Still others are teenagers about to enter college who need advanced placement courses or adults who want to finish their high school degrees (Robbins, 2009). Across the board, many of the 4,000 students enrolled in IUHS simply did not fit in the traditional U.S. high school setting.

Take 16-year-old Evren Ozan (www.ozanmusic.com), the Native American flute prodigy whose music I've enjoyed for several years. I'm listening to him as I write this sentence. Many of Evren's vast accomplishments—he's been recording music since he was 7 years old—would not have been possible without the online and distance education experiences he benefited from during his teen years when most of his peers were attending traditional high schools. Also attending IUHS is 15-year-old Ania Filochowska, a Polish-born violinist who has studied with several great masters of the violin in New York City since 2005. Similarly, Kathryn Morgan enrolled in IUHS so she could continue her quest to become a professional ballerina. With the flexibility of online courses and degrees, Kathryn danced full-time and pursued an apprenticeship with the New York City Ballet.

Then there is the amazing story of Bridey Fennell. Bridey completed four IUHS courses while enjoying a five-month sailboat journey with her parents and two sisters from Arcaju, Brazil, to Charleston, South Carolina. Ship dock captains and retired teachers proctored her exams in port, and she practiced her French lessons on different islands of the Caribbean. Her sister Caitlin posted updates about their daily activities to her blog, and elementary students in the Chicago area monitored the family's journey and corresponded with Caitlin.

We All Learn

All this raises the question of why so many people only see the benefits of online learning for musicians, dancers, athletes, and other performers or for those affected by some calamity. I personally benefited from nontraditional education a quarter of a century ago when I was taking correspondence and televised courses from the University of Wisconsin. Back then, I was a bored accountant, and distance learning was my only way out. It got me into graduate school and changed my life. I now speak, write books, and teach about the benefits of distance learning.

The 21st century offers us far more options to learn and grow intellectually. Today more than a million people in the United States alone are learning online.

To make sense of the vast array of Web-based learning opportunities possible today, I have developed a framework based on 10 *openers*—10 technological opportunities that have the potential to transform education by altering where, when, and how learning takes place. The openers form the acronym WE-ALL-LEARN.[1] They include

- **W**eb searching in the world of e-books.
- **E**-learning and blended learning.
- **A**vailability of open-source and free software.
- **L**everaged resources and open courseware.
- **L**earning object repositories and portals.
- **L**earner participation in open information communities.
- **E**lectronic collaboration.
- **A**lternate reality learning.
- **R**eal-time mobility and portability.
- **N**etworks of personalized learning.

Online and blended learning opportunities are just one opener (opener #2). Lets look at two more.

Web Searching in the World of e-Books

A decade ago, books were limited to being physical objects. Today, all that has changed. Government, nonprofit, and corporate initiatives are placing greater emphasis on digital book content.

The digital textbook project in Korea (www.dtbook.kr/eng), for instance, is being piloted in 112 schools with hopes of making textbooks free for all Korean schools by 2013. Digital textbooks include such features as dictionaries, e-mail applications, forum discussions, simulations, hyperlinks, multimedia, data searching, study aids, and learning evaluation tools.

Right behind Korea is California, which is steeped in a huge deficit. Governor Arnold Schwarzenegger is seeking ways out. One direction is a greater emphasis on digital education (Office of the Governor, 2009). By using digital books, California not only addresses its budgetary problems, but also assumes a leadership role in online learning. Officials in the state plan to download digital textbooks and other educational content into mobile devices that they will place in the hands of all students.

Some digital book initiatives are taking place at the district level. Vail School District in Arizona has adopted an approach called Beyond Textbooks (http://beyondtextbooks.org), which encourages the use of Web resources and shared teacher lesson plans geared to meet state standards (Lewin, 2009). Rich online videos, games, and portals of Web materials as well as podcasts of teacher lectures extend learning at Vail in directions not previously possible.

Innovative companies and foundations are also finding ways to offer free textbooks. Flat World Knowledge (www.flatworldknowledge.com) offers free online textbooks and also sells print-on-demand softcover textbooks, audio textbooks, and low-cost ancillary or supplemental materials, such as MP3 study guides, online interactive quizzes, and digital flashcards connected to each book. Using an open-content, Web-based collaborative model, the CK-12 Foundation (http://ckl2.org) is pioneering the idea of free FlexBooks that are customizable to state standards.

Digital books on mobile devices will move a significant chunk of learning out of traditional classroom settings. Hundreds of thousands of free e-books are now available online. You can search for them at places like Google; Many-Books.net (http://manybooks.net); LibriVox (www.librivox.org); the World Public Library (http://worldlibrary.net); the Internet Archive (www.archive.org); Bookyards.com (www.bookyards.com); and other e-book sites. Ironically, the majority of the top 25 best sellers on the Kindle are actually free (Kafka, 2009). We have entered the era of free books.

Real-Time Mobility and Portability

Mobile learning is the current mantra of educators. More than 60,000 people around the planet get mobile access to the Internet each hour (Iannucci, 2009), with 15 million people subscribing each month in India alone (Telecom Regulatory Authority of India, 2009). Also, if just one percent of the 85,000 applications for the iPhone (Marcus, 2009) are educational, thousands of possible learning adventures are at one's fingertips. It's possible to access grammar lessons, language applications, Shakespearean plays or quotes, physics experiments, musical performances, and math review problems with a mobile phone.

Online classes and course modules as well as teacher professional development are now delivered on mobile devices. As mobile learning advocate John Traxler (2007) points out, mobile professional development options are especially important in developing countries in Africa.

Mobile learning is not restricted to phones, of course. Laptops, iPods, MP3 players, flash memory sticks, digital cameras, and lecture recording pens all foster mobile learning pursuits as well as greater learning engagement. Educators need to thoughtfully consider where, when, and how to use such devices.

For instance, rather than ban mobile technologies, school officials might encourage students to record lectures with their pens or digital devices and listen to them while studying for quizzes and final exams. Or teachers might make available snippets of content that students can download to their mobile devices—such as French grammar lessons or quick guides to concepts in the study of chemistry, the human nervous system, or cell biology (Bonk, 2009).

When we think about mobile learning, we often just think of a mobile learner. But the deliverer of the learning might also be mobile. With the Web, our learning content might come from a climb up Mount Everest, expeditions to the Arctic or Antarctic, research at the bottom of an ocean, NASA flights far above us, or sailing adventures across the planet.

Michael Perham (www.sailmike.com) and Zac Sunderland (www.zacsunderland.com), for instance, each blogged and shared online videos of their record-setting solo sailing journeys around the globe. Amazingly, they each completed their adventures last summer at the tender age of 17. I could track their daily experiences and post comments in their blogs. They were my highly mobile teachers. I also learn from Jean Pennycook, a former high school science teacher who now brings scientific research on penguins in the Antarctic to classrooms around the world (see www.windows.ucar.edu/tour/link=/people/postcards/penguin_post.html).

Trends in the Open World

Given these myriad learning opportunities on the Web, you might wonder what is coming next. Here are some predictions.

- *Free as a book.* Digital books will not only be free, but readers will also be able to mix and match several of their components. E-books and classrooms will increasingly embed shared online video, animations, and simulations to enhance learning.
- *The emergence of super e-mentors and e-coaches.* Super e-mentors and e-coaches, working from computer workstations or from mobile devices, will provide free learning guidance. As with the gift culture that we have seen in the open source movement over the past two decades, some individuals will simply want to share their expertise and skills, whereas others may want practice teaching. Many will be highly educated individuals who have always wanted opportunities to teach, coach, or mentor but who work in jobs that do not enable them to

do so. Those with the highest credibility and in the most demand will have human development or counseling skills (perhaps a master's degree in counseling); understand how to use the Web for learning; and have expertise in a particular domain, such as social work, nursing, accounting, and so forth.

- *Selecting global learning partners.* Peers don't need to live down the street; they could be anywhere on the planet. Tools like Ning (www.ning.com) and Google Docs and resources like ePals (www.epals.com) and iEARN (International Education and Research Network; www.iearn.org) make global interactions ubiquitous. Global peer partners will form mini-school communities and unique school-based social networking groups. Projects might include learning how to cope with natural disasters, engaging in cultural exchanges, designing artwork related to human rights, exploring the effects of global warming, and learning about threats to animal habitats.
- *Teachers everywhere.* Soon students will be able to pick their teachers at a moment's notice. Want a teacher from Singapore, the Philippines, the United Kingdom, or Israel? They will be available in online teacher or mentor portals as well as preselected and approved by local school districts or state departments. Some will be displayed on a screen as students walk into school; students might consult this individual during a study hall period or review session.
- *Teacher as concierge.* The notion of a teacher will shift from a deliverer of content to that of a concierge who finds and suggests education resources as learners need them.
- *Informal = formal.* Informal learning will dramatically change the idea of "going to school," with a greater percentage of instructors being informal ones who offer content, experiences, and ideas to learners of all ages. Such individuals will include explorers on expeditions, researchers in a science lab, and practitioners in the workplace.
- *International academic degrees.* Consortia of countries will band together to provide international education using online courses and activities with the goal of offering a high school or community college degree.
- *Dropouts virtually drop back in.* The U.S. government will offer free online courses for high school dropouts and those needing alternative learning models (Jaschik, 2009). Such courses, as well as multiple options for learning, may lure students back to pick up a secondary or postsecondary degree. Interactive technology enhancements will appeal to teenagers and young adults savvy with emerging tools for learning.
- *The rise of the super blends.* As schools are faced with continued budgetary constraints and with the plethora of free courses, learning portals, and delivery technologies available, blended learning will become increasingly prevalent in K-12 education. Determining the most effective blend will be a key part of effective school leadership.
- *The shared learning era.* In the coming decade, the job of a K-12 teacher will include the willingness to share content with teachers in one's school district as well as with those far beyond. Teachers will also be called on to evaluate shared content.

- *Personalized learning environments.* Open educational resources (OER) and technologies like shared online videos podcasts, simulations, and virtual worlds will be available to enhance or clarify any lesson at any time (Bonk & Zhang, 2008). For example, Wendy Ermold, a researcher and field technician for the University of Washington Polar Science Center, conducts research in Greenland and in other northern locations on this planet. While out on the icebreakers or remote islands, she listens to lectures and reviews other OER content from MIT, Stanford, Seattle Pacific University, and Missouri State University to update her knowledge of physics and other content areas. The expansion of such free and open course content options will personalize learning according to particular learner needs or preferences.

- *Alexandrian Aristotles.* Learners will emerge who have the modern-day equivalent of the entire ancient library of Alexandria on a flash memory stick in their pocket or laptop. They will spend a significant amount of time learning from online tools and resources, will be ideal problem finders and solvers, and will set high personal achievement standards.

Open for Business

The world is open for learning. In addition to blended learning, e-books, and mobile learning, we are witnessing an increase in learner generation of academic content, collaboration in that content generation, and customization of the learning environment at significantly reduced costs and sometimes for free.

The 10 openers I suggest, push educators to rethink models of schooling and instruction. They are converging to offer the potential for a revolution in education—which is already underway.

Endnote

1. For a full discussion of the We-All-Learn framework, see my book, *The World Is Open; How Web Technology Is Revolutionizing Education* (Jossey-Bass, 2009).

References

Bonk. C.J. (2009). *The world is open: How Web technology is revolutionizing education.* San Francisco: Jossey-Bass.

Bonk, C. J., & Zhang, K. (2008). *Empowering online learning: 100+ activities for reading, reflecting, displaying, and doing.* San Francisco: Jossey-Bass.

Huang, R., & Zhou, Y. (2006). Designing blended learning focused on knowledge category and learning activities: Case sudies from Beijing. In C. J. Bonk & C. R. Graham (Eds.), *Handbook of blended learning: Global perspectives, local designs* (pp. 296–310), San Francisco: Pfeiffer.

Iannucci, B. (2009, January 7). *Connecting everybody to everything.* Nokia Research Center, Stanford University POMI (Programmable Open Mobile Internet), NSF research advisory meeting.

Jaschik, S. (2009, June 29). U.S. push for free online courses. *Inside Higher Ed.* Available: www.insidehighered.com /news/2009/06/29/ccplan.

Kafka, P. (2009, December). The secret behind the Kindle's best-selling e-books: They're not for sale. *CNET News.* Available: http://news.cnet.com/8301-1023_310422538-93.html.

Lewin, T. (2009, August 9). In a digital future, textbooks are history, *The New York Times.* Available: www.nytimes.com/2009/08/09 /education/09textbook.html.

Marcus, M. B. (2009, October 5). Pull yourself from that iPhone and read this story. *USA Today.* Available: www.usatoday.com /printedition/life/20091005/appaddiction05_st.art.htm.

Mississippi Department of Education. (2005, September). *Katrina recovery information.* Available: www.mde.k12.ms.us/Katrina.

Office of the Governor. (2009, May 6). Gov Schwarzenegger launches first-in-nation initiative to develop free digital textbooks for high school students (Press Release). Sacramento, CA: Author. Available: http://gov.ca.gov/press-release/12225.

Robbins, R. (2009, June 9). Distance students are "a varied and interesting lot." *Herald Times Online.* Available: www .heraldtimesonline.com/stories/2009/06/08/schoolnews .qp2930970.sto.

Sloan-C (2006, August 8). The Sloan Consortium honored for post-hurricane delivery of online courses. The Sloan semester. Available: www.sloan-c.org/sloansemester.

Telecom Regulatory Authority of India. (2009, June). Information note to the press (Press Release No 54/2009). Available: www.trai.gov.in/WriteReadData/trai/upload/PressReleases/687 /pr1june09no54.pdf.

Traxler, J. (2007, June). Defining, discussing, and evaluating mobile learning: The moving finger writes and having writ . . . *International Review of Research in Open and Distance Learning,* 8(1). Available: www.irrodl.org/index.php/irrodl /article/view/346/875.

Critical Thinking

1. Make a list of the ways that you use technology to learn or teach.

2. Work with a small group of peers to share your technology-use lists. Make a team list of all the ways you can teach or learn with technology.

3. Go online and open the Horizon Report: www.nmc .org/pdf/2010-Horizon-Report.pdf. Select one of the Six Top Technologies to research further. Explain how you might use the new information in your school.

CURTIS J. BONK is Professor of Instructional Systems Technology at Indiana University. He is the author of *The World Is Open: How Web Technology Is Revolutionizing Education* (Jossey-Bass, 2009) and coauthor, with Ke Zhang, of *Empowering Online Learning: 100+ Ideas, for Reading, Reflecting, Displaying, and Doing* (Jossey-Bass, 2008). He blogs at TravelinEdMan (http://travelinedmanblogspot .com); curt@worldisopen.com.

What Middle School Educators Should Know about Assistive Technology and Universal Design for Learning

This article reflects the following *This We Believe* characteristics: High expectations for every member of the learning community— Students and teachers engaged in active learning—Multiple learning and teaching approaches that respond to student diversity.

VICTORIA ZASCAVAGE AND KATHLEEN G. WINTERMAN

In the new millennium, the No Child Left Behind Act (2001) and the Individuals with Disabilities Education Improvement Act (IDEIA) (2004) ask educators to maximize opportunities for students with disabilities to succeed in inclusive classrooms. To make autonomy and integration seamless, many students with special needs will need to make use of assistive technology. The Individuals with Disabilities Education Act (IDEA) (1990) established the working definition of assistive technology as

> Any item, piece of equipment or product system, whether acquired or commercially off the shelf, modified or customized, that is used to increase, maintain, or improve the functional capabilities of children with disabilities.

(20 U.S.C. 1401 25, Sec. 300.5)

Since a technology decision is part of every Individual Educational Plan (IEP) for every student with a disability (Individuals with Disabilities Education Act Amendment, 1997), students who have sensory disabilities, such as hearing or vision, arrive at the middle school comfortable with their use of assistive technology devices. For the students with a specific learning disability who may not have needed technology at the elementary level, facing the increased demands of middle school can make a big difference. According to Gargiulo (2006), a majority of students with specific learning disabilities have reading and writing delays. Whereas, in the elementary years, students may not have needed the additional support, in middle school, technologies such as word prediction, spell check, graphic organizers, or books on tape may be necessary to facilitate successful adjustment.

Most middle school general educators are familiar with computer-enhanced instruction and the use of technology for research projects, presentations, and interactive learning software. As we restructure to meet the demand for equitable education for all students (No Child Left Behind, 2001), Universal Design for Learning becomes an important tool. Universal Design for Learning (UDL) is research-based model for curricular design that ensures participation in the general educational program of all students, including those with disabilities (Center for Applied Special Technology (CAST), 2007). UDL emerged from the original work of Ron Mace, a renowned architect, whose work changed the blueprint of American architectural design. He designed buildings based on the needs of the intended users of the space (CAST, 2007). Mace's overarching principle was to accommodate the widest spectrum of users, including those with disabilities, without the need for subsequent adaptation or special design. In the early 1990s the staff at CAST began to expand Mace's principle to incorporate the concept of Universal Design to adapt curricula that met the needs of all learners. The goal was information accessibility for all learners. UDL supports learners by providing teachers with varying methodology options for presenting information and content. The incorporation of technology has been one way to make this happen.

In the inclusive middle school, the principles of UDL, a form of differentiated instruction, allow all students access to the methods, materials, and technology that will maximize their learning. The framework of a UDL classroom begins with curricula designed to maintain high expectations for all types of learners. In this manner, UDL uses technology to supplement and enhance individualized assessment and instruction (CAST, 2007).

Overview of Assistive Technology

The 1997 amendments to IDEA assigned the final responsibility for the decisions on assistive technology services provided to students and their families to the Individualized Education Plan (IEP) team. Since 1997, we no longer confine evaluation for assistive technology to disability issues of such a severe nature that assistive technology becomes an easily recognizable need. Technology access is now an entitlement for all students protected by IDEA (i.e., students with IEPs). The IDEA Amendments of 1997, PL 105-17, state that *schools* will provide service to assist the individual with a disability to select, acquire, or use appropriate assistive technology. This includes (a) evaluation of need; (b) purchasing, customizing, and maintaining the assistive technology selected; (c) coordinating use with other services, interventions, or therapies; and (d) training the family, the teacher, and the child with a disability to use the equipment (20 U.S.C. 1401 (26)).

The first step for the selection of assistive technology starts with determination of need. Middle school teachers looking for ways to individualize, provide repetition and feedback, objectively measure progress, collect data to analyze performance, and increase their students' interest and engaged time look to computer assisted instruction (Kilgore, Griffin, Sindelar, & Webb, 2002). Middle school teachers who need to increase students' (a) ease of access to important information, (b) ability to explore and generate information independently, (c) decoding and reading comprehension skills, and (d) productivity of written assignments look to assistive technology (Forgrave, 2002). See Figure 1 for an overview of the process for selecting technology in a language arts classroom.

Assistive Technology in the UDL Classroom

This article focuses on the inclusion of students with learning disabilities who are demonstrating difficulties in reading and writing in middle school classrooms. Assistive technology to build academic strength and independence for students with learning disabilities in literacy focuses on speech recognition programs, screen reading software, organizational software, and word prediction programs used in conjunction with access to spelling and grammar check on a personal computer.

Speech Recognition Programs

Speech recognition software works well for students with a written language disability or with a deficit in short-term memory. A Southwest middle school student, Austin, who has learning disabilities in written language, handwriting, and spelling, would initially enter into the computer his handwritten papers using speech recognition software. The computer would correctly spell the words for Austin and provide him with a legible copy of the composition for editing. Eventually, Austin would

use the computer to dictate the assignment. Dictation helped Austin get his ideas on paper before he forgot what he wanted to say. Austin's parents purchased the technology so that he could use it for his homework assignments. As Austin's fine motor skills matured and he gained confidence in his writing ability, he used the computer keyboard more often when composing.

Speech recognition software lets the student control the computer by speaking into a microphone. Students can write using speech recognition software and the computer's standard word processing program. The voice file is user specific and stores patterns of word usage for the student. Speech recognition programs sell for under $100 and work with newer computer hardware. The greatest expense may well be the cost of training for teachers and ongoing support; initial training could take up to five hours per teacher. The software manufacturer or distributor of *Speaking to Write* (Special Needs Opportunity Window, 2007) often provides the training session free.

In the UDL middle school, the speech recognition software is often located in a common location such as the library. Since the technology is sensitive to noise, a busy classroom is not the optimum place for this tool. All students who have a need for a close examination of their written work or who feel they can be more creative using speech recognition software are encouraged to make use of the technology. Voice recognition software improves reading comprehension, spelling, and word recognition scores for the typical student (Higgins & Raskind, 2000).

Text-to-Speech Technology

Timothy, a middle school student from an affluent suburban community in the Southwest, had a learning disability in reading: specifically word recognition, word analysis, and comprehension. When Timothy entered middle school, he did not want to spend time isolated in a resource classroom taking corrective reading. Timothy read several grade levels below his classmates, despite extensive private tutoring. Timothy was struggling to keep up academically, but he was adamant about being a "regular kid." He would not do any work that made him look different. By having Timothy's textbooks, assignments, and classroom handouts scanned into the computer, he could read independently in the regular classroom. Because the teachers understood the importance of Universal Learning Design, several classrooms in Timothy's sixth grade created a learning center based on auditory input. The center, decorated in student-friendly décor, had books on tape, computers with outstanding headphones, and comfortable chairs. It was a privilege to be able to spend time in the Auditory Center. Students who liked to draw while they listened to the assigned chapter could program the computer to scan and read the chapter. Students using text-to-speech could download books from the Internet and click on unfamiliar words as they read. In content areas in which technical vocabulary can be difficult to pronounce, this software took the guesswork out of decoding complex vocabulary, leaving more time for understanding new concepts. Students who had visual impairments or who needed to use auditory enhancement also found the Auditory Center very useful.

Text-to-speech technology reads the words from a computer document in an audible, computerized voice. This technology also works in conjunction with optical character recognition software (scanners) and reads aloud the documents scanned into the computer. It also reads standard word processing documents and, depending upon the program, it will read the text boxes on the Internet. Text-to-speech is not a screen reader, as it does not read system information. This software is commonly available in PC accessories packages and is a standard feature on most computers today. For a more soothing voice production, you must purchase other software programs. This form of technology may be a hand held device such as the Quick Link Pen by Wiz Com, which has a text-to-speech package combined with an optical scanner and an audio package. Text-to-Speech programs also read word-by-word as the student types, or sentence-by-sentence. To allow students to benefit from this technological intervention, there is a large commitment to daily organization, scanning of text, and computerized versions of presentation and lessons. The software packages range in price from free to more than $1,000.

More than half of the students with learning disabilities have reading problems (Lerner, 2003; Garguilo, 2006). Heward (2006) suggested 90% of students with learning disabilities also have issues with reading. Problems in comprehension, word recognition, phonological awareness, and word analysis are examples of reading problems that might benefit from technology intervention. Studies have verified that the use of text-to-speech provides remedial benefits by increasing word recognition and decoding abilities. The multisensory use of auditory stimulation and visual input raises both reading and comprehension levels (Forgrave, 2002) and is an effective teaching strategy to support all learners.

Technology to Facilitate Written Composition

George, a middle school student labeled as severely language disabled, transferred in the seventh grade to a suburban school in the Southwest from a rural school in the Southeast. When George arrived, he had no experience with assistive technology, typed with two fingers, tested at the first grade level in spelling, but could read proficiently at the 10th grade level. George wrote nothing and had a negative attitude toward writing. Had it not been for assistive technology, George would have had extreme difficulty keeping up in an inclusive classroom. The challenge the special education team met was convincing

Figure 1 Selection process for technology use in the language classroom

1. **The Lesson and the Learner**
   a. What do you want the student to do? Example: write a short story, investigate Web sites on environmental issues, have an interactive chat about the Civil War. _____
   b. Will technology increase the interest level of the typical student? Y / N
   c. Will technology create a distraction from the purpose of the activity for the typical student? Y / N
   d. What are the concerns within the classroom for students with special needs for this lesson: hearing _____, vision _____, movement _____, attention _____, and/or reading level _____?
   e. Is technology access essential for the student with special needs to participate? Y / N If so, which students? _____

2. **Group Work**
   a. Are the students going to work in groups or on their own? _____
   b. Will technology enable the students with a disability to participate in the activity and/or in the group? Y / N If so, which students? _____
   c. How will the technology make participation possible? (For example, will the use of an Alpha Smart word processor enable the student with dysgraphia to take notes for the group?) _____

3. **Availability**
   a. How are students going to share the available hardware? (For example, are all 20 students going to need access to a software-based graphic organizer to collect their thoughts for a project?) _____ (sign up sheet, time slots, etc.)
   b. Do the students with disabilities have available the technology specified in their individualized education plan? _____
   c. Who is going to assist students with disabilities in accessing the technology? The teacher _____, peers _____, paraprofessional _____, special education co-teacher _____, other _____?
   d. What level of assistance do we expect to make technology use possible for the student with disabilities: full-time involvement _____, occasional involvement _____, or planning only _____?
   e. What level of assistance do we expect to make technology use possible for the typical student: full-time involvement _____, occasional involvement _____, or planning only _____?
   f. Who is going to assist the typical student in accessing the technology? The teacher _____, peers _____, paraprofessional _____, special education co-teacher _____, other _____?

4. **Assessment**
   a. Did the use of technology increase interest in the activity? Y/ N If so, how? _____
   b. Did the use of technology benefit learning? Y / N If so, how? _____
   c. Did the use of technology allow all students to participate? Y /N If so, how? _____
   d. What would I do differently the next time? _____

George to try composing using invented spelling and a word processor. The first step in this persuasion was to let George use the Paint Software to draw out science concepts such as Newton's Laws of Motion. George understood the concepts; he just had no way to convey this understanding in a written form. With some positive reinforcement and very caring, patient teachers, George moved gradually into using the pictures and the diagrams in Inspiration, a graphic organizer software package, to convey his thoughts. George was a very creative writer who had kept vivid, imaginative stories locked inside. Once he trusted the technology, George tried invented spelling with the word prediction software. Due to his advanced reading skills, he easily found the correct word and substituted it for his imagined spelling. As George matured as a writer, he used the spell check function more often than word prediction. At the end of seventh grade, George was writing short stories and plays about a ferocious world of imaginary creatures. Although a standardized test of spelling revealed at the end of the year that he was still on a second grade level, his plays composed with the aid of assistive technology and typed with two fingers, were organized, descriptive, and written on a ninth grade level.

Word prediction software assists with text entry by predicting the word you are attempting to type. Predictions rely on the statistics of word frequency within specific context and grade level. For example if you type the letter "g" it will give you a selection of common words beginning with "g" (go, get, gap, got, give), which, when highlighted, will be placed into your word processing document. Word prediction without speech output is a very useful tool for individuals with a written language disability who read at, or slightly below, grade level. Additional options of a word prediction package may include spell checks, speech synthesis, and hotkeys for frequently used words. Supplementary features (e.g., vocabulary expansion using interactive or semantic categories) bolster the language competence of students with a language disability. This system, if combined with a text-to-speech software package, synthesizes visual, auditory, and kinesthetic reinforcement to augment word retrieval skills (Assistive technology products, SNOW, 2006).

Word prediction technology can also work in conjunction with the standard spell check and grammar check on the personal computer. Students writing reports, presenting projects, detailing experiments, and composing original short stories are typical of middle school students. Word prediction helps the marginal speller work independently. Students are also encouraged to take advantage of the computer's spell check and grammar check features. Gaining confidence and independence in written work is a challenge for all middle school students progressing through the stages of written language proficiency.

Students with a learning disability in written language typically use simple sentence structure within truncated, poorly organized paragraphs (Hallahan, Lloyd, Kaufman, Weiss, & Martinez, 2005). Inspiration, a software package, helps students create picture-enhanced outlines and concept mapping for thought organization. This flexible technology is an example of a Universal Learning Design concept, as it is of value to both students with a learning disability and those without. Both groups of

Figure 2 Technology in a UDL classroom

Provides a variety of ways the student can demonstrate a skill, (e.g., written, oral recording, video presentation, word process).

Supplements limited background knowledge by using graphic organizers such as pictures downloaded to a computer file. This visual can be accessed either from a picture file already on the computer or from the Internet. Access for some children might involve using a variety of switches, head controls, or voice recognition software.

Diversifies by using multiple media and formats for lessons (e.g., text version of book, books on tape, online or digital resources, interactive computer module with immediate feedback).

Encourages students to use computer highlighting features to mark important material and help all the students prioritize. Highlighting critical features is a best practice teaching method for students with attention problems.

Offers all children the choice to wear headphones and listen to music or soft background sounds during quiet seatwork or testing. Some children become overstimulated or distracted by the environment.

students can use the outlines format, hyperlinks, Web enhancements, and progressive complexity to organize their thoughts. For all students, but particularly for students with learning disabilities who frequently exhibit deficits in metacognition, this writing technology helps focus attention, clarify purpose, and monitor personal achievement (Garguilo, 2006).

Teachers and Assistive Technology Decisions

To meet the mandates of NCLB and to implement the concept of Universal Learning Design in education, the typical middle school teacher will need to be computer literate, knowledgeable about current technology, and aware of the learners' specific assistive technology needs (CAST, 2007; Resta, Bryant, Lock, & Allan, 1998). Technology changes so rapidly that keeping up with the most recent technology applications challenges the most capable teacher. It is a challenge even for specialized technology personnel. Ideally, each school will have its own core Assistive Technology (AT) Team and not have to rely on a small group of experts disbursed throughout an entire district. Depending on your school district and the needs of individuals with a learning disability, the AT Team might include any or all of the following professionals:

- Occupational therapist: access issues and advise on curriculum
- Educators, special and regular: academic aptitudes, study habits, learning styles, adaptations and accommodations, and curriculum-based assessments
- Speech pathologist/therapist: communication and language problems
- County Educational Service Center expert on assistive technology

- Administration: funding issues and timeline on requested technology; arrangements for staff development for technology use
- The students' parents

Many schools already have this core group of professionals in place. These educators typically act as part of the Intervention Assistance Teams (IAT) or are part of each child's IEP educational team. Additional resources are not necessary to develop an Assisted Technology (AT) Team.

AT teams initially may be frightened away from suggesting the use of AT due to the perceived costs. There is a wide spectrum in levels of technology in AT from no technology to high technology. Providing students with AT is an important part of the "free and appropriate public education" that is guaranteed in IDEA (2004). Families and students cannot bear the burden of the costs associated with the child's education. School districts can access a variety of providers to assist with acquiring AT for students. In Ohio, the Special Education Regional Resource Centers (SERRC) loan devices to school districts free of charge. Ohio School Net is an agency that offers technological support as well as devices for all students including those with disabilities. The county Educational Service Centers also loan devices to schools and provide technical support. Other supports to schools and families regarding AT include the Bureau for Children with Medical Handicaps (BCMH), Family Resource Services, Medicaid, and private insurance.

Daily classroom technology decisions made by general educators are an essential part of instructional planning. These decisions affect all children in the class, with or without exceptionalities. Depending on the type of technology chosen, the teacher must be aware of environmental issues such as noise, distraction, or potential academic compromises (Can they use it to cheat?) that this technology will bring to the classroom.

When we look at the concept of the word "universal" in Universal Learning Design, it becomes apparent that one methodology will not work for all students. Answers to the question: "What are the student's cognitive abilities and how will they interface with technology?" will assist general educators, special educators, and the assistive technology team in working together to provide an inclusive environment for all students. Figure 2 summarizes the role of assistive technology in UDL classrooms.

The transition from elementary school to middle school is a challenge for all students. For students with learning disabilities, the complexity of their distinct learning needs magnifies the transition. In the past, the term "universal design" simply meant eliminating the physical barriers to learning by providing accessibility. IDEIA and NCLB require reducing barriers to cognitive access to learning. This has created a paradigm shift in the manner in which teachers design and implement their lessons. The challenges teachers face center around meeting the dynamic needs of a variety of learners while maintaining rigorous standards for all. UDL is a research-based framework for designing curricula (CAST, 2007). Both IDEIA and NCLB mandate high-quality standards for all students, yet neither law

addresses implementation. UDL establishes a framework for designing lessons that meet the needs of all learners. Through word prediction software, access to spelling and grammar check on a personal computer, and simple devices such as a tape recorder, curricula can be developed that allow each child to demonstrate his or her knowledge and understanding. Throughout this article, descriptions detailed how middle school teachers have been successfully using technology in the UDL classroom for the benefit of their students. In today's middle school, teachers provide the expertise, UDL provides the philosophy, and technology provides the tools to enable all students to become productive members of their class.

References

Center for Applied Special Technology (CAST). (2007). What is Universal Design for Learning? Retrieved March 1, 2007, from www.cast.org/research/udl/index.html.

Forgrave, K. (2002). Assistive technology: Empowering students with learning disabilities. *The Clearing House, 75*(3), 122–126.

Garguilo, R. (2006). *Special education in contemporary society.* Belmont, CA: Thomson & Wadsworth.

Hallahan, D., Lloyd, J., Kaufman, J., Weiss, M., & Martinez, E. (2005). *Learning disabilities: Foundations, characteristics and effective teaching* (3rd ed.). Boston: Pearson Education.

Heward, W. L. (2006). *Exceptional children: An introduction to special education* (8th ed.). New York: Prentice-Hall.

Higgins, E. L., & Raskind, M. H. (2000). Speaking to Read: The effects of continuous vs. discrete Speech Recognition Systems on the reading and spelling of children with learning disabilities, *Journal of Special Education Technology, 15*(1), 19–30.

Individuals with Disabilities Education Act 1990, 34 CFR 300.6 (Authority: 20 U.S.C 1401 2); 300.308 (Authority: 20 U.S.C 1412 (a)(12)(B)(i).

Individuals with Disabilities Education Act Amendments 1997, Pl-105-17; 34 CFR 300.6 (Authority: 20 U.S.C 1401 2): 300. 308 (Authority: 20 U.S.C 1412 (a)(12)(B)(i).

Individuals with Disabilities Education Improvement Act of 2004, Pl-108-446. Retrieved May 9, 2007, from www.nichcy.org /reauth/Pl.108-446.pdf.

Kilgore, K., Griffin, C., Sindelar, P., & Webb, R. (2002). Restructuring for inclusion: Changing teaching practices (Part II). *Middle School Journal, 33*(3), 7–13.

Lerner, J. (2003). *Learning disabilities* (9th ed.). Boston: Houghton Mifflin.

No Child Left Behind Act of 2001, Pl-107-110. Retrieved February 24, 2007, from www.ed.gov/policy/elsec/leg/esea02/index .html.

Resta, P., Bryant, P., Lock, R., & Allan, J. (1998). Infusing a teacher preparation program in learning disabilities with assistive technology. *Journal of Learning Disabilities, 31*, 55–66.

Special Needs Opportunity Window (SNOW). (2006). Assistive Technology. *Assistive technology products.* Retrieved October 2, 2006, from http://snow.utoronto.ca/technology/product.

Special Needs Opportunity Window (SNOW). (2007). Assistive Technology. *Speaking to Write.* Retrieved February 2, 2007, from http://snow.utoronto.ca/technology/product.

Critical Thinking

1. Reread the definition of assistive technology (AT) at the beginning of the article. Now make a list of the items found in most K-12 classrooms that might fit the definition of AT. Compare your list with others in the class and add items you missed.

2. Consider the grade level or content area that you teach or will teach. What AT would be most useful to all of your students, including those with disabilities? Refer to Figure 2 in the article for support of your choices. Also, several articles in this unit offer additional technology tools that will help you build UDL teaching activities and learning experiences.

3. Explain how Universal Design for Learning can provide support to teachers as they implement No Child Left Behind (NCLB) and Response to Intervention (RTI).

4. Visit the web page at www.cast.org/teachingeverystudent/tools/main.cfm?t_id=10. Here you can participate in an activity that will help you understand the brain research that supports UDL. What did you learn during the interactive activity that supports the information in this article? How will the activity help you develop learning activities for your students?

VICTORLA ZASCAVAGE is an assistant professor of secondary education and special education services at Xavier University, Cincinnati, Ohio. E-mail: zascavagev@xavier.edu. KATHLEEN G. WINTERMAN is an assistant professor of secondary education and special education services at Xavier University, Cincinnati, Ohio. E-mail: wintermank1@xavier.edu.

Tech Tool Targets Elementary Readers

A Game Boy-like device now being used by 40,000 students in 15 states aims to improve the reading skills of K-2 students.

KATIE ASH

Much attention has been paid to how mobile-learning devices can be incorporated into middle and high schools, but Seth Weinberger is targeting a different set of students: kindergartners through 2nd graders.

"The sweet spot of literacy is kindergarten to 2nd grade," says Weinberger, the executive director of Innovations for Learning, the Evanston, Ill.-based nonprofit organization that developed a mobile-learning device called the TeacherMate. "If you get them [reading on grade level] early, there's a real chance that you can keep them at grade level."

TeacherMates are now being used by more than 40,000 students in 15 states, says Weinberger, and there are plans to adapt the TeacherMate software into applications for the iPod touch or iPad. And the decision to target the devices at elementary youngsters has attracted the attention of ed-tech researchers, some of whom say the elementary grades are where such devices could have their greatest impact on improving reading skills.

Cathleen A. Norris, a professor of learning technologies at the University of North Texas and the chief education architect for the Ann Arbor, Mich.-based company GoKnow, which provides educational technology, software, and curriculum to K-12 schools, says that "what you must do is catch [the students] at the early grades and make them successful. When children are experiencing success in early grades, they spend more time with [the subject]."

On the heels of the One Laptop Per Child initiative, which aims to provide low-cost laptop computers to students in developing countries, Weinberger wanted to create a relatively affordable, easy-to-use mobile-learning device for students in the United States. "Schools are unbelievably strapped for cash," says Weinberger.

The TeacherMate device itself costs about $40, although with the reading and math software that has been developed for it, the total cost is about $100 per device. That's not cheap, but it's well below the cost of putting a laptop or netbook computer in the hands of all those youngsters.

Evaluating Effectiveness

Preliminary data on the effectiveness of the device are promising, although more research is needed, says William H. Teale, a professor of education in the department of curriculum and instruction at the University of Illinois at Chicago. His review of a pilot program, which put TeacherMates in 176 1st grade classrooms in the 409,000-student Chicago school district, found that students who used the devices performed higher on their end-of-year reading tests in three categories than those who did not have the devices.

Still, Teale cautions in his review: "Because of its design, this study does not speak to the issue of a causal connection between the use of the hand-held learning systems . . . and enhanced early reading achievement."

And no research is currently available on the effectiveness of the math software for TeacherMates.

The Game Boy-like device fits into the palm of a student's hand and is controlled by eight buttons. It includes a speaker that both plays back sounds and allows students to record their own audio, a screen, and a USB slot to synchronize the devices with the teacher's computer.

To use TeacherMates, teachers need a USB cable and a computer with an Internet connection where they can sync the devices, change the levels of the software that the students are working on, check on how well students are using the software, and listen to what the students have recorded during their lessons.

Instead of teachers' needing to incorporate the Teacher-Mate into the curriculum, the TeacherMate is equipped to align directly with whatever math or reading curriculum the teacher is using, says Weinberger. That aspect of the device appeals to Patti Beyer, a 1st grade teacher at the 750-student New Field Elementary School in Chicago.

"The stories that they're working on are the stories we're reading. The letters [on the device] are the letters that we're working on." she says. "Every concept we hit is addressed by the TeacherMate."

And not only is the device easy for teachers to use. it's easy for students to pick up and learn, too, says Jenna Kelsey, a 1st grade teacher at the 750-student James Russell Lowell Elementary School, also in Chicago. She uses the devices for 15 to 20 minutes a day, usually as part of rotating centers where students spend some time reading on their own, with a teacher, and with the TeacherMate.

"They're so used to hand-held games as it is that they are able to just play the game without much assistance," she says. As a result, Kelsey is freed up to work with pupils one-on-one or in small groups.

Reinforce and Practice

Although students can usually navigate the TeacherMate software by themselves, the devices are not designed to be used on their own but to accompany teachers' lessons, says Weinberger of Innovations for Learning, which developed the devices. Rather than being used to introduce new material and concepts to students, TeacherMates are intended to reinforce and practice skills that students are actively learning in their teacher-led classes, he says.

X. Christine Wang, an associate professor of learning and instruction at the State University of New York at Buffalo, is not familiar with the TeacherMate specifically, but she speculates that hand-held devices used for reinforcement and practice may not be making use of their full educational potential.

"The majority of researchers and teachers are now against the drill-practice type of learning" with technology, she says. "When we take children's active thinking out of learning, we take children's curiosity out of learning."

Hand-held tools that allow access to the Internet, which do not include the TeacherMate, not only can be appropriate for elementary youngsters, but also can help foster collaboration and expand the walls of the classroom, says Wang.

But Kelsey, the teacher at Lowell Elementary in Chicago, sees the lack of Internet capability as an advantage of the TeacherMate. Because students can only access the software that she has downloaded and put on the devices, she can be sure that all her students are on task, unlike in the computer lab, where she has to monitor what each child is doing.

"I already know what's going on [the devices] because I put it there," she says.

Because each student has his or her own device, it's easy to differentiate instruction, says Beyer, from New Field Elementary.

"It's all individualized," Beyer says, and it takes away the stigma of some students' needing more reinforcement of a concept than others do.

Throughout the year that Kelsey has used the devices, they have malfunctioned occasionally, but usually just require a restart, she says. Innovations for Learning provides technical support if teachers run into more serious issues, she says.

Going Global

TeacherMates are also making their way into the hands of children around the world, thanks to the efforts of Paul Kim, the chief technology officer for Stanford University. Over the past year, Kim has traveled to Costa Rica, Mexico, Nicaragua, Rwanda, and other countries to provide educational materials, including TeacherMates, to children who are not receiving any formal education.

"I found it very useful because kids love them, and I don't have to teach them anything," he says. Even children who had never seen similar technologies can pick one of the devices up and start learning, he says. The software's game-based approach, says Kim, helps youngsters learn on their own and engages those who may not be used to traditional instructional methods.

The platform that runs the software, which uses Flash, a multimedia platform popular for creating animations and interactivity, also makes it easy to develop new software for the TeacherMate, he says.

The durability of the devices has also made the TeacherMate a good candidate for Kim's project.

"There is a growing digital divide, and we are leaving a big chunk of our society behind," he says. "I like to give these children who have no access whatsoever to have an opportunity to reach their potential by giving them [this technology]."

Critical Thinking

1. What is a TeacherMate? How is it being used in K-2 classrooms?

2. Do you think that technology is appropriate for children in K-2 classes to use to complete reading activities? Provide a rationale for your answer.

Digital Readers: The Next Chapter in E-Book Reading and Response

E-books have the potential to unveil an array of new teaching and learning possibilities as traditional and new literacy skills are integrated in meaningful ways.

LOTTA C. LARSON

A visit to a local bookstore or online book vendor will undoubtedly confirm the recent bombardment of digital readers, also known as digital reading devices or e-book readers. A digital reading device stores hundreds of books, newspapers, magazines, and blogs; allows for quick look-up of information through its built-in dictionary, Wikipedia, or internal search capabilities; and offers customizable settings to suit each unique reader. Although the Amazon Kindle, Sony Reader and Barnes & Noble Nook are common, other,l esser-known products are also available, each offering varying features and capabilities (see Table 1).

As an avid Kindle reader and teacher educator, I am intrigued by the potential of using digital readers in classroom settings. Recent studies of e-book reading and response behaviors suggested that e-book reading may support comprehension and strengthen both aesthetic and efferent reader response (Larson, 2008, 2009). This article recognizes the continued evolution

of e-book technologies by taking a closer look at children's involvement with and response to digital readers. In particular, I will explain the basic features of digital reading devices and discuss how they can advance e-book readership among primary students by offering new avenues for accessing and interacting with a wide array of texts.

Digital Reading and Responding

In today's classrooms, reading instruction, along with the broader notion of literacy instruction, is undergoing tremendous transformations as new technologies demand new literacy skills (Leu, Kinzer, Coiro, & Cammack, 2004). The International Reading Association (IRA; 2009) emphasized the importance of integrating information and communication technologies (ICTs) into current literacy programs. A first step toward integrating new literacies into existing reading programs often involves redefining the notion of what constitutes *text,* as teachers seek alternative text sources including digital texts and electronic books (Booth, 2006; Kucer, 2005).

Traditionally, text was seen as "a passage of print or a slice of speech, or an image" (Lankshear, 1997. p. 45). Thus, texts were perceived as written-down messages and symbols in the forms of books, magazines, and newspapers. Today, texts are professed as much more than written words or images.

Bearne (2005) argued that most children are immersed in multimodal experiences and, therefore, have a keen awareness of the possibility of combining modes and media to create a message. This awareness results in an urgent need for teachers and researchers to address the discrepancy between the types of literacy experiences students encounter at school and those they practice in their daily lives outside the school environment.

Although early forms of electronic books have been available for almost two decades, studies examining how students

Table 1   Digital Readers

Device/brand	Manufacturer	For more information
Kindle	Amazon	www.amazon.com
Nook	Barnes & Noble	www.barnesandnoble.com
Sony Reader	Sony	www.sonystyle.com
Cybook OPUS	Bookeen	bookeen.com/ebook/ebook-reading-device.aspx
iLiad	IREX	www.irextechnologies.com
iPad	Apple	www.apple.com/ipad

interact with and respond to e-book texts are still few and results are somewhat conflicting. Although multimodal features (animations, sounds, etc.) of interactive e-books may potentially distract children as they read and make sense of the story (Burrell & Trushell, 1997; Matthew, 1996), reading motivation appears higher after children interact with multimodal texts, especially among children with reading difficulties (Glasgow, 1996).

Fasimpaur (2004) proposed that students find e-books to be "a new and unique medium" (p. 12) and consequently often read more when having access to e-books. Furthermore, because e-books can be presented in an individualized format, students with special needs (ELL, visually impaired, struggling readers) may benefit from the additional text tools available with the use of electronic texts.

The transactional theory of reader response (Rosenblatt, 1938, 1978) supports that readers "make sense" of reading experiences as they apply, reorganize, revisit, or extend encounters with text and personal experiences. Central to this theory is the interaction of the reader, author, and text as the reader engages in personal meaning-making of the text (Hancock, 1993). Although a reader may not physically change print text, digital texts can literally transform as the reader uses tools and settings available within the digital text format (Eagleton & Dobler, 2007).

Some forms of electronic books, with their potential for multimodal texts and multidimensional representations of a message, challenge the linear, right-to-left and top-down processing that is the norm for most written texts (Leu, 2002; Reinking, 1998). At first glance, digital readers present texts in a traditional format: the screen of a digital reader looks like a "traditional" book. However, as will be discussed later in this article, a plethora of tools and features allow the reader to physically interact with and manipulate the text, making the reading experience interactive and engaging.

Rooted in cognitive constructivist theory, the New Literacies perspective (Leu et al., 2004) acknowledges that new literacies are persistently evolving and challenges teachers to transform reading instruction in response to emerging ICTs. Traditional definitions of reading and writing are insufficient in today's world as today's students encounter and interact with new digital literacies, including digital texts such as e-books (IRA, 2009). This study builds upon past research of transactional reader response theory, while recognizing the need for future studies as textual transformations continually occur with the arrival of new literacies and emerging ICTs.

Methodology, Participants, and Data Collection

The site of this study is located in the Midwestern United States in a K–12 district serving approximately 6,000 students. Mrs. Miles, the classroom teacher, is an avid proponent of technology integration who encouraged her 17 second graders to read online texts, blog about their reading experiences, and engage in online literature discussions.

With only one classroom computer, Mrs. Miles relied heavily on a ceiling-mounted LCD projector to display the computer screen during whole-class instruction. Through shared literacy experiences, her students frequently read and responded to digital texts. During weekly visits to the school's computer lab, the second graders practiced independent computer skills or engaged in Internet explorations. In addition, Mrs. Miles encouraged her students to use the class blog to share their opinions about books that they read in class.

Prior to this study, Mrs. Miles had heard about digital readers but had no personal experience with this technology. After briefly exploring an Amazon Kindle, Mrs. Miles visited Amazon.com to select and download books that were of interest to and at appropriate reading levels for her second graders.

With access to only two Kindles, Mrs. Miles explained to her students that they would take turns using the digital readers. With the help of a visual presenter and LCD projector, she read aloud and modeled the basic functions of the Kindle. She explained how to turn it on and off, insert notes, change the font size, and use the dictionary. Students were told that they were welcome to use any of these functions but not required to do so. She also identified the following two girls, Amy and Winnie (pseudonyms), of diverse reading levels and ethnic/linguistic backgrounds, on which this small case study would focus:

- Amy was a 7-year-old Caucasian girl who, in October, read at a beginning second-grade level and expressed strong verbal and written communication skills. She viewed herself as a "good, but not very fast reader." She explained that she loves books about animals. Her teacher described her as outgoing, funny, and social.
- Winnie was an 8-year-old Asian girl who is fluent in Chinese and speaks English as a second language. At the beginning of second grade, Winnie read independently at a fifth-grade level and was described by her teacher as quiet, calm, and very serious. Winnie considered herself a "very good reader" and her favorite books included the Harry Potter series.

Mrs. Miles suggested that both girls would read *Friendship According to Humphrey* by Betty G. Birney (2006). Recommended for grades 2–4, this book is written from the perspective of a classroom pet hamster who resides in Mrs. Brisbane's

---

Pause and Ponder

- How do digital readers support reader response, vocabulary development, and reading comprehension?
- How can teachers use the insights gained from students' response notes to plan for future reading instruction?
- Picture your own classroom. How could digital readers meet the unique needs of each of your students? Which student(s) would benefit the most from using e-book readers?

classroom. For three weeks, I observed Amy and Winnie read and respond to the Kindle edition of *Friendship According to Humphrey* for 40 minutes daily. While reading, Amy and Winnie physically interacted with the text by using tools and features unique to the Kindle. For example, the girls adjusted the font size, listened to parts of the story by activating the text-to-speech feature, highlighted key passages or vocabulary, used the built-in dictionary, and searched for keywords or phrases within the book.

Using the keyboard included with the Kindle, the girls also added annotations, or notes, to the text (much like writing notes in the margin of a book) in response to what they were reading. Both participants had access to their own Kindle on which their notes and markups were saved each day.

Questions guiding this study included the following:

- How can wireless digital reading devices support primary readers in their reading processes as they read and respond to digital texts?
- How do wireless digital reading devices advance e-book readership as they offer new avenues for accessing and manipulating texts?

Data collection and analysis were ongoing and simultaneous. This study used qualitative case study techniques (Stake, 2000). Using categorical aggregation, multiple sources of data were examined in search of emerging categories of information and meanings. Data sources include my field notes and interviews with participating students, their classroom teacher, and their respective parents. Students' digital notes, or markups, were also collected for careful examination and analysis for emerging reader response themes and patterns.

Findings

Findings suggested that using digital reading devices with second-grade students promotes new literacies practices and extends connections between readers and text as engagement with and manipulation of text is made possible through electronic tools and features. The Kindle tools invited Amy and Winnie to engage with the text and put the reader in greater control than when reading printed text.

Literature Response

The digital note tool offered insights into the reader's meaning-making process as the text unfolded and served as a conduit to ongoing response writing. While using the note tool, the second graders seemed unconcerned with proper writing conventions and mechanics. Rather, they focused on transferring their thoughts into written annotations as quickly and effectively as possible, resulting in extensive use of invented spelling. Overall, the notes reflected a sense of spontaneity and impulsiveness as they expressed the voice and mood of the individual reader while revealing an understanding of the story or expressing a desire for additional information or clarification of the emerging plot.

While reading the story, Amy and Winnie inserted 43 and 33 notes respectively. The note tool provided them with a literature-response mechanism that suited their individual needs and purposes as readers. Close examination of their inserted notes suggest the following five categories of response notes:

1. Understanding of story (retelling; personal commentary)
2. Personal meaning-making (text-to-self connection; character identification)
3. Questioning (desire for information; indication of lack of understanding)
4. Answering (answers to questions in the text)
5. Response to text features/literary evaluation

Table 2 details the frequency of each response type for each reader. What follows is a discussion of each of these response categories, including authentic examples produced by Amy and Winnie.

Response Category 1: Understanding of the Story

These responses indicate the reader's current understanding of the characters and plot through personal commentary or retelling of parts of the story (Hancock, 1993). Ten out of Winnie's 33 notes (30%) fit into this category. As a character in the book waved goodbye to his classroom pet, Og the Frog, and shouted, "Catch you later, Oggy," Winnie inserted a note, "see you later oggy poggy." When another character, Gail, affectionately grabbed a classmate, Heidi, by the hand, Winnie inserted a note stating, "i think heidi and gail are friends now."

The interpretation of the budding friendship among characters was correct and confirmed by Winnie's note. Eighteen of Amy's 43 notes (42%) expressed understanding of the story primarily by retelling, or restating, facts and events as the plot unfolds. Examples included, "she has a stepsister," "yay a field trip," "she has a baby," and "he has a notebook." Amy's understanding of the story was also confirmed by her response to

Table 2 Types of Response Notes

Student	1. Understanding of story (retelling; personal commentary)	2. Personal meaning-making (text-to-self; character identification)	3. Questioning (desire for more information; lack of understanding)	4. Answering (response to questions in the text)	5. Text features/literary evaluation	Total
Amy	18 (42%)	6 (14%)	11 (25%)	0 (0%)	8 (19%)	43 (100%)
Winnie	10 (30%)	18 (55%)	1 (3%)	3 (9%)	1 (3%)	33 (100%)

what Humphrey, the hamster, calls "giant circles of lace." In a note, Amy candidly explained, "it's called snow."

Response Category 2: Personal Meaning-Making

In these reader-centered responses the readers expressed thoughts and feelings about the reading experience as they relate to plot and characters (Wollman-Bonilla & Werchadlo, 1995). As indicated in Table 2, Winnie responded to the story through personal meaning-making 55% of the time. Comments such as "i don't like crickets either," "i want to be a layer [lawyer] when in [I] grow up," and "I would like to go outside too" illustrated Winnie's ability to relate to the story and its characters.

Winnie felt empathetic toward Humphrey, the hamster, as he fought with Og the frog: "don't worry Humphrey i have a terrible life with my sister." She also recognized the advantages of being a classroom pet: "i would like someone to clean my room for me. humphrey is so lucky." Only 14% of Amy's notes expressed personal meaning-making. Like Winnie, she related to events and characters in the book: "i acshayli [actually] like bugs a lot," "i woude be scared too," and "i woude like to be a techer to." In one note, she also showed empathy toward the hamster: "i am sad that Humphrey is egnored."

Response Category 3: Questioning

Twenty-five percent (11) of Amy's notes consisted of questions relating to the book: "what dose that mene [mean]," and "wye do thay kepe doing that," suggesting some confusion about the unfolding plot. Other questions, such as, "i wonder what garths house looked like," and "i wonder what she thinks about Humphrey," revealed a longing for deeper understanding beyond what was offered through literal interpretation of the text.

On the other hand, Winnie's notes contained only one question indicating confusion about the text. As Principal Morales chuckles, "Muy inteligente," Winnie wrote, "is that spanish." Interestingly, while Winnie does not have personal experience with Spanish, she is a fluent speaker of both Chinese and English and clearly recognized the presence of a foreign language.

Response Category 4: Answering

Although Amy asked multiple questions during her reading experience, Winnie provided answers to questions asked in the book by various characters. For example, when Mrs. Brisbane asked her class, "What do you think, class? Do some people think frogs are odd?" Winnie inserted a note answering, "i do." In response to, "Tell me your friends and I'll tell you who you are, (Assyrian proverb)," Winnie listed her friends "jazmyn ashton lola xander brady." Such literal conversations with the author indicated a strong involvement with the text.

Response Category 5: Text Features/Literary Evaluation

Hancock (1993) explained that even young readers may indicate praise or criticism of the author, writing style, and literary genre. At the end of the book, Winnie inserted a note stating, "that was a great book, i thought it was fantastic and bumbastic." Amy commented on the author's writing style through

comments like, "that is a lot of names." In response to the sentence "According to Mandy, my beautiful golden fur was actually brown. . . ." Amy wrote, "thats how the book starts," clearly relating to the book's title *Friendship According to Humphrey*.

On numerous occasions, Amy also wondered about the author's use of conventions or specific text features. She noticed a dash used as a sentence break ("what dose that line mene"), lines used for emphasis ("i wonder wye thay put thos lines there"), parentheses ("what are thos lins for") and the use of an apostrophe in "Yes, ma'am" ("that is werd [weird]"). She also paid close attention to the division of chapters, commenting as she entered each new chapter ("im on chapter seven; im on the last chapter").

Previous studies in which primary students used literature response journals suggested that individual readers respond distinctively to the literature, often favoring a personal response style (Dekker, 1991; Wollman-Bonilla & Werchadlo, 1995). In this study, the digital notes provided a unique glimpse into the minds of individual readers. For Amy, the challenging text sparked her to ask questions, retell her understanding of plot and characters, and wonder about the author's use of conventions and writing style. Winnie, on the other hand, transacted with the text at a deeper level by conversing with the author and engaging in personal meaning-making as the plot unfolded.

New Literacies at Work

Analysis of all data sources indicated that the participants used new literacy skills and strategies to envision and access the potential of the digital reading device. To support their comprehension processes, the second graders consistently did the following:

- Adjusted the font size
- Accessed the built-in dictionary to look up meanings of words and to review the phonetic spelling of words to help "sound out" text
- Activated the text-to-speech feature to listen to words that they found difficult or to reread text passages

Font Size

The Kindle provides a choice of six different font sizes. During this study, Amy generally kept her font at a larger size than Winnie. In an interview, she explained that it helped her "read faster when the text was large." The varying text size did create some challenges on days when the girls decided to partner read, as the visual layout of their Kindle "pages" differed. The girls quickly learned to synchronize their settings when reading together.

Built-in Dictionary

The Kindle features a readily accessible built-in dictionary (*The New Oxford American Dictionary*) which was accessed during this study for two purposes: 1) to look up the meaning of words, and 2) to help decode words. Winnie accessed the dictionary periodically while reading independently to look up the meaning of words. When encountering "Muy inteligente," she turned to Amy and stated, "I tried the dictionary and it didn't work." (Subsequently, she inserted a note asking, "is that spanish.")

Amy primarily used the dictionary to help her decode words. For example, when reading out loud, she struggled with the word *accomplishment*. After accessing the dictionary, she read the word out loud, explaining that the dictionary "chunks the words for you so you can read them." For Amy, the dictionary seemed particularly helpful with multisyllabic words such as *audience, magician, prosperity, produced,* and *cabinet.* The dictionary did not appear as helpful when she encountered short, unfamiliar words such as *eerie.* In this instance, after attempting to use the dictionary, she simply stated, "I still can't tell what that word is."

Text-to-Speech Feature

The Kindles text-to-speech feature allows readers to listen to the text in a somewhat robotic male or female voice. In this study, Winnie and Amy were both aware of this feature and were allowed to use it at any time. When initially introduced to the text-to-speech function, the girls listened to the story for approximately 10 minutes before removing their headphones, requesting to read on their own.

In an ensuing interview, the girls explained that they did not like to listen to the "Kindle's voice." Winnie elaborated, "he just didn't sound the way the story reads in my head." During subsequent sessions, Amy occasionally accessed text-to-speech to help her decode individual words or navigate through difficult text passages.

Sociophysical Settings

Rosenblatt (1978) considered nonlinguistic factors to be of great influence on the reading experience. This includes the sociophysical settings, or the conditions or environment in which the actual reading takes place. During previous studies involving e-book reading on laptop or desktop computers, I have found that the reading venue, or physical environment, context, and even reading position, largely affects the overall reading experience (Larson, 2007).

For example, when reading on laptops or desktop computers, readers often express physical discomfort or say they miss the feel of "snuggling up" with a real book. In this study, no similar sentiments were expressed, as the second graders used digital reading devices similar in size and shape to traditional books. Like most readers, the girls simply positioned themselves on the floor in a quiet corner of the library. In the opinions of Winnie and Amy, the convenience and "coolness factor" gained from reading on a Kindle outweighed any lost sentiments of reading a traditional text.

Interviews with Amy and Winnie, their parents, and the classroom teacher revealed notable changes in reading dispositions and personas. For example, prior to participation in this study, Amy expressed that she did not like to read, especially chapter books. According to her mother, reading on the Kindle made Amy excited about reading and the experience "gave her confidence in herself."

Similarly, Winnie, an avid reader, explained that she preferred reading on the Kindle "because you can take notes in it, but you can't take notes in a regular book." After reviewing Winnie's notes and markups, Mrs. Miles reported that the notes disclosed "a whole new side of Winnie." Winnie's notes often expressed humor and a sense of whimsy, which seemed to contradict her otherwise serious and shy personality.

Implications for the Classroom

Hancock (2008) explained that technology offers "a new vision and dimension of reader response" as teachers think of ways to merge new literacies and traditional literature in the classroom (p. 108). In the cases of Winnie and Amy, the digital readers clearly provided new opportunities and extended possibilities for individual engagement with and interpretation of the text. The girls' voices blended with the voice of the author as they engaged in an active, constructive experience where personal meaning became the collaborative product of reader and text during the act of reading.

By carefully examining the children's responses and their use of Kindle tools, Mrs. Miles gained valuable insights into each child's reading behaviors and comprehension skills. When the response notes indicated that Amy struggled to understand the emerging plot or specific text features, Mrs. Miles was able to answer her lingering questions and support her individual needs as a reader. Amy's use of Kindle tools supported her ability to independently decode unfamiliar or multisyllabic words with the help of the built-in dictionary, along with a larger font size.

Winnie's response notes indicated deep transactions with the text, while unveiling a previously disguised sense of humor and outgoing personality. Thus, Mrs. Miles broadened Winnie's selection of future reading materials and encouraged her to express her sense of humor and socially interact with her peers. The digital readers proved to be a valuable tool that will be useful as Mrs. Miles continues her quest to differentiate reading instruction and provide her students with the individual support they deserve.

E-books in general, and digital readers in particular, have the potential to unveil an array of new teaching and learning possibilities as traditional and new literacy skills are integrated in meaningful ways. In today's world of increased accountability and strong focus on individualized student support systems, digital reading devices may provide much needed support to both students and teachers. The lack of research published on this topic hinders the efforts made by educators and administrators who wish to integrate digital texts into their current curricula or school libraries.

Although a small case study, this study advances past research on e-book reading and response and clearly shows that there is more to digital readers than just their portability and incredible storage capacity. Digital readers show promise in supporting struggling readers through multiple tools and features, including manipulation of font size, text-to-speech options, expandable dictionary, and note capabilities.

The rapidly changing nature of e-books and digital reading devices demands a progressive research agenda that examines the use of new technologies in authentic school settings. Teachers must explore the potential of digital readers, as one

Take Action!

1. To get started, you should communicate closely with school administrators and technology staff to develop common literacy and technology goals. Discuss funding options for acquiring digital readers and subsequent e-books (i.e., grants, PTA/PTO support, or fundraisers). You must also decide how to effectively use the digital readers during whole-class instruction, literature circles, and individual reading experiences. If the access to digital readers is limited, download multiple book titles on each device, which can be shared by several students. Use a visual presenter and projector to initially introduce the e-book reader's many tools and features. During ensuing lessons, students may further use this technology to share digital notes or favorite text passages with their classmates.

2. Craft a schedule that allows each student frequent blocks of uninterrupted reading time. Establish class expectations for note taking and markings in the e-books, particularly if multiple students share a digital reader. Decide if students have the right to access one another's books and if they can read one another's notes. Also, consider if multiple students may add notes in the same book—possibly responding to one another's notes and comments.

3. As students read and respond to e-books, it is important that teachers carefully observe their reading behaviors. Note how students access and use e-book tools and features (e.g., font size, dictionary, text-to-speech). Review students' notes and markups on a regular basis. Carefully consider types of notes written, as well as strategies for nudging students toward a broader repertoire of response options. Encourage students to share how the digital readers support their individual reading processes.

device can potentially take the place of hundreds of printed books and allow for unique transactions between the reader and the text. Although print books are the world's oldest means of communication and the Internet one of the newest, digital readers merge the two media in innovative and interesting ways as they integrate "the portability of books with the search and storage capabilities of personal computers" (Goldsborough, 2009, p. 11).

Although research on the use of this medium is in its infancy, the results from this study appear promising in using digital reading devices as a means to foster literacy development and offering a glimpse into the unique minds of individual readers.

ReadWriteThink.org Lesson Plan

- "Going Digital: Using E-Book Readers to Enhance the Reading Experience" by Lotta C. Larson

IRA Books

- *Teaching and Learning Multiliteracies: Changing Times, Changing Literacies* by Michèle Anstey and Geoff Bull
- *Trading Cards to Comic Strips: Popular Culture Texts and Literacy Learning in Grades K–8* by Shelley Hong Xu

References

Bearne, E. (2005). Multimodal texts: What they are and how children use them. In J. Evans (Ed.), *Literacy moves on: Popular culture, new technologies, and critical literacy in the elementary classroom* (pp. 13–29). Portsmouth, NH: Heinemann.

Booth, D.W. (2006). *Reading doesn't matter anymore: Shattering the myths of literacy.* Portland, ME: Stenhouse.

Burrell, C., & Trushell, J. (1997). "Eye-candy" in "interactive books"—A wholesome diet? *Reading, 31*(2), 3–6.

Dekker, M.M. (1991). Books, reading, and response: A teacher-researcher tells a story. *The New Advocate, 4*(1), 37–46.

Eagleton, M.B., & Dobler, E. (2007). *Reading the web: Strategies for Internet inquiry.* New York: Guilford.

Fasimpaur, K. (2004). E-books in schools: Check out the reasons why e-books are gaining in popularity in K–12 schools. *Media & Methods, 40*(5), 12.

Glasgow, J.N. (1996). It's my turn! Part II: Motivating young readers using CD-ROM storybooks. *Learning and Leading With Technology, 24*(4), 18–22.

Goldsborough, R. (2009). The latest in books and the Internet. *Tech Directions, 68*(10), 11.

Hancock, M.R. (1993). Exploring the meaning-making process through the content of literature response journals. *Research in the Teaching of English, 27*(4), 335–368.

Hancock, M.R. (2008). The status of reader response research: Sustaining the reader's voice in challenging times. In S. Lehr (Ed.), *Shattering the looking glass: Challenge, risk, and controversy in children's literature* (pp. 97–116). Norwood, MA: Christopher-Gordon.

International Reading Association. (2009). *New literacies and 21st-century technologies: A position statement of the International Reading Association.* Newark, DE: Author.

Kucer, S.B. (2005). *Dimensions of literacy: A conceptual base for teaching reading and writing in school settings* (2nd ed.). Mahwah, NJ: Erlbaum.

Lankshear, C. (with Gee, J., Knobel, M., & Searle, C.) (1997). *Changing literacies.* Buckingham: Open University Press.

Larson, L.C. (2007). *A case study exploring the "new literacies" during a fifth-grade electronic reading workshop.* Doctoral dissertation, Kansas State University. Retrieved February 19, 2010, from krex.k-state.edu/dspace/handle/2097/352.

Larson, L.C. (2008). Electronic reading workshop: Beyond books with new literacies and instructional technologies. *Journal of Adolescent & Adult Literacy, 52*(2), 121–131. doi:10.1598/JAAL.52.2.3.

Larson, L.C. (2009). E-reading and e-responding: New tools for the next generation of readers. *Journal of Adolescent & Adult Literacy, 53*(3), 255–258. doi:10.1598/JAAL.53.3.7.

Leu, D.J. (2002). The new literacies: Research on reading instruction with the Internet. In A.E. Farstrup & S.J. Samuels (Eds.), *What research has to say about reading instruction* (3rd ed., pp. 310–336). Newark, DE: International Reading Association.

Leu, D.J., Kinzer, C.K., Coiro, J., & Cammack, D.W. (2004). Toward a theory of new literacies emerging from the Internet and other information and communication technologies. In R.B. Ruddell & N. Unrau (Eds.), *Theoretical models and processes of reading* (5th ed., pp. 1570–1613). Newark, DE: International Reading Association.

Matthew, K.I. (1996). The impact of CD-ROM storybooks on children's reading comprehension and reading attitude. *Journal of Educational Multimedia and Hypermedia, 5*(3–4), 379–394.

Reinking, D. (1998). Synthesizing technological transformations of literacy in a post-typographical world. In D. Reinking, M.C. McKenna, L.D. Labbo, & R.D. Kieffer (Eds.), *Handbook of literacy and technology: Transformations in a post-typographic world* (pp. xi–xxx). Mahwah, NJ: Erlbaum.

Rosenblatt, L.M. (1938). *Literature as exploration.* New York: Appleton-Century-Crofts.

Rosenblatt, L.M. (1978). *The reader, the text, the poem: The transactional theory of the literary work.* Carbondale: Southern Illinois University Press.

Stake, R.E. (2000). Case studies. In N.K. Denzin & Y.S. Lincoln (Eds.), *Handbook of qualitative research* (2nd ed., pp. 435–454). Thousand Oaks, CA: Sage.

Wollman-Bonilla, J.E., & Werchadlo, B. (1995). Literature response journals in a first-grade classroom. *Language Arts, 72*(8), 562–570.

Critical Thinking

1. Have you personally used a digital reader? How did you use it? Reflect on your experience and how that will influence your use of digital readers as a teacher.

2. Digital readers offer students and teachers new ways to interact with text. Which of the interactive ways Amy and Winnie used the e-book was most interesting to you? Explain why.

3. Your principal purchased enough digital readers for each of your students to have one. How will you integrate them into your content area? As you answer this question, refer back to the article on AT and Universal Design for Learning.

Larson teaches at Kansas State University, Manhattan, USA; e-mail ell4444@ksu.edu.

Literature Cited—Birney, B.G. (2006). *Friendship according to Humphrey* (Kindle ed.). New York: Puffin.

Digital Tools Expand Options for Personalized Learning

Digital tools for defining and targeting students' strengths and weaknesses could help build a kind of individualized education plan for every student.

KATHLEEN KENNEDY MANZO

Teachers have always known that a typical class of two dozen or more students can include vastly different skill levels and learning styles. But meeting those varied academic needs with a defined curriculum, time limitations, and traditional instructional tools can be daunting for even the most skilled instructor.

Some of the latest technology tools for the classroom, however, promise to ease the challenges of differentiating instruction more creatively and effectively, ed-tech experts say, even in an era of high-stakes federal and state testing mandates. New applications for defining and targeting students' academic strengths and weaknesses can help teachers create a personal playlist of lessons, tools, and activities that deliver content in ways that align with individual needs and optimal learning methods.

For educators who struggle to integrate technology into their daily routines and strategies, the notion of a kind of individualized education plan for every student is more pipe dream than prospect. Yet the most optimistic promoters of digital learning say the vision of a tech-immersed classroom for today's students—one that offers a flexible and dynamic working environment with a range of computer-based and face-to-face learning options customized for each student—is not far off.

Several examples of such customization have recently emerged across the country, and are garnering widespread interest and some encouraging results.

"Those examples are a crude picture of a future scenario, where there's a student playlist of learning experiences, some of which happen in something that looks like a classroom, some with a computer, and some at a community resource, like a library, museum, college, or workplace," says Tom Vander Ark, a former executive director of education for the Seattle-based **Bill & Melinda Gates Foundation** who has advocated for years that schools should take a more individualized approach to learning. He is now a partner in **Vander Ark/Ratcliff,** an education venture-capital firm. "Their day could look like an interesting variety of activities, driven by their learning needs, not by the school's limitations."

'Feedback to Children'

Vander Ark says that supplemental-service providers, like private tutoring companies or after-school programs, have taken the lead in offering tailored instruction. The ways those providers use assessment tools to gather and process data and then suggest a roster of activities for each student could pave the way for similar approaches within the school day, he says.

Creating a Custom Playlist for Learning

Technology experts recommend that teachers utilize a variety of tools and activities to address individual student learning needs:

Class Lessons

Traditional lessons for the whole class help introduce a lesson or reteach material as needed.

Assessments

Teachers conduct regular formative assessments, using some quick digital applications and analytic tools, to determine students' skills and academic needs.

Skill-Building Games

Computer-based games that focus on developing specific skills like vocabulary or multiplication facts.

Group Projects

Students collaborate on assignments using technology and traditional research and presentation tools.

Online Courses

Virtual learning could give students access to credit-recovery or accelerated courses, as well as enrichment and intervention activities.

Tutoring

One-on-one or small-group tutoring sessions, on-site or virtually, aid students who are struggling academically.

Museum Site Visit

Students can tap into outside educational resources, such as museums, libraries, and local historical sites.

Blogs

Students can write blog entries to demonstrate what they've learned, outline their research, and communicate with their teachers.

Independent Research

Assignments outside of class using online and traditional resources give students the chance to guide their own learning.

He points to one widely publicized model: New York City's **School of One.**

The pilot program at Dr. Sun Yat Sen Middle School in Chinatown provided math lessons that were customized every day to meet the individual needs, and progress, of the 80 incoming 7th graders who volunteered to attend the five-week session this past summer. The School of One combined face-to-face instruction, software-based activities, and online lessons designed to move each new 7th grader through a defined set of math benchmarks at his or her own pace.

As students entered school each morning, they could view their schedules for the day on a computer monitor—similar to the arrival-and-departure monitors at airports—and proceed to the assigned locations. A student's schedule could include traditional lessons from a certified teacher, small-group work, virtual learning, or specific computer-based activities, most of them offered in converted space in the school library.

After each half-day of instruction, teachers entered data on students' progress and instructional needs into a computer program that recommended the next day's tasks.

Preliminary data showed significant student progress toward mastering the skills targeted in the program, officials say. The district is continuing to track participants' progress.

The school—named one of the 50 best inventions of 2009 by *Time* magazine—expanded in the fall to three middle schools in the city as an after-school program, and is set to guide the school-day math course at one of them this spring.

"When we ask ourselves how much instruction during the course of a typical school day does each student get exactly on the skill they're working on, and in the amount that is right for them, the answer is very little," says Joel Rose, a former teacher who has been instrumental in the development and expansion of the School of One.

"By leveraging technology to play a role in the delivery of instruction," he says, "we can help to complement what live teachers do."

The San Diego Unified School District is betting that the bulk of a recent $2 billion bond measure for technologies designed to transform teaching and learning through a more personalized approach will yield academic improvements.

The five-year plan for the 135,000-student district started this school year in 1,300 math classrooms. The students, in grades 3 and 6 and in high school, were issued netbook computers, and teachers were required to complete 39 hours of training on instructional strategies using technology. Classrooms throughout the district were also equipped with a variety of interactive technology tools.

After introducing content, teachers can immediately test students using remote devices attached to their netbooks. Students are then assigned to appropriate practice activities or more in-depth lessons.

"The wait time for getting feedback to children is sliced significantly. This is about the speed of learning and the depth of learning," says Sarah Sullivan, the principal of San Diego's Pershing Middle School. "This is the first time I've seen the promise of technology appearing to be paying the dividends we want."

San Diego plans to expand the program next year to other grades and into other subject areas.

Making the Transition

Experts caution, however, that instituting such large-scale change is not simply a matter of putting new tools in place. As in San Diego, most teachers will need extensive professional development to use digital tools and learn the best ways of teaching with technology.

"In many ways, the challenge we face with technology is similar to the challenge we face with data," says Stephanie Hirsch, the executive director of the Dallas-based **National Staff Development Council.** "We have more and more of both with little support to help educators know how to use it . . . to advance their effectiveness and student success."

A number of teachers have found their own ways to harness some of technology's potential to get a closer gauge of their students' work, and to provide a range of options for them to consume required content and demonstrate knowledge.

For several years, Shelly Blake-Plock has asked students in his Latin, English, and art history classes to summarize what they've learned from class and document their progress on assignments in daily blog entries. The students at The John Carroll School, a Roman Catholic secondary school in Bel Air, Md., can post Web links they used in their research, photos and drawings, or short videos that show their work.

Blake-Plock, who writes the popular **Teach Paperless** blog and has a large following among educators on social-networking sites, says the entries are a continuous source of formative data that he can use to evaluate how students are doing.

If he observes a lack of basic understanding or language skill in some students' work, he says, he can suggest online resources and activities to get them on track. When students reveal their personal interests—such as one student's passion for painting and another's talent for music—he can craft assignments that allow them to explore the content through those areas.

"Before I went paperless and used the blogs to get information from them, I would only see students' work if they wrote an essay or turned in a quiz or test," Blake-Plock says. "Now I'm seeing what they're working on all the time, . . . and I'm finding it's a lot easier for me to tell if a student is having problems early on."

'Lack of Innovation'

The advantages for students are potentially more compelling, given the widespread enthusiasm among young people for using technology to create and consume media, ed-tech experts say.

"We have this generation of students that yearns to customize everything they come into contact with," says Steve Johnson, a technology facilitator at J.N. Fries Middle School in Concord, N.C. His book *Engaging All Learners With 21st Century Tools* is due out from Maupin House Publishing this coming summer.

The educational technology market is slowly responding with the kinds of products that can help teachers track and target their students' learning needs.

Wireless Generation Inc., a New York City-based technology company, created its **Burst Reading** program in response to teachers' comments about the need to vary basic literacy lessons for the many students who did not fit the developmental patterns assumed by lockstep reading lessons.

The company, which helped build the technology applications for the School of One, designed an assessment schedule for K-3 reading schedules that gives feedback and recommends lessons for small groups of similarly skilled students every 10 days. Although the Burst program suggests only face-to-face

lessons for students, its underlying assessment relies on sophisticated digital tools for gathering and analyzing data from individual students.

"It's this model of deeply analyzing the data in a way that no human teacher would have time to do, and mapping lessons to kids' abilities, that's fundamental to what education is going to look like in the future," predicts Wireless Generation's chief executive officer, Larry Berger. (Berger serves on the board of Editorial Projects in Education, the nonprofit corporation that publishes *Education Week Digital Directions*.)

The company is working on similar products for middle school reading and elementary math.

At the same time, traditional textbook publishers are starting to adapt their products for greater personalization as well. **McGraw-Hill Education,** for example, has developed the K-6 CINCH math program for use on interactive whiteboards that includes differentiation options.

The slow pace of development of customizable content and tools is frustrating, though, to some in the field, particularly in light of the widespread adoption of such strategies for training in the U.S. military, or their entrance into the mainstream in public schooling in other developed countries, Vander Ark says.

"This is not science fiction," he says. "None of the technology we're talking about is really advanced, . . . but the fact that it doesn't exist yet on a large scale in education is just a reflection of a lack of innovation in that sector."

Critical Thinking

1. Write a 50–75 word abstract for the article regarding tools for individualizing instruction.

2. Review the list of digital tools that are suggested as options for individualizing instruction. Select three of these tools to research. Go to the Internet and find two or three examples of each tool. Create an annotated bibliography of these tools to share with peers in your class.

Differentiate Teaching and Learning with Web 2.0 Tools

KIMBERLY LIGHTLE

How do you differentiate instruction? We asked the Middle School Portal 2: Math and Science Pathways project (http://msteacher2.org) 21st Century Teacher Leaders about their favorite tech tools for differentiating instruction. Here's what they had to say:

Todd Williamson is a National Board Certified teacher (early adolescent science) at Broad Creek Middle School in Newport, North Carolina. He teaches seventh grade science.

A key to differentiating instruction is having a multitude of strategies to use with students on different learning paths. The strategy that works brilliantly with a few students might self-destruct with another group.

Jumping from one strategy to another on our laundry list of differentiation practices is time-consuming and frequently inefficient. When working with middle grades students, it's important to recognize that they are developing the ability to advocate for themselves and can have some level of input into the strategies that best help them learn.

The Internet offers students a plethora of tools to use according to the situation. Just as a carpenter uses a broad range of tools in the construction of a house, our students should have a broad range of options for demonstrating their learning. Here are few that I especially like.

MakeBeliefsComix.com allows students to create a short comic strip. There are many characters to choose from, each featuring four different expressions. Students can add speech or thought bubbles, resize characters, add items to each frame, and e-mail their finished comics to their teacher. Alternatively, students can print out the comic strips and color in background objects to get their point across. This is a great entry point for students who claim they "can't draw."

VoiceThread.com encourages group conversations around images. Students or teachers can post images to the thread and other users can add text, spoken, or videoed comments about the images. This way students can discuss a topic asynchronously and perhaps even across multiple classes.

Animoto.com and *JayCut.com* provide for video creation and editing, respectively. Using Animoto, students create professional-looking video slideshows set to music in a short amount of time. Students can upload images, add text slides, and select music, then let Animoto do the rest. With JayCut, students work with short video segments and edit them online, much like Windows MovieMaker but without the platform issues, since it's a web-based tool.

Rather than giving students a couple of options, the Internet and technology tools offer infinite potential if we just take the time to explore and let our students discover what works best for them.

Eric Biederbeck is in his tenth year of teaching math, science, and social studies at Essex Middle School in Essex Junction, Vermont.

Differentiation has been a buzzword in our district the past few years. As we have begun our districtwide implementation of differentiated techniques, most of our training and ideas have revolved around differentiating for readiness. Recently, however, we began to consider differentiating for learning style and interest as well.

Technologies, particularly the many Web 2.0 tools available, help with this process. One tool I've used to help differentiate for learning style and interest is *Glogster.*

Glogster (www.glogster.com) provides students with opportunities to express themselves and their interests.

For example, during a unit on ancient civilizations of Latin America, students might choose activities from a board about European conquest, including creating a Glog about diseases that Europeans brought to the New World to a Glog that includes a Venn diagram comparing Cortes to Pizzaro.

After students have been introduced to Glogster and have had the opportunity to use it a few times, they often use it for open-ended projects. I asked my math students to create a visual describing a miniature golf hole they created as part of a geometry project. Many used Glogster to show examples of their golf hole using digital pictures they took and included text explaining the angles and scale of the hole.

Glogster also provides opportunities for students to work within their learning style. Glogster appeals to students who are visual learners by allowing them to create their own posters. Students have options to add background, color, pictures, and videos. Glogster allows them to highlight text and have it "pop" out.

Glogster also gives students a choice in the type of multimedia they use. Students can find pictures and music to incorporate into their Glog. They can find videos on YouTube.com, which they can embed into a Glog. In my classroom, students created Glogs about particular arctic animals. Some incorporated video or audio of their animal while others stayed with pictures.

Students who are auditory learners can create podcasts, which they can then embed in their Glog. In math, I have students create a podcast explaining a particular math strategy such as prime factorization. Students often opt to embed this podcast into a Glog and might also include information in text form that discusses everyday uses of prime factorization. The many options Glogster provides allow students of different learning styles to thrive.

Tom Jenkins is a National Board Certified teacher at Indian Valley Middle School in Enon, Ohio, where he teaches STEM and technology to fifth through eighth graders.

One of my favorite tools in the classroom is an ***MP3 player.*** Users can easily upload and organize many essential and complementary pieces of information onto this digital media device.

To create original audio files, I prefer to use **Audacity.** This free software is a cross platform digital audio and recording application available from SourceForge.

net. To create images I prefer to use **GIMP,** which is also free software and is available at GIMP.org.

Please keep in mind that although my preference is to use a digital media device, one could also accomplish many of the same objectives by allowing the students access to a computer.

To differentiate for students who have difficulty taking class notes, I record all class notes during the lecture part of the lesson. By breaking the lecture into "chapters," I don't create a 30-minute MP3 file for students. I post the lectures in an archive form so the students can listen on the computer or download the files to their own MP3 players.

To differentiate for students who have difficulty reading, I have a peer read and record the material. Although an instructor can do the same thing, I've found that students prefer hearing their peers read. It also creates an environment in which the exemplar reader takes a mentoring role with the struggling reader. This option can be used with a reading selection, a lab, or even a test if an aide should be unavailable to provide the modification.

When student-led, this particular activity lends itself to enrichment for the students in the higher end of the spectrum. The students who need to be challenged can take on more of a leading role and reinforce their own knowledge while helping students who need assistance with the lesson.

To differentiate for students who are visual learners, consider multimedia players. Many devices are equipped to play music, show pictures, and even movie clips. You can create or copy pictures (with permission, of course) and then store them to the device for subsequent viewing during a lecture or to reinforce concepts. You can include diagrams to provide visuals during labs and other activities.

You may even choose to download media from Teachertube.com or use a site such as Kickyoutube.com to download videos from Youtube.com that complement the lesson.

These have all proven to be very successful tools in my classroom; MP3 players provide the students access to the entire scope of the lesson while allowing them to focus on the parts of the lesson in which they need assistance. The students are allowed to use an instrument in an educational setting that for many of them is an essential part of their everyday life. It helps enrich the material and in many cases makes the lesson fun!

Make Connections

For more information about these resources and other digital tools, please visit the MSP2 social network at http://msteacher2.org.

Critical Thinking

1. Explore Web 2.0 websites that would be appropriate for your content area or grade level. Make a list of these websites with a brief explanation of how you might use them.

2. What are the likely outcomes of ignoring these technologies and continuing to teach with paper texts and teacher-centered activities?

3. Explain which of the Web 2.0 tools might be appropriate for your content or grade level. Provide a rationale for your answer.

4. Based on what you have learned in the articles in this unit, will you allow your students to use technology, Internet searches, and blogs as a routine part of their daily learning activities? Why or why not?

KIMBERLY LIGHTLE is director of digital libraries, School of Teaching and Learning, College of Education and Human Ecology, The Ohio State University. E-mail: lightle.16@osu.edu.

From *Middle Ground*, February 2011, pp. 8–9. Copyright © 2011 by National Middle School Association. Reprinted by permission.

Effects of Video-Game Ownership on Young Boys' Academic and Behavioral Functioning: A Randomized, Controlled Study

Robert Weis and Brittany C. Cerankosky

Exposure to violent video games is associated with aggressive behavior among children (Anderson & Bushman, 2001; Carnagey, Anderson, & Bushman, 2007). Meta-analyses show significant associations between violent video-game play and aggressive thoughts ($r = .27$), feelings ($r = .18$), and actions ($r = .20$). These associations can be seen in experimental, correlational, and longitudinal studies involving children, adolescents, and adults (Anderson et al., 2008; Anderson, Gentile, & Buckley, 2007; Carnagey & Anderson, 2005). Furthermore, theoretical models based on learning, social cognitive, and neoassociative network theories have been developed to explain how violent video games might prime immediate aggressive behaviors and make them more accessible and appealing to children over time.

Although parents and children are beginning to recognize the risks of overtly violent video-game exposure, the risks associated with less violent video games, particularly those marketed to young children, are not as evident (Kutner, Olson, Warner, & Hertzog, 2008). Emerging data indicate that video games marketed to young children may also have adverse effects on child development by interfering with academic functioning. Assuming that time spent in after-school activities is zero-sum, recreational video-game play may displace activities that might have greater educational value (Vandewater, Bickham, & Lee, 2006). Indeed, recent studies have found significant relationships between the duration of video-game play and the academic performance of students in elementary school (Anderson et al., 2007), middle and high school (Gentile, 2009; Gentile, Lynch, Linder, & Walsh, 2004; Willoughby, 2008), and college (Anderson & Dill, 2000).

Further support for the displacement hypothesis comes from several recent population-based studies that have monitored children's time use. These studies indicate that children who own video games spend more time playing these games, spend less time engaged in after-school educational activities, and earn lower grades than comparison children (Schmidt & Vandewater, 2008).

For example, Sharif and Sargent (2006) found that middle-school students' exposure to video games on weekdays, but not weekends, was associated with their academic performance. Similarly, Valentine, Marsh, and Pattie (2005) determined that adolescents' after-school video-game play competed with the time they devoted to studying. In their analysis, video-game exposure was associated with decreased academic achievement scores on standardized tests. Most recently, Cummings and Vandewater (2007) found that video-game players spent 30% less time reading and 34% less time completing homework than did children who did not play video games.

Data supporting the displacement hypothesis are limited by the fact that they have been obtained chiefly through cross-sectional research (Cummings & Vandewater, 2007). It is possible that struggling students may simply decide to spend less time reading and completing homework and more time playing video games. Without data from randomized, controlled studies that monitor children's functioning over time, we cannot infer a causal relationship between video-game ownership, increased play, and changes in academic performance.

To remedy this limitation, we conducted a randomized, controlled study of the short-term effects of video-game ownership on the academic and behavioral functioning of young boys. At baseline, none of the boys owned a video-game system, but all of their parents expressed an interest in purchasing a system for them. To control for participant bias, we told parents that the purpose of the study was to examine boys' development, not to study the effects of video-game ownership. Parents were promised a video-game system as incentive for participation. After baseline assessment of boys' functioning, families were randomly assigned to an experimental group, in which members received the video-game system immediately, or to a control group, in which members received the system 4 months later, after follow-up assessment.

Evidence supporting displacement would come from significant differences in boys' duration of video-game usage, duration of after-school academic activities, and academic achievement as a function of experimental condition. Additional support would come from data showing video-game play mediating the relationship between experimental condition and achievement outcomes. We also examined whether boys in the experimental group showed more behavior problems at follow-up than boys in the control group. Such evidence would indicate that video-game ownership places young children at risk for behavior problems, even when they play games marketed to children their age.

Method

Participants

Sixty-four boys, 6 to 9 years of age ($M = 7.89$, $SD = 0.82$) participated. Boys were included in the study if they (a) were enrolled in a first-grade (33%), second-grade (44%), or third-grade (23%) class; (b) did not have a video-game system in their home; (c) had a parent interested in purchasing a system for their use; and (d) had no history of developmental, behavioral, medical, or learning problems. Ethnicities included White (89%), African American (6%), Asian American (3%), and Latino (2%). Approximately 79% of boys came from two-parent families. Paternal education included elementary school (5%), high school (70%), college (15%), and graduate or professional education (10%).

Measures

The Kaufman Brief Intelligence Test—2nd edition (KBIT–2; Kaufman & Kaufman, 2004) was used to estimate boys' intellectual ability ($M = 100$, $SD = 15$). The Woodcock–Johnson—III: Tests of Achievement (WJ–III; McGrew & Woodcock, 2001) were used to assess boys' academic functioning. The WJ–III yields three composite scores ($M = 100$, $SD = 15$): Broad Reading, Broad Mathematics, and Broad Written Language.

The Parent Rating Scale (PRS) and Teacher Rating Scale (TRS) were used to assess boys' behavior at home and school, respectively (Reynolds & Kamphaus, 2004). Both scales yield three composite scores ($M = 50$, $SD = 10$): Externalizing Problems, Internalizing Problems, and Adaptive Skills. The TRS yields one additional composite, School Problems, indicative of Attention Problems (i.e., distractibility, difficulty concentrating) and Learning Problems (i.e., difficulty reading, writing, spelling).

The Afterschool Time Diary (Hofferth, Davis-Kean, Davis, & Finkelstein, 1997) was used to estimate the duration of boys' video-game play and academic activities after school. Parents were asked to report boys' activities from the end of the school day until bedtime for the 2 previous weekdays. Average duration of video-game play was calculated by summing the duration of video-game play across the 2 days and dividing by 2. Average duration of academic activities was calculated by summing the total time spent engaged in after-school education, homework, reading, listening to stories, and writing, divided by 2.

Procedure

In early autumn, boys were recruited through newspaper advertisements to participate in an "ongoing study of boys' academic and behavioral development." In exchange for their participation, parents were promised a PlayStation II (PSII), controllers, and three games rated E (Everyone) by the Entertainment Software Rating Board. The games, *Nicktoons: Battle for Volcano Island, Shrek Smash N' Crash Racing,* and *Sonic Riders,* reportedly contain mild cartoon violence and comic mischief.

Only boys were included in the study, to increase the effectiveness of the experimental manipulation. Because our study was naturalistic, we could not directly manipulate the frequency and duration of children's video-game play. We worried that girls assigned to the experimental condition might not play significantly more than girls assigned to the control condition or play enough to potentially influence their academic or behavioral functioning. Indeed, naturalistic studies often show restricted range in girls' frequency and duration of video-game play (Gentile, Saleem, & Anderson, 2007). In contrast, boys play video games more often and for longer duration than do girls (Roberts, Foehr, & Rideout, 2005). Boys are also more likely to select games with violent content and display physical aggression (Ostrov, Gentile, & Crick, 2006). Furthermore, survey data indicate that boys are more likely to displace after-school academic activities with video games (Cummings & Vandewater, 2007), and approximately twice as many boys as girls report skipping homework or performing poorly on tests because of their video-game play (Gentile, 2009).

All parents who expressed an interest in the study were interviewed by telephone to determine whether their children met demographic criteria. Researchers also informed parents of the incentive for participation and asked, "Does your child want a PSII or do you already have a video-game system in your home?" Only parents who reported that the family did not own a system and who said that they intended to give the PSII to their child were scheduled for baseline assessment.

Children completed the KBIT–2 and WJ–III, and parents completed the PRS. The TRS was mailed to teachers. After baseline assessment, boys were randomly assigned to experimental or control conditions. Only boys whose baseline scores indicated academic achievement within normal limits and no significant behavior problems were randomized. Parents of boys assigned to the experimental condition were telephoned the day after randomization and told that the PSII was available immediately and that it would be delivered to their home.

Families participated in follow-up assessment 4 months after baseline. Boys completed the WJ–III, parents completed the PRS and Afterschool Time Diary, and teachers were mailed the TRS. Boys in the control condition were awarded the PSII, and parents were debriefed. Figure 1 provides a flowchart of the steps in the experimental procedure and the number of participants after each step.

Results

Baseline Characteristics and Manipulation Check

There were no significant differences between the experimental and control groups at baseline (see Table 1). Time from baseline to follow-up was similar for boys in the experimental ($M = 135$ days, $SD = 18.34$ days) and control ($M = 133$ days, $SD = 19.11$ days) conditions, $t(62) = 0.240$, $p = .811$. At follow-up, all of the boys in the experimental condition continued to play the video-game system. Ninety percent of boys in the experimental condition acquired additional games ($M = 2.28$, $SD = 1.49$). The most popular games were

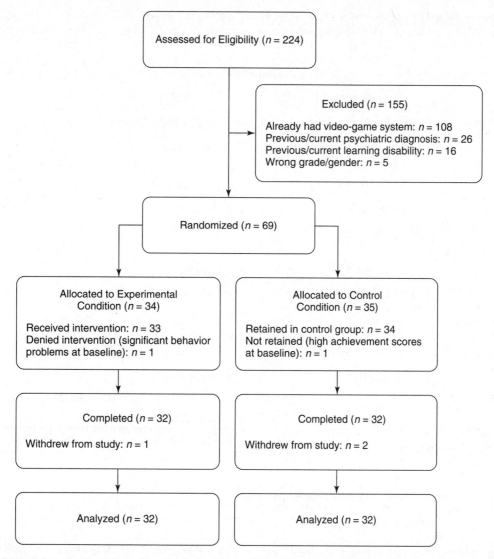

Figure 1 Consolidated Standards of Reporting Trials flowchart of the procedure. Eligible participants were assigned to either the experimental condition, in which they immediately received the video-game system, or the control condition, in which they received the system 4 months later, after assessment. All participants were assessed at follow-up.

rated E (Everyone): *Madden NFL, Lego Star Wars,* and *Pac-Man World 3.* The latter two games reportedly contain mild cartoon violence. Fifty-three percent of boys acquired at least one game rated E10+ (Everyone 10 and older); the most popular game was *Lego Star Wars II,* which reportedly contains cartoon violence and crude humor. Two boys acquired *Pirates of the Caribbean,* rated T (Teen), which reportedly contains alcohol references and violence. No boy in the experimental group owned games rated M (Mature), and no boy in the control group acquired a video-game system during the study.

Average duration of video-game play was longer for boys in the experimental condition ($M = 39.38$ min/day, $SD = 22.13$ min/day) than the control condition ($M = 9.37$ min/day, $SD = 12.65$ min/day), $t(62) = 6.65$, $p < .001$, $d = 1.66$. Also at follow-up, average duration of after-school academic activities was lower for boys in the experimental condition ($M = 18.28$ min/day, $SD = 15.11$ min/day) than for boys in the control condition ($M = 31.64$ min/day, $SD = 20.05$ min/day), $t(62) = 3.01$, $p = .004$, $d = 0.75$.

Effects of Video-Game Ownership

Three multivariate analyses of covariance (MANCOVAs) were conducted to determine the effects of video-game ownership on boys' functioning. In these MANCOVAs, the dependent variables were boys' (a) academic achievement, (b) parent-reported behavior, and (c) teacher-reported behavior at follow-up, respectively. The independent variable was experimental condition. Boys' baseline scores and IQ scores served as covariates. In each analysis, we followed up significant multivariate effects with univariate tests using Bonferroni adjustment to control for family-wise error.

In the first analysis, boys' three achievement scores at follow-up served as dependent variables. Results yielded a significant multivariate effect, Wilks's $\Lambda = .749$, $F(3, 56) = 6.26$, $p = .001$, $\eta_p^2 = .25$. Analyses of covariance (ANCOVAs; see Table 2), evaluated at $p < .017$ to control for error, indicated that boys in the experimental condition earned significantly lower Reading and Written Language scores at follow-up than did boys in the control condition.

Table 1   Characteristics of the Participants at Baseline

	Condition		
Variable	Experimental (*n* = 32)	Control (*n* = 32)	χ^2
Child's age (in months)	*M* = 95.36 (*SD* = 9.52)	*M* = 93.92 (*SD* = 10.16)	
Child's intelligence[a]	*M* = 100.97 (*SD* = 9.24)	*M* = 102.22 (*SD* = 9.02)	
Child's grade in school			0.790 (*df* = 2)
First	*n* = 10 (31.3%)	*n* = 11 (34.4%)	
Second	*n* = 13 (40.6%)	*n* = 15 (46.8%)	
Third	*n* = 9 (28.1%)	*n* = 6 (18.8%)	
Child's ethnicity			0.160 (*df* = 1)
White	*n* = 28 (87.4%)	*n* = 29 (90.6%)	
African American	*n* = 2 (6.3%)	*n* = 2 (6.3%)	
Asian American	*n* = 2 (6.3%)	*n* = 0	
Latino	*n* = 0	*n* = 1 (3.1%)	
Parents' marital status			0.097 (*df* = 1)
Married	*n* = 26 (81.3%)	*n* = 25 (78.1%)	
Father's education			0.721 (*df* = 1)
Finished college	*n* = 7 (21.9%)	*n* = 10 (31.3%)	
Child taking medication[b]	*n* = 3 (9.4%)	*n* = 4 (12.5%)	0.160 (*df* = 1)

Note: The experimental and control groups did not differ in age, *t*(62) = 0.584, or intelligence, *t*(62) = 0.547.
[a]Intelligence was estimated using the Kaufman Brief Intelligence Test—2nd edition (Kaufman & Kaufman, 2004).
[b]All children were taking nonpsychotropic medication for medical problems (e.g., asthma).

In the second MANCOVA, parent-reported behavioral outcomes were the dependent variables. Results did not show a significant multivariate effect, Wilks's Λ = .947, *F*(3, 56) = 1.04, *p* = .384. ANCOVAs (see Table 2) revealed no differences in parent-reported outcomes as a function of condition.

In the final MANCOVA, the four teacher-reported behavior scores served as dependent variables. Results did not show a significant multivariate effect, Wilks's Λ = .882, *F*(4, 54) = 1.81, *p* = .141. However, ANCOVAs (see Table 2), evaluated at $p \leq .0125$ to control for error, indicated a tendency for boys in the experimental condition to display greater School Problems than boys in the control condition. To explore this finding, we conducted two ANCOVAs (controlling for IQ and baseline scores) examining differences on the Attention Problems and Learning Problems subscales as a function of experimental condition. Results showed no difference in Attention Problems at follow-up, *F*(1, 60) = 0.030, *p* = .857. However, boys in the experimental condition showed greater Learning Problems at follow-up (*M* = 52.99, *SD* = 11.33) than did boys in the control condition (*M* = 45.88, *SD* = 7.00), *F*(1, 60) = 9.37, *p* = .003, η^2 = .12.

Mediation

We examined whether average duration of video-game play would mediate the relationship between video-game ownership and boys' Reading and Written Language scores at follow-up, adjusting for scores at baseline (Baron & Kenny, 1986; MacKinnon & Fairchild, 2009).

A test of the unmediated model showed that experimental condition predicted boys' Reading scores at follow-up, *b* = −5.17, β = −0.208, *F*(1, 58) = 9.55, *p* = .003. Experimental condition predicted duration of video-game play, *b* = 29.23, β = 0.629, *F*(1, 58) = 42.29, *p* < .001, and play predicted Reading outcomes, *b* = −0.158, β = −0.296, *F*(1, 57) = 12.59, *p* = .001. After controlling for video-game play, the relationship between condition and Reading outcomes was no longer significant, *b* = −0.542, β = −0.022, *F*(1, 57) = 0.073, *p* > .05. Confidence intervals at 95% (95% CIs) for the indirect effect fell outside zero, indicating significant mediation (95% CI = −7.78, −1.93).

A test of the unmediated model showed that experimental condition predicted Written Language scores at follow-up, *b* = −6.21, β = −0.287, *F*(1, 58) = 12.17, *p* = .001. A test of the mediated model showed that condition predicted video-game play, *b* = 29.23, β = 0.629, *F*(1, 58) = 42.29, *p* < .001, and play predicted Written Language outcomes, *b* = −0.134, β = −0.288, *F*(1, 57) = 7.36, *p* = .009. After controlling for video-game play, the relationship between experimental condition and Written Language was not significant, *b* = −2.29, β = −0.106, *F*(1, 57) = 1.07, *p* > .05. Confidence limits for the indirect effect also fell outside zero (95% CI = −5.67, −0.81).

Table 2 Academic Achievement and Behavior as a Function of Condition and Time ($N = 64$)

Variable and testing time	Experimental		Control		F^a	p	η^2
	M	SD	M	SD			
Academic achievement							
Reading							
Pretest	97.81	9.57	98.37	11.20	0.05	n.s.	
Posttest	96.43	12.66	101.60	11.83	9.55	.003	.042
Mathematics							
Pretest	102.69	9.68	102.19	10.26	0.04	n.s.	
Posttest	104.29	11.04	106.24	9.75	1.67	n.s.	
Written Language							
Pretest	94.09	8.80	95.53	9.71	0.39	n.s.	
Posttest	95.19	9.28	101.40	11.29	12.17	.001	.081
Parent-reported behavior							
Externalizing Problems							
Pretest	52.47	8.01	50.75	7.29	0.81	n.s.	
Posttest	51.76	9.20	52.12	8.69	0.07	n.s.	
Internalizing Problems							
Pretest	48.16	8.97	48.59	6.39	0.05	n.s.	
Posttest	49.13	9.71	47.15	8.54	2.49	n.s.	
Adaptive Skills							
Pretest	50.34	8.20	48.13	8.62	1.11	n.s.	
Posttest	49.89	8.07	50.55	7.83	0.32	n.s.	
Teacher-reported behavior							
Externalizing Problems							
Pretest	47.88	6.45	50.84	7.30	2.97	n.s.	
Posttest	50.33	6.89	50.89	9.14	0.19	n.s.	
Internalizing Problems							
Pretest	47.38	7.69	47.22	6.05	0.01	n.s.	
Posttest	50.13	8.39	50.02	7.52	0.06	n.s.	
School Problems							
Pretest	46.53	5.71	48.69	6.64	1.94	n.s.	
Posttest	51.87	9.37	47.47	7.31	5.89	.018	.064
Adaptive Skills							
Pretest	51.13	8.22	48.88	7.62	1.29	n.s.	
Posttest	50.13	6.56	51.90	7.91	2.56	n.s.	

Note: Pretest means are unadjusted; posttest means are adjusted for pretest and Kaufman Brief Intelligence Test—2nd edition (KBIT–2) scores (Kaufman & Kaufman, 2004). The same number of participants was analyzed at pretest and posttest; change in degrees of freedom from pretest to posttest reflects adjusting for pretest and KBIT–2 scores in posttest analyses. All scores are standardized. The mean score was 100 for achievement ($SD = 15$) and 50 for behavior ($SD = 10$). Eta-squared was calculated by hand so that total variance explained equals 1.00.

[a]The degrees of freedom for the analyses of variance were as follows—academic achievement and parent-reported behavior: $df = 1, 62$ for the pretest and $df = 1, 58$ for the posttest; teacher-reported behavior; $df = 1, 62$ for the pretest and $df = 1, 57$ for the posttest.

Discussion

Our study represents the first randomized, controlled test of the effects of video-game ownership on the academic and behavioral functioning of young boys. Our findings provide initial support for the notion that video-game ownership among boys is associated with decreased academic achievement in the areas of reading and writing. Overall, boys who received the video-game system at the beginning of the study showed relatively stable and somewhat below average reading and writing achievement from baseline to follow-up. In contrast, boys in the control group showed increased reading and writing achievement across the duration of the study.

The effect size for reading was moderate, reflecting approximately two fifths of a standard deviation difference in achievement scores at follow-up, whereas the effect size for written language was large, reflecting more than one half of a standard deviation difference at follow-up (Cohen, 1988). Furthermore, the lower academic achievement scores displayed by boys in the experimental condition were observable by teachers; boys who received the video-game system earned significantly higher Learning Problems scores, which reflect delays in reading, writing, spelling, and other academic tasks. These early reading and writing problems are particularly salient to young, elementary-school age children, because they can interfere with the acquisition of more advanced reading comprehension and writing composition skills later in development (Rayner, Foorman, Perfetti, Pesetsky, & Seidenberg, 2001). Altogether, our findings suggest that video-game ownership may impair academic achievement for some boys in a manner that has real-world significance.

Our findings also support displacement as a mechanism by which video-game ownership might influence boys' academic achievement. Boys in the experimental condition spent more time playing video games and less time engaged in after-school academic activities than did boys in the control condition. Furthermore, video-game play mediated the relationship between video-game ownership and boys' reading and writing outcomes. Our findings are consistent with survey research that shows video-game play to be extensive among young boys who own video-game systems (Roberts et al., 2005) and with cross-sectional studies indicating that video games displace children's after-school academic activities (Cummings & Vandewater, 2007; Schmidt & Vandewater, 2008; Vandewater et al., 2006).

Boys' Mathematics scores did not differ as a function of experimental condition. One explanation is that the displacement of homework by video games may not affect the development of math skills as much as reading and writing skills. For example, in one population-based study, the amount of time young children spent completing homework was strongly associated with their basic reading skills but not their math calculation or problem-solving skills (Hofferth & Sandberg, 2001). Another possibility is that young children may not engage in many math-based after-school activities in the first place. Whereas it is easy to imagine a young child reading or listening to stories at bedtime, it is more difficult to imagine a child completing math worksheets for pleasure. Young children may simply have fewer math-based recreational activities for video games to displace.

In our study, video-game ownership was not associated with increased behavior problems among boys. It is likely that boys in the experimental condition were exposed to at least moderate levels of video-game violence, given the tendency of the Entertainment Software Rating Board to underestimate the degree of illegal, harmful, and violent behavior in games rated E and E10+ (Walsh & Gentile, 2001). It is possible that these games did not have enough violent content to prime, model, or reinforce behavior problems. It is also possible that boys' behavior did change, but the omnibus rating scales used in this study were not sensitive to these changes. A third possibility for the null findings is that the study lacked sufficient power to detect differences in boys' behavior

as a function of game ownership. Given the extensive evidence supporting the association between violent video-game play and aggression, future experimental studies conducted in naturalistic settings are necessary to explore these possibilities.

Future research is also necessary to replicate and extend the current study to examine the long-term effects of video-game ownership on children. For example, we do not know whether video-game ownership would continue to displace academic activities and impair achievement beyond 4 months. Furthermore, we do not know whether video-game ownership might influence the academic and behavioral functioning of girls. Girls appear to play video games for different reasons, to select games with different content, and to manifest aggressive behavior following play in different ways than boys (Ostrov et al., 2006). Although recent research has shown few gender differences for the effects of violent video-game play on children's behavior, the base rate of girls' video-game play and physical aggression may be too low to observe a relationship between video-game ownership and girls' functioning in naturalistic settings (Gentile et al., 2007).

Finally, future research might also explore other mechanisms, besides displacement, that might explain the relationship between video-game ownership and boys' academic outcomes. For example, video-game play may affect the development of executive functioning or information-processing skills. Children may become accustomed to the fast pace of video games and have difficulty engaging in slower, academic tasks that require sustained concentration (Bailey, West, & Anderson, 2009). Alternatively, children may become conditioned to the frequent and immediate schedule of reinforcement inherent in many video games and show low motivation to learn academic skills that are reinforced in a less consistent and more delayed fashion (Ennemoser & Schneider, 2007).

We believe that our study extends the existing research literature through its focus on games marketed to young children, its examination of academic outcomes, and its reliance on experimental methodology in naturalistic settings. Our findings provide the first experimental evidence that video-game ownership may displace academic activities and hinder the academic achievement of young boys. We hope that our findings can be added to this growing body of research so that parents can make informed choices regarding their family's media consumption.

Acknowledgments

Portions of the data were presented at the 2009 meeting of the Midwestern Psychological Association, Chicago, Illinois.

Declaration of Conflicting Interests

The authors declared that they had no conflicts of interest with respect to their authorship or the publication of this article.

Funding

This research was supported by the J. Reid and Polly Anderson Fund for Science Research and the Fairchild Foundation of Denison University.

References

Anderson, C.A., & Bushman, B.J. (2001). Effects of violent video games on aggressive behavior, aggressive cognition, aggressive affect, physiological arousal, and prosocial behavior: A meta-analytic review of the scientific literature. *Psychological Science, 12,* 353–359.

Anderson, C.A., & Dill, K.E. (2000). Video games and aggressive thoughts, feelings, and behavior in the laboratory and in life. *Journal of Personality and Social Psychology, 78,* 772–790.

Anderson, C.A., Gentile, D.A., & Buckley, K.E. (2007). *Violent video game effects on children and adolescents: Theory, research, and public policy.* New York: Oxford University Press.

Anderson, C.A., Sakamoto, A., Gentile, D.A., Ihori, N., Shibuya, A., Yukawa, S., et al. (2008). Longitudinal effects of violent video games on aggression in Japan and the United States. *Pediatrics, 122,* e1067–e1072.

Bailey, K., West, R., & Anderson, C.A. (2009). A negative association between video game experience and proactive cognitive control. *Psychophysiology, 47,* 34–42.

Baron, R.M., & Kenny, D.A. (1986). The moderator-mediator distinction in social psychological research: Conceptual, strategic, and statistical considerations. *Journal of Personality and Social Psychology, 51,* 1173–1182.

Carnagey, N.L., & Anderson, C.A. (2005). The effects of reward and punishment in violent video games on aggressive affect, cognition, and behavior. *Psychological Science, 16,* 882–889.

Carnagey, N.L., Anderson, C.A., & Bushman, B.J. (2007). The effect of video game violence on physiological desensitization to real-life violence. *Journal of Experimental Social Psychology, 43,* 489–496.

Cohen, J. (1988). *Statistical power analysis for the behavioral sciences.* Mahwah, NJ: Erlbaum.

Cummings, H.M., & Vandewater, E.A. (2007). Relation of adolescent video game play to time spent in other activities. *Archives of Pediatric and Adolescent Medicine, 161,* 684–689.

Ennemoser, M., & Schneider, W. (2007). Relations of television viewing and reading: Findings from a 4-year longitudinal study. *Journal of Educational Psychology, 99,* 349–368.

Gentile, D.A. (2009). Pathological video-game use among youths ages 8 to 18: A national study. *Psychological Science, 20,* 594–602.

Gentile, D.A., Lynch, P.J., Linder, J.R., & Walsh, D.A. (2004). The effects of violent video game habits on adolescent hostility, aggressive behaviors, and school performance. *Journal of Adolescence, 27,* 5–22.

Gentile, D.A., Saleem, M., & Anderson, C.A. (2007). Public policy and the effects of media violence on children. *Social Issues and Policy Review, 1,* 15–61.

Hofferth, S., Davis-Kean, P.E., Davis, J., & Finkelstein, J. (1997). *The Child Development Supplement to the Panel Study of Income Dynamics.* Ann Arbor, MI: Institute for Social Research.

Hofferth, S.L., & Sandberg, J.F. (2001). How American children spend their time. *Journal of Marriage and the Family, 62,* 295–308.

Kaufman, A., & Kaufman, N. (2004). *Kaufman Brief Intelligence Test, Second Edition manual.* Circle Pines, MN: American Guidance Service.

Kutner, L.A., Olson, C.K., Warner, D.E., & Hertzog, S.M. (2008). Parents' and sons' perspectives on video game play. *Journal of Adolescent Research, 23,* 76–96.

MacKinnon, D.P., & Fairchild, A.J. (2009). Current directions in mediation analysis. *Current Directions in Psychological Science, 18,* 16–20.

McGrew, K.S., & Woodcock, R.W. (2001). *Woodcock-Johnson III technical manual.* Itasca, IL: Riverside.

Ostrov, J.M., Gentile, D.A., & Crick, N.R. (2006). Media exposure, aggression and prosocial behavior during early childhood: A longitudinal study. *Social Development, 15,* 612–627.

Rayner, K., Foorman, B.R., Perfetti, C.A., Pesetsky, D., & Seidenberg, M.S. (2001). How psychological science informs the teaching of reading. *Psychological Science in the Public Interest, 2,* 31–74.

Reynolds, C.R., & Kamphaus, R.W. (2004). *Behavior Assessment System for Children, Second Edition manual.* Circle Pines, MN: American Guidance Service.

Roberts, D.F., Foehr, U.G., & Rideout, V. (2005). *Generation M: Media in the lives of 8–18 year-olds.* Washington, DC: Kaiser Family Foundation.

Schmidt, M.E., & Vandewater, E.A. (2008). Media and attention, cognition, and school achievement. *The Future of Children, 18,* 63–85.

Sharif, I., & Sargent, J.D. (2006). Association between television, movie, and video game exposure and school performance. *Pediatrics, 118,* 1061–1070.

Valentine, G., Marsh, J., & Pattie, C. (2005). *Children and young people's home use of ICT for educational purposes.* London: Department for Education and Skills.

Vandewater, E.A., Bickham, D.S., & Lee, J.H. (2006). Time well spent? Relating television use to children's free-time activities. *Pediatrics, 117,* 181–191.

Walsh, D.A., & Gentile, D.A. (2001). A validity test of movie, television, and video-game ratings. *Pediatrics, 107,* 1302–1308.

Willoughby, T. (2008). A short-term longitudinal study of Internet and computer game use by adolescent boys and girls: Prevalence, frequency of use, and psychosocial predictors. *Developmental Psychology, 44,* 195–204.

Critical Thinking

1. Summarize the data from the research study on the effects of video game ownership. What do you conclude from this data?

2. A father, who enjoys playing video and Facebook games, is seeking your advice about allowing his son to play games and use social media. What will you tell him?

From *Psychological Science,* February 18, 2010, pp. 1–8. Copyright © 2010 by the Association for Psychological Science. Reprinted by permission of Sage Publications via Rightslink.

Test-Your-Knowledge Form

We encourage you to photocopy and use this page as a tool to assess how the articles in *Annual Editions* expand on the information in your textbook. By reflecting on the articles you will gain enhanced text information. You can also access this useful form on a product's book support website at www.mhhe.com/cls

NAME: _____   DATE: _____

_____

TITLE AND NUMBER OF ARTICLE:

_____

BRIEFLY STATE THE MAIN IDEA OF THIS ARTICLE:

_____

_____

LIST THREE IMPORTANT FACTS THAT THE AUTHOR USES TO SUPPORT THE MAIN IDEA:

_____

_____

WHAT INFORMATION OR IDEAS DISCUSSED IN THIS ARTICLE ARE ALSO DISCUSSED IN YOUR TEXTBOOK OR OTHER READINGS THAT YOU HAVE DONE? LIST THE TEXTBOOK CHAPTERS AND PAGE NUMBERS:

_____

_____

LIST ANY EXAMPLES OF BIAS OR FAULTY REASONING THAT YOU FOUND IN THE ARTICLE:

_____

_____

LIST ANY NEW TERMS/CONCEPTS THAT WERE DISCUSSED IN THE ARTICLE, AND WRITE A SHORT DEFINITION:

We Want Your Advice

ANNUAL EDITIONS revisions depend on two major opinion sources: one is our Advisory Board, listed in the front of this volume, which works with us in scanning the thousands of articles published in the public press each year; the other is you—the person actually using the book. Please help us and the users of the next edition by completing the prepaid article rating form on this page and returning it to us. Thank you for your help!

ANNUAL EDITIONS: Education 12/13

ARTICLE RATING FORM

Here is an opportunity for you to have direct input into the next revision of this volume.
We would like you to rate each of the articles listed below, using the following scale:

1. **Excellent: should definitely be retained**
2. **Above average: should probably be retained**
3. **Below average: should probably be deleted**
4. **Poor: should definitely be deleted**

Your ratings will play a vital part in the next revision.
Please mail this prepaid form to us as soon as possible.
Thanks for your help!

RATING	ARTICLE
	1. 'Quality Education Is Our Moon Shot'
	2. Duncan's Strategy Is Flawed
	3. Grading Obama's Education Policy
	4. Dictating to the Schools
	5. Response to Intervention (RTI): What Teachers of Reading Need to Know
	6. Responding to RTI
	7. The Why Behind RTI
	8. A Diploma Worth Having
	9. Who Are America's Poor Children?: The Official Story
	10. Teacher's Perspectives on Teaching Students Who Are Placed At-Risk
	11. Dismantling Rural Stereotypes
	12. Examining the Culture of Poverty: Promising Practices
	13. Exploring Educational Material Needs and Resources for Children Living in Poverty
	14. Print Referencing during Read-Alouds: A Technique for Increasing Emergent Readers' Print Knowledge
	15. Supporting the Literacy Development of Children Living in Homeless Shelters
	16. Integrating Children's Books and Literacy into the Physical Education Curriculum
	17. You Gotta See It to Believe It: Teaching Visual Literacy in the English Classroom
	18. Strategies for Teaching Algebra to Students with Learning Disabilities: Making Research to Practice Connections
	19. Do Girls Learn Math Fear from Teachers?
	20. The Power of Positive Relationships
	21. Teachers Connecting with Families—In the Best Interest of Children
	22. Motivation: It's All About Me
	23. Start Where Your Students Are

RATING	ARTICLE
	24. Leaving Nothing to Chance
	25. She's Strict for a Good Reason: Highly Effective Teachers in Low-Performing Urban Schools
	26. What Educators Need to Know about Bullying Behaviors
	27. Meeting Students Where They Are: The Latino Education Crisis
	28. What Does Research Say about Effective Practices for English Learners?
	29. Strategies and Content Areas for Teaching English Language Learners
	30. Teaching Photosynthesis with ELL Students
	31. Literacy and Literature for 21st Century Global Citizenship
	32. Using Guided Notes to Enhance Instruction for All Students
	33. Strategies for Every Teacher's Toolbox
	34. Methods for Addressing Conflict in Cotaught Classrooms
	35. "For Openers: How Technology Is Changing School"
	36. What Middle School Educators Should Know about Assistive Technology and Universal Design for Learning
	37. Tech Tool Targets Elementary Readers
	38. Digital Readers: The Next Chapter in E-Book Reading and Response
	39. Digital Tools Expand Options for Personalized Learning
	40. Differentiate Teaching and Learning with Web 2.0 Tools
	41. Effects of Video-Game Ownership on Young Boys' Academic and Behavioral Functioning: A Randomized, Controlled Study

BUSINESS REPLY MAIL
FIRST CLASS MAIL PERMIT NO. 551 DUBUQUE IA

POSTAGE WILL BE PAID BY ADDRESSEE

McGraw-Hill Contemporary Learning Series
501 BELL STREET
DUBUQUE, IA 52001

ABOUT YOU

Name _____   Date _____

Are you a teacher? ☐ A student? ☐
Your school's name _____

Department _____

Address _____ City _____ State _____ Zip _____

School telephone # _____

YOUR COMMENTS ARE IMPORTANT TO US!

Please fill in the following information:
For which course did you use this book?
_____

Did you use a text with this ANNUAL EDITION? ☐ yes ☐ no
What was the title of the text?
_____

What are your general reactions to the Annual Editions concept?
_____

Have you read any pertinent articles recently that you think should be included in the next edition? Explain.
_____

Are there any articles that you feel should be replaced in the next edition? Why?
_____

Are there any World Wide Websites that you feel should be included in the next edition? Please annotate.
_____

May we contact you for editorial input? ☐ yes ☐ no
May we quote your comments? ☐ yes ☐ no

NOTES

NOTES

NOTES

NOTES